IBSEN, SCANDINAVIA AND THE MAKING OF A WORLD DRAMA

Henrik Ibsen's drama is the most prominent and lasting contribution of the cultural surge seen in Scandinavian literature in the later nineteenth century. When he made his debut in Norway in 1850, the nation's literary presence was negligible, yet by 1890 Ibsen had become one of Europe's most famous authors. Contrary to the standard narrative of his move from restrictive provincial origins to liberating European exile, Narve Fulsås and Tore Rem show how Ibsen's trajectory was preconditioned on his continued embeddedness in Scandinavian society and culture, and that he experienced great success in his home markets. *Ibsen, Scandinavia and the Making of a World Drama* traces how Ibsen's works first travelled outside Scandinavia and studies the mechanisms of his appropriation in Germany, Britain and France. Engaging with theories of book dissemination and world literature, and re-assessing the emergence of 'peripheral' literary nations, this book provides new perspectives on the work of this major figure of European literature and theatre.

NARVE FULSÅS is Professor of Modern History at the University of Tromsø – The Arctic University of Norway, where his work focuses on Norwegian cultural and intellectual history in the nineteenth and twentieth centuries. He has edited Ibsen's letters for the new critical edition, *Henrik Ibsens skrifter* (2005–2010), and is chief editor of the journal *Historisk tidsskrift*.

TORE REM is Professor of British Literature at the University of Oslo. He has been head of the board of the Centre for Ibsen Studies and has published on Victorian literature, book history and the early English-language appropriations of Ibsen. He is editor of the new Ibsen editions in the Penguin Classics series.

IBSEN, SCANDINAVIA AND THE MAKING OF A WORLD DRAMA

NARVE FULSÅS

University of Tromsø

TORE REM

University of Oslo

CAMBRIDGE
UNIVERSITY PRESS

CAMBRIDGE
UNIVERSITY PRESS

University Printing House, Cambridge CB2 8BS, United Kingdom

One Liberty Plaza, 20th Floor, New York, NY 10006, USA

477 Williamstown Road, Port Melbourne, VIC 3207, Australia

314–321, 3rd Floor, Plot 3, Splendor Forum, Jasola District Centre, New Delhi – 110025, India

79 Anson Road, #06–04/06, Singapore 079906

Cambridge University Press is part of the University of Cambridge.

It furthers the University's mission by disseminating knowledge in the pursuit of
education, learning, and research at the highest international levels of excellence.

www.cambridge.org
Information on this title: www.cambridge.org/9781107187771
DOI: 10.1017/9781316946176

© Narve Fulsås and Tore Rem 2018

First published 2018

Printed in the United Kingdom by Clays, St Ives plc

A catalogue record for this publication is available from the British Library.

Library of Congress Cataloging-in-Publication Data
NAMES: Fulsås, Narve, 1953- author. | Rem, Tore, author.
TITLE: Ibsen, Scandinavia and the making of a world drama / Narve Fulsås,
University of Tromsø, Norway ; Tore Rem, University of Oslo, Norway.
DESCRIPTION: First edition. | New York, NY : Cambridge University Press, 2017. |
Includes bibliographical references and index.
IDENTIFIERS: LCCN 2017027457 | ISBN 9781107187771 (Hardback)
SUBJECTS: LCSH: Ibsen, Henrik, 1828-1906–Criticism and interpretation. |
Ibsen, Henrik, 1828-1906–Appreciation–Scandinavia. | Ibsen, Henrik,
1828-1906–Appreciation–Europe. | Ibsen, Henrik, 1828-1906–Influence.
CLASSIFICATION: LCC PT8895 F85 2017 | DDC 839.822/6–dc23
LC record available at https://lccn.loc.gov/2017027457

ISBN 978-1-107-18777-1 Hardback

Contents

Figures

Acknowledgements

The end of the nineteenth century experienced what may be called a Scandinavian moment in world literature. This moment's most prominent feature and lasting contribution were the plays of Henrik Ibsen. When Ibsen made his literary debut in Norway in 1850, the nation's literature was negligible. By 1890, he had become one of the most famous authors of Europe and made Nordic literature a marketing brand. How was such an extraordinary trajectory possible?

Our contribution to answering that question has emerged from our involvements in two large publishing projects, namely the new critical edition of Ibsen's complete works, *Henrik Ibsens skrifter* (HIS) and the new *Penguin Classics Ibsen* edition. It has been completed within the research project 'The Scandinavian Moment in World Literature', supported by the Norwegian Research Council and UiT The Arctic University of Norway, and is, more generally, indebted to our long-time work within reception studies, book history, intellectual history and world literature and drama.

Shorter parts of this book rework and expand materials previously published elsewhere. These include Narve Fulsås' articles 'The de-dramatization of history and the prose of bourgeois life', *Nordlit*, no. 34 (2015), 83–93 (Chapter 2), 'Ibsen misrepresented: Canonization, oblivion, and the need for history', *Ibsen Studies*, vol. 9, no. 1 (2011), 3–20 (Chapter 5) and *Innledning til brevene: Forfatterrett og utgivelsespolitikk – 1890-årene: Det tyske markedet*, www.ibsen.uio.no/brev (Chapter 7).

The starting point for our collaboration was HIS, and we would like to thank its main editor, Vigdis Ystad, as well as Christian Janss, Ståle Dingstad and Aina Nøding. Many people have contributed comments and input on a number of different occasions. We would also like to thank all those who have either hosted us or participated in our own seminars in the course of this process. We would like to express our gratitude to our PhD students Maria Purtoft and Henning Hansen for helping to create a stimulating research environment.

We are indebted to the Scandinavian Department at University of California, Berkeley, St Catherine's College, Oxford and Christ Church, Oxford, for hosting us at various points; to the Centre for Ibsen Studies for co-organising a seminar on the 'Modern Breakthrough' in the autumn of 2013; and to Fondet for dansk-norsk samarbeid for facilitating a stay at their wonderful Schæffergården near Copenhagen. We have received generous financial support from the Norwegian Research Council, as well as from the Norwegian Non-fiction Writers and Translators' Association and St Catherine's College, Oxford.

Special thanks go to those who have read and commented on drafts of the manuscript at different stages: Terence Cave, Peter D. McDonald, Martin Puchner, Kirsten Shepherd-Barr and Cambridge University Press's two anonymous readers. Our editor Kate Brett has throughout the process been wonderfully supportive, competent and efficient.

Note on the Text

Quoting Ibsen in English necessarily involves the use of a number of different editions. For Ibsen's plays, two editions have been particularly important. For Ibsen's *early* plays, we have (mostly) used *The Oxford Ibsen* (1960–77), edited by James W. McFarlane. For Ibsen's *contemporary* plays, we have, where available, quoted the *New Penguin Classics* edition (3 vols., 2014–), edited by Tore Rem. We have also adopted the Penguin edition's new English title *Pillars of the Community* for the play usually called *The Pillars of Society*, unless the reference is to an English translation or production with that last title.

Of Ibsen's *letters*, just a small selection of those considered most important are translated. When a letter already exists in English translation, we have quoted it from the two main editions: *Letters and Speeches*, trans. Evert Sprinchorn (1965) and *Letters of Henrik Ibsen*, trans. John Nilsen Laurvik and Mary Morison (1908). Otherwise, the footnotes will only give the addressee and date of the letter, and often having 'with comment(s)' added, referring to the critical and commented edition of Ibsen's letters in *Henrik Ibsens skrifter* vols. 12–15, ed. Narve Fulsås (2005–10), digital edition: www.ibsen.uio.no/brev. In these cases, translations are ours. To those able to navigate Norwegian, the comments will provide additional references to those listed in the bibliography.

Other translations into English are also ours, unless otherwise stated.

In the nineteenth century the name of the Norwegian capital was 'Christiania', gradually replaced by 'Kristiania' from the 1870s before becoming Oslo in 1925. We have opted for consistently using Kristiania for the capital while alternating according to the institutions' own practices for institutional names, like *Christiania Theater*, where the old spelling was preserved until the theatre was closed down in 1899 and replaced by *Nationaltheatret*.

Chronology

1828–1843: Skien
1828, 20 March: Born

1843–1850: Grimstad
1850, 12 April: *Catiline* (*Catilina*) published

1850–1851: Kristiania (Oslo)
1850, 26 September: *The Burial Mound* (*Kjæmpehøien*) performed
                                (published January–February 1854)
1851, 1 and 8 June: *Norma, or: The Love of a Politician* (*Norma eller
                                en Politikers Kjærlighed*) published

1851–1857: Bergen
1853, 2 January: *St John's Night* (*Sancthansnatten*) performed
                                (published 1909)
1855, 2 January: *Lady Inger* (*Fru Inger til Østeraad*) performed
                                (published May–August 1857)
1856, 2 January: *The Feast at Solhoug* (*Gildet paa Solhoug*)
                                performed (published 19 March 1856)
1857, 2 January: *Olaf Liljekrans* performed (published 1902)

1857–1864: Kristiania (Oslo)
1858, 25 April: *The Vikings at Helgeland* (*Hærmændene paa
                                Helgeland*) published
1860, January: The poem 'On the Heights' ('Paa Vidderne')
                                published
1862, 23 February: The poem 'Terje Vigen' published
1862, 31 December: *Love's Comedy* (*Kjærlighedens Komedie*)
                                published
1863, October: *The Pretenders* (*Kongs-Emnerne*) published

1864–1868: Rome

1866, 15 March:	*Brand* published
1867, 14 November:	*Peer Gynt* published

1868–1875: Dresden

1869, 31 September:	*The League of Youth* (*De unges Forbund*) published
1871, 3 May:	*Poems* (*Digte*) published
1873, 17 October:	*Emperor and Galilean* (*Kejser og Galilæer*) published

1875–1878: Munich

1877, 11 October:	*Pillars of the Community* (*Samfundets støtter*) published

1878–1879: Rome and Amalfi
1879–1880: Munich

1879, 4 December:	*A Doll's House* (*Et dukkehjem*) published

1880–1885: Rome

1881, 13 December:	*Ghosts* (*Gengangere*) published
1882, 28 November:	*An Enemy of the People* (*En folkefiende*) published
1884, 11 November:	*The Wild Duck* (*Vildanden*) published

1885–1891: Munich

1886, 23 November:	*Rosmersholm* published
1888, 28 November:	*The Lady from the Sea* (*Fruen fra havet*) published
1890, 16 December:	*Hedda Gabler* published

1891–1906: Kristiania (Oslo)

1892, 12 December:	*The Master Builder* (*Bygmester Solness*) published
1894, 11 December:	*Little Eyolf* (*Lille Eyolf*) published
1896, 15 December:	*John Gabriel Borkman* published
1899, 19 December:	*When We Dead Awaken* (*Når vi døde vågner*) published
1898–1900:	*Collected works* (*Samlede værker*) vols. 1–9 published
1906, 23 May:	Dies

For a detailed chronology, see Ståle Dingstad and Aina Nøding: 'Tidstavle 1828–1906', in Narve Fulsås, ed., *Biografisk leksikon til Ibsens brev – med tidstavle*. Acta Ibseniana X–2013 (Oslo: Centre for Ibsen Studies, 2013), 483–555.

Abbreviations

BL: British Library, London
NLN: National Library of Norway [Nasjonalbiblioteket], Oslo
NLS: National Library of Sweden [Kungliga biblioteket], Stockholm
PRO: Public Record Office, London
RDL: The Royal Danish Library [Det Kongelige Bibliotek],
       Copenhagen
VAM: Victoria and Albert Museum, London

Introduction

After having been met with nothing but misunderstanding, bordering on persecution, Henrik Ibsen left his native country in 1864, becoming an exile. First in Italy and later in Germany, he encountered a European modernity which changed the course of his work and gave him the necessary impulses to become the 'Father of Modern Drama'. Through his twenty-seven years of exile, Ibsen managed to escape the provincial conditions and mentalities at home, completely freeing himself from his backward and restrictive domestic contexts. Meanwhile in Scandinavia, he was championed by the Danish critic Georg Brandes, who helped bring about the so-called Modern Breakthrough on his behalf. The conservative and puritan forces were defeated, at least for a short while. Ibsen, the autonomous, self-made artist, became the exemplary European avant-gardist, hailed by those in the vanguard of theatrical and literary innovation (Figure I.1).

The main features of this master narrative of Ibsen's career originated in the author's own time, and were in part created by himself. They have enjoyed endless uncritical reproduction ever since. We could cite numerous instances of this interpretive pattern, and we will return to some of them, but we trust that anyone even faintly familiar with Ibsen will recognise the existence and power of this narrative. 'Ibsen had the misfortune', to quote just one Ibsen scholar, of being 'born into a provincial, limiting, and repressive society from which he spent his lifetime liberating his imagination'.[1]

Ibsen, Scandinavia and the Making of a World Drama is a history about the Scandinavian origins and early European appropriations of Henrik Ibsen's plays. Its aims are threefold. First, it fills a gap in the field of Ibsen

---

[1] Brian Johnston, *Text and Supertext in Ibsen's Drama* (London: Pennsylvania State University Press, 1989), 8; see also Johnston's 'Introduction' to the Norton edition of *Ibsen's Selected Plays* (London: Norton, 2004), xv.

Figure I.1   Ibsen at Karl Johan's street in 1891, with the Parliament building (*Stortinget*)
in the background.

On his return to Kristiania, basic elements of the overall narrative of Ibsen's troubled
relationship to Norway were confirmed. The poem by the Ibsen biographer Henrik Jæger
installed in Gustav Lærum's picture reads: 'As stepmother Norway's poor son / you went
far away. / Europe's jubilation was your reward / before coming "home from the world". /
In spite of hardships victory will eventually be won / by the spirit whole and strong – / that
lesson we learn from your life's long day / and from your noble works.'

studies between predominantly biographical approaches on the one hand
and literary and performance studies on the other. In this gap, areas like
publishing history, author's economy, copyright, translations and other
issues of 'book history' have remained largely unexplored. Second, taking
up these fields of inquiry leads to a questioning of several dominant

narratives and interpretations informing Ibsen studies, from the author's own time up until the present. This holds particularly for the largely negative perceptions of Ibsen's relationship to his originating cultures. Third, the Ibsen case will serve to question and challenge some influential theories and models within literary and theatre studies, as well as within the field of world literature.

We set out to challenge the narrative of exile and rupture in the first part of this book. Our account then moves on to the first attempts at disseminating Ibsen beyond Scandinavia, his European breakthrough by the late 1880s and early 1890s, and end by considering his position in Scandinavian and major European literatures and theatre cultures by the turn of the century.

In Chapter 1, we will revalue the overwhelmingly negative account of Ibsen's time spent in the service of the Norwegian theatre in the 1850s and early 1860s. Alongside emphasising the extraordinary training and occupational opportunities this project offered, we will underline the transnational context of this theatre project and also how this came to shape Ibsen's publishing strategy when he transferred his attention to the book market in the latter part of the 1860s.

We continue by addressing the exile topos which has informed the understanding of Ibsen's move from Norway and his twenty-seven-year stay in Italy and Germany. 'Exile' implies both an initial traumatic break and a barrier to return; Ibsen's stay abroad had none of these characteristics. There were certainly real obstacles to the unfolding of Ibsen's creativity at home, and moving away helped him overcome some of these. His residence in Europe should not, however, be equated with a break with Scandinavian literature, culture and society.[2] Rather, we should recontextualise the way Ibsen, after leaving Norway, rephrased authorship in terms of vocation and antagonism between artist and society, and also realise that his first 'European' experiences were not just about liberation but as much about defeat and alienation.

In Chapter 3 we question the commonly held assumption that Ibsen with *Emperor and Galilean* (1873) definitely left the historical play behind and decided to take up contemporary drama. We bring out the many competing plans he was entertaining by the middle and late 1870s, complicating the impression of a unidirectional movement towards 'the

---

[2] In the last major Ibsen biography Ivo de Figueiredo adds nuance to the received picture of Ibsen's suffering at home, but nevertheless concludes that 'When [Ibsen] left Norway and went to Rome, he cut his ties to Norwegian society', *Masken* (Oslo: Aschehoug, 2007), 507.

social plays'. With *Pillars of the Community* (1877), Ibsen was signaling a reorientation, but this reorientation was consolidated only with the gravity unfolding from the Scandinavian 'Literary Left', which formed independently of Ibsen at the end of the 1870s.

Chapter 4 takes *A Doll's House* (1879) to be a decisive turning point in Ibsen's authorship. We argue that this play and the following *Ghosts* (1881) and *An Enemy of the People* (1882) had predominantly Scandinavian contexts of origin. Literary and political tensions overlapped to spur a literary dynamic which enabled Ibsen to overcome aesthetic restrictions, articulate his political-social reasoning in a dramatically productive way, and regain the position as the leading Scandinavian author, a position which had been questioned by the late 1870s. Very soon, however, Ibsen set out to distance himself from the party affiliation bestowed upon him by these early 'social plays'.

The Modern Breakthrough in Scandinavian literature was permeated by an avant-garde rhetoric. In Chapter 5, we will show how this, by being uncritically appropriated by so much later scholarship, has obscured the astonishing commercial success of Ibsen's contemporary plays. We attribute the extraordinary attention paid not just to Ibsen but to the whole 'golden age' generation of Norwegian literature to the importance of literary prestige for a small and young nation seeking recognition and a sense of equality.

Moving beyond Scandinavia in Chapter 6, we relate Ibsen's own, early and largely unsuccessful efforts to promote his work in German. We argue that it was only with the contemporary plays that Ibsen acquired a potential for 'European' relevance, and that his breakthrough was made possible only when he was appropriated by local agents as an asset in their struggle to change existing aesthetic hierarchies and norms. A common denominator among his mediators was a shared commitment to a revival of 'literary drama' and a perception of a widening gap between book and theatre. Apart from that, they were highly divergent and ended up constructing very different 'Ibsens'.

Chapter 7 gives an account of the remarkable European position obtained by Ibsen in the 1890s and shows the importance of intellectual property regimes to the different European dissemination patterns. One reason Ibsen existed in such a variety of circuits was, we argue, the transitory state of copyright, the author being protected in all his Scandinavian home markets while being unprotected beyond.

In Chapter 8 we assess Ibsen's status in European cultures by the turn of the century and the impact made by his drama outside of Scandinavia.

A threefold pattern can be discerned. In northern Europe, Ibsen was already firmly appropriated both as book and theatre. In Britain, his existence was conditioned on the still-existing divide between literature and theatre, with Ibsen soon being established as literature, while belonging to the 'independent', minority theatre sector; in France, he remained a minority interest both as book and performance.

To make our case, we will highlight areas which have largely been ignored and under-researched, such as the issues of Ibsen's finances and publishing history. These tell a story very different from that of indifference or hostility. But this is also an account of how literature became its own primary context, that is, how Scandinavian literature developed into a relatively autonomous field of cultural production. Ibsen's turn to contemporary prose plays, the plays which made his name in Europe, would not have happened without it. This is not to say that we now pretend to give *the* contextual account of Ibsen's achievement. Contexts are never closed, they are always constructed anew from changing historical vantage points, and they always come in the plural. We have, for example, to a large extent left out intellectual and aesthetic discourses and influences, not because we deem them irrelevant, but because we have wanted to emphasise significant areas which we think have been given far too little attention, and which will help us reconsider a number of earlier contextualisations, both explicit ones, and, equally often, implicit ones.

Relating this history in a basically chronological order, the approaches, issues and emphases will vary between and within the different chapters and will include elements of biography, political history, book history, theatre history, with some ventures into literary interpretation. Our over-arching ambition is to explain 'the Ibsen phenomenon', to address the question of how a world drama arose from such seemingly inauspicious origins.

Ibsen poses a challenge to our own efforts at contextualisation and has forced us to rethink basic theoretical assumptions about modern literature and its institutional settings. In the last part of this introduction we would like to single out four of our recurrent theoretical concerns. The first one is paying attention to Ibsen's poetics: How did he construct and reconstruct his authorship and what Michel Foucault called 'the author function': the 'author' as the privileged offspring and unifying principle of the literary work?[3] This is an area which has been prone to the essentialisation of a

---

[3] Michel Foucault, 'What Is an Author?', in David Finkelstein & Alistair McCleery (eds.), *The Book History Reader*, 2nd edn (London: Routledge, 2006), 281–91.

handful of authorial statements, not least those about Ibsen being 'a fighter in the intellectual vanguard' and always 'at least ten years ahead of the majority'.[4] We will try to demonstrate that this avant-garde rhetoric belongs to a restricted phase of Ibsen's authorship, the time around *Ghosts* and *An Enemy of the People*, and that we should be careful in giving it a wider or even general reach. There are certainly signs of a poetics of distance, emerging by the early 1860s, in sharp contrast to his poetics of the 1850s.[5] But this poetics undergoes a series of significant reformulations, from the dichotomous opposition between art and society in the 1860s to the bourgeois artists of the late plays. These reformulations are indications of the degrees of artistic autonomy experienced at different stages, we will suggest, and should be re-historicised in that perspective. What is remarkable is that already by the early 1880s the author-function 'Ibsen' was so powerful that his publisher strongly advised against compromising it with biographical information. Ibsen was asked to cultivate elevation and silence.

A second concern is the relevance and at the same time the limitations of the theory of the literary field. According to this theory, the world of literature is an instantiation of the market of symbolic goods, organised around the opposition between small-scale and large-scale circulation. This makes literature an 'economic world reversed', not only distinguishing between, but opposing sales and literary recognition. In Pierre Bourdieu's analyses of French literature and art, Gustave Flaubert and others 'affirmed the autonomy of literature from the market in the second half of the nineteenth century, by claiming the superiority of the judgement of their peers and other specialists over those of the uninitiated public'.[6] As the wider theory of symbolic goods indicate, however, there is nothing completely new or particularly French about the opposition between aesthetic value and commercial value. The Danish philosopher Søren Kierkegaard held the quality of a book to stand in an inverse relationship to its number of readers. He oscillated between deploring this fact and cultivating the idea of authorship as sacrifice. When *Enten-Eller* (*Either-Or*) immediately

---

[4] Ibsen, Letter to G. Brandes, 12 June 1883, *Letters and Speeches*, ed. Evert Sprinchorn (London: MacGibbon & Kee, 1965), 220.

[5] The poetics of distance has been underlined, but not historicised, by Bjørn Hemmer, *Ibsen* (Bergen: Vigmostad & Bjørke, 2003), 19, 557.

[6] Gisèle Sapiro, 'Autonomy Revisited: The Question of Mediations and Its Methodological Implications', *Paragraph*, vol. 35, no. 1 (2012) 34; Pierre Bourdieu, *The Rules of Art*, trans. Susan Emanuel (Stanford: Stanford University Press, 1996); see also Bourdieu, 'The Field of Cultural Production', in Finkelstein & McCleery (eds.), *The Book History Reader*, 99–120.

sold out on its first publication in 1844 and the publisher suggested a new edition, Kierkegaard first opposed the idea 'on principle'.[7] The later Modern Breakthrough relied on a rhetoric of the split audience and the opposition between 'free art' and 'bourgeois demand'. It is imperative that we acknowledge the productive role of this discourse in framing literary positions, oppositions and possibilities. It certainly had a transformative effect on Ibsen's authorship. But it is equally important to realise that this logic does not correspond to actual circulation. Ibsen could not, like Kierkegaard, afford to neglect the market; in fact, his contemporary plays consolidated his position not just at the top of the literary hierarchy but also as a bestseller. As indicated, we will suggest that a major reason for this success was the national importance of and the national stakes in literature in Norway. It was, then, the intersection of the 'law of the field' and the logic of national literature that made Ibsen possible; his literary drama could never have emerged from within a Scandinavian avant-garde.

A third recurring concern regards cultural asymmetries. Asymmetries were used by the literary agents at the time as a means of positioning themselves in cultural struggles at home and abroad.[8] At home, they would often resort to the language of 'Scandinavian backwardness' while positioning themselves as 'European', as in the often quoted introduction to Georg Brandes's famous *Hovedstrømninger i det 19de Aarhundredes Litteratur* (*Main Currents in Nineteenth-Century Literature*, 1872): 'we are this time, as usual, forty years behind Europe.'[9] Abroad, however, Brandes would more than once attack 'the provincialism of the centre', an accusation that Ibsen in fact directed precisely against Brandes himself and what *he*, as a Norwegian writer, perceived to be the 'Copenhagen parochialism' of *Main Currents*. While we direct attention to such highly situated uses of centre-periphery rhetoric, we also acknowledge that asymmetries represented very real obstacles for authors trying to achieve literary autonomy and, eventually, a place within 'world literature'. They wrote in marginal languages, worked in less developed and differentiated cultural environments, and would often be immediately exposed to political and national pressures. However, we should not from such restrictions draw the general conclusion that 'being peripheral' is antithetical to having agency and that 'periphery'

---

[7] Joakim Garff, *Søren Kierkegaard*, trans. Bruce H. Kirmmse [2007] (Princeton: Princeton University Press, 2013), 508, see also 513–19 and 545–48.

[8] Stefan Nygård & Johan Strang, 'Facing Asymmetry: Nordic Intellectuals and Center-Periphery Dynamics in European Cultural Space', *Journal of the History of Ideas*, vol. 77, no. 1 (2016), 75–97.

[9] Georg Brandes, *Hovedstrømninger i det 19de Aarhundredes Litteratur* (Copenhagen: Gyldendal, 1872), 15.

and 'province' are only positions of disadvantage. In Pascale Casanova's *The World Republic of Letters*, there seems to be three ideal-typical strategies available for peripheral authors: total assimilation to a dominant culture and language, joining the strategy of nationalising language, literature and theatre, or breaking with the national model in order to pursue recognition in the literary centres, notably Paris, as a way of obtaining autonomy.[10] Her model has been much criticised, but it corresponds well with the critical orthodoxy which has never really considered Scandinavia as the primary context of origin of Ibsen's modern drama. The master narrative related above has depicted Scandinavia as a restricting, not as an enabling environment, and the Modern Breakthrough as initiated by import. Against such perceptions we will highlight certain 'advantages of backwardness', or 'resources of the periphery', such as, not least, the continued existence of drama as a vital literary genre – without which Ibsen's achievement is hard to imagine in the first place – as well as the national importance attached to literature. Furthermore, we will argue that Norway and Scandinavia were, with expanding markets, rapid urbanisation and extended education, able to provide a relatively high degree of literary autonomy and to facilitate something like a homegrown modern literature far beyond what Brandes had imagined at the beginning of the 1870s.

Finally, a central aim of *Ibsen, Scandinavia and the Making of a World Drama* is to reintroduce historical contingency to inherited narratives. In canonised authorships, the power of teleology and closure is overwhelming. Indications of this power is the recurring tendency in Ibsen biography and Ibsen scholarship to harmonise apparent 'deviations' and contradictions, for example, by explaining that 'essentially' Ibsen was radical all the time and that what may 'look like' socially affirmative plays are more subversive than they appear.[11] The ideas of 'habitus' and 'field' might actually help underpin such notions, by suggesting an all-encompassing mode of making intellectual subjects.[12] Our aim is rather to underline discontinuity and situational variation. That is one reason why we, to take one example, have wanted to draw attention to the 1870s, highlighting the indeterminacy of Ibsen's situation through most of that decade and trying to restore the sense of surprise with which *A Doll's House* and *Ghosts* were met at the time.

[10] Pascale Casanova, *The World Republic of Letters*, trans. M.B. DeBevoise (Cambridge, Mass.: Harvard University Press, 2004), 173—347.
[11] This has been done, for example, with respect to *The League of Youth* and *Pillars of the Community*, see on the first, Helge Rønning, *Den umulige friheten* (Oslo: Gyldendal, 2006), 193–94 and on the latter, James W. McFarlane, *Ibsen and Meaning* (Norwich: Norvik Press, 1989), 85, 89.
[12] Henning Trüper, *Topography of a Method* (Tübingen: Mohr Siebeck, 2014), 221.

1

From Stage to Page

The overwhelmingly negative assessment of Ibsen's years in Norway, and his years in the theatre in particular, originated in the author's own time. In the English-reading world it has been cemented not least by Michael Meyer's major Ibsen biography.[1] Here, Ibsen's departure from Norway in 1864 is the great turning point, introduced under the heading 'Out of the tunnel', followed by sections entitled 'Italian spring' and 'German seed-time'. In addressing this narrative, we ought not to conceal the very real obstacles Ibsen faced in Norway and the limitations of the institutions within which he worked. However, this needs to be balanced against the extraordinary opportunities for employment and training he was offered, and the continuous rise in his literary status. Furthermore, we will high-light the entangled Scandinavian and European character of Ibsen's early dramatic and literary efforts.

Norwegian State, Danish Culture

In order to understand the preconditions for Ibsen's rise to world status, it is vital that we establish a few key cultural and political contexts. In the beginning of the nineteenth century, the Napoleonic wars had redrawn the political geography of Scandinavia. In 1808 Sweden lost Finland to Russia and in 1814, the Danish King was forced to give up the centuries-old union between Denmark and Norway. Norway entered into a new but much looser royal union with Sweden, with a separate constitution, parliament and government. In the post-Napoleonic 'restoration' period, the Swedish King repeatedly tried to revise the constitution in order to strengthen royal power and the Norwegian parliament fought as

---

[1] Michael Meyer, *Ibsen* (London: Penguin, 1974), originally published in three volumes: *The Making of a Dramatist, 1828–1864* (1967), *The Farewell to Poetry, 1864–1882* (1971) and *The Top of a Cold Mountain, 1883–1906* (1971) (London: Rupert Hart-Davis).

consistently, and successfully, to defend the constitution and its power in relation to the King. In some respects, this situation served to prolong and strengthen the age-old cultural ties to Denmark. Danish continued to be the written, vernacular language in the new Norwegian state and Norway continued to be part of and dominated by Danish literature and theatre.

Two basic cultural characteristics were common to the Nordic countries. First, they all had high levels of literacy, not least due to the concerted efforts by the Protestant states to promote popular religious reading.[2] Secondly, the Nordic countries were open literary economies and, strikingly so, cultures of translation. Comparing translation activity in a number of European countries in the first half of the nineteenth century, Franco Moretti has shown that Denmark regularly comes out on top.[3] In one perspective, this dominance of translation over domestic production and export attests to the peripheral status of the Scandinavian countries in the international circulation of literature. In another perspective, Scandinavian readers were enjoying the advantages of what Goethe in the late 1820s called 'world literature': the intensified circulation of books, journals and ideas facilitated by increased economic exchange.[4]

The European novel came to Norway via Denmark, on a wave of translations in the 1830s: Cooper, Marryat, Bulwer-Lytton and soon Dickens, Scott, H.B. Stowe, A. Dumas *père*, E. Sue, George Sand and others.[5] Denmark experienced its own literary 'golden age' in this period, with authors like Hans Christian Andersen, Søren Kierkegaard and a series of popular novelists who were also read in Norway throughout the century.[6] In Norway, the native novel arrived slightly later, however. Camilla Collett's *The District Governor's Daughters*, published 1854–55, is considered the first Norwegian bourgeois novel, while the firm establishment of the novel as a serious, modern genre only took place in the 1870s.[7]

The late arrival of the novel had its counterpart in the persistent popularity of the drama. There were dramatic societies all over the country, reflected in the fact that both private libraries and the libraries of

[2] Loftur Guttormsson, 'The Development of Popular Religious Literacy in the Seventeenth and Eighteenth Centuries', *Scandinavian Journal of History*, vol. 15 (1990), 7–35.

[3] Franco Moretti, *Atlas of the European Novel 1800–1900* (London: Verso, 1998), 151–58, 174–84.

[4] Johann Wolfgang (von) Goethe, 'On World Literature (1827)', in Theo D'haen, Cesar Domínguez & Mads Rosendahl Thomsen (eds.), *World Literature* (London: Routledge, 2013), 9–15; David Damrosch, *What Is World Literature?* (Princeton: Princeton University Press, 2003), 6–15.

[5] Harald L. Tveterås, *Bokens kulturhistorie* (Oslo: Cappelen, 1986), 118–25.

[6] Among them, B.S. Ingemann, Steen Steensen Blicher, Thomasine Gyllembourg, Carl Bernhard, and Carit Etlar (J.C.C. Brosbøll).

[7] Per Thomas Andersen, *Norsk litteraturhistorie*, 2nd edn (Oslo: Universitetsforlaget, 2012), 246.

reading societies had substantial selections of play texts.[8] In the leading public library in Kristiania, the Danish-Norwegian playwright Ludvig Holberg (1684–1754), Shakespeare and Schiller were among the most popular authors in the 1820s.[9]

As a young reader Ibsen was exposed to this influx of translated novels and Danish golden age literature, alongside the continued presence of the drama. He does not seem to have inherited particular literary or theatrical interests or dispositions, but evidence clearly suggests that he read widely from his childhood and youth.[10] His friend in Grimstad, Christopher Due, says that Ibsen 'had certainly read remarkably much, incredibly much considering the limited accessibility of literature in the circumstances in which he lived'.[11] Due does not go into detail but claims that among the works being eagerly studied in these years were *Either-Or* and other books by Kierkegaard and the tragedies of the Danish playwright Adam Oehlenschläger. He also notes that Ibsen had a preference for Voltaire.

Ibsen himself admitted to having read Oehlenschläger and Holberg in Grimstad, 'besides novels', but no other dramatists.[12] However, the first extant Ibsen letter, from 1844, seems to be referring to Schiller's play *Wilhelm Tell*.[13] At least there is no doubt about the importance of Oehlenschläger and Holberg. Oehlenschläger, also a Danish 'golden age' author and generally considered the initiator of national romanticism in Danish and Nordic literature, was widely read and played in Norway. He used material from Nordic mythology, saga and ballads for poetry and stories, and laid the foundation for the new history drama. Ibsen's second printed poem, 'The Skald of Valhalla', was written on the occasion of Oehlenschläger's death in 1850, and the influence of this dramatist is evident in the first Ibsen play to reach the stage later that year, *The Burial Mound*.

There was, then, nothing peculiar in Ibsen choosing poetry and drama as his main genres. But even though drama enjoyed a high prestige and was

---

[8] Elisabeth S. Eide, *Bøker i Norge* (Oslo: Pax, 2013), 89, 106, 116, 132, 165–66, 169, 173, 238.

[9] Nils Johan Ringdal, *By, bok og borger* (Oslo: Aschehoug, 1985), 47.

[10] Jon Nygaard, '... *af stort est du kommen*' (Oslo: Akademika, 2013), 120–28.

[11] Chr. Due, *Erindringer fra Henrik Ibsens Ungdomsaar* (Copenhagen: Græbes bogtrykkeri, 1909), 39, quoted in Kristian Smidt, *Silent Creditors* (Oslo: Aschehoug, 2004), 8. For a survey of Ibsen's possible reading, see Vigdis Ystad, *Innledning til Catilina: Bakgrunn*, www.ibsen.uio.no/skuespill.

[12] Henrik Jæger, 'Henrik Jægers opptegnelser fra samtaler med Ibsen', in Hans Midtbøe, *Streiflys over Ibsen og andre studier* (Oslo: Gyldendal, 1960), 162; see also Henrik Jæger, *Henrik Ibsen* (Copenhagen: Gyldendal, 1888), 45.

[13] Ibsen, Letter to P. Lieungh, 20 May 1844, *Letters and Speeches*, 7.

still common reading, it was not at all a blooming genre in terms of published titles. The last 'serious' Norwegian drama published before *Catiline* was Henrik Wergeland's *Venetianerne* in 1843, and alongside *Catiline* just one other Norwegian play was published in 1850.[14] But the slim production of drama was basically a reflection of the overall weakness of Norwegian literary production. In the first national bibliography, covering the period up to 1847, it was estimated that just 147 books were published in Norway that year, of them 23 in the category 'Fine Sciences and Arts'.[15] Norwegian literature was, in other words, in its infancy.

Breaking the Danish Hegemony: The Norwegian Theatre Project

Ibsen's first period as dramatist is framed by two major political events, the 1848 revolution and its Norwegian aftermath and the 1864 war between Denmark and Prussia-Austria over Schleswig-Holstein. The first event, 1848, had a double impact on Ibsen. Like most students, he sympathised with the revolution and in Kristiania he befriended one of the leaders of its Norwegian offspring, the so-called Thrane movement, and also became involved in its activities.[16] There were some contacts between the liberal, parliamentary opposition against the government and the Thrane movement, but under the impression of the reinstalment of order in the rest of Europe, the movement was brought down by the police in the summer of 1851 and its leaders arrested and later convicted. The leaders of the parliamentary opposition were driven to rather humiliating retreats and Ibsen scorned them, for example, in his early and largely unknown three-act parody of parliamentary debates, *Norma; or the Love of a Politician* (*Norma; eller en Politikers Kjærlighed*) (1851).[17]

The revolution was also, however, the source of inspiration for the Norwegian theatre project. One visible aspect of the continued Danish cultural dominance in Norway was the fact that up until the middle of the century, the Norwegian stage was dominated not just by Danish plays but also by Danish actors and consequently by Danish spoken language. A couple of initiatives to train and use Norwegian actors had been taken, but none had survived for long. The first significant move to alter the

[14] Ystad, *Innledning til Catilina: Bakgrunn*, www.ibsen.uio.no/skuespill.
[15] Martinus Nissen, 'Statistisk Udsigt over den Norske Litteratur fra 1814 til 1847', *Norsk Tidsskrift for Videnskab og Literatur* (1849), 181, quoted in Eide, *Bøker*, 22.
[16] Ibsen later commented on his relation to the movement in a letter to J.B. Halvorsen, 18 June 1889, *Letters and Speeches*, 14.
[17] Published in *Andhrimner* 1851, nos. 9 and 10; www.ibsen.uio.no/skuespill/Norma.

situation was made in Bergen in 1850, followed by the capital Kristiania in 1852. Bergen's famous violin virtuoso Ole Bull, invigorated by experiencing the 1848 revolution in Paris to fight for Norwegian 'independence' by promoting Norwegian culture at home and abroad, came to Bergen to support the theatre cause.[18] On 15 October 1851 the Students' Society in Kristiania organised a concert in support of the Bergen theatre project, after Bull's effort to gain financial support from the parliament, *Stortinget*, had failed. Ibsen had written the prologue and also the text to a song, 'Kunstens Magt' ('The Power of Art'), for which Bull had composed the music. Bull was impressed and immediately offered Ibsen a position at the theatre.[19]

On his arrival in Bergen Ibsen's responsibility was specified as pertaining to 'assisting the theatre as dramatic writer', and a bit later he was appointed 'stage director'. In April 1852 Ibsen signed a contract which allowed him to travel to Copenhagen and Dresden to study theatre, while obliging him to stay in Bergen for five years. He carried out the study trip from the middle of April until the end of July 1852. In 1853, his duties were once more expanded and he was appointed 'stage manager'. During these years, Ibsen became practically acquainted with almost every aspect of theatre management, from directing to accountancy.

In 1857, after first having prolonged his Bergen contract for one year, Ibsen was allowed to leave in order to take over a position as artistic director at the Norwegian Theatre in Kristiania. Ibsen stayed in his new position in Kristiania until the theatre had to close for financial reasons in June 1862. From the beginning of January 1863 Ibsen had a part-time post as 'aesthetic consultant' at Christiania Theater, which was now once again the only theatre in the capital, but with a growing number of Norwegian actors. In September 1863 Ibsen was awarded a state travel grant to go to Paris and Rome. In June the following year he left for Rome and began what would turn out to be a twenty-seven-year period of residence in Italy and Germany.

---

[18] Bull's involvement in and importance for the project has probably been overestimated. In a recently discovered letter from November 1857, just after Ibsen had left Bergen and an antagonistic conflict between Bull and the theatre board had broken out, Ibsen wrote that 'the false impression of Ole Bull's importance as founder, must be corrected'. Ibsen wholeheartedly supported the board against Bull and offered to write the history of the Bergen theatre. Unfortunately, he never did; Ibsen, Letter to D.C. Danielssen, 18 November 1857 (original in Bergen Museum). See also Knut Nygaard, *Holbergs teaterarv* (Bergen: Eide, 1984), 121–22; and Ellen Karoline Gjervan, 'Ibsen Staging Ibsen', *Ibsen Studies*, vol. 11, no. 2 (2011), 125.

[19] Ståle Dingstad, *Den smilende Ibsen* (Oslo: Akademika, 2013), 65–66.

National Theatre in a Transnational Context

The 'Norwegianness' of the new theatres in Bergen and Kristiania had a number of distinctive features. The most salient was the use of Norwegian actors and the introduction of Norwegian spoken language on the stage. While still a student in 1851, Ibsen said this about the student theatre: 'It is us who will make the people used to hearing the Norwegian tongue from the stage.'[20] Pascale Casanova notes that drama, by occupying 'an intermediate position between the spoken and written language', has generally played an important part in standardising the language, settling the boundaries of an oral language, and transforming 'a popular audience into a national audience': 'In many newly formed literary spaces, the accumulation of popular heritage, the demand for (and reinvention of) a national language distinct from the language of colonisation, and the founding of a national theater go hand in hand.'[21]

By the nineteenth century philology too had become more concerned with spoken language, and the Danish scholar Rasmus Rask argued that orthography should follow contemporary pronunciation rather than etymology and tradition. In Norway this 'orthophony principle' was picked up by Knud Knudsen and, applying that principle, he had started using the term 'the Norwegian language' (1845).[22] Knudsen was appointed as a member of the board of the Norwegian Theatre in Kristiania and functioned as its language consultant.

No clear-cut reform strategy followed from this orthophony principle, however, since pronunciation was varied in different parts of the country. Knudsen's own suggestion was to base a reform of the written language on a form of 'received pronunciation' ['den landsgyldige norske uttale'], a pronunciation he thought was generally acceptable or understandable throughout the country, soon referred to as 'educated everyday speech' ['dannet dagligtale']. This in effect meant the spoken language of the upper class as it had emerged in the eighteenth century, with vocabulary and grammar similar to Danish but with a different pronunciation. Ivar Aasen went for another strategy, grounding a new language in rural dialects with echoes of Old Norse. This meant a vocabulary more different from Danish and in some respects closer to Swedish, and also with a slightly different

---

[20] 'Om Samfundstheatret' (1851), www.ibsen.uio.no/sakprosa.
[21] Casanova, *World Republic*, 228.
[22] For short introductions to these questions, see Eric Papazian, 'Språkreformatoren Knud Knudsen', *Språknytt*, vol. 40, no. 2 (2012), 19–22; Arne Torp, 'Skandinavisten Knud Knudsen', ibid. 23–25; Erlend Lønnum, 'Knudsen og Ibsen', ibid. 29–31.

grammar. Knudsen himself thought that Aasen and he were working towards the same goal, only along different routes. Knudsen was controversial in his own time, but the great orthographical reforms of 1907 and 1917, laying the foundation for today's majority language 'bokmål' ['book language'], meant that his strategy finally won out, while Aasen's 'landsmål' ['country language'], later called 'nynorsk' ['New Norwegian'], has remained a minority language.

It ought to have been easy to apply some clear-cut basic differences to a new Norwegian stage language, like replacing 'soft' Danish consonants 'd', 'g' and 'b' with the 'hard' Norwegian 't', 'k' and 'p' in words like 'gade' [gæːðə]/'gate' [gaːtə] (street), 'bog' [boʊ]/'bok' [buːk] (book) and 'åbne' [oːbnə]/'åpne'[oːpnə] (to open).[23] But applying the principle consistently was far from easy, and many other seemingly trivial changes in pronunciation, for example from 'sø' [søː] to 'sjø' [ʃøː] (sea) or from 'skov' [sgoʊ] to 'skog' [skuːg] (forest), or taking up distinctly Norwegian words, could take on revolutionary significance and be felt like a descent into barbarism. Danish continued to set the norm for what should be considered 'poetic', 'serious' and 'high'.[24] Ibsen soon learnt that 'the people' were not at all that happy to hear 'the Norwegian tongue from the stage'. It seems that the reforms introduced were not very radical[25]; even so, in 1861 Ibsen was disappointed at a common complaint 'that the language of the Norwegian theatre is raw and offensive'. He noted that it had been associated with a Kristiania working-class dialect ('Piperviksdialekt') and was therefore seen as 'unsuitable in all true artistic representation'.[26]

The actual development of a Norwegian stage language came to be influenced by the regional recruitment of actors. As it turned out, the Bergen project became of vital importance for the gradual replacement of Danish actors by Norwegian ones. Laura Svendsen (later Gundersen), born in Bergen, became the first Norwegian actress at Christiania Theater in 1850. Several of the actors that came from Bergen and gained their schooling at the Norwegian theatre in Bergen eventually came to join her. This resulted in the notion that Norwegian spoken with a polished Bergen accent, with uvular 'rs' and softer consonants than in the east, was particularly well suited for the stage. Olaf Hansson, who made his second

[23] Kirsten Shepherd-Barr, 'The Development of Norway's National Theatres', in S.E. Wilmer (ed.), *National Theatres in a Changing Europe* (Houndmills: Palgrave Macmillan, 2008), 87–9.

[24] Andersen, *Norsk*, 92.

[25] Thoralf Berg, 'Debatten om et norsk scenespråk i Christiania 1848–1853', unpublished thesis (Trondheim: Universitetet i Trondheim, NLHT, 1977).

[26] 'De to Theatre i Christiania III' (1861), www.ibsen.uio.no/sakprosa.

debut as Stensgaard in *The League of Youth* in 1877, was the first to gain
acceptance for quotidian, urban, southeastern dialect, while actors with
other linguistic backgrounds, like the Trøndelag dialects, had to erase their
regional roots to be accepted.

The other basic aspect of the programme for a Norwegian theatre was to
perform Norwegian plays written by Norwegian authors. Ibsen wrote
40 theatre articles and reviews before leaving Norway, in addition to
commenting on the theatre in many letters, and they show that he fully
identified with the Norwegian theatre project and that, at the time, he also
embraced the accompanying expressivist-essentialist vocabulary associated
with Herderian nationalism. The national author, he wrote in 1851, 'is the
one who understands how to endow his work with the keynote that
chimes towards us from mountains and valleys, from hillsides and sea-
shores, but most of all from our own inner beings'.[27] In 1857 he main-
tained that 'the people', as opposed to the usual theatre audience, did not
care about poetic subjectivity and did not seek to be entertained by new
situations and plots. The 'new' would only be attractive to the people if it
was at the same time 'old': 'it must not be invented, but *re*invented'. The
mission of the national author was to wake up 'memories which sort of lay
in our inner being, fermenting in obscure and indefinite ways until the
poet came and put them into words.'[28] His colleague and rival
Bjørnstjerne Bjørnson's style in his peasant tales, Ibsen explained a year
later, did not belong to the author in any other sense than that Bjørnson
was the first who had used it. The sense of relief with which Bjørnson's
peasant tales had been met showed that his style 'already in advance had
been a dormant demand in the people and a completely adequate expression of the notion of nationhood in our times'.[29]

Ibsen, furthermore, advocated the idea of a Norwegian language totally
distinct from Danish: 'The spirit of these brother languages is just as
different as the nature, history and other linguistic conditions of the two
countries.'[30] He also engaged wholeheartedly in the polemics against the
'foreign tendencies' and 'unpopular activity' at the 'Danish' Christiania
Theater.[31] Even so, he acknowledged the great contribution that Danish

[27] '"Huldrens Hjem," originalt skuespil i tre akter med sange og chor' (1851), ibid.
[28] 'Om Kjæmpevisen og dens Betydning for Kunstpoesien' (1857), ibid.
[29] '["See Tiden an"]' (1862), ibid.
[30] 'De to Theatre i Christiania III' (1861), www.ibsen.uio.no/sakprosa.
[31] In 1857 Christiania Theater first accepted *The Vikings at Helgeland*, but then found that they could
not afford to produce it after all. Ibsen wrote a series of polemical articles, the first of which were
entitled 'Et Træk af Christiania Danske Theaters Bestyrelse' (1858), ibid.

actors had made to Norwegian theatre. He wrote tributes to a couple of
them upon their return to Copenhagen, partly under the impression of the
growing demand for Norwegian actors.[32] Ibsen also acknowledged
Oehlenschläger as the one who first had realised the need to give national
art a national foundation by using sagas and ballads.[33]

In Ibsen's most extended discussion of these matters, 'On the Heroic
Ballad and Its Significance for Poetry' ('Om Kjæmpevisen og dens Betydning for Kunstpoesien', 1857), he argued that the ballads were better suited
as raw material for drama than the sagas, because the saga 'is a large, cold,
completed and self-contained epic'.[34] The ballads had the advantage of
allowing for 'Mystery, the enigmatic, the inexplicable'. The ballads, he
continued, suggested a spiritual kinship between the different branches of
the 'great Germanic tribe' – the Scandinavian, the German, the English,
the Scottish. The heroes and themes of Scandinavian poems were clearly
recognisable in, for example, the 'Niebelungenlied' and 'The Song of
Roland'. Ibsen claimed that their origin went all the way back to 'a time
which lies *before* the Germanic tribe's immigration to Europe, a time, in
other words, when this great tribe made up a unified whole'. Everything
suggests that Ibsen was a follower of the Norwegian historians' 'immigration theory', according to which the originally 'Germanic' and 'Nordic'
had been best preserved in Norway and Iceland and was primarily a Norse-
Norwegian inheritance. In this perspective, the struggle for a 'Norwegian'
theatre was an attempt to reconquer a precious source of cultural prestige
that had so far been appropriated and exploited primarily by Danes and
Swedes.[35]

Ibsen contributed to this programme during his whole time in Norway,
before his departure for Italy in 1864. After his first play in Bergen, *St
John's Night* (1853), with a contemporary setting,[36] his second contribution was a revised version of *The Burial Mound* (1854). The next were:
Lady Inger of Ostrat (premiere 1855, printed 1857), subtitled 'historical
drama'; *The Feast at Solhaug* (1855, 1856), with a certain basis in historical
events in the early fourteenth century, but according to Ibsen just as much
inspired by medieval ballads[37]; and finally *Olaf Liljekrans* (premiere 1857,

---

[32] 'Anton Wilhelm Wiehe' (1857), ibid. and 'Til en Bortdragende Kunstner' (1863/1871), www.ibsen.uio.no/dikt.
[33] 'Om Kjæmpevisen', www.ibsen.uio.no/sakprosa.   [34] Ibid.
[35] This is the general thrust of the conclusion, ibid.
[36] Ibsen later repudiated the authorship of this play, see Ibsen, Letter to J. Elias, 19 September 1897, *Letters and Speeches*, 329.
[37] 'Fortale til anden udgave', www.ibsen.uio.no/skuespill/Gildet.

unpublished until 1902), based on legends and ballads of the Black Death. In Kristiania he wrote *The Vikings at Helgeland* (printed and performed 1858), relying on Icelandic 'family' sagas, but with invented characters and intended to 'give a picture of life in the age of the sagas more generally'.[38] After the contemporary verse drama *Love's Comedy* (published 1862), Ibsen concluded the national-historical cycle with *The Pretenders* (published October 1863, performed January 1864), subtitled 'historical play' and with characters and events taken from early thirteenth-century Norwegian history, generally considered to be the climax of the Norwegian medieval state.

Even though both Bjørnson and Ibsen made a substantial contribution to 'national' drama, the Norwegian theatres were not even close to nationalising their repertoires. Norwegian theatre continued to be dominated by Danish and French plays. During Ibsen's five full seasons in Bergen, 122 new plays were performed: 62 French, 28 Danish, 16 Norwegian, 11 German, and 5 others. In terms of genre the repertoire for the whole period in which the theatre operated, 1850–1863, was dominated by light comedy ('lystspill') (35 per cent), vaudeville (20 per cent), comedy (14 per cent), farce (3 per cent), and 'musicals' (4 per cent). Ten per cent were classified as 'plays' and 8 per cent as 'drama'. The most frequently played author was, by far, Eugène Scribe (40 plays), but Nordic plays achieved the highest number of performances.[39]

The composition of the repertoire is the most obvious evidence that the struggle for a national theatre took place in a thoroughly transnational context. From the very start the ambitions of the project were also self-consciously formulated in transnational terms. Reviewing a vaudeville at Christiania Theater in the spring of 1851, Ibsen called for something new: 'We ourselves produce nothing, nor do the Danes. Scribe has become stale.'[40] Six years later it was much the same. There was a general complaint, he wrote, that the time of the great scenic artists were over. The Théâtre Français had its period of excellence, the Danish theatre adored its own past and Germany no longer had the likes of Eckhoff, Iffland or Schröder. Those to blame, Ibsen thought, were the dramatic authors,

---

[38] Ibsen, Letter to C. Hauch, 8 February 1858.
[39] Jan Olav Gatland, *Repertoaret ved Det Norske Theater 1850–1863* (Bergen: Universitetsbiblioteket i Bergen, 2000), iv–vi.
[40] '["En blaseret Herre"]' (1851), www.ibsen.uio.no/sakprosa, quoted and trans. in McFarlane, *Ibsen and Meaning*, 109.

and particularly those of the new dramatic trend in France; these in technical terms perfect pieces of art that annually emanate from the Parisian authors' workshops and that to such a sad degree contribute to promoting virtuosity at the expense of art, – these laceworks that are calculated only to create effect through the 'delivery of lines' cannot but degrade art to a lower region – that of sensation.[41]

It is not quite clear which new trends Ibsen referred to. But the European theatre market was highly synchronised at this time. Émile Augier, for example, was first performed at Christiania Theatre in 1855 with *Le Gendre de Monsieur Poirier* (*Hr. Poiriers Svigersøn*, trans. Glückstad) – written with Jules Sandeau – appearing only a year after its Paris production. *Un beau Marriage* (*Et godt Parti*, trans. H. Arentz) was staged in 1860, that too only a year after Paris, and *Les Effrontés* (*Den offentlige Mening*, trans. unknown) in 1863, two years after its French premiere. Ibsen himself produced Victorien Sardou for the first time in Norway, with *Pattes de Mouche* (*Et farligt Brev*, trans. A. Recke) at Kristiania Norwegian Theatre in the autumn of 1860. It was one of Sardou's first successes in Paris that same year.[42] Where the translators have been identified, at least some of them seem to be Norwegian. But whether the translations were made directly from French or were adaptions from Danish or other languages is not known, nor how the plays were acquired.

The national theatre project clearly aimed at raising the theatre to an art institution, and this ambition was conceived in a European context, more particularly in the context of a French theatre hegemony that needed to be challenged. Bjørnson explicitly perceived the Norwegian historical drama as a transitional stage towards a renewal of bourgeois drama. He had, he wrote in 1861, 'an ill-fated passion for the bourgeois drama, which at this very moment all over the world is in need of radical development, even though it seems that no one wants to start'. In Norway, he thought, 'it would in many respects be harmful if this drama came before the historical one; without it [the historical drama] the bourgeois drama would tend towards a sentimentality and pettiness that would be more suffocating than refreshing'.[43] In 1865 Bjørnson wrote what is considered to be the first bourgeois play in Norway, *The Newly Married*, but it was only with his two plays of 1875,

[41] 'Anton Wilhelm Wiehe' (1857), ibid.
[42] Anker, Øyvind, *Christiania Theater's Repertoire 1827–99* (Oslo: Gyldendal, 1956); Øyvind Anker, *Kristiania Norske Theaters Repertoire 1852–1863* (Oslo: Gyldendal, 1956).
[43] Bjørnstjerne Bjørnson, Letter to Ditmar Meidell, [Summer 1861], *Gro-tid*, ed. Halvdan Koht (Kristiania: Gyldendal, 1912), 255–56; we would like to thank Ann Schmiesing for identifying this reference.

Figure 1.1   The Norwegian Theatre in Kristiania, where Ibsen served as artistic director
1857–62.
The contemporary xylography shows a scene from A. Duval's *Snedkeren i Lifland, eller:
Peter den Stores Reise* (*Le Menuisier de Livonie, ou: Les Illustres Voyageurs*, 1805), performed
five times in the 1852/53 season (Øyvind Anker: Kristiania Norske Theaters Repertoire,
Oslo: Gyldendal 1956, 38).

A Bankruptcy and *The Editor*, that he definitively initiated the turn of
Scandinavian drama towards contemporary middle-class society.

There are good reasons to argue that the way Ibsen empowered modern
drama owes much to his craftsmanship learnt in the service of the national
theatre. Many have pointed to the continuity in his constellations of
characters and the affinities between his female heroines, for example.
Exploiting the techniques of 'the well-made play', he fused them with
the tragic, the heroic, the passionate, the 'demonic' that he found in his
'native' literary heritage. But 'bourgeois' transcended a national frame of
reference. By moving from the heroic national past to the un-heroic
middle-class present, Ibsen was able to contribute to national and European culture at the same time. His contemporary prose plays no longer

appealed to nationally specific 'memories' or 'a peculiarity of outlook belonging to us and nobody else',[44] but to experiences that could be transnationally recognised and appreciated.

How Bad Were Ibsen's Theatre Years?

The master narrative informing Ibsen biography imposes a double-entry bookkeeping on the account of his theatre years, resulting in a highly negative balance. In James W. McFarlane's introductions to *The Oxford Ibsen* – arguably, due to its appearance in English, the most influential scholarly Ibsen edition of the twentieth century[45] – we read this about the start of Ibsen's theatre career: 'For a young and ambitious author to be invited at the age of twenty-three to join this exciting new enterprise was on the face of it a stroke of amazing good fortune; even today it is difficult to believe that the effect on his career was other than wholly beneficial'.[46] Only 'on the face of it', since at this point we have already learnt that Ibsen's early plays 'help to define the nature of a kind of intellectual bondage from which it took him long years to break free. Summarily expressed, the two things that mainly held him fettered were the Norwegian Myth and the *pièce bien faite*.'[47]

If Bergen had been bad, Kristiania turned out worse, 'far more chilling to his spirit than anything he had experienced in Bergen, or Grimstad, or Skien', according to Michael Meyer.[48] McFarlane acknowledges *The Pretenders* as 'Ibsen's first and incontrovertible masterpiece', and credits the warm sympathy Ibsen met with in Bergen during the choral festival in June 1863 for the creative mood that enabled him to write it. But this turns out to be the exception to the general experience of 'frustration, hostility, misunderstanding, and growing artistic isolation'.[49] Arriving at the crisis of 1864, the narrative voice merges completely with Ibsen's own fierce condemnation of Norwegian 'betrayal' and 'cowardice' and no further explanation of the nature of the Danish-German conflict or Norwegian and Swedish politics are given. The transfer to Rome can, accordingly, take on the character of a romance; a transition from darkness to light, from nationalism to culture, from bondage to freedom, from heteronomy to authentic self-expression.

---

[44] Ibsen et al., Letter to the Storting, 25 October 1859, quoted and translated in McFarlane, *Ibsen and Meaning*, 144.
[45] The introductions are collected in McFarlane, ibid.   [46] Ibid. 108.   [47] Ibid. 104.
[48] Meyer, *Ibsen*, 157.   [49] McFarlane, *Ibsen and Meaning*, 164–66.

Again, there is no denying that this narrative can find ample evidence from Ibsen himself and his supporters.[50] When leaving Bergen in 1857 to take up his new position in Kristiania, Ibsen wrote that 'the conditions at the Bergen theater have for a long time now oppressed and inhibited me. Every path in which I might have accomplished something has been closed to me.'[51] In 1867, after three years in Rome, Ibsen wrote to Bjørnson: 'For a poet, working in a theater is equivalent to repeated, daily abortions.'[52] Throughout the years he turned down every offer he was given to return to Kristiania and take up a position at the theatre. Based on Ibsen's own statements and actions, the view of McFarlane and numerous other authors certainly seems reasonable and well founded.

Even so, the overall negative assessment needs to be reconsidered and, above all, Ibsen's theatre experiences deserve some comparative perspectives. Starting with the response to his own plays, Ibsen might seem to have met with little understanding. In Bergen, most of his plays were only on for two nights. But this was, after all, the fate of the majority of plays.[53] *The Feast at Solhoug*, which Ibsen later called 'a study which I have disowned',[54] was his only clear success, performed five times in its premiere season. This should not, however, be taken to indicate that the taste of the Norwegian audience was particularly unsophisticated; *The Feast at Solhoug* was actually also the first Ibsen play to be performed outside Norway, at the Royal Theatre in Stockholm in 1857 and at the Casino theatre in Copenhagen in 1861.

When *The Vikings at Helgeland*, generally thought of as Ibsen's best play from the 1850s, was not put on by Christiania Theater, Ibsen ventured on an extended newspaper campaign against the theatre. But this time as well the Norwegian reception seems quite sympathetic within a Scandinavian context. When Ibsen sent *The Vikings* to the Royal Theatre in Copenhagen it was turned down by the censor and leading dramatic authority in Scandinavia, Johan Ludvig Heiberg. The conclusion of Heiberg's report has entered the repertoire of spectacularly failed predictions: 'A Norwegian theatre will probably not appear from the laboratory of these experiments;

---

[50] See Ståle Dingstad, 'Mytene etableres', in Astrid Sæther et al. (eds.), *Den biografiske Ibsen* (Oslo: Unipub, 2010), 79–101.

[51] Ibsen, Letter to the Director of the National Theater in Bergen, 23 July 1857, *Letters and Speeches*, 25.

[52] Ibsen, Letter to Bjørnson, 28 December 1867, ibid. 71.   [53] Gatland, *Repertoaret*, iv–v.

[54] Ibsen, footnote to Letter to P. Hansen, 28 October 1870, *Letters and Speeches*, 101. Even so, in 1883 Ibsen made a new version of the play.

the Danish does happily not need them.'⁵⁵ When Ibsen himself produced the play at the Norwegian theatre in Kristiania during the season of 1858–59, it achieved a respectable eight performances.

In terms of his practical schooling in drama, Ibsen's theatre years were invaluable. He was involved in staging 122 new plays in Bergen, and around 200 in all before he left the country. He became acquainted with everything relating to the creation and use of the stage, technically and artistically.⁵⁶ In Bergen, he had the unique privilege of having every piece he wrote rehearsed and tried out on the stage. Furthermore, he worked with many highly talented actors. In 1862 Ibsen claimed that 'our theatre history will be able to show up an amount of talent and many-sided giftedness that few others can equal'.⁵⁷ He later found support for his opinions. After visiting Christiania Theater in 1876, Georg Brandes wrote: 'There were evenings where, in this small, inconspicuous and ugly theatre, they were not behind Théâtre Français in their comedy.'⁵⁸

The *literary* value of Ibsen's theatre experience has generally been downplayed with reference to the inferior repertoire. Ibsen was largely forced to reproduce what he in 1851 termed 'Scribe and Co.'s sugar-candy dramas'.⁵⁹ The total reliance on box office receipts meant an extremely high turnover in the repertoire and subjection to the popular demand for entertainment. But when Ibsen himself, in the early 1860s, was met with the charge of running a 'vaudeville theatre' nurtured on 'the so-called lower dramatic arts',⁶⁰ he turned on his critics. The French, he said, produced half of what any theatre in Europe, big or small, put on.⁶¹ A 'good repertoire' was a repertoire that suited the resources available and a good execution of bad drama was preferable to destroying a masterpiece. A 'good repertoire' also had to be diverse: 'it has to vary between Mallefille, Oehlenschläger, Birch-Pfeifer, Shakespeare, Iffland, Molière, Barriere, and partly, Holberg.'⁶²

On a couple of occasions at the beginning of the 1860s, Ibsen also noted the relative merits of French plays. In 1862 he contrasted plays with stereotypical characters with plays where the actors could supply the

---

⁵⁵ Quoted in J.B. Halvorsen, *Norsk Forfatter-Lexikon 1814–1880* (Kristiania: Den norske Forlagsforening, 1892), vol. 3, 39.
⁵⁶ Gjervan, 'Ibsen Staging', 130.   ⁵⁷ '[Theaterkrisen]' (1862), www.ibsen.uio.no/sakprosa.
⁵⁸ *Levned* (Copenhagen: Gyldendal, 1907), vol. 2, 214.
⁵⁹ '"Haarpidsk og Kaarde", Skuespil i 5 Akter af K. Gutzkow' (1851), www.ibsen.uio.no/sakprosa.
⁶⁰ 'De to Theatre i Christiania' (1861), ibid.
⁶¹ 'Lidt, men nok om Theaterafhandlingen i *Christianiaposten*' (1861), ibid.
⁶² 'De to Theatre i Christiania IV' (1861), ibid.

characters with 'a thousand individual shades'. Plays of the first kind were
overwhelmingly represented in German and Swedish literature and in the
majority of the Parisian repertoire 20–25 years ago. He even suggested that
'the entire genre of tragedy, according to its definitions, belongs to the
same category; it is at least certain that one cannot exempt most of
Oehlenschläger's tragedies.' Another kind of play, he argued, was found
in the light comedy of recent French and Danish literature. Their quality
was totally dependent on performance and they required that each actor
knew the whole dialogue, not just the individual part.[63] Later the same
year he reviewed Augier's *Diane* (*Diana*, tr. unknown, 1852) at Christiania
Theater. The play was originally written for Rachel and is considered a
failed effort in the genre of the historical drama,[64] but Ibsen compared it
favourably with 'German art'. And he praised Louise Brun as Diane and
Chr. Jørgensen as Richelieu in a minor but, according to Ibsen, important
scene: 'The interaction between him and Diane makes the scene into the
most excellent thing dramatic art has achieved in this country. Why does
one not produce *Macbeth*?'[65]

It is generally acknowledged that Ibsen's technique owes a lot to Scribe
and 'the well-made play'. Here, he learnt how to construct a clear, logical
and conceivable chain of events, with the uncovering of a hidden truth as a
major device. There are reasons to claim, then, that the most valuable
experience from these years might have been exactly what in one sense was
a failure, namely that they exposed Ibsen to and made him learn the whole
range of the 'low', 'illegitimate drama'.[66]

Even so, Ibsen clearly felt that the theatre was more and more of a
restriction. The poem On the Heights (1860) was, as Ibsen later expressed
it, pervaded by a desire for freedom.[67] In this poem he developed a poetics
of distance, organised around the opposition between 'high mountain life'
('høyfjellsliv') and 'low country life' ('lavlandsliv'), making distance and
cold the necessary preconditions for reaching a higher perspective and
giving aesthetic form to subjective pain. We will return to how Ibsen on
several occasions rephrased this poetics in response to changing conditions

[63] '[Der gives en hel stor Klasse af Theaterstykker]' (1862), ibid.
[64] 'Augier, Guillaume Victor Émile', *Salmonsens Konversationsleksikon*, 2nd ed. (Copenhagen: J.H. Schultz, 1925), vol. 2; see also comment to Ibsen, '[Christiania Theater]' (1862), www.ibsen.uio.no/sakprosa.
[65] '[Christiania Theater]' (1862), ibid. In 1855 Bjørnson too had praised what he called the 'naturalist' plays of Musset, Augier and Dumas *fils* at the expense of Scribe, see Meyer, *Ibsen*, 139.
[66] Gjervan, 'Ibsen staging', 131–32.
[67] Ibsen, Letter to P. Hansen, 28 October 1870, *Letters and Speeches*, 101.

of production and reception. It clearly marks a departure from the expressivism and collectivism of his writings of the 1850s.

There is no doubt that economic factors presented a major challenge for the Norwegian theatre project, and that economic concerns and box office considerations took on an overwhelming importance. Repeated applications for state support were turned down and after 1860 theatre attendance fell.[68] Ibsen was quite pleased to report in 1861, after having received some criticism, that under his leadership the incomes of the Norwegian theatre in Kristiania had increased year by year.[69] But the next year he commented bitterly that the public had been indifferent to the closure of the theatre[70] and that the audience preferred amusement to art and national endeavour.[71] The hardships of the theatre, furthermore, directly affected his private economy. The last part of his salary from the Norwegian Theatre was never paid, and when he was engaged as consultant for Christiania Theater from 1863, his payment was made dependent on the overall income. Again he had to write much occasional poetry as well as articles and reviews for newspapers and periodicals, like other Norwegian writers of this time. He was forced to change residence frequently, and his last address was in a 'slum-like' neighbourhood.[72]

Ibsen's financial problems cannot, however, be attributed purely to bad theatre economy, nor even to low incomes generally. During his time at the Norwegian Theatre in Kristiania, Ibsen was paid 635 specie dollars the first season (1857–58) and 664 the last one (1861–62). In between these two his salary varied from 711 to 767. In addition to this, he might have had something like 100 specie dollars from literary work.[73] This should have provided him with a solid economy; his contractual minimum income alone, 600 specie dollars, put him on the same level as a master craftsman and above a Principal Officer (byråsjef).[74] Ibsen's annual income in Kristiania was above what he had received in Bergen and should have been sufficient even after he got married in 1858 and his son Sigurd was born in 1859. But Ibsen had started to accumulate debt already in Bergen, and in Kristiania he began to neglect the maintenance obligation for his illegitimate son in Grimstad, even though less than 30 specie dollars were left to pay.[75] From 1857 to 1864, thirteen lawsuits were raised against him,

---

[68] Anette Storli Andersen, 'In the Right Place, at the Right Time', *Ibsen Studies*, vol. 11, no. 2 (2011), 105.

[69] '[I det forløbne Spilleaar]' (1861), www.ibsen.uio.no/sakprosa.

[70] '[Den forestaaende Theatersæson]' (1862), ibid.   [71] '[Christiania Theater]' (1862), ibid.

[72] Per Kristian Heggelund Dahl, *Streiflys* (Oslo: Ibsen-museet, 2001), 40.   [73] Ibid. 36–7.

[74] Ibid. 104.   [75] Ibid. 104–5.

ten of them by 1861.[76] By the time the Norwegian Theatre had to give up in 1862, Ibsen's debt amounted to 400 specie dollars. A year later, it had grown to over 500.[77] The politician Ludvig Daae, a relative of Ibsen's wife Susanna, wrote in his diary 3 February 1863: 'On the way home . . . I met Ibsen. He looks fairly dissipated; patchy overcoat, patchy hat and an almost copper-red face. It may be accidental that he looked like this today, but it made a disturbing ['uhyggeligt'] impression on me.'[78] Other sources confirm that Ibsen had built up a reputation for drunkenness.[79]

Ibsen's application for an annual stipend in line with Bjørnson's was rejected in March 1863, but in the course of the year his fortune turned in many respects. In May he was awarded a domestic travel grant (100 specie dollars), and in September a grant to go abroad (400 specie dollars), something which had been indicated already when his application for the regular annual stipend was denied. In September he received 150 specie dollars for the publication of *The Pretenders*. In 1864 the performance of this play earned him almost 190 specie dollars from Christiania Theater, and in addition to this Bjørnson and Bernhard Dunker managed to collect 700 specie dollars which were paid him in monthly rates from April 1864 until January 1865.

Overall, Ibsen was in a privileged position during his years in Norway, even during the last period in Kristiania. The causes of his economic troubles are mixed and not altogether clear. Furthermore, they seem not to have severely affected the quality of his literary work. If *The Vikings at Helgeland* is Ibsen's best work of the 1850s, this was improved upon in the 1860s, with the long poems On the Heights (1860) and Terje Vigen (1862), the verse drama *Love's Comedy* (1862) and the historical drama *The Pretenders* (1863) as high points. And his works were appreciated. Ibsen himself put great emphasis on the hostility against *Love's Comedy* in the preface to the new edition issued in 1867: 'I made the mistake of publishing the book in Norway.' It took ten years before the play was finally performed at Christiania Theater (1873), but from then on it became one of his most popular plays. It has often been assumed that he was refused an annual grant because of *Love's Comedy*,[80] but this was flatly denied by Ibsen himself.[81] The next play after *Love's Comedy*, *The Pretenders*, was an

[76] Ibid. 11.
[77] Ibid. 33–5. See also Ibsen, Letter to the King, 10 March 1863, *Letters and Speeches*, 32.
[78] Ludvig Daae, *Politiske dagbøker og minner* (Oslo: Grøndahl, 1934), vol. 1, 216.
[79] See Meyer, *Ibsen*, 197.   [80] For example, McFarlane, *Ibsen and Meaning*, 166–67.
[81] Ibsen, Letter to F.V. Hegel, 8 March 1867, *Letters and Speeches*, 62.

immediate and considerable success. The publisher produced a relatively large edition of 1250 copies, and at the theatre, under Ibsen's own instruction, it was played for seven nights in the spring of 1864.

Ibsen had clearly acquired a solid position by 1863, as witness for instance the celebration he received during the above-mentioned choral festival in Bergen in 1863. Here he was a leading cultural personality alongside other authors and composers like Bjørnson, Andreas Munch and Ole Bull. His fame also reached outside the two largest cities. On his return from Bergen Ibsen was greeted with a speech by the mayor of Kristiansand when the Kristiania delegation made a stop there.[82] When he left Norway Ibsen was on his way up, both financially, socially and artistically.

We could, finally, adopt a broader comparative perspective and ask what chances a character like Ibsen would have stood in a more advanced theatre culture. What would his prospects have been, for example, in the theatre capital of the world, Paris? Of ten playwrights elected to the Académie Française over the period 1855–88, all except two were born in Paris. Their fathers had all pursued professional careers and they themselves had attended prestigious educational establishments in Paris and mostly gone on to study for degrees. Nearly all had connections in theatrical or literary circles. Even so, it was extremely hard to be let in because everything suggested that it was wiser to go for an established name than to gamble on a new one. The younger Dumas had to wait four years until he had one of the greatest theatre successes of the century, *La Dame aux Camélias*, accepted by the Vaudeville, in spite of the name and connections of his father. Victorien Sardou, another of the most highly esteemed playwrights and one of the richest, 'led a life of dire poverty between 1854 and 1859, a period during which he was starving and shabby and never knew how he was to pay the rent for his room'.[83] Émile Zola was highly disfavoured by these circumstances; Ibsen would simply have lacked every quality required to enter into this world. In Norway, on the contrary, all available dramatic talent was mobilised to build a Norwegian theatre, just when Ibsen stood poised at the start of his career. The timing was 'a stroke of amazing good fortune', indeed, not just 'on the face of it'.

---

[82] *Beretning om den femte store Sangerfest afholdt i Bergen 14–18 Juni 1863* (Kristiania: Joh. D. Behrens, 1963), 1–2, 61, 89, 121–22, 172.

[83] F.W.J. Hemmings, *The Theatre Industry in Nineteenth-Century France* (Cambridge: Cambridge University Press, 1993), 242–43; the sociological data are from a study by Christophe Charle.

1864 and the Crisis of the Pan-Scandinavian Movement

Ibsen left Norway under the impression of another major event which coloured Scandinavian political and intellectual life for years, and Danish politics for decades. In 1864, Denmark was defeated by the allied military forces of Prussia and Austria and lost the two duchies of Schleswig and Holstein (in Danish Slesvig and Holsten). Ibsen would later describe his transfer to Rome as a voluntary exile caused by growing isolation, as well as anger at Norway and Sweden for not supporting Denmark with military forces. Ibsen had been a supporter of the Pan-Scandinavian movement (*Skandinavismen*) and had seen Scandinavian solidarity in this conflict as a true test. When Denmark was left alone, the crisis became a major blow to Scandinavianism and to Ibsen a disillusionment even darker than 1848.

The Norwegian policy on the war issue, however, was dictated by rather straightforward reasons. The King had instilled hopes for military support to Denmark, but he had never had the backing of either the Swedish or the Norwegian government. The leader of the Norwegian government, Frederik Stang, would not involve Norway in continental politics to defend Danish interests in Schleswig, and made Norwegian support of Denmark conditional on British support. Stang thought Schleswig should be divided along nationality lines, while the Danish policy was to include the whole of the duchy under the Danish constitution and introduce Danish in administration, church and school. It was only in the northern parts of Schleswig that Danish-speakers were in a majority; the conflict was very much an internal civil war between the Danish-speaking and the German-speaking parts of the duchy. The overall majority in Schleswig was German and it was not obvious to all Norwegians that Danish nationalism was more ideal and principled than German nationalism. The remarkable thing about Ibsen's rhetoric is indeed how one-sided it was.

If we take the emotional temperature in Ibsen's rhetoric seriously, the question remains: Why did Scandinavianism matter that much to him? At first glance it seems contradictory, since the Norwegian theatre project with which he had identified had such a clear anti-Danish tendency. Furthermore, by the 1860s Scandinavianism had ceased to be primarily a liberal movement and had turned into an instrument for the dynastic ambitions of the Bernadottes, the Swedish royal family, as a military programme against Russia and Prussia.[84]

---

[84] Bo Stråth, *Union og demokrati* (Oslo: Pax, 2005), 189–95.

Even so, there was a consistency to the attitude of Ibsen and many other Norwegian intellectuals. First, Ibsen, like other Norwegian supporters of the pan-Scandinavian movement, always insisted that working for closer Nordic unity and solidarity, had to go hand in hand with the struggle for national 'liberation'. The Scandinavian idea, Ibsen claimed, made it a 'duty' for Norwegians to act as a free nation, politically and culturally.[85] Nordic unity presupposed independence and coequality.[86] Expressing Norwegian individuality and working for closer Nordic unity were two sides of the same coin.

The second motive was that Scandinavianism promoted a northern cultural orientation, as opposed to the traditional German-Continental orientation that was predominant in Denmark. In his speech in Rome in 1865 on the occasion of the unveiling of a monument of the Norwegian historian P.A. Munch, Ibsen encouraged the Danes to stop looking south, to erase from their art and literature 'that party in your country which with such strangely sympathetic ties feel pulled towards the South, that party in your country which do all its exercise ['Idræt'] with their eyes directed there, as if it *there* had its allied country ['Frændeland'], the country of its own tribe ['Stammeland'].'[87] A northern orientation had a lot to offer Norwegian academics, artists, and authors since it implied the cultivation of a glorious past of myth, religion, Vikings and medieval kings where Norway could claim not just coequality with its neighbours, but even a certain priority and superiority.

A similar motive can, thirdly, explain why the struggle for a Norwegian language could coexist with efforts to promote Scandinavian language cooperation. The kind of Danish-Norwegian hybrid language that was advocated by Knud Knudsen could be conceived of as an ideal Scandinavian 'middle language'. The orthophonic reforms he suggested would all contribute to narrowing the gap between Danish and Swedish.[88]

All these reasons were conjoined in a fourth strong motive for Ibsen's Scandinavianism: it was a perfect ideological underpinning for entering the Scandinavian book market.

The Transition to Danish Gyldendal

Bjørnson was instrumental not only in making it possible for Ibsen to go to Rome, but also for his transition to Gyldendal. In 1860, Gyldendal

---

[85] 'De to Theatre i Christiania' (1861), www.ibsen.uio.no/sakprosa.
[86] Ibsen, 'Endnu et Indlæg i Theatersagen' (1858), ibid.
[87] 'Korrespondence fra Rom til Nyhedsbladet' (1865), ibid.   [88] Torp, 'Skandinavisten', 23.

published a new edition of Camilla Collett's *The District Governor's Daughters*. At that time Bjørnson too had decided to go to the Copenhagen publisher Frederik V. Hegel, head of the Gyldendal company since 1850. This was a turning point with far-reaching consequences for literature and publishing in the whole of Scandinavia. Bjørnson was strongly encouraged to take this step by the Danish critic Clemens Petersen after the success of his peasant tale *Synnøve Solbakken* in Denmark. It was not at all an easy step since it was in obvious conflict with the whole national rhetoric of building a Norwegian theatre and a Norwegian literature – in opposition to the age-old Danish hegemony. But the advantages were many. Publishing in Copenhagen had a cultural prestige that added value to a Norwegian book in the home market, while at the same time facilitating access to the Danish market. Within the still existing cultural hierarchy, Norwegian publishers had a disadvantage in the Danish market that Danish publishers did not have in the Norwegian. Neither were there any Norwegian publishers at the time with visions and financial muscle to provide for a considerable expansion of Norwegian literature. Hegel, on his side, had the means to be generous with advance payments. Bjørnson's offer to introduce Ibsen to Hegel and ask for an advance on his behalf fell on fertile ground since Ibsen's financial sources had all dried up by the spring of 1865.

So it was that, starting with Collett, Bjørnson and Ibsen, the writers of the 'golden age' of Norwegian literature became Copenhagen publishing commodities while Frederik V. Hegel became the main publisher of the literature of the Modern Breakthrough and the foremost literary publisher in Scandinavia. From 1860 to 1890, around 90 Norwegian authors chose Gyldendal and other Danish publishers.[89] The result was that the great majority of 'native language' books circulating in Norway in the nineteenth century continued to be books printed in Denmark.[90]

The move to Gyldendal had several important consequences. One was that it stabilised the relationship between author and publisher. Until Ibsen went to Gyldendal, his publishing pattern had been new book, new publisher. But after some initial misunderstandings concerning *Brand*, the loyalty and mutual understanding between Ibsen and Gyldendal were cemented and unbroken for the rest of his career.

The transition to a Danish publisher also had major consequences in linguistic terms. In a wider perspective, the fact that the most prestigious part

[89] Harald L. Tveterås, *Norske forfattere på danske forlag, 1850–1890* (Oslo: Cappelen, 1964), 409.
[90] Eide, *Bøker*, 23, 110, 184.

of Norwegian literature in the late nineteenth century was published in Denmark, might have contributed to prolonging the Danish hegemony over Norwegian written language. The major spelling reforms, adjusting the written language to Norwegian pronunciation, came, as already noted, only in 1907 and 1917. When a Norwegian author opted for a Danish publisher, it clearly meant a rejection of Aasen's radical linguistic strategy, but it also made Knudsen's strategy difficult to apply. Ibsen participated in the Nordic spelling reform meeting in Stockholm in 1869 and immediately took up its few and rather meagre proposals, like changing to lower case in the spelling of nouns, and replacing the double vowel 'aa' with the 'Swedish' 'å'. Hegel had no problem with this and he was pleased that Ibsen did not follow Bjørnson's more radical approach. Ibsen replied that 'I would regret it very much if Bjørnson sticks to his decision of supporting the Knudsen method; this is the most unpopular one in Norway and in the case of Denmark and Sweden the most incomprehensible and offensive one.'[91]

It is hard to find a discernible strategy behind Ibsen's linguistic development. *Catiline* was written in more or less plain Danish and Ibsen's manuscripts from the 1850s reveal inconsistencies and hesitations. He followed Knudsen some of the way, but was reluctant when it came to the 'hard consonants'.[92] But even though Ibsen might seem rather cautious in his reform efforts, he clearly had an identity as a Norwegian writer, and just as importantly: He was conceived of as such in Denmark. A Norwegian linguistic identity was bestowed upon him by Danish authorities almost from the start. When *The Pretenders* was reviewed by the censor of the royal theatre in Copenhagen in 1863, the playwright Carsten Hauch, he remarked that the language was partly incomprehensible and 'even madder than with the other Norwegian-Norwegian Norwegians'. Hauch gave several examples of words and expressions that he thought came from

> various peasant dialects which have now been adopted by the Norwegian writers in order to hastily acquire a language which differs from Danish; with us it can hardly appear except in translation, and least so in a theatre whose task it is, among other things, to guard the purity of the language.[93]

In 1866 a more sympathetic Danish author published an eighty-eight page dictionary of Norwegian aesthetical literature since 1842,[94] containing

[91] Ibsen, Letter to F.V. Hegel, 12 February 1870.   [92] Lønnum, 'Knudsen', 29–31.
[93] Quoted in Edvard Agerholm, 'Henrik Ibsen og det kgl. Teater', *Gads danske Magasin* (1910–11), 277.
[94] A. Listov, *Ordsamling fra den norske æsthetiske literatur siden Aaret 1842, alfabetisk ordnet og forklaret* (København: Gyldendal, 1866).

common words in Norwegian popular language, often stemming from
Old Norse but no longer present in Danish; words from Danish literary
language gone out of use in Denmark; and words deviating in spelling or
content from corresponding Danish ones.

Being treated as a foreign author could only reinforce Ibsen's sense of
national difference, and to the extent that it was based on a sense of
superiority, also his anger at what he conceived as Danish indifference
and arrogance. During the first years at Gyldendal he called Copenhagen
'the real Scandinavian centre',[95] he said that his intention was 'as much as
possible to tie myself to Denmark',[96] that 'our Scandinavian literary
activity' had to be concentrated as much as possible in the Danish
capital,[97] and that he figured he would settle there.[98] As it turned out,
he never went to live in Copenhagen, and during the 1870s his ambivalence about what he took to be Copenhagen's hegemonic pretentions
seems to have grown in proportion to the advancement of his own literary
reputation. His most explicit formulations on this issue came in a letter to
Georg Brandes in 1874. Ibsen commented on the plans for the journal
which came to be *Det Nittende Aarhundrede* (The Nineteenth Century),
accusing Danes of being ignorant about what was going on in the other
Nordic countries, of regarding it 'as almost an act of grace to acknowledge
that what is strictly Norwegian has the right to express itself in literature',
and always supposing 'that Denmark sets the standard':

> The Copenhagen ignorance of Scandinavian affairs surpasses everything but
> Copenhagen arrogance [. . .] Your population of two million cannot sup-
> port a periodical. If it is to succeed, you must not, in your Copenhagen
> superiority, overlook the four million Swedes, the two million Norwegians,
> the one million Finns, and the almost equally large Scandinavian popula-
> tion in America. This makes a public of about ten million in all. Give up
> your Copenhagen particularism. Write for them all. Then I will join you.[99]

Ibsen acknowledged that Brandes too was 'antagonistic to this "Copenha-
genism"', but that he nevertheless was affected by it: 'The whole first
volume of your *Main Currents in Nineteenth-Century Literature* is more an
attack upon Copenhagen narrow-mindedness than upon the narrow-
mindedness of Scandinavia in general.'

[95] Ibsen, Letter to M. Thoresen, 3 December 1865, *Letters of Henrik Ibsen,* trans. John Nilsen Laurvik
     & Mary Morison (New York: Duffield & Comp. 1908), 93.
[96] Ibsen, Letter to F.V. Hegel, 7 March 1866.
[97] Ibsen, Letter to F.V. Hegel, 22 August 1866, *Letters of,* 123.
[98] Ibsen, Letter to G. Brandes, 25 April 1866, ibid. 109.
[99] Ibsen, Letter to G. Brandes, 20 April 1874, *Letters and Speeches*, 148.

Speaking from a position on the periphery of the periphery, Ibsen performed a double distancing from Brandes. He both stressed the need, obvious for an author aware of being from a small nation, of transcending one's national context, and he attacked the 'provincialism of the centre', the confidence that in the centre 'the world comes to you anyway'.[100]

Ibsen repeated his criticism when a new issue of the journal was out by the beginning of 1875 – it is one of the rare occasions of him immediately answering a letter from Brandes. Although having found much of great interest in the new issue, he could still not 'help thinking that your magazine is far too exclusively Danish, or rather Copenhagenish, when your aim should absolutely be to take in all of Scandinavia'.[101] Ibsen advised Brandes to seek assistance in Norway and Sweden, and registered that there was one Swedish contribution, appearing in Danish translation:

> do you Copenhageners believe that the Swedes will read original Swedish articles in Danish translation? Are the Danes really still so ignorant of Swedish that communications from that country cannot be understood unless they are translated? If so, the outlook for the most important of all our causes is very bad.[102]

For Ibsen, 'the most important of all our causes' was the Scandinavian idea, and to him that idea had two basic components: it aimed at levelling the internal cultural hierarchy between the Nordic countries, and it meant that Scandinavian readers should get used to reading each other's literature in the original languages. Ibsen always stuck to this principle and he was able to enforce it with the mutual Scandinavian agreements on copyright by the end of the 1870s. In practical terms, it meant that he would not authorise translations into Swedish for other purposes than theatre productions.

A strategy like this was probably only conceivable from a Norwegian position, thought of as a position in the middle, between Danish and Swedish. But even in Norway Ibsen's strategy meant a radical departure from established cultural practices. In Norway Swedish literature was read in translation, if read at all. In Norwegian book collections from the eighteenth and nineteenth centuries there are hardly books in Swedish and even few books by Swedish authors. The only contemporary Swedish author widely read in Norway before the middle of the nineteenth century was Esaias Tegnér with his hugely popular *Frithjofs Saga*; published in

---

[100] Martin Puchner, 'Goethe, Marx, Ibsen and the Creation of World Literature', *Ibsen Studies*, vol. 13, no. 1 (2013), 32.
[101] Ibsen, Letter to G. Brandes, 30 January 1875, *Letters and Speeches*, 154.   [102] Ibid.

Swedish in 1825 and translated and published in Norway the following year.[103] Conversely, Ibsen's strategy probably restricted his own dissemination in the Swedish book market, making his readership there smaller than what it might have been if he had allowed translations.

Another occasion for expressing his Norwegian identity came in 1878, when Ibsen wrote to the author, and later the model for Nora, Laura Kieler. Kieler was a Norwegian living and publishing in Denmark and she had been attacked in the Danish press. A reviewer had criticised her spelling of vowels, using short spellings instead of composite in accordance with Norwegian pronunciation, for example 'gåt' for 'gået' (gone), 'lamslåt' for 'lamslået' (paralysed); '[Just] because Ibsen's language is moving towards Swedish, Danish writers ought not to do it.'[104] Kieler had answered that her mother tongue was Norwegian and that the expressions she used was not only part of 'educated Norwegian speech, but also the written language, without in any way belonging to the "New Norwegian"'. The reviewer regretted that Norwegian authors always came up with this answer and thought that as long as Norwegian authors were published in Copenhagen, the Danish should have a say in the matter of language. In fact, criticism ought to be even stricter and should demand from the Norwegians that if they wanted to uphold the common literature they ought also to uphold the common language. If not, what would happen to Danish in the end? Major authors like Bjørnson and Ibsen were in a position to dictate their own conditions, the Danish critic admitted. But every year inferior authors joined them and with the great productivity of Norwegian literature they might one day make up half of what was published in Denmark. By that time it would be too late to 'protect the purity of our own language':

> The good Norwegians would prefer, and we cannot blame them, to be free of Danish speech on their stages. Nor would we want to have Norwegian in our books. Exceptions will always be made in respect to the literary heroes, but if the lesser spirits in the future want to enjoy the material advantages which a Danish publisher can offer, they will have to speak and write Danish.[105]

Ibsen was critical of a manuscript that Kieler had sent him, but he supported and encouraged her in this particular matter. He told her not to let anyone influence her: 'There is so much inane correctness in Denmark. Be on your guard against it and similarly be on your guard

---

[103] Eide, Bøker, 39, 214, 288; Fredrik Paasche, Norges litteratur (Oslo: Aschehoug, 1932), 37.
[104] Quoted in Tveterås, Norske, 409.   [105] Quoted in ibid. 410.

against acting like a Dane, do not be ashamed of continuing to think and feel in Norwegian; one can obviously make you un-Norwegian, but you will not therefore become Danish.'[106]

Norwegian authors were constantly reminded that they were on someone else's linguistic ground and not 'legitimate heirs' to the literary language.[107] They were immigrants, maybe even intruders, expected to comply with the owner's rules and regulations, not language users with full and equal rights of citizenship. The uneasiness of this situation is indicated by Ibsen's reluctance to give his language a national name. This was a common problem in Norway throughout the nineteenth century and Ibsen was in accordance with general practice when he usually settled for terms like 'the common' or 'the written language'. There are, however, examples of Ibsen using the double national designation: to a German he used 'the Norwegian-Danish language' and to a Dane 'the Danish-Norwegian language'.[108] In his late correspondence he would even resort to calling his language 'Norwegian', but never when writing to Danes.[109]

Ibsen was, then, located in the middle of a tension between the received vernacular language and literature and the demand for a new national language and literature, caused by the redrawing of the political state map by the beginning of the century.[110] His response was to resist enrolment on either side. This situation, although conflict-ridden, may also be considered highly privileged and productive for a writer; if we return to the resources available in this particular periphery, it may even be seen as a competitive advantage. The Norwegian 'language struggle' was accompanied by a heavily essentialist rhetoric of the sort we have also found in Ibsen in the 1850s, but the effect was nevertheless the opposite: Language was thoroughly denaturalised and politicised. The Royal Theatre in Copenhagen was set to protect the purity of the language; the mission of the Norwegian theatre, and Norwegian literature, was to reform it. Language was not self-evident and natural for Norwegian authors; language stood out as a problem in its own right. No matter what particular choice was taken on the issue – opting either for Aasen, Knudsen, moderate adaptation, or the Danish status quo – it was a matter of choice, not a matter of course. All talk of 'purity' was to Ibsen 'inane correctness', because language to him was always under construction, impure – something that constantly had to be reflected upon.

---

[106] Ibsen, Letter to L. Kieler, 26 March 1878.   [107] Casanova, *World Republic*, 262, 272.
[108] Ibsen, Letters to E. Brausewetter, 18 February 1886 and to J. Hoffory, 16 November 1888.
[109] Ibsen, Letters to R. Darzens, 6 May 1890, G. Vollmar, 22 August 1890, R.A. Armstrong, 4 May 1891, and G. af Geijerstam, 29 March 1892.
[110] Alexander Beecroft, 'World Literature without a Hyphen', *New Left Review*, no. 54 (2008), 96–7.

With reference to Ireland, Terry Eagleton describes this kind of linguistic situation as 'being stranded between two tongues'. He takes it to be an important reason why Ireland experienced a 'flourishing native modernism, as opposed to one imported from abroad'.[111] Being caught between different cultures and languages can only spur verbal self-consciousness; Joyce, notes Eagleton, 'observed that it was his freedom from English convention, including linguistic convention, that lay at the source of his talent'. Many Irish writers recognised a similarity between the Irish and the Norwegian literary and linguistic situation and felt, even though interpreting this situation in very different ways, a deep affinity with Ibsen in particular. Such will be the situation for any writer in fraught political circumstances; it is only in the 'centre' that language appears settled and natural.

A final far-reaching consequence of Ibsen's transition to Gyldendal was that it made him prioritise the book. His first two publications at Gyldendal, *Brand* (1866) and *Peer Gynt* (1867), were written as verse dramas primarily for reading. They gave Ibsen his Scandinavian breakthrough in the book market, at a time when he had still not been performed at The Royal Theatre in Copenhagen and only one play, *The Feast at Solhoug*, had been produced by The Royal Theatre in Stockholm (1857). With *The League of Youth* Ibsen went back to writing for the theatre. By the end of 1867, Hegel in fact asked Ibsen if he would not consider returning to 'dramatic writing for the theatres, which are lacking in new plays'.[112] Ibsen soon confirmed that this was his intention, and that publishing therefore had to wait. In October 1868, he wrote that publication was not to be considered 'until next autumn or winter, since the play is intended for the theatres; I will of course send you a transcript ['afskrift'].'[113] Hegel then offered to have the play set and printed as 'manuscript', that is: in just three copies for the theatres in Kristiania, Copenhagen and Stockholm. If it was accepted, the play should be available as a book after five performances.[114] The major reason for doing it in this order was that the theatres would not pay for published plays, or at least not very much; the theatre in Stockholm had even been criticised for having paid Bjørnson for the already printed *The Newly Married*.

By the beginning of 1869 Hegel reminded Ibsen that he was about to be too late for the present theatre season, but Ibsen had already realised this

---

[111] Terry Eagleton, 'An Octopus at the Window', *London Review of Books*, vol. 33, no. 10 (2011), 24.
[112] See comment to Ibsen, Letter to F.V. Hegel, 24 February 1868.
[113] Ibsen, Letter to F.V. Hegel, 10 October 1868.
[114] See comment to Ibsen, Letter to F.V. Hegel, 22 December 1868.

and had a plan: 'If it could be sent in to the theatres in May, then it would be possible to have it performed in September, and have it in the book-shops by October.'[115] Hegel replied that it might be impossible for the printer to have the set standing that long, and asked if the whole edition could be made at once if only he guaranteed that just the three copies, plus one for Ibsen himself, came out.[116] Ibsen had no objection. Hegel advised him to demand that the play be staged by September since it ought to be on the book market by October. Ibsen answered: 'If the play is accepted in Copenhagen, there can be no question of waiting for the performance there – the book must, of course, come out in the autumn; and I am quite prepared to be paid less by the theatre in consequence of this.'[117]

It all ended with the original plan being reversed – and never repeated. The priority of the book was underpinned by the expansion of the book market in the 1870s, a topic to which we will return. It was also strengthened by the state of copyright legislation. In the 1870s, when Ibsen was still not treated as a native author by Danish and Swedish theatres, the lack of protection could only motivate him to give priority to the book market. And when mutual protection was put into effect, his market value was such that increasing costs did not scare off the major theatres in Copenhagen and Stockholm.

This chapter has shown that the restrictions and opportunities facing Ibsen and other Norwegian authors were framed by a particular set of tensions between 'Norwegian', 'Danish' and 'international'. When the political union with Denmark ended in 1814, the two countries had shared a vernacular culture for centuries. Applying the new state borders to the established and contemporary practices of cultural production made the received tradition 'Danish' and 'foreign', just as Denmark itself had to reconstruct its cultural history and identity on national grounds. However, the vernacular system of cultural circulation did not disappear with the redrawing of state borders; in some respects, it was reinvigorated. In Norway, the written language continued to be basically Danish and from the 1860s, Copenhagen again became Norway's publishing capital, giving Norwegian authors access to a Danish-Norwegian book market. In the history of literature, the national principle took hold already in the nineteenth century and it has had a profound impact ever since. One of the effects of this bias has been to obscure the co-existence and tensions

---

[115] Ibsen, Letter to F.V. Hegel, 20 February 1869, *Letters of*, 163.
[116] See comment to Ibsen, Letter to F.V. Hegel, 14 March 1869.
[117] Ibsen, Letter to F.V. Hegel, 10 June 1869, *Letters of*, 168–69.

between the vernacular and the national throughout the whole of the nineteenth century. Norwegian authors have been excluded from the Danish history of literature, even if they wrote in Danish, were published in Copenhagen and had a wider Danish readership than those of native authors. On the other hand, the Danish publishing history of Norwegian literature has been treated more as an external issue than as something integral to its existence.

At the same time, the restrictions of Ibsen's theatre experience have tended to be associated primarily with a national program and a Norwegian, supposedly provincial audience. But it seems more apt to suggest that the restrictions Ibsen experienced were the restrictions of European theatre in general, and particularly the artistic limitations imposed under the commercial hegemony of the French theatre industry. In this respect, the most important aspect of Ibsen moving abroad and his move to a new publisher was that it meant an 'exile' from the institution of the theatre.[118] In 1864, Ibsen broke with the theatre as the institutional setting for playwriting. He later came back to the theatre, but when he returned, it was from the distanced position of literature. This was how he came to revolutionise both drama and theatre – at home and beyond.

[118] We want to thank Martin Puchner for helping us make this point.

2

No Escape

Leaving Norway in 1864 and moving to Rome, and to Gyldendal, Ibsen was, after a year of struggling with formal concerns, able to produce his two masterpieces of verse drama, *Brand* (1866) and *Peer Gynt* (1867). Far from home and relieved of the burdens of theatre business, Ibsen's creative energies seem to have been released. The narrative of liberating 'exile' tends, however, to downplay or conceal other important dimensions of Ibsen's European experiences during these years. First, we need a more exact understanding of the nature of his residence abroad and what Rome and Dresden more precisely had to offer him. Furthermore, we must recognise that Ibsen's experiences were to a large extent experiences of defeat and alienation and that he, by the early 1870s, developed a more and more conservative, if not to say outright reactionary, political identity. This all has implications for our reading of his plays, for our understanding of Ibsen's strained relation to Georg Brandes and thus for a proper understanding of Ibsen's location in the new political-literary configuration emerging in Scandinavia in the late 1870s.

From Norway to Rome

Ibsen's move to Rome in 1864 was not in any way exceptional; going abroad was something that was expected from Scandinavian artists and writers. As related in the previous chapter, Ibsen was awarded a grant to go abroad in 1863, and his application stated that his intention was 'to spend a year, for the most part in Rome and Paris, studying art and the history of art and literature'.[1] In addition to a literature and a theatre strongly characterised by translation, another aspect of the openness and import nature of Norwegian culture in the nineteenth century owed to the fact that there were few national institutions that could provide training and

---

[1] Ibsen, Letter to the King, 27 May 1863, *Letters of,* 73–4.

employment. The university was young (founded in 1811) and small, and
in the arts there were no national academies. Norwegian artists primarily
went to Germany to receive formal or informal instruction; painters
mainly to Düsseldorf and later to Munich – before Paris took over as
the main destination from the 1880s – while musicians went to Leipzig.
Authors too went abroad; Ibsen's contemporaries Bjørnson and Jonas Lie
for years, Lie for even longer than Ibsen and mainly in Paris.[2]

The main destination for scholars, writers and artists by the middle of
the century was still Rome. Nordic visitors and residents in Rome formed a
separate community, always with the Danes in a majority. A formal
Scandinavian Society was founded in 1860, and this society became
Ibsen's primary social environment during his time in Rome. During his
first winter, in 1867, there were about a hundred Scandinavians in the city,
but not all attended the Society regularly, and women only had access on
Saturday evenings.[3] The Scandinavians were one of many foreign commu-
nities, each group socialising more with fellow countrymen than with
Romans. Most of the young Scandinavian artists and scholars, wrote the
historian P.A. Munch, 'may have lived here for many years without having
seen the inside of a single respectable Italian house'.[4]

It was not life in a big city with advanced arts and literature that made
Rome attractive. Ibsen hardly made any literary connections in Rome and
remained largely ignorant of contemporary Italian literature, although it
seems he learned to speak Italian. The attraction lay in Rome's ancient
culture and the conception of Rome as a city where time was frozen.[5] By
1850 Rome had 171,000 inhabitants, far below its antique maximum.
Inside the ancient city walls around half of the land had been transformed
into fields, vineyards and pasture. The landowners made up a nobility
open to new merchant and banking families, while a bourgeois middle-
class hardly existed. The city was outmoded in every respect, with mostly
lanes and alleys, without paving stones or street lighting. Only three
bridges crossed the Tiber and the river was not confined, causing floods
almost every year. The swampland made malaria a constant threat.[6]

What Rome offered Ibsen was primarily distance. In a country as small
as Norway, and with literature in an initial stage of development, an author
was immediately and directly exposed to social and political pressures.

---

[2] Lie lived in Germany 1878–82 and then in Paris until 1906.
[3] Vilhelm Bergsøe, *Rom under Pius den niende* (Copenhagen: Gyldendal, 1877), 327–28, 511.
[4] Quoted in Per Jonas Nordhagen, *Henrik Ibsen i Roma* (Oslo: Cappelen, 1981), 156.   [5] Ibid. 7.
[6] Anne Eriksen, *Minner fra Den evige stad* (Oslo: Pax, 1997), 47–66.

Already in 1852, in Bergen, Ibsen had written: 'Our very conditions place great hindrances in the way of the dramatic author. Our society is so small that any place in the country, any town, any district with all its social and family relations is known to everyone.'[7] Nor was the capital Kristiania a metropolitan alternative to Bergen. By the early 1850s the Norwegian capital still only had around 30,000 inhabitants. The claustrophobia felt by Ibsen, exaggerated no doubt by his reputation for drunkenness and his general sensitivity, is spelled out in his recurrent praise of distance in his letters from Rome in the late 1860s. By the end of 1865 he wrote to his mother-in-law Magdalene Thoresen: 'At home I was afraid, when I stood in that clammy crowd and sensed their evil smiles behind my back.'[8] Two years later, in a letter to Bjørnson, he explained why he could not go back home: 'Were I to go home now, one of two things would happen: within a month I would make an enemy of everyone there; or else I would worm my way back into favor again, using all sorts of disguises, and thus become a lie both to myself and others.'[9] He strongly advised Bjørnson to go abroad again, '[b]oth because distance gives one perspective, and because it is good to be out of the sight of one's public.' An author could not live in Kristiania, he explained to Hegel, 'unless he coolly manages to reject all parties and take up his own stance.'[10] To both Peter Hansen and Edmund Gosse he claimed that *Peer Gynt* could only have been written at a distance from his readers: 'Being so far away from one's future readers makes one reckless. This poem contains much that is reminiscent of my own youth. For Aase my own mother – with necessary exaggerations – served as model.'[11] Honesty and authenticity, in other words, required a social and political distance that was only achieved through migration.

The Ethos of Vocation

Ibsen's generation of intellectuals experienced the 1850s as utterly unheroic and materialistic. Becoming a student in the early 1850s, wrote his friend Lorentz Dietrichson, was like 'arriving at a feast at the moment when the guests are saying goodnight'.[12] Another of Ibsen's Kristiania

---

[7] '[C.P. Riis og H.Ø. Blom]' (1852), www.ibsen.uio.no/sakprosa.
[8] Ibsen, Letter to M. Thoresen, 3 December 1865, *Letters and Speeches*, 50.
[9] Ibsen, Letter to Bjørnson, 28 December 1867, ibid. 71.
[10] Ibsen, Letter to F.V. Hegel, 16 July 1869.
[11] Ibsen, Letter to P. Hansen, 28 October 1870, *Letters and Speeches*, 102; see also letter to E. Gosse, 30 April 1872, ibid. 124.
[12] Lorentz Dietrichson, *Svundne Tider* (Kristiania: Cappelen, 1896), vol. 1, 169.

friends, the historian Ernst Sars, later described the decade under the heading: 'New political reaction. – A foregrounding of business and practical-economic interests'.[13] Throughout the 1850s and 1860s Ibsen frequently expressed his disdain for the concern with 'purely' material progress. He repeatedly complained about Norwegian insularity and a lack of idealism and ambitions.[14] In his application for a state grant in 1866, addressed to the Swedish King, Ibsen made it his God-given mission to arouse 'the people of our nation and urg[e] them to think great thoughts'.[15]

From the 1860s he would, however, articulate the creative impulse behind his 'uplifting' mission more in 'negative' than 'positive' terms, referring to what he sometimes called his 'illness' as a major source of his creativity. This 'negativity' is what came to constitute his early identity as 'satirist'. One major instance is *Brand*, and Ibsen depicted the work's negative impulse in the image of the scorpion he kept in a glass on his desk while writing: 'Now and then the little creature became ill. Then I would give it a piece of soft fruit. It would attack it furiously and empty its poison into it – after which it was well again. Does not something of the same kind happen with us poets?'[16]

All from the start of his career Ibsen's sense of social alienation had driven him towards doomed rebels and the semantic field of 'vocation' or 'calling'. The opening lines of his first published play, *Catiline*, state this in manifesto-like fashion:

> I must! I must! Deep down within my soul
> A voice commands, and I will do its bidding; . . .
> I feel I have the courage and the strength
> to lead a better, nobler life than this . . .
> one endless round of dissipated pleasures![17]

Although the word 'calling' ('kald') is not in the play, it is a main concern. Later both the word and the concept became central in *Lady Inger* (1855), *The Pretenders* (1863), and particularly in *Brand* (1866), as well as, albeit in an inverted sense, in *Peer Gynt* (1867).

---

[13] Ernst Sars, *Norges Politiske Historie 1815–1885* (Kristiania: Oscar Andersens Bogtrykkeri, 1904), 343.

[14] Ibsen, Letter to Bjørnson, 4 March 1866, *Letters and Speeches*, 53.

[15] Ibsen, Letter to the King, 15 April 1866, ibid. 56–7.

[16] Ibsen, Letter to P. Hansen, 28 October 1870, ibid. 102.

[17] Ibsen, *Catiline* (1850), trans. and ed. James W. McFarlane and Graham Orton, *The Oxford Ibsen* (London: Oxford University Press, 1970), vol. 1, 39.

Vocation has a prominent place in Ibsen's social and political critique as well as in his way of conceptualising authorship. Ibsen famously said that 'Brand is myself in my best moments',[18] thus making himself a context for the play while at the same time contextualising himself through the play. This invites us to read *Brand* not just as his confrontation with Norway after the Danish-German War in 1864, but just as much as an investigation into the demands of authorship and literary autonomy at this stage of his career.[19]

One reason why authorship is conceptualised in the heroic language of calling, sacrifice, duty, vocation and service must certainly be the fact that no objective basis for authorship existed. There was not at this time a market that could have provided an author with sufficient incomes to be economically independent; neither had Ibsen inherited a fortune that could have made literature a leisure activity. Furthermore, the language of calling was something that united him with at least part of his family.[20] The opening lines of *Catiline* could almost have been an expression of the agony of a revivalist Christian. But with the religious intensification of their different choices, the ethos of calling could only drive the family apart when they chose to serve different 'gods'. The revivalist movement in Skien that his siblings Hedvig and Ole Ibsen joined, in fact started as a protest against the visit of a touring theatre company in 1853.[21] At the time, the affinities between Søren Kierkegaard's criticism of conventional Christianity and the uncompromising Brand were immediately pointed out. Kierkegaard was well off and could afford to neglect the business side of writing, but he too cultivated his minority position and thought isolation the destiny of the intellectual. He saw authorship as sacrificial, and suffering and torture as the main sources of productivity.[22]

In *Brand*, Ibsen elaborated the logic of calling to its utmost consequences. He insisted that it was insignificant that Brand was a priest: 'The demand of "All or Nothing" is made in all domains of life – in love, in art,

---

[18] Ibsen, Letter to P. Hansen 28 October 1870, *Letters and Speeches*, 102.

[19] Kjetil Jakobsen makes a related point in his system-theory approach to Ibsen. Ibsen's strategy for gaining autonomy, argues Jakobsen, was emigration and self-objectification. In *Brand* and *Peer Gynt* Ibsen won reflexive autonomy by objectifying the power structures of the literary field, and the two dramas can be considered Ibsen's dramas of autonomy; *Kritikk av den reine autonomi*. Doctoral dissertation (Oslo: University of Oslo, 2004), 29, 235. What is missing from this argument, however, is attention to the material foundations of literary autonomy. If we pay attention to these, Ibsen's Scandinavian contexts must be given priority over exile, and we must stress the limitations of his 'Roman autonomy'.

[20] Nygaard, '… af stort', 129–63,

[21] Einar Østvedt, *Fra 1814 til ca. 1870: Skiens historie* (Skien: Skien kommune, 1958), vol. 2, 381–2.

[22] Garff, *Kierkegaard*, 428, 431–4, 498–500, 632–6, 760–5.

etc.'[23] However, the play shares the basic Christian presupposition that the 'natural self' is worthless and must be opposed and transcended if life is to gain meaning and purpose: 'What awful, overwhelming avalanche of guilt / Hangs suspended on that little word – the one word, Life!', says Brand.[24] It is only through subordination to a 'god', something as absolutely commanding as the divine, that the self can obtain value. The individual then becomes a battleground between a higher and a lower self. Peer Gynt is 'Emperor of Self' but leaves life without individual identity because he has not realised that 'To be one's self is to kill one's self', or, as the Buttonmoulder rephrases it: 'to show unmistakably / The Master's inten-tion whatever you're doing.'[25]

Vocation is not, then, just a question of choosing a cause to serve; the relation to the cause or 'god' is of vital importance.[26] The vocation is objectively given, it is 'The Master's intention', and the relation to the cause has to have the character of absolute necessity and obedience. After *Brand*, Ibsen wrote to a Danish critic that: 'it is no longer a question for me of "want to be" but of "must be." You have helped me across that yawning gulf.'[27] To Georg Brandes three years later he observed that: 'then you will do what you must do. A nature such as yours has no choice.'[28] 'Freedom' to Ibsen, at this time, meant being subjected to a form of necessity, not being 'free to choose'. His concern was with weakness and empowerment: He sought to discipline the depraved and vain self. Since the primary battleground was the individual self, political freedom was not a major concern. '[T]he only thing I love about liberty is the struggle for it', he explained to Brandes, 'I care nothing for the possession of it'.[29]

Since the demands of calling are absolute and tolerate no compromise, their implications are radically antisocial, and they are spelled out to the bitter end in *Brand*. Brand is not only opposed to the everyday concerns of the commoners and to the petty officials representing the state, the church and bourgeois society. His natural family and all his social inheritance are also burdens to be overcome.[30] Appeals to 'humanism' and 'Christian mercy' are taken as excuses and convenient escape routes. Brand demands

[23] Ibsen, Letter to P. Hansen, 28 October 1870, *Letters and Speeches*, 102.
[24] Ibsen, *Brand*, trans. James Kirkup in collaboration with James W. McFarlane, in J.W. McFarlane (ed.), *The Oxford Ibsen* (London: Oxford University Press, 1972), vol. 3, 110.
[25] Ibsen, *Peer Gynt*, trans. Christopher Fry and Johan Fillinger, ibid. 411.
[26] Harvey Goldman, *Politics, Death, and the Devil* (Berkeley: University of California Press, 1992), 178–84.
[27] Ibsen, Letter to C. Petersen, 9 March 1867, *Letters and Speeches*, 64.
[28] Ibsen, Letter to G. Brandes, 20 December 1870, ibid. 106.   [29] Ibid.
[30] *Brand, Oxford Ibsen*, vol. 3, 115.

that his dying mother give away everything and refuses to see her when she will go no further than nine-tenths of the way. The cruel logic of absolute ethics drives him to sacrifice both his son and his wife. Showing particular concern for his family is idolatry to Brand: 'I have no right / To set my family up as gods.'[31]

The great sociologist of vocation, Max Weber, would later spell out the meaning of the 'absolute ethic' of the Sermon on the Mount in exactly the same way: 'Where this ethic is concerned, it is a case of all or nothing if anything other than trivialities is to come out of it. [...] The gospel's command is unconditional and unambiguous: give what you have – *everything*, quite simply.'[32] Such a demand may be deemed socially sense-less as long as it does not apply to everyone. However, Weber argues, the nature of the ethical command is that it '*does not ask* about this at all. [...] One must be a saint in *all things*, or at least intend to be; must live like Jesus, the apostles, Saint Francis and others like him. *Then* this ethic is meaningful and the expression of dignity; *not otherwise*.'

Can this be anything but idealism gone mad? The problem with such an interpretation is that Ibsen clearly admires Brand: the opponents he confronts Brand with are generally easy matches for his hero. But while Ibsen esteems Brand, he also drives him all the way into social isolation, to the frontiers of madness and to death – and with no certain outcome. How are we to interpret the words of the concluding 'Voice': 'He is deus caritatis'? Is Brand being damned or saved? For 150 years, interpreters have been in disagreement over the answer to that question.[33]

Read as a reworking of the demands of authorship, *Brand* suggests that Ibsen at this time held art and bourgeois life to be incompatible. Ibsen lived for his calling, and enjoyed it intensely, at the expense of all social obligations. He reported that while writing *Brand*, 'I was indescribably happy, even in the midst of all my pain and misery. I felt the exultation of a Crusader; I would have had the courage to face anything on earth.'[34] He had spent the economic means that had been provided for him. He had a wife and a son to care for and nothing to live on, and he even entertained

---

[31] Ibid. 127.
[32] Max Weber, 'Politics as a Vocation', *Max Weber's Complete Writings on Academic and Political Vocations*, trans. Gordon C. Wells (New York: Algora Publishing, 2007), 197 (italics in the original).
[33] See Erik Bjerck Hagen, 'Brand-resepsjonen 1866–1955', in Erik Bjerck Hagen (ed.), *Ibsens Brand* (Oslo: Vidarforlaget, 2010), 11–32.
[34] Ibsen, Letter to Bjørnson, 4 March 1866, *Letters and Speeches*, 53; see also Letter to M. Birkeland, 4 May 1866, ibid. 58.

the idea that *Brand* would jeopardise the only foreseeable way of providing
for his family: the award of a permanent state grant. He wrote to Bjørnson
that the satire and polemics in *Brand* would not make the politicians more
sympathetic towards him, but he would not compromise, 'no matter what
these "pocket-edition" souls think of it. Let me rather be a beggar all my
life'.[35]

On several occasions, Ibsen repeated his dichotomous view on vocation
and social obligations. 'When you invest in a calling and mission in life', he
wrote to Brandes, 'you cannot afford to keep friends.'[36] In the autumn of
1871, when Brandes was preparing the famous lectures usually considered
the inauguration of literary modernity in Scandinavia, Ibsen told him that
productivity and 'egoism' would be 'the medicine that will drive the
disease out of your system':

> Energetic productivity is an excellent remedy. What I recommend for you is
> a thoroughgoing, full-blooded egoism, which will force you for a time to
> regard yourself and your work as the only things of consequence in this
> world, and everything else as simply nonexistent. Now, don't take this as
> evidence of something brutal in my nature! There is no way in which you
> can benefit society more than by coining the metal you have in yourself.
> I have never really had a very great feeling for solidarity. [. . .] If one had the
> courage to throw it overboard altogether, one would be getting rid of the
> ballast that weighs most heavily on the personality.[37]

To Bjørnson Ibsen explained that underneath 'my foolishness and swin-
ishness, I have always taken life seriously. Do you know that I have entirely
separated myself forever from my own parents, from my whole family,
because being only half understood was unendurable to me?'[38] Literary
'seriousness' was incompatible with 'natural' family solidarity.

Reconstructing Authorship

Brand is one articulation of a new poetics emerging in the 1860s. We have
seen that in the 1850s Ibsen more or less denied the value of individual
authorship, asking for a literature which articulated what was already
'objectively' given in 'the people'. In the poem 'On the Heights' ('Paa
Vidderne') (1860), he started to develop his poetics of distance. After

[35] Ibsen, Letter to Bjørnson, 12 September 1865, ibid. 46.
[36] Ibsen, Letter to G. Brandes, 6 March 1870, ibid. 93.
[37] Ibsen, Letter to G. Brandes, 24 September 1871, ibid. 114.
[38] Ibsen, Letter to Bjørnson, 9 November 1867, ibid. 68.

Brand, yet another important contribution came in an often-quoted letter to the Danish critic Peter Hansen in 1870, where Ibsen appropriated his whole 'national' production for his individual biography. Hansen had asked Ibsen for information for an anthology of author portraits – itself a contribution to the rising cult of the author. In his answer to Hansen's request, Ibsen set out to provide 'the inner history' of his authorship, stating that '[e]verything that I have created as a poet has had its origin in a frame of mind and a situation in my life'.[39] His first play, *Catiline* (1850), had been written in 'a little provincial Philistine town' – Grimstad –where he could not find adequate expression for 'all that was fermenting in me' and where he had to fight his battles alone.[40] *Lady Inger of Østraat* (1855) was the result of a 'hastily entered into and violently broken off' love affair. *The Vikings at Helgeland* (1858) was written while he was engaged to be married, and for Hjørdis he had used the same model as later for Svanhild in *Love's Comedy* (1862): his wife Susanna.

Not until he was married, Ibsen continued, did he take life more seriously. The first fruit of this change was 'On the Heights'. But the desire for freedom pervading this poem did not receive its full expression until *Love's Comedy*. This work gave rise to a lot of gossip in Norway, Ibsen claimed, 'and my reputation suffered considerably'. The only person who approved of the book was Susanna, 'a woman of great character [. . .] and an almost violent hatred of all petty considerations. All this my countrymen did not understand, and I did not choose to make them my father-confessors. So they excommunicated me. Everybody was against me.'[41]

Ibsen's last play before leaving Norway was *The Pretenders* (1863), appearing just as Frederick VII of Denmark died and the Danish-Prussian war began. As a response to the crisis, Ibsen wrote a poem, 'En broder i nød' ('A Brother in Need'), but it 'had no effect against the Norwegian Americanism that had driven me back at every point. That's when I went into exile ['landflygtighed']!' In Rome he created *Brand* (1866) and *Peer Gynt* (1867), and later in Dresden his contemporary prose play *The League of Youth* (1869). Comparing his Roman and German creations, Ibsen thought they bore witness to the influence of environment upon literary form: 'Cannot I, like Christoff in [Holberg's] *Jacob von Tyboe*, point at *Brand* and *Peer Gynt*, and say, "See, the effects of wine"? And is there not something in *The League of Youth* which reminds one of *Knackwurst und Bier*?'[42]

---

[39] Ibsen, Letter to P. Hansen, 28 October 1870, *Letters and Speeches*, 100.   [40] Ibid. 101.
[41] Ibid.   [42] Ibid. 102.

From the perspective of the problematic of life and works, the major attitude towards Ibsen's letters has always been that there is not enough of this kind of material. Ibsen's letters have been considered too business-like and as revealing too little about the personal background of the works and the secrets of the creative process.[43] Taking a step back, we might want to take notice of the contexts Ibsen does *not* mention in his letter. He says nothing about intertextuality: what other works influenced him, of which sources did he avail himself? He says nothing about the institutional and economic contexts: for most of this period he was engaged by theatres to write drama. And he does not comment on the reasons why he wrote national and historical drama in the first place. Instead, he puts the emphasis on the origin of his products in his personal biography and experiences and he associates his poetics of distance and freedom with starting to take life more 'seriously'.

Here Ibsen can be seen retrospectively to appropriate and unify his production by installing the author as its principal, originating source. The way he now conceived creativity was no longer to be found in a compact between author and nation but in the distance between them, not in affinity with the people's longing for self-expression but in 'illness' and 'egoism', not in being a vehicle for the collective but in individual experiences and personal pain. Lady Inger's and King Haakon's callings had been to national causes; Brand's calling is radically antisocial. Authorship was now framed in terms of exiled distance, biography and individual vocation.

The Award of a State Grant

It is hard to decide how much coquetry there is in Ibsen thinking that *Brand* could jeopardise his prospect of a state grant. As it turned out, it was the great success of *Brand* that made the grant go through. To Hegel, the success was completely unexpected. Bjørnson had given Hegel the impression that his colleague's new book would be a historical drama. When the publisher saw part of the manuscript, it made him doubt. He wrote to Ibsen that he thought it would not be 'understood by the great mass and that sales will not be such that it will be right at first to opt for such a considerable print run as 1250 copies'.[44] It was too late to change the plan, however, and Hegel's panic was proven unfounded. Not only did the first

---

[43] Halvdan Koht, the first editor of Ibsen's letters, notes that 'Henrik Ibsen was no great letter writer – quantitatively nor qualitatively', *Samlede verker* (Oslo: Gyldendal, 1940), vol. 16, 9.

[44] Quoted in comment to Ibsen, Letter to F.V. Hegel, 7 March 1866.

edition sell out immediately, Hegel had to print three more editions so that during its first year *Brand* had been issued in a total of 3000 copies. This success created a veritable race to give Ibsen a state grant.

A few leading authors of the previous generation had been given official positions to live off; the state grants represented a new stage in the state's facilitation of authorship. Ivar Aasen, the collector of linguistic and folkloristic material and also an author, was from 1850 paid 300 specie dollars from a public fund and from 1860 the sum was raised by the parliament to 400 specie dollars a year. In 1863 Bjørnson applied for a similar grant and was immediately supported by the head of the ministry. The ministry's reasoning was that Bjørnson would develop more freely and form his works to greater perfection if he 'in addition to the return from his literary activities, can rely on a regular, if relatively modest income'.[45] Parliament decided to support the ministry's recommendation for the coming three-year term, and in 1866 the grant was made permanent.

Ibsen too had applied for an annual salary of 400 specie-dollars in 1863. In his letter to the King he stated that '[i]t is impossible in this country to live exclusively or even principally on one's writings'.[46] He was turned down at this point, but three years later his cause was supported from almost all sides. Proposals were put forward from his old friends in Kristiania, from Bjørnson and from a group of liberal representatives, and they immediately found support from the government and from the King personally.[47]

Although the ministry held 400 specie-dollars, from 1875 converted to 1600 *kroner*, to be a 'modest' income when it was awarded Bjørnson, it was by no means an insignificant sum. It was equal to half the starting salary of a professor and the grant enabled Ibsen from now on to concentrate fully on his dramatic and poetic work, leaving occasional poetry and journalism almost completely behind. Equally important was the great symbolic value attached to the arrangement. The grant was soon called a 'writers' salary' ('diktergasje'), and even though 'gasje' might initially have been used to create prosaic connotations, these connotations soon gave way to the conception of an honorary award.[48] The importance of the arrangement in both economic and symbolic terms is attested to by the efforts other authors, like Alexander Kielland, Arne Garborg, Magdalene Thoresen, and Amalie Skram, made to be included, in their cases without

---

[45] Both quotations in Geir Vestheim, '(. . .) *der er Gift paa Pennen hans*' (Oslo: Unipub, 2005), 20.
[46] Ibsen, Letter to the King, 10 March 1863, *Letters and Speeches*, 31.
[47] See comment to Ibsen, Letter to the King, 15 April 1866.   [48] Vestheim, '*der er Gift*', 23–6.

success. When Ibsen in 1869 asked his friend Lorentz Dietrichson to write a biographical note that could be used to introduce him in Germany, he recommended Dietrichson to '[f]orget about the sufferings of the starving poet – no one is interested in that nowadays. Say rather that I have received grants from the government and the Storting [parliament]'.[49]

Antipolitics

As Ibsen's literary and financial position became more consolidated, a distance between him and Bjørnson was emerging, signalling different literary strategies and conflicting political orientations. This conflict merits some attention because it has implications for our understanding of the 'prehistory' of the Modern Breakthrough and of Ibsen's position in Scandinavian literature by the late 1870s.

Ibsen and Bjørnson always had a complicated relationship, but in some respects they had been close. Bjørnson had, for example, been godfather to Sigurd Ibsen when he was baptised in 1860, when they had also lived in the same house. During his last winter in Norway and during his first years in Rome Bjørnson was Ibsen's main patron. He organised money collections, applied on Ibsen's behalf for grants and introduced him to Hegel. The situation of dependence in which this put Ibsen was probably in itself enough to create tensions between the two. It is as if Ibsen sought an occasion to restore the balance and found it in the Danish critic Clemens Petersen's review of *Peer Gynt*. It may at first glance be hard to understand Ibsen's fury. Petersen criticised him for an inclination to allegory and did not like the fourth act, but Brandes said much the same, without Ibsen pouring his anger out on him. Ibsen blamed Bjørnson for Petersen's review, and although he came to regret his immediate outburst, this event initiated the break between the two writers that came to last until 1882. Bjørnson on his side responded as an offended patron, blaming his client for a lack of 'gratitude'.

From here on, Bjørnson and Ibsen chose different strategies in both literary and political matters. Their attitudes to royal orders serve as an illustration. During their exchange over Petersen's review in 1867, the republican Bjørnson tried to win Ibsen over to a common boycott strategy in the event that they were offered royal decorations. Ibsen refused. As long as the budgetary authority paid them money, he argued, he could not see why they should not accept a sign of honour from the royal authority. Of

---

[49] Ibsen, Letter to L. Dietrichson, 19 June 1869, *Letters and Speeches*, 80–1.

course, he assured Bjørnson, he had no 'real desire for such finery'.[50] This was disingenuous; Ibsen did in fact take the initiative towards getting his first two royal orders, from Sweden in 1869[51] and from Denmark in 1870,[52] and he went to great lengths to make sure that he received a Turkish order he had been promised as member of the Norwegian-Swedish delegation at the opening of the Suez canal in 1869.[53] Usually he would explain his enthusiasm upon receiving such honours by noting that royal signs of recognition would strengthen his literary position in Norway. But he also ordered miniature copies of his decorations so that he could always take them with him on his travels, in case a suitable occasion should occur.

Bjørnson and Ibsen were also aiming at different audiences. Around the time they fell out, Bjørnson became strongly influenced by the Danish clergyman N.F.S. Grundtvig, both by Grundtvig's 'popular orientation' and by his 'bright' form of Christianity. Bjørnson wanted at least some of his own books to reach a popular audience, and was concerned that they should not be too expensive. For this reason, he also continued to publish his peasant tales in Gothic type until the beginning of the 1880s.[54] Ibsen was set in Gothic type as long as he was published in Norway, but the shift to Gyldendal meant a decisive shift to Roman type. By the middle of the 1860s the general transition to Roman type was well under way, but types still had social connotations, and Roman type signalled an orientation towards the educated public.

Finally, Bjørnson and Ibsen parted ways politically. From 1866, Bjørnson was the editor of *Norsk Folkeblad* ('The Norwegian People's Magazine'), which he made into a central press organ for the opposition against the government and which made him an important player in Norwegian politics. Ibsen, however, was not so much on the other side, at least not in the late 1860s, as he was against politics itself. Another of the attractions of Rome was that it offered him an asylum from politics. By the middle of the nineteenth century, after the upheavals of the 1848 revolutions, it was a deliberate policy of the Catholic Church to resist all kinds of changes. When Italy was united in 1860, Rome was chosen as the capital, but the Church State managed to stay outside the Italian state for another

---

[50] Ibsen, Letter to Bjørnson, 28 December 1867, *Letters and Speeches*, 72.
[51] See comment to Ibsen, Letter to J.H. Thoresen, 24 September 1869.
[52] See Ibsen, Letters to A. Klubien, 9 September 1870 and 8 January, 1 February, and 13 February 1871, with comments.
[53] Ibsen, Letter to O. Demirgian, 23 November 1870, with comments.
[54] Tore Rem, 'Bjørnson, bønder og lesning', *Edda*, vol. 92, no. 3 (2005), 243–58.

decade. Ibsen appreciated the situation. The population were 'undoubtedly people who cannot do much and do not know much, but they are indescribably beautiful, and sound, and calm'.[55] He hoped politics would be left out of it, but in 1870, when the Church State finally fell and Rome was taken over by the Italian nation state, the idyll was over. 'They have finally taken Rome away from us human beings and given it to the politicians', he complained to Brandes; 'Where shall we take refuge now? Rome was the one sanctuary in Europe, the only place that enjoyed true freedom – freedom from the tyranny of political freedom.'[56]

Ibsen's antipolitics was founded on the conception of the modern state as a machine for equalisation and homogenisation that threatened to eradicate individuality. The modern state gained power from disempowering the individual;[57] '[T]he state is the curse of the individual', he famously put it to Brandes.[58] In his 'Balloon-letter to a Swedish Lady' from Dresden on Christmas Eve 1870, likening his own situation to that of the beleaguered population of Paris, he described modern Prussia by invoking the orientalist image of the soulless, dead, un-individuated ancient Egypt. He virtually fled from the consolidation of state power across the European continent, only to be relentlessly caught up, first in Rome, then in Dresden. When the Ibsen family moved to Dresden in 1868, it was because Susanna wanted Sigurd to attend a protestant school. Dresden, the capital of Saxony, was known as 'The Florence of the North', or *Elbflorenz*, and like Rome it offered an environment of classicist culture. Saxony had sided with Catholic Austria against Prussia in the war of 1866, but when the Franco-Prussian war broke out in 1870, Saxony participated wholeheartedly in the resulting unification of the German Empire. When the family moved southwards again in 1875, this time to Munich, Ibsen complained that in northern Germany the state and politics 'have subjected all forces to its service and appropriated all interests'.[59] Moving to Munich would again take them further from home, he wrote, 'but to make up for this I shall be nearer to Italy, and I shall also have the advantage of living among Catholics, who, in Germany, are decidedly to be preferred to the Protestants.'[60]

[55] Ibsen, Letter to M. Thoresen, 3 December 1865, *Letters of*, 94.
[56] Ibsen, Letter to G. Brandes, 20 December 1870, *Letters and Speeches*, 106.
[57] Ibsen, Letter to F.G. Knudtzon, 19 February 1871.
[58] Ibsen, Letter to G. Brandes, 17 February 1871, *Letters and Speeches*, 108.
[59] Ibsen, Letter to E. Gosse, 10 March 1875.
[60] Ibsen, Letter to L.L. Daae, 4 February 1875, *Letters of*, 282.

There are multiple paradoxes in Ibsen's attitudes. He hailed the heroism of Garibaldi, the foremost romantic revolutionary hero of the nineteenth century, and held his followers up as a glorious counterexample to the misery and cowardice at home.[61] But he was simply annoyed when personally confronted with disorderly conduct, as in 1867, when on his return from southern Italy back to Rome, Italian nationalists had destroyed parts of the railway in a new attack on the Church State, and Ibsen was caught up for several days in San Germano: 'Damn all war! [. . .] Hope our usual circumstances won't be too much upset by this.'[62] In the Franco-German war he saw no heroism at all, only a war machine of numbers and regiments and a general staff without poets: the Prussian chief of staff Helmuth von Moltke had 'murdered warfare's poesy', as Ibsen put it.[63]

Antiliberalism

There are similarities between Ibsen's antipolitics and the stance taken by writers like Baudelaire and Flaubert in this period. The failure of the revolution of 1848 and the experiences of the Second Empire led them, writes Pierre Bourdieu, to a 'disenchanted vision of the political and the social world' and an 'undifferentiated condemnation of all those who sacrifice to the cult of good causes'.[64] However, there are major differences as well. For Flaubert and Baudelaire, their disenchanted vision led them to a 'heroic', although ambivalent, rejection of all signs of social recognition,[65] while Ibsen explicitly pursued such recognition. Furthermore, Ibsen's antipolitics evolved into a more and more distinctly conservative position during the 1870s. It would be an overstatement to ascribe to him a systematic political philosophy, but there is at least a series of utterances pointing in a clearly conservative direction and his political criticism was always primarily directed against the liberals. It is in no way obvious why this should be. On the issue of Norwegian support to Denmark in 1864, for example, it was the Norwegian government, as we have seen, which had been completely against involving Norway in a continental war as long as Denmark was not supported by Britain. However, Ibsen did not direct his anger at the government. His main target was always the opposition,

---

[61] Ibsen, Letter to M. Thoresen, 3 December 1865, *Letters and Speeches*, 49.
[62] Ibsen, Letter to J. Bravo, 4 November 1867.
[63] Ibsen, *Ibsen's Poems*, in a version by John Northam (Oslo: Norwegian University Press, 1986), 110.
[64] Bourdieu, *Rules*, 59, 81.   [65] Ibid. 60–3.

and he would claim more than once that 'the liberals are the worst enemies of freedom'.[66]

In *The League of Youth*, written in Dresden and published in 1869, liberal politicians are portrayed in the least flattering manner. The negative protagonist, attorney Stensgaard, founds a new party, The League of Youth, while attacking the local magnate, Chamberlain Bratsberg. Bratsberg mistakes Stensgaard's speech as being directed against his rival Monsen and invites Stensgaard home. Stensgaard, having courted Monsen's daughter Ragna until then, immediately redirects his interest towards Bratsberg's daughter Thora. And so it goes, with a series of misunderstandings and turns, and with Stensgaard revealing himself as a complete opportunist in matters of both love and politics.

Before the publication of *The League of Youth*, Ibsen wrote that his new play was 'peaceable' and written in 'a peaceful and happy frame of mind'.[67] He prided himself of his technical achievements in this play, having here already constructed a realist dialogue completely without asides.[68] But it is hard to imagine that the violent reactions *The League of Youth* caused in liberal circles in Norway came as a complete surprise. Bjørnson felt himself personally attacked, recognising that some of his own rhetoric had been put into the mouth of Stensgaard only to be parodied, denounced and ridiculed.[69] The actor playing Stensgaard at The Royal Theatre in Copenhagen had been working in Norway for several years and even put on a Norwegian accent. When giving public readings of the play, another Danish actor clearly tried to resemble Bjørnson in the Stensgaard part.

The session of the Storting of 1869, the year when *The League of Youth* was published, marks a decisive turning point in Norwegian political history. That year Johan Sverdrup achieved support from the agrarian leader Søren Jaabæk to introduce annual gatherings of the parliament. This strengthened the parliament against the government and was seen as a step towards parliamentary rule. Consequently, the political field became more polarised and in the next decade there was an escalating power struggle between the government with its supporters in Stortinget and the parliamentary majority. While in the late 1860s Ibsen had declared the necessity of staying independent, he now took sides. He wrote to Brandes

---

[66] Ibsen, Letter to G. Brandes, 4 April 1872, *Letters and Speeches*, 122.
[67] Ibsen, Letter to F.V. Hegel, 31 October 1868, ibid. 75.
[68] Ibsen, Letter to G. Brandes, 26 June 1869, ibid. 84.
[69] Bjørnson was furious in private letters, for example, to R. Schmidt, *Brevveksling med danske 1854–1874*, ed. Øyvind Anker, Francis Bull, and Torben Nielsen (Copenhagen: Gyldendal, 1972), vol. 2, 289.

in 1872 that he was not afraid of being regarded as partisan: 'I do not really understand why I am considered as belonging to no party.'[70] Since this was written to the radical Brandes, and accompanied in other letters by statements like 'anything is better than the existing state of affairs',[71] it might be difficult to identify exactly what 'party' Ibsen had in mind. But it was definitely not the Norwegian liberal opposition to the government. From 1871, Ibsen had a lawsuit going against the printer H.J. Jensen for what Ibsen held to be illegal reprints of two of his older plays, and he had no objection to letting this law suit feed on the general Left-Right antagonism. Jensen printed some of the leading liberal newspapers and Ibsen thought it was a brilliant idea to take Emil Stang, the son of the head of government Frederik Stang, as his lawyer, and to capitalise on Stang's 'natural hatred towards the person in question'.[72] He would also declare that 'I loyally stand by the government and support it with my pen and all my abilities',[73] and that he sided with the guardians of order, only regretting that the government was too soft on the opposition when they allowed people like Bjørnson and Jaabæk to operate freely.[74]

While siding with 'order', Ibsen's antimass rhetoric grew more and more radical in the early 1870s. 'The masses, both at home and abroad, have absolutely no understanding of higher things', he declared to Brandes.[75] After meeting Ibsen in Dresden in 1872, Brandes reported that the playwright considered all parliamentary politicians – explicitly not a man like Bismarck – to be liars, hypocrites and dilettantes for their outdated preoccupation with political matters. The only decisive thing, he declared, was social freedom, freedom of thought and conscience, which could be promoted just as well under modern forms of absolutism. He expressed his hatred of Norwegian national-liberals and called Norwegian peasant free-holders 'all a filthy and self-interested mob'.[76] Believing strongly in a monarchy that would uphold an aristocratic spirit and destroy the liberals, he was furious about Bjørnson's republicanism. Writing home, Brandes complained: '[Ibsen's] hatred of false struggles for freedom is on its way to

---

[70] Ibsen, Letter to G. Brandes, 23 July 1872, *Letters and Speeches*, 126.
[71] Ibsen, Letter to G. Brandes, 4 April 1872, ibid. 123.
[72] Ibsen, Letter to J.H. Thoresen, 22 February 1872.
[73] Ibsen, Letter to O. Demirgian, 23 November 1870, *Letters and Speeches*, 105
[74] Ibsen, Letter to J.H. Thoresen, 27 September 1872, ibid. 129.
[75] Ibsen, Letter to G. Brandes, 24 September 1871, ibid. 115.
[76] Georg Brandes, Letter to his Parents, 19 September 1872, *Breve til Forældrene 1872–1904*, ed. Morten Borup and Torben Nielsen (Copenhagen: Reitzel, 1994), vol. 1, 15–17.

repress his interests in true struggles for freedom. If he were not my friend, he would be my enemy.'[77]

After a new meeting with Ibsen in Dresden in 1874, still in a cordial atmosphere, Brandes felt rather depressed. He complained that Ibsen lacked 'any kind of solid *Bildung*' and that he consequently was 'completely restricted': 'Imagine that he seriously believes in a time when "the intelligent minority" of the countries will "be forced with the aid of chemistry and medicine to poison the proletariat" in order not to be politically inundated by the majority. And this universal poisoning has his sympathy.'[78] Brandes's report is so astonishing that it is hard to believe that it is entirely accurate; it nevertheless speaks volumes on how the leading figure of modern Scandinavian literature perceived Ibsen at this time.

The Ironies of History

Even though he experienced moving to Rome in 1864 as a liberation, and even if the conditions at home were 'small', Ibsen's basic 'European' experiences during these years were the experiences of defeat, alienation and aspirations misfiring. The Danish nationalism in Schleswig, which Scandinavianism was mobilised to support, had produced exactly the opposite of what it had aimed for. The 1864 war not only led to the loss of Schleswig but also initiated the course of events that led to the unification of Germany under Prussian leadership. In 1870 Ibsen, like most Scandinavians, sided with France, hoping a German defeat would lead to the renegotiating of Denmark's southern borders. The 'Balloon-letter' of Christmas 1870 marks Ibsen's low point of isolation and estrangement.

European politics continued to mock him. Ibsen had written to Brandes that the state had to go, and the Paris commune in the spring of 1871 seemed to effect just that. But attacking the life and property of the ruling classes was not exactly what Ibsen had had in mind, and he lamented that his excellent no-state theory had been corrupted: 'The idea is now ruined for a long time to come. I cannot even proclaim it in verse with any decency. But there is a sound core in it. [...] And someday it will be put into practice, without any caricature.'[79]

---

[77] G. Brandes, Letter to his Parents, 20 September 1872, ibid. 20
[78] G. Brandes, Letter to C.J. Salomonsen, 21 June 1874, Georg and Edvard Brandes, *Georg and Edv. Brandes brevveksling med nordiske forfattere og videnskabsmænd*, ed. Morten Borup (Copenhagen: Gyldendal, 1939), vol. 1, 313.
[79] Ibsen, Letter to G. Brandes, 18 May 1871, *Letters and Speeches*, 112.

In 1871 Ibsen was attacked in the German press for anti-German statements in some of his poems, among them the 'Balloon-letter', and he had to defend himself publicly.[80] From then on, he started a reorientation. In a letter to his first German translator P.F. Siebold in 1872 he claimed that he recognised the greatness of Bismarck.[81] In another letter from the same year he called the unification of Germany the greatest event of the century and declared that he had changed his mind on the matter.[82] In a poem on the occasion of the supposed millennium of the unification of Norway in 1872, Ibsen sent new signals back home: 'Observe time's law! It may not be denied. / Cavour and Bismarck wrote it as *our* guide.'[83] In one sense it was a repetition of the Scandinavian message of unity and a warning against separatism. But Bismarck, the former arch enemy, and Cavour, the politician who had initiated Italian unification – the two foremost symbols of the consolidation of state power – had now become Ibsen's guiding stars.

At this time Ibsen began making a few literary connections in Dresden and he started to attend meetings in the city's *Literarischer Verein*. The literary society had engaged in patriotic activities during the Franco-German war and would hardly have been attractive to Ibsen at that time. He registered as a member in 1873, but does not seem to have entered into discussions, even if he reported that his authorship had been the subject of lectures in the society.[84] Even so, it seems that Ibsen left Dresden in 1875 without being widely known, almost as unnoticed as Dostoevsky, who had left the city four years earlier. In the first society history, published in 1889, Ibsen is not even mentioned. From the 1890s that changed; in 1903 Ibsen was made honorary member and in 1908 a plaque was put on the house where he had finished *Emperor and Galilean* in 1873.[85]

It was only by the spring of 1871, when German unification was accomplished, that Ibsen came to grips with the Julian theme – the story of the 'apostate' Roman emperor of the middle of the fourth century. Even though emperor for only two years, no other Roman ruler has left behind as many contemporary sources, including many writings of his own.[86]

---

[80] See Ibsen, Unaddressed Letter, dated 23 November 1871.

[81] Ibsen, Letter to P.F. Siebold, 6 March 1872, *Letters and Speeches*, 116.

[82] Ibsen, Undated and Unaddressed Letter [1872]. [83] Ibsen, *Poems*, 134.

[84] Ibsen, Letter to A. Strodtmann, 20 March 1873.

[85] See Narve Fulsås and Ståle Dingstad, *Innledning til brevene: Bosteder: Dresden 1868–1875*, www.ibsen.uio.no/brev.

[86] See Hubert Cancik and Hildegard Cancik-Lindemayer, '"Was ich brauche, sind Fakta" (Ibsen)', in Richard Faber and Helge Høibraaten (eds.), *Ibsens "Kaiser und Galiläer"* (Würzburg: Königshausen & Meumann, 2011), 39–64.

They provide a very divided picture: 'Hellenistic' supporters portraying a philosopher on the throne and a reformer who wanted to restore religious freedom and tolerance; Christians portraying an 'apostate' and a persecutor of Christianity. Later, Christian historiography incorporated the legend of Julian's last words being 'You have conquered, Galilean', which are included also in Ibsen's play, although not as Julian's very last utterance. Ibsen's two-part drama embraces both interpretations of Julian. In the first, located in the West, we meet the prince who is disgusted by Christian sectarian violence and hypocrisy and attracted to Neoplatonic mysticism, and who ends by abandoning his old faith. In the second part, located in the East, Emperor Julian starts by proclaiming full religious freedom but ends by persecuting the Christians and gradually descends into madness. At the end, he and his army are trapped by the Persians and Julian is eventually killed by a childhood friend, now a Christian soldier.

Ibsen had become interested in this material already in 1864, just after arriving in Rome, when Lorentz Dietrichson read the story to him as related by the Roman historian Ammianus Marcellinus.[87] Since then he had announced several times that he intended to take up this material, but every time other literary projects came in his way and acquired priority. The experiences of the preceding years seem to form an important part of the background to the final preparation of the play. In a letter to Hegel with a list of people who were to receive the book when it was printed, Ibsen wanted a copy sent 'to Bishop Monrad, if this is acceptable, since I am not so honoured as to know him personally'.[88] D.G. Monrad was one of the leading national-liberals in Denmark. He had been central in drafting the first free constitution in 1849, and had later served in the Government. In December 1863, when war with Prussia had become unavoidable, he took over as the head of Government and became responsible for the military defeat and the loss of Schleswig in the peace negotiations. He stepped down in July 1864 and in 1865 went to New Zealand as a settler. After four years he returned to an incumbency outside Copenhagen and from 1871 he was again bishop in the Danish church. He published on religious and political matters, among other things on the relationship between Christianity and politics.

The counterfinality of Danish politics is probably one reason Ibsen wanted Monrad to receive his new drama. The title, *Emperor and Galilean*, also indicates that the conflict between the temporal and the spiritual powers is a key concern. Julian returns more than once to the 'enigma'

---

[87] Dietrichson, *Svundne*, vol. 1, 336.   [88] Ibsen, Letter to F.V. Hegel, 6 October 1873.

of the 'Galilean's' saying: 'Give the Emperor what belongs to the Emperor – and God what belongs to God'. But while Ibsen said that the 'positive philosophy of life which the critics have demanded of me will finally be given to them',[89] critics have struggled at least as hard as in *Brand* with identifying a 'positive' meaning.

The play encompasses several characteristically and rather straightforward tragic plots. There is a conflict of values, one 'god' fighting another, held by the philosopher Hegel to be the essence of tragedy. There is also the theme of excess, transgression and 'overreaching', common to the rebel and the tyrant.[90] Julian starts as a rebel and ends as a tyrant, Ibsen thereby showing the affinity and continuity between the two positions. He was immediately criticised, though, for making Julian so depraved in the second part that any kind of heroism seemed to fade away altogether.[91]

Emperor and Galilean also thematises a conflict between imagination and reality. Julian is attracted to a vision of 'Hellenic' joy of life ('livsglede') which he confronts with the reigning Christian denial of life ('livsfornektelse'). Christianity had been appropriated by the Roman emperor to serve imperial power, Julian contends, and he can well understand why Constantine embraced a doctrine 'which so cramps men's wills'.[92] No bodyguard could so effectively protect the imperial throne as 'this bemusing faith, forever pointing beyond man's earthly life'. The Christians, says Julian, 'spend their lives in morbid brooding, stifling every stirring of ambition; the sun shines for them, and they do not see it; the earth offers them its abundance, and they do not desire it; their only desire is to renounce and suffer, so that they may die'. While at first considering Christianity and Greek 'paganism' incompatible, Julian is led by several mystical prophesies into trying to found a 'third empire', synthesising the 'empire of knowledge' and the 'empire of the cross'. But this only leads to catastrophe: megalomania, hermeneutic delirium and tyranny.

One reason for the complexity of the play, we will suggest, is that it is not just a play on a historical subject or a historical allegory, but that 'historicity', the experience of history, is itself a major issue with which Ibsen is trying to come to terms. Commenting on the generic classification of the play, Ibsen wrote to his English middleman Edmund Gosse, who had criticised him for abandoning verse, that in general 'the dialogue must

---

[89] Ibsen, Letter to F.V. Hegel, 12 July 1871, *Letters and Speeches*, 113.

[90] Rebecca Bushnell, *Tragedy* (Malden, Mass.: Blackwell, 2008), 88–95.

[91] See Asbjørn Aarseth, *Innledning til Kejser og Galilæer: Utgivelse*, www.ibsen.uio.no/skuespill.

[92] Ibsen, *Emperor and Galilean*, trans. James W. McFarlane and Graham Norton, in J.W. McFarlane and G. Norton (eds.), *The Oxford Ibsen* (London: Oxford University Press, 1963), vol. 4, 310–11.

conform to the degree of idealisation which pervades the work as a whole. My new drama is no tragedy in the ancient sense. What I sought to depict were human beings, and therefore I would not let them talk the "language of the Gods".[93] Ibsen repeatedly claimed that he had been truthful to history, and that his interest had been directed towards 'the characters, their conflicting plans, the [*history*]'.[94] What would it mean, then, to read history and realism against tragedy in this play?

The Christian reading offers one possibility. History tells us that Julian failed and that Christianity was consolidated. The play also shows that Julian in the end only strengthened the spiritual power of his opponents. This qualification turns the tragedy into a subplot in a Divine comedy, with Julian as an instrument of Providence. The concluding lines of the play, with the Christian characters Basil and Macrina contemplating the 'mystery of election', lend themselves to such an interpretation. The victims of Julian's persecution come to realise that Julian 'was a rod of correction ... not for our death, but for our resurrection'. 'Fearful is the mystery of election', Macrina says, but concludes: 'Oh, brother, let us not seek to the bottom of this abyss.'[95]

Against such a Christian interpretation we can argue, however, that there is disagreement between the characters as to what mission Julian has served. Just before the above exchange, Maximus the Mystic has made other, highly enigmatic claims. There is also the statement Ibsen made in a letter, explaining that the sub-title 'world-historical drama' should denote that it was about 'a struggle between two irreconcilable powers in the history of the world – a struggle that will always repeat itself'.[96] This suggests that Ibsen's concept of historical temporality was closer to Nietzsche's 'eternal recurrence' than it was to providential or progressive history. It might even suggest that the ending of the play, with a new Christian emperor on the throne, only brings us back to the beginning, characterised by violent sectarian struggle among different branches of Christianity.

---

[93] Ibsen, Letter to E. Gosse, 15 January 1874, *Letters and Speeches*, 145.

[94] Ibsen, Letter to G. Brandes, 24 September 1871, ibid., 115, which has 'plot' for Ibsen's emphasised '*historie*', thereby obscuring the argument we want to make by distinguishing between 'tragedy' and 'history'.

[95] Ibsen, *Emperor and Galilean, Oxford Ibsen*, vol. 4, 459. In a recent contribution, Jørgen Haugan argues that Ibsen in this play manages to work his way through conventional and state church Christianity to the truly Evangelical call for truth and love, *Dommedag og djevlepakt* (Oslo: Gyldendal, 2014), 217.

[96] Ibsen, Letter to L.L. Daae, 23 February 1873, *Letters and Speeches*, 135.

Such a concept of historical temporality would mean that Ibsen's vision was incompatible with contemporary national-liberal history of the kind supported and endorsed by Bjørnson at the time. In the same year that Ibsen finished *Emperor and Galilean*, Ernst Sars, alongside Bjørnson a leading ideologist of the national-liberal opposition, published the first volume of his monumental *Udsigt over den norske Historie* (*Survey of the History of Norway*, 1873–1891). Sars set out to emplot Norwegian history into one coherent story, starting in the Viking era and culminating in his own time. There was no doubt about the meaning of this narrative – it was all about the growth towards full national independence, a task that it was left to the contemporary generation to fulfil. Sars's history, wrote Bjørnson in 1874, was 'the first attempt to conquer the past for the future'.[97] Whatever one might say of the 'invented' character of such histories, the one that Sars produced served the liberal party well as a master narrative during their struggles to get out of the union with Sweden. The dissolution of the union in 1905 in the end made it the most 'realistic' interpretation of national history.[98]

In *The Pretenders*, Ibsen had made the medieval king Haakon Haakonsson a hero fit for national-liberal history. 'Norway was a *kingdom*', Haakon says, 'it shall become a *nation*'. 'Impossible,' responds his rival Skule, 'Norway's Saga has never dreamt such a thing!' Haakon dismisses him: 'Impossible for *you*; for you are only capable of recreating the *old* saga. But for me it is as easy as for a hawk to cleave the skies.'[99] Haakon is a Hegelian hero – in him the subjective and the objective spirit meet. In *Emperor and Galilean*, the subjective and the objective are driven apart to such a degree that a position like the one occupied by Haakon seems unavailable. Julian wants to create history, and moulds himself on great forerunners such as Alexander and Julius Caesar. But the more powerful he gets, and the higher his ambitions, the more powerless he becomes. At the end, in a 'moment of truth', Julian conceives of himself as an instrument for some external force to which he will never gain access, 'a mysterious power outside us which essentially determines the outcome of human endeavour'.[100] The distance between action and history turns history, for Julian, into an empty, unsignifying space – a space where meaning is withdrawn; it is 'sign against sign', until finally '[a]ll the omens are silent'.[101]

[97] Quoted in Trygve Ræder, *Ernst Sars* (Oslo: Gyldendal, 1935), 127.
[98] Narve Fulsås, *Historie og nasjon* (Oslo: Universitetsforlaget, 1999), 276–81.
[99] Ibsen, *The Pretenders*, trans. Evelyn Ramsden and Glynne Wickham, in J. W. McFarlane (ed.), *The Oxford Ibsen* (London: Oxford University Press, 1962), vol. 2, 283–84.
[100] Ibsen, *Emperor and Galilean*, *Oxford Ibsen*, vol. 4, 457.   [101] Ibid. 441.

Where the scholarly historian Sars emplotted history into an easily recognisable romantic national narrative, the dramatist Ibsen depicted a history where no clear overall plot was discernible. Where Sars closed the gap between action and history, Ibsen widened it. On this reading, a 'realistic', 'historical' qualification of tragedy would lead to what Northrop Frye describes as the archetypal ironic and satirical vision that 'heroism and effective action are absent, disorganised or foredoomed to defeat, and that confusion and anarchy reign over the world'.[102] Following Frye's further distinction between irony and satire, *Emperor and Galilean* would lean towards irony: 'satire is militant irony: its moral norms are relatively clear, [...] whenever a reader is not sure what the author's attitude is or what his own is supposed to be, we have irony with relatively little satire'.[103]

There is one form of clearly appreciated heroism in the play, however, namely the primitive martyr version of Christianity that Julian's persecution reproduces and reinvigorates. While at the start Julian saw the other-worldliness of the Christians as a tool for social pacification, he himself has turned the Christians into spiritually invincible opponents: 'Yes, this Jesus Christ is the greatest rebel who has ever lived', recognises Julian; 'For he is alive on earth, Maximus, [...] he is alive in men's rebellious minds; he is alive in their defiance and scorn of all visible power.'[104] Is this, then, Ibsen's 'positive vision'? If so, Julian's megalomaniac absolutism is being opposed by the sacrificial service to another absolute, the way to redemption. It is still about the need to serve and to find what one is 'elected' to serve. And Ibsen clearly values only the sacrificial side of rebellion, not its transformative, not to say utopian side. One of his derogatory terms for the liberal leaders was 'our demagogic political millennialists'.[105]

A basic ingredient in Ibsen's criticism seems to be a kind of unarticulated antihistoricism – if by 'historicism' we mean any kind of search for coherence, meaning or explanatory relations in history. This antihistoricism is reminiscent of what we find in Ibsen's great Russian contemporaries, Dostoevsky and Tolstoy. In *Notes from the Underground*, written and published in early 1864, Dostoevsky's narrator claims to be living in 'the Schleswig-Holstein period of human history'. He rejects history: 'In short, you can say anything you like about world history, anything that might enter the head of a man with the most disordered imagination. One thing, though, you cannot possibly say about it: you cannot say that it is

---

[102] Northrop Frye, *Anatomy of Criticism* [1957] (Princeton: Princeton University Press, 1971), 192.
[103] Ibid. 223.   [104] Ibsen, *Emperor and Galilean*, *Oxford Ibsen*, vol. 4, 399–400.
[105] Ibsen, Letter to M. Birkeland, 10 October 1871, *Letters of*, 222.

sensible.'[106] In *War and Peace*, published in the years 1863–69, Tolstoy attacks the 'great man approach' of Napoleonic historiography in particular and ends up rejecting rational historical understanding in general. The philosophy of history advocated in the novel claims that anything that happens is caused by an endless chain of events, which makes them predetermined from eternity.[107] 'History' makes things happen, even though we may feel perfectly free in our individual lives. The most reasonable attitude we can adopt is the kind of passivity demonstrated by the completely unheroic General Kutuzov. As head of the Russian army in the utmost crisis he does almost nothing, but ends up saving Russia, destroying Napoleon and liberating Europe.[108] In fact, Kutuzov may be perceived as the perfect counterimage of Julian.

Ibsen himself drew similar 'fatalist' conclusions from *Emperor and Galilean*. While preparing his lecture series in Copenhagen in the autumn of 1871, and feeling that a lot was at stake, Brandes seems to have asked Ibsen to send a 'signal' to the younger generation by way of moral support. We do not know the exact content of Brandes's letter, only Ibsen's answer. Here he rejected Brandes's call for him to 'raise a banner', arguing that it would be like 'putting on the same kind of performance Louis Napoleon did when he landed at Boulogne with an eagle on his head. Later, when the hour of his destiny struck, he didn't need any eagle. In the course of my work on Julian, I have become a fatalist in a way.'[109] Louis Napoleon attempted a coup d'état in 1840. He landed in Boulogne with sixty men, and an eagle is reported to have been trained to circle over his head. He was sentenced to life imprisonment but escaped easily in 1846 and in 1848, the revolutionary year, he won the presidential election in December with an overwhelming majority. Two years later he carried out a successful *coup d'état* and proclaimed himself emperor. Ibsen's conclusion seems to be that when time is ripe, appropriate action will take place, but for reasons that are beyond comprehension. It is in vain to try to create the appropriate situation, to

---

[106] Fyodor Dostoevsky, *Notes from the Underground*, trans. David Magarshack, in *Great Short Works of Fyodor Dostoevsky* (New York: Harper & Row, 1968), 287. Both Ibsen and Dostoevsky lived in Dresden during the Franco-German war, and there are similarities in their reactions, see Ibsen, Letter to G. Brandes, 20 December 1870 and J.H. Thoresen 21 November 1870; *Selected Letters of Fyodor Dostoyevsky*, trans. Andrew R. MacAndrew, ed. Joseph Frank & David I. Goldstein (London: Rutgers University Press, 1987), 338–9.

[107] Leo Tolstoy, *War and Peace*, trans. Rosemary Edmonds (Harmondsworth: Penguin, 1982), 715–19, 1400–44.

[108] See also Hayden White, 'Against Historical Realism', *New Left Review*, no. 46 (July–August 2007), 89–110.

[109] Ibsen, Letter to G. Brandes, 24 September 1871, *Letters and Speeches*, 115.

'create history', or to create a reasonable prognosis of its course and act accordingly. What is left for contemplation is only 'the mystery of election'.[110]

In the Conservative Camp

In spite of all its complexities, and in spite of its high sales price, *Emperor and Galilean* was a new, extraordinary success. When the work was about to be published in 1873, Hegel thought that such a huge and expensive book – 512 pages for 1 specie dollar and 78 shillings (6, 60 kroner) – was not likely to be sold out for a while.[111] He was immediately proven wrong: the whole edition sold out on the day of publication. Bookshops in Norway, Denmark and Sweden had preordered more than 3,200 copies, Hegel informed Ibsen: 'The rest was disposed of on the day of the 17th, mostly to booksellers in Copenhagen. It is quite an extraordinary case in my own practice, supposedly in the history of our book trade.'[112] The author and critic Arne Garborg noted on the occasion of *Emperor and Galilean*:

> He is read with interest, almost with extreme eagerness; his books are sold out with a speed unheard of in our literary world; as soon as it is merely rumored that a new work of his is expected, the public is seized with an excited anticipation that at times comes close to fever, and when the book is out and read, nothing else is spoken of for a long time in any circle that has the least interest in such things.[113]

It is harder to locate the work within Ibsen's oeuvre. In our reading, *Emperor and Galilean* is not the great turning point and herald of modernism, as claimed by several Ibsen scholars during the last decades.[114] The notion that it has an affinity to and even should be considered a response

[110] Karl Marx, in contrast, presented a rational, and therefore contestable, explanation of these events in *The Eighteenth Brumaire of Louis Bonaparte* (1852). Marx stressed the isolation of the Parisian working class, the interests of the peasantry and the lower middle class, the appeal of the Napoleonic legend, the self-destructive undermining of parliamentary institutions by royalists and liberals, and so on.
[111] F.V. Hegel, Draft of letter to Ibsen, 2 October 1873, RDL, NKS 3742, 4°, II, 'Fr. Hegels Concepter'.
[112] F.V. Hegel, Draft of Letter to Ibsen, 19 October 1873, ibid.
[113] Quoted and translated in Halvdan Koht, *Life of Ibsen*, trans. and ed. Einar Haugen and A.E. Santaniello (New York: B. Blom, 1971), 289.
[114] McFarlane claims that Brandes's *Main Currents of Nineteenth Century Literature* (1872) and *Emperor and Galilean* are 'startlingly dissimilar and yet strangely related', 'born of a shared vision and of a common sense of purpose', *Ibsen and Meaning*, 362–63; Toril Moi sees *Emperor and Galilean* as one of the first major responses to Brandes's lectures of 1871 and discusses the play

to Brandes's call for a new literature, does not find support in the contemporary reception. Ibsen himself thought Brandes would be rather sceptical of *Emperor and Galilean,* and he was right: Brandes did not like it at all.[115] As for their personal relationship, we have seen that Ibsen and Brandes were drifting more and more apart by the middle of the decade.

The move from militant satire to a more ironic attitude in *Emperor and Galilean* could perhaps be taken to anticipate the pervasive mood in Ibsen's later, 'modern' plays. But, as we will argue in the next two chapters, there was no unidirectional and imminent path leading from *Emperor and Galilean* to *Pillars of the Community* and further on to *A Doll's House.* This is not to say that Ibsen by this time had been accommodated to and reconciled himself with bourgeois society. The ironic philosophy of history in *Emperor and Galilean* was incompatible not just with Norwegian national-liberal history but also with the German euphoria over the new Empire. Even though accepting and maybe even appreciating the reality of the new German state, Ibsen's whole attitude would again be closer to Nietzsche and his 'untimely' warning about the dangers inherent in the triumph over France.[116] But Ibsen's alienation at this time disposed him to radicalism of a primarily right-wing bent and first and foremost to disgust at everything that proclaimed itself as 'progressive' and 'liberal'.

In Scandinavian public opinion, there was no doubt about Ibsen's conservative political identity and *Emperor and Galilean* seems in no way to have altered that image. Ibsen's political position was further underlined during his visit to Norway in 1874 and on his twenty-five-year anniversary as author in 1875. On the former occasion Ibsen was mainly in company with his old friends from the 'erudite Holland' circle, now staunch conservatives, and he was invited to parties by other prominent conservatives in press and politics. The celebration of Ibsen's jubilee in 1875 was dominated by the same circles.[117] This company put Ibsen on the sideline of the main current of Scandinavian literature by the middle of the 1870s.

Ibsen's poetics of distance and vocation, his quest for royal decorations, and his fierce opposition to politics were all parts of his struggle for literary autonomy. His response to national pressure and political setbacks was the opposite of Bjørnson's, who immersed himself in Norwegian politics. This

---

under the heading 'Becoming modern', *Ibsen and the Birth of Modernism* (Oxford: Oxford University Press, 2006), 188–222.

[115] See Ibsen, Letter to F.V. Hegel, 13 November 1873, with comment.

[116] See Narve Fulsås, *Innledning til brevene: Litteratur, kultur og politikk i Tyskland: Bildungsbürgertum og borgerlig-protestantisk kulturhegemoni,* www.ibsen.uio.no/brev.

[117] See comment to Ibsen, Letter to J.H. Thoresen, 28 March 1875.

meant that the two leading figures of Norwegian literature became antag-
onists as the 1870s wore on. In retrospect, Ibsen has come out as the
hallmark of modern Scandinavian literature while Bjørnson has descended
into a figure of mainly national importance. But in the 1870s Bjørnson's
literary politics put him on the more straightforward path towards the
Modern Breakthrough, while Ibsen's antipolitics from afar almost sent him
astray. What brought him back in the end was what he despised the most –
Scandinavian liberal politics and its interference with the dynamics of
Scandinavian literature.

3

Open Futures

The reorientation of Ibsen's authorship in the latter half of the 1870s may seem straightforward enough, and as such it has generally been presented. Early in 1875 Ibsen informed his publisher that he had made plans for a new contemporary play ('nutidsskuespil') in five acts.[1] In August he reported that the scheme was all worked out,[2] and in October he announced that the title would be *Pillars of the Community*, that the first act was ready, and that it would 'probe into several of the more important questions of the day'.[3] Two years later, in October 1877, the play was published. Two years after that again *A Doll's House* came out, and for the rest of his career Ibsen's modern prose plays were published with an astonishing regularity.

However, looking more closely at Ibsen's publishing history, his strategic considerations and the variety of projects he entertained during the middle of the 1870s, the course towards *Pillars of the Community* appears as far more complicated and open-ended. Nor was *Pillars of the Community* itself, in its contemporary reception, welcomed as a major turning point by his literary colleagues.

Recirculation and Copyright

First, we should note that although Ibsen had experienced considerable and growing success with his publications at Gyldendal, it is in fact not obvious when he confidently settled for a future as full-time, professional playwright. In 1872, commenting on a rumour, unfounded as it turned out, that Ibsen would be offered a professorship, Susanna's sister, who had lived with the Ibsens in Dresden, wrote: 'Ibsen can after all not live exclusively for his authorship [...] would it not be convenient for Ibsen

---

[1] Ibsen, Letter to F.V. Hegel, 20 February 1875.   [2] Ibsen, Letter to F.V. Hegel, 22 August 1875.
[3] Ibsen, Letter to F.V. Hegel, 23 October 1875, *Letters and Speeches*, 159.

in many, many ways?'[4] In the same year, Ibsen himself said that he needed 'continual sidelines'.[5] By the end of the year that he finished *Emperor and Galilean*, he wrote to J.H. Thoresen, the brother-in-law who was responsible for his economic affairs at home, that he was now without debt and even had 'a few thousand' placed in government securities; 'so I look forward to a time, and it is not far away, when I can live exclusively off my interest and my grant'.[6] On one occasion in 1875 he claimed that 'It is on the new editions of my books that I will mainly be living'.[7]

This claim is supported by the efforts he put into recirculation in the 1870s, and the work spent on revising earlier editions. His strategy was closely connected to his fight for copyright and the emergence of a Norwegian legal framework to protect authors' rights. The matter had already been discussed at the first Nordic booksellers' meeting in 1856. Denmark had a substantial book production, the need for regulation was urgent, and a law was passed in 1857. In Norway, few literary works were published, and even fewer were of a kind that led to reprinting.[8] Authors sold their manuscripts outright; the challenge was to get a publisher at all and explicit agreements on future relations between author and publisher were not made. But the literary success of Bjørnson, first, and later of Ibsen, made the question of copyright urgent also in Norway. Bjørnson was the first to be subjected to unauthorised reprints in the wake of his success with *Synnøve Solbakken*.

Moving to Gyldendal made Ibsen a Danish author in legal terms and there were never any ambiguities in his dealings with Hegel. From the beginning of their relationship, Hegel paid Ibsen for the right to publish a specified number of copies of a work. The price varied with the size of the book and the numbers printed. With each new edition, there was therefore a new payment. Trying to bring his older Norwegian publications over to Gyldendal, however, was a more complicated matter, and Ibsen never had a clear grasp of all the intricacies of copyright legislation.

After the success with *Brand*, Ibsen wanted Hegel to bring out a slightly revised version of *Love's Comedy*. Hegel answered that he assumed Ibsen was the owner of the rest of the Norwegian edition, which would have to be destroyed. It was not that simple, however, since the ownership had already passed through many hands. The rest of the print run came up for

---

[4] Marie Thoresen, Undated letter to Susanna Ibsen, [1872], NLN, Letter coll. 200.
[5] Ibsen, Letter to F.V. Hegel, 15 September 1872.
[6] Ibsen, Letter to J.H. Thoresen, 12 December 1873.
[7] Ibsen, Letter to A.E. Erichsen, 7 April 1875.   [8] Tveterås, *Bokens*, 416.

sale, and because of Ibsen's increased market value, Hegel, on Ibsen's behalf, had to pay more for it than he had first anticipated.[9] In 1870, Hegel informed Ibsen that he had bought the copyright to *The Pretenders* from Johan Dahl, who had published the play in Norway. Only when Hegel explicitly asked him about the contract with Dahl, did Ibsen realise that Hegel had bought something Dahl, the author now claimed, had never owned.[10]

In 1871, Ibsen started the long legal battle with the Norwegian printer H.J. Jensen, mentioned earlier, when Jensen issued a reprint of *The Vikings at Helgeland* and announced his intention to do the same with *Lady Inger of Østraat*. Jensen had been the owner of the journal *Illustrered Nyhedsblad* where *Lady Inger* and *The Vikings* had originally been published. Ibsen charged him for illegal reprinting, and the process dragged out until 1876 when Ibsen finally won after a ruling in the Supreme Court. This case contributed to exposing the outdated legal regulations of the field in Norway: the only law pertaining to the case was from 1741. A modern law was now prepared and worked out by Norway's leading authority on intellectual property, O.A. Bachke, one of Ibsen's old friends from Kristiania. The law (*Lov om beskyttelse af den saakaldte Skrifteiendomsret*) was passed in 1876 and stated unequivocally that the right to print a written work belonged exclusively to the author, for the author's lifetime plus fifty years. This legal consolidation lay a firm basis for Ibsen's recirculation strategy. More importantly, however, as we will see later, it was a precondition for stabilising his whole Scandinavian home market.

Some of the new Gyldendal editions of Ibsen's older plays were quite successful – *Love's Comedy* (Gyldendal editions 1867, 1873, 1877), *The Pretenders* (1870, 1872, 1875, 1879), and *The Vikings at Helgeland* (two 1873 editions, 1875, 1878) – while other endeavours to make his former production yield new profit brought modest results. In 1874, Ibsen reworked *Lady Inger* for its first Danish edition. He particularly had The Royal Theatre in Copenhagen in mind, and when suggesting the play for Hegel, he thought that after the rewriting it would become 'one of my best books'.[11] The Royal Theatre was not impressed, however, and rejected it this time as they had done with the first edition in 1857, while in Kristiania and Stockholm it was performed without much success. Ibsen was not put off by the meagre success. After reissuing *Lady Inger* he immediately suggested a new edition of *Catiline* on the occasion of the

[9] Tveterås, *Norske*, 104–5. [10] Ibsen, Letter to F.V. Hegel, 12 February 1870, with comment.
[11] Ibsen, Letter to F.V. Hegel, 6 February 1873, *Letters of*, 251.

twenty-fifth anniversary of its publication in 1875. *Lady Inger* and *Catiline* both had only one print run in the short term, and *Lady Inger* in particular was a disappointment for the publisher. The success of *The Vikings* spurred Hegel to order 4,000 copies of *Lady Inger*, which it took him seventeen years to get rid of, while the slightly more modest edition of *Catiline* (3,000) was in stock for sixteen years.[12]

National-Historical Revival?

Much of this revision and recirculation work took place before the announcement of *Pillars of the Community*, but there were several other plans which competed directly with the composition of the new play. In May 1875, Ibsen promised Georg Brandes that he would become a regular contributor to the latter's new journal, *The Nineteenth Century*. He even assured Brandes that this would be 'my exclusive occupation for some time to come' and that he would send him a poem every month.[13] Ibsen eventually sent only one poem and one 'rhyme letter', published in the July and August-September issues. Brandes immediately forwarded the rhyme letter, which he called 'melancholy', to the Danish poet Holger Drachmann, whom he wanted to write 'a bold answer [...] an answer from us young ones'. Brandes feared that the poem's reference to a 'corpse in the cargo' could be appropriated by the conservatives to mean modern disbelief, and he encouraged Drachmann to show, though in circumstantial wording, that the real corpse was 'the religion of the past and the social structures of the past'.[14] Drachmann did not respond, however; nor did Ibsen send any further contributions. It is impossible to decide whether this was caused solely or partly by his dissatisfaction with Brandes's language policy for the journal, of which he had been critical from the beginning.

More surprising is another plan also launched in 1875. Almost simultaneously with suggesting the new 'contemporary play', Ibsen, in a letter discovered only in 2011, wrote that he was working on a new play based on medieval Norwegian history.[15] This might have been overlooked as a sudden and soon forgotten impulse, but an order sent at the same time to his friend the historian L.L. Daae for translations of *The King's Mirror*,

---

[12] Tveterås, *Norske*, 195–96.   [13] Ibsen, Letters to G. Brandes, 2 May and 8 June 1875.
[14] G. Brandes, Letter to H. Drachmann, 19 July 1875, *Breve fra og til Holger Drachmann*, ed. Morten Borup (Copenhagen: Gyldendal 1968–1970), vol. 1, 124–25.
[15] Ibsen, Letter to D.C. Danielssen, 26 February 1875, Bergen Museum.

the kings' sagas and a pamphlet attributed to King Sverre, suggests that his plan was more than a lofty idea.[16] This information clearly unsettles the standard chronology of the development of Ibsen's authorship. The usual assumption is that Ibsen had left behind the writing of national-historical plays with *The Pretenders* in 1863 and historical plays altogether with *Emperor and Galilean* ten years later. But these letters suggest that he had abandoned neither the historical nor the national at this late stage.

The plan for a new historical play has left no other traces than these two letters, so we cannot decide how much work Ibsen put into it. But there is also other evidence that he had not left his national-historical inheritance behind. In 1874, as part of his recycling strategy, he asked Edvard Grieg to compose music for *Peer Gynt*. What was originally written as a dramatic poem, not to be performed, became a huge success with Grieg's music at Christiania Theatre in 1876. This success gave Ibsen the idea for another national-romantic project. In 1877–78, Ibsen started work on an opera libretto based on his early *Olaf Liljekrans*, and Grieg was again to compose the music. The idea may have been stimulated by all the interest surrounding the first Wagner festival at Bayreuth in 1876. Grieg attended the festival and Ibsen and Grieg seem first to have discussed the plan in Gossensass in 1876, upon Grieg's return from Bayreuth.[17] Again, this is an example of a plan not materialising, but this time most probably only because Ludvig Josephson had to leave Christiania Theatre. The entrepeneurial Swedish director had been instrumental in bringing *Peer Gynt* to the stage, but when he left the theatre, opera was put off the playbill. Ibsen was intensely opposed to this shift in artistic direction and boycotted the theatre for a year.[18]

Ibsen's German Strategy

During most of 1876 *Pillars of the Community* was put completely aside because Ibsen's primary interest now became oriented towards the German market. Throughout that year he constantly complained that it was unattractive to write for Scandinavian theatres, and in particular felt that he was badly treated by the theatres in Copenhagen and Stockholm.

---

[16] Ibsen, Letter to L.L. Daae, 4 February 1875, *Letters of*, 281–82.
[17] Vigdis Ystad, *Innledning til [Olaf Liljekrans] [1877/78]: Tilblivelse*, www.ibsen.uio.no/skuespill.
[18] See Ibsen, Letters to F.V. Hegel, 23 August 1877 (*Letters of*, 302–303), and H. Holst, 2 November 1878.

In March 1876, he registered as a member of the *Deutsche Genossenschaft Dramatischer Autoren und Componisten*, a special interest organisation and theatre agency founded in 1871.[19] At the same time, he engaged in preparing a German translation of *The Vikings at Helgeland*. The play was published at his own cost in commission by Th. Ackermann in Munich, where Ibsen now lived, and it was performed in both Munich and Vienna. In Munich the occasion was celebrated in Paul Heyse's literary circle, which Ibsen had been welcomed into and seems to have enjoyed.[20] The Norwegian playwright even received a greeting from the eccentric Wagnerian on the throne, Ludwig II of Bavaria.[21] Simultaneously, the Meiningen company were preparing their production of *The Pretenders*, already translated by Adolf Strodtmann, for Berlin. Ibsen attended their guest performance there in June, followed by an invitation to the holiday palace of the 'theatre duke' George II with a Knight's Cross as reward. In July Ibsen wrote to his attorney in the case against the 'pirate' Jensen: 'I am now seriously on my way to becoming a German writer; this means that I am arranging original German editions of my books. This undoubtedly pays better than writing at home.'[22]

Ibsen refused to give up *Lady Inger*, which was also translated into German and published in commission by Ackermann, in 1877. The Germans were no more attentive to its supposed virtues than the Scandinavians, but the first major blow to Ibsen's German strategy only came when he had finally completed *Pillars of the Community* in 1877 and had that play too immediately translated into German. *Stützen der Gesellschaft* was the third 'original' edition that he published in commission by Ackermann, all of them translated by Emma Klingenfeld in Munich under Ibsen's supervision.

Ibsen based his German strategy on his membership in the German society of dramatic authors and on presenting his authorised translations as 'original' German editions. He thought this would secure him 10 per cent of the net income. But the German authors' society was not very effective, and, more importantly: the legal fiction 'original German edition' put no one off. For every German translator or publisher who wanted it, the Danish edition was there to be taken, and the Society was not in a position to boycott theatres which did not respect their members' interests, particularly

[19] Narve Fulsås & Ståle Dingstad, *Innledning til brevene: Eksil, forfatterrett og oversettelser – 1870-årene: Deutsche Genossenschaft Dramatischer Autoren und Componisten*, www.ibsen.uio.no/brev.
[20] See Narve Fulsås, *Innledning til brevene: Bosteder: München 1875–80*, www.ibsen.uio.no/brev.
[21] See Ibsen, Letter to J. Løkke, [April 1876].   [22] Ibsen, Letter to E. Stang, 12 July 1876.

not when the translators might themselves be among its members. Ibsen's *Stützen der Gesellschaft* immediately had at least two much cheaper 'pirate' competitors. The play was a huge success on German stages: In Berlin alone it ran simultaneously in five theatres in 1878. But most theatres availed themselves of the unauthorised translations, of which one was a version heavily adapted to accommodate popular conventions. Georg Brandes thought Ibsen lost 15,000 Mark (13,350 kroner) from more than twenty theatres by not being protected[23] – but the theatres might of course have chosen not to produce the play if they had had to pay not just the translator, but the author as well.

In the meantime, important regulations came in place in Scandinavia. When new laws had been passed in all countries, the stage was settled for agreements on mutual recognition and protection of authors' rights. An agreement between Norway and Sweden came into effect by January 1878. The two countries, being in royal union, went on to sign a joint agreement with Denmark which became effective from January 1880. The most disputed provision in the law stated that Swedish, Danish and Norwegian should be considered dialects of the same language, which in effect made unauthorised translations between the Scandinavian languages equivalent to illegal reprints. The most important consequence of this provision was that the Swedish Ibsen market was reserved for the Danish Gyldendal edition.

These regulations were important both for Ibsen and his publisher. To Ibsen it put an end to his grievances with Danish and Swedish theatres; from now on Scandinavian theatres had to offer all Scandinavian authors the same terms of pay. This change is reflected in the rhetoric of Ibsen's correspondence with the royal theatres. *The League of Youth* was Ibsen's Scandinavian breakthrough on the stage. The Royal Theatre in Stockholm had first produced the play in 1869, without paying him. When the play had been performed twenty-one times by 1875, the year Ibsen celebrated his twenty-fifth anniversary as author, the director Erik af Edholm felt bad about it and went directly to the King, asking 'most graciously' for permission to pay Ibsen 1,000 kroner as a sign of 'the gratefulness and high regard of the board of directors'. Ibsen thanked Edholm, asking him to express to the King his most 'humble thanks' for the attention bestowed upon him by his highness.[24] After the copyright agreement, the tone in the correspondence

[23] G. Brandes, Letter to V. Pingel, 14 April 1878; Georg Brandes & Edvard Brandes, *Georg og Edv. Brandes brevveksling med nordiske forfattere og videnskabsmænd*, ed. Morten Borup (Copenhagen: Gyldendal, 1940), vol. 3, 273–74.

[24] Ibsen, Letter to E. Edholm, 13 May 1875; Stig Torsslow, *Ibsens brevväxling med Dramatiska teatern* (Stockholm: [Kungliga dramatiska teatern], 1973), 9.

with the Stockholm theatre changed. Appeal to royal favour was replaced by plain business, with covering letters basically saying: 'This is my new play. If you want it, these are my conditions'.[25] We have ample evidence that Ibsen was in full command of the rhetoric of the patronage economy, but he also seems to have felt relieved to move to the plain prose of market transactions.

Pillars of the Community: Social Criticism in a Comic Mode

It was a fraught way to the final preparation of *Pillars of the Community*, then; only by spring 1877, it seems, was Ibsen fully dedicated to its completion. Furthermore, it is up for debate where best to locate *Pillars* in Ibsen's literary development. At the time, it was more of a commercial than a literary success, if by the latter we refer to the recognition by peers.

When Ibsen first announced the title of his new play to Hegel, saying it would 'probe into several of the more important questions of the day', he also called it 'a counterpart of *The League of Youth*'.[26] *The League of Youth* is a comedy, ending with the social order being restored after the ruptures caused by the newcomer Steensgaard. Nothing suggests that Ibsen at this time was struggling to achieve something like a modern, realist prose tragedy. All his tragedies had been set in the past and their protagonists had been what protagonists of tragedies had always been: aristocrats. As soon as Ibsen moved to contemporary society, he had moved to the 'lower' genres thought fitted for the un-heroic present – parody, satire, comedy – and/or he had resorted to verse, as in *Love's Comedy*, *Brand* and *Peer Gynt*.[27] These three plays firmly established that Ibsen, when turning to polemics and responding to the demand for topical relevance, was first and foremost a satirical poet.

At the same time, however, Ibsen had struggled to overcome verse. In 1863, while preparing *The Pretenders*, he wrote to Clemens Petersen: 'I am now working on a historical play in five acts, but in prose; I cannot write it in verse.'[28] *The Pretenders* is a prose play, but was immediately criticised by Brandes, who otherwise held the play in high esteem, for Ibsen's repeated recourse to monologues and asides. It was against this background that

---

[25] Örjan Lindberger, 'Ibsen och två svenska teaterchefer', *Nordisk tidskrift för vetenskap, konst och industri*, vol. 40, no. 6 (1964), 386.
[26] Ibsen, Letter to F.V. Hegel, 23 October 1875, *Letters and Speeches*, 159.
[27] Sally Ledger: '"Serious" drama was never written in prose, and it was always concerned with people of high estate. The idea that a tragedy could be written in prose, or that it could be about ordinary nineteenth-century people, was unheard of', *Henrik Ibsen* [1999] (Tavistock: Northcote, 2008), 16.
[28] Ibsen, Letter to C. Petersen, 10 August 1863, *Letters and Speeches*, 34.

Ibsen took such great pride in having written what he considered a consistently realist dialogue in *The League of Youth* and later in *Emperor and Galilean*. But even after *The League of Youth* Ibsen asserted, almost complainingly: 'I present life's richness better / for the verse's fetter'.[29]

By the middle of the 1870s, then, Ibsen had achieved both the writing of realist, 'de-idealised' prose tragedies on 'serious', historical topics and of realist prose comedies and dramatic poems on contemporary matters. What he had not done, and not even conceived, it seems, was a new realist, contemporary prose tragedy.

Pillars of the Community is, as Ibsen himself noted, closer to *The League of Youth* than to tragedy, ending as it does on a conciliatory note with Bernick acknowledging his sins and being forgiven and reintegrated into society and family. Its style is not as 'low' as the style of *The League of Youth*, it is more 'serious', but primarily in a moralising sense. The pity Ibsen shows Bernick is striking when compared to his harsh treatment of Lady Inger. Her great sin is her moment of passionate love and her subsequent devotion to her illegitimate son, whose real identity she has to hide and whose death she causes by a cruel misunderstanding. For her there is no mercy. The sins of Bernick are not just bad; they are deliberate. But he is nevertheless allowed back into society, family and business.

The 'uplifting' character of *Pillars of the Community* surprised the critic and author Arne Garborg, who had been accustomed to Ibsen's work being characterised by the 'sick and fiercely bitter'.[30] This was a play more in line with Bjørnson's idealism than with the image of Ibsen as satirist. In March 1875, a month after stating his own intention of writing a new contemporary play, Ibsen asked Hegel to send him Bjørnson's two plays *A Bankruptcy* and *The Editor*. *The Editor* was accused of being a personal attack, and for that reason rejected by most theatres. *A Bankruptcy*, on the other hand, became a huge success in Scandinavia as well as in Germany. Georg Brandes hailed the two Bjørnson plays, albeit camouflaged as a report he had received from someone else, as the introduction of a new era: 'Finally! – Finally it seems that we in the Nordic countries are close to getting a cycle of plays in which those two great powers, the now and reality, are being respected and allowed to come into their own right.'[31]

---

[29] Ibsen, 'Rhyme-Letter to Mrs. Heiberg' (1871), *Poems*, 113.
[30] Quoted in de Figueiredo, *Masken*, 175.
[31] 'Literatur: Bjørnstjerne Bjørnson: "En Fallit" og "Redaktøren"', *Det nittende Aarhundrede* (1875), 241.

Brandes's response is in full accord with what he had otherwise advocated in his criticism. In his introduction to the first volume of his published lectures, *Emigrantliteraturen* (1872), he had famously stated: 'That a literature in our day is alive shows by the way in which it subjects problems to debate.' But his examples, it is generally forgotten, had been authors like George Sand on marriage, Voltaire, Byron and Feuerbach on religion, Proudhon on property, Dumas *fils* on gender relations, and Émile Augier on social conditions.[32] He had not even mentioned authors like Stendhal, Balzac or Flaubert. As examples of 'modern foreign plays' dealing with social questions that existed in social reality but not in 'our literature', he chose, in the same introduction, Dumas' *Le Fils naturel* (1858) and Augier's comedies *Les Effrontés* (1861) and *Le Fils de Giboyer* (1862).

Pascale Casanova has suggested that Brandes in these lectures presented French 'naturalism' as a model of autonomy for Scandinavian authors to follow,[33] but clearly he did not; at this time Brandes was primarily occupied with romanticism. The Augier plays he mentions attack shady businessmen and the 'lowering of manners'. *Les Effrontés* is about corrupt journalism, exposing the link between manipulation of the stock exchange and the press. The play created the character Giboyer, followed up in the anticlerical *Le Fils de Giboyer*.[34] In France at the time, George Sand was Baudelaire's *bête noire* as an example of authors 'who sacrifice to the cult of good causes',[35] while Augier's 'idealist', 'bourgeois' theatre was rejected by those fighting for 'realist' and 'social' art.[36] Dumas, in a more 'realist' manner than Augier, addressed problems like money, marriage and prostitution with moralising intentions. In the preface to *Le Fils naturel* he explicitly opposed the separation of art and morality represented by Baudelaire: 'All literature which does not aim at perfectibility, the raising of moral standards, the ideal – and in a word, the useful – is a scrawny, unhealthy, stillborn literature.'[37] It is a poetics to which Bjørnson could have subscribed.

What would happen in Scandinavian literature around 1880 was, therefore, beyond the horizon of expectation of *Emigrantliteraturen*. What Brandes had asked for was nothing more than the kind of idealist and

---

[32] The list of authors mentioned is slightly changed in later editions, Voltaire for example being left out and Turgenev and Spielhagen brought in.

[33] Casanova, *World Republic*, 97–98. Only later, by the 1880s, would Brandes engage with Zola and naturalism.

[34] 'Augier, Émile', *The Cambridge Guide to Theatre*, ed. Martin Banham (Cambridge: Cambridge University Press, 1995), 56–7.

[35] Bourdieu, *Rules*, 81.   [36] Ibid. 70.   [37] Quoted in ibid. 72.

moralising social criticism found in the contemporary boulevard melo-drama. As we have already seen, several Augier plays had been produced in Kristiania before Ibsen left Norway, among them *Les Effrontés* (*Den offentlige Mening*, unknown tr.) in 1863, while *Le Fils de Giboyer* (*Fader og Søn*, tr. Chr. Grüner) was put on in 1865.[38] Furthermore, Bjørnson had already in his theatre criticism in the 1850s voiced the demand for a drama 'more responsive to contemporary modes of thought'.[39] He had, in accordance with Ibsen's theatre criticism at the time, pointed to Musset, Augier and Dumas *fils* as better models than Scribe, and he had called for 'naturalism', 'individualisation', and 'truth'. So neither did Brandes intro-duce authors who were unknown in Scandinavia by the beginning of the 1870s, nor anything resembling the 'realism' fought for by the most autonomous sectors of French literature. His examples rather suggest that Brandes himself, at this time, thought that literature ought primarily to be socially and politically useful.

In 1877, Ibsen was quite confident about the market potential of his new play. He called it 'modern in all respects and completely in tune with the times; and it is probably composed with more skill and artistry than any of my other works'.[40] He predicted that it would 'create a good deal of excitement', which would only serve to speed up sales.[41] He even wondered if they dare put it up in 'a city like Gothenburg', Sweden's shipping capital, and there was undoubtedly something to this slightly affected pretension of being controversial.[42] Ibsen sent the play to Johanne Luise Heiberg, who had introduced him at The Royal Theatre in Copen-hagen with *The League of Youth* and *The Pretenders*. In her reply, she expressed her opposition to 'the new realistic subject matter'.[43] When entering the theatre, she thought, people wanted to be released from 'the reality of real life', not to be confronted with it once again, this time 'idealised through the power of art'. The pack of crooks that had made money into their god did not deserve the attention of a talented poet but to be handed over to police and justice. She acknowledged that the play had been a box office success, though, and that the theatre badly needed one.

---

[38] Øyvind Anker, *Christiania Theater's repertoire*, 17, 33.
[39] Frederick J. Marker and Lise-Lone Marker, *The Scandinavian Theatre* (Oxford: Basil Blackwell, 1975), 155–56.
[40] Ibsen, Letter to F.V. Hegel, 29 July 1877, *Letters and Speeches*, 165.
[41] Ibsen, Letter to F.V. Hegel, 23 August 1877, ibid. 166.
[42] Ibsen, Letter to F.V. Hegel, 28 October 1877.
[43] J.L. Heiberg, Letter to Ibsen, 21 November 1877, NLN, Ms. 4° 2590, 279.

Ibsen and the Emergence of the Literary Left

The responses in the literary world were, for different reasons, largely negative, and they were influenced by Ibsen's perceived conservatism. It seems clear that Ibsen himself sensed that the times were changing, and that he was in need of adjusting his direction. A first sign of this came when, by the end of 1875, he had started subscribing to the leading liberal newspaper *Dagbladet*. A more significant step came at the beginning of 1877, and it was directly related to his financial interests. That year he wrote to the leader of the opposition, Johan Sverdrup, in order to request a rise in his state grant. He did not think, he revealed to Sverdrup, 'that the government entertains any deeper, rooted interest in such affairs and partly I have no reason to assume that the government's course these days will be the way by which we can expect the most certain, safe and favourable decision about our proposal'.[44] If Sverdrup, however, as President of Parliament, would decide to back the proposal, 'a happy result would be given'. In the first part of the 1870s Ibsen had stood 'firmly behind the government' against people like Sverdrup. Now the political centre of gravity in Norway moved towards parliament, and Ibsen followed.

Bjørnson's turn to contemporary drama and the polarisation of the political field led to the forming of new alliances, bringing together Brandes and Bjørnson and thereby marginalising Ibsen. Via Hegel Ibsen sent *Pillars of the Community* with a conciliatory letter to Bjørnson, thanking him for his statement on Brandes's departure from Denmark, which he said 'has gladdened and deeply moved me'.[45] Bjørnson did not care to answer him. The occasion for Ibsen's approach was that by this time several attempts to secure Brandes the professorship in aesthetics in Copenhagen had failed, and in 1877, Brandes finally decided to go to Berlin and try to live there as a man of letters. Supporters published an address expressing their regret that Brandes had been forced to take this step and that Denmark let such a talent go. Ibsen did not sign it, nor did Bjørnson, but Bjørnson joined the address in an article published 20 October 1877. Shortly afterwards Bjørnson also gave a much publicised speech which inaugurated his break with Christianity. These events consolidated the friendly relations which had emerged between Bjørnson and Brandes since 1875. In May 1875, when Ibsen had asked Brandes to introduce him to Paul Heyse in Munich, Brandes wrote to Heyse: 'He does not like

---

[44] Ibsen, Letter to J. Sverdrup, 4 February 1877.
[45] Ibsen, Letters to Bjørnson and F.V. Hegel, 28 October 1877.

Bjørnson, who is his rival, and therefore you must not tell him that B. and I are reconciled now. He will know that soon enough.'[46]

Keeping Brandes out of the university unintentionally contributed to a higher degree of literary autonomy in Denmark. The Copenhagen professorship in aesthetics had been an institutional link between academia, literature and the theatre. The Romantic poet and playwright Adam Oehlenschläger had held it, and after him the dramatist and for some years censor of The Royal Theatre, Carsten Hauch. When Brandes was excluded, this could only serve to further the institutional differentiation between literature and academy.

Just before Brandes's departure from Denmark, Ibsen, for his part, was being made honorary doctor by the University of Uppsala on the occasion of its 400th anniversary. On 6 September 1877 the professor of literature and guardian of idealist aesthetics, Carl Rupert Nyblom, placed a laurel wreath on Ibsen's head in Uppsala Cathedral in the presence of the King. The symbolic distance between these two events measures the gap that had emerged between Ibsen and the literary camp now headed by Brandes and Bjørnson. It would indeed have been hard to predict that Ibsen in a couple of years would be firmly identified with the same camp.

Georg Brandes was, however, quite positive towards *Pillars of the Community*. He thought highly of its technique and found 'much daring' in its demonstration that 'the better ones in the country' had to migrate from the 'stuffed-in air'. Society was depicted as 'completely hypocritical', but he agreed that it was 'unnatural that the Consul is converted at the end'.[47] His brother Edvard, on the other hand, was outright disappointed: 'I have this against *Pillars of the Community* that it is so extraordinarily cautiously constructed. [. . .] The play makes it possible for both the press and public to pretend that it has no purpose ['tendens'] whatsoever'.[48] In Denmark, Edvard claimed, its effect as oppositional drama 'equals nill' and he absolutely preferred a play like *The King*, Bjørnson's unmistakably republican drama of 1877. Ibsen, he thought, was 'so anxious not to cause provocation that there is no greatness to his play. [. . .] But it is of course brilliant technically and, with the exception of the fourth act, makes a great impact on stage'. Taking the capacity to provoke as the foremost criterion,

[46] G. Brandes, Letter to P. Heyse, 6 May 1875, *Correspondance de Georg Brandes*, ed. Paul Krüger (Copenhagen: Rosenkilde & Bagger, 1966), vol. 3: *L'Allemagne*, 105.

[47] G. Brandes, Letter to his parents, 2 November 1877, *Forældrene*, vol. 1, 135, see also 132.

[48] E. Brandes, Letter to G. Brandes, 30 November 1877, Georg Brandes & Edvard Brandes, *Georg og Edv. Brandes brevveksling med nordiske forfattere og videnskabsmænd*, ed. Morten Borup (Copenhagen: Gyldendal, 1940), vol. 2, 5–6.

the critic V. Pingel shared Edvard Brandes's assessment: 'a rather kindly constructed Grocer's drama',[49] while the novelist J.P. Jacobsen thought that Ibsen 'is only half his own self and has forgotten what was written between the lines in *Catiline*'.[50]

Bjørnson shared this verdict and considered Ibsen too weak to be willing to risk his social reputation. In June 1878, Bjørnson informed Georg Brandes that Ibsen had written to him and that he had not answered. He thought Ibsen's 'behaviour towards me mean', and he found him 'a petty businessman with titles and honours and the most despicable letters to every small man who praises him in the smallest paper'.[51] Ibsen had initially been in another camp, Bjørnson noted, but he was insecure, doubtful and 'angrily ungenerous'. When wrong was done against him, while he was drinking and getting into debt, Ibsen's mistrustful, weak and wretched nature drove him over to the conservatives: 'now flattery keeps him there, in spite of "Pillars" etc. He would, it seems, have preferred to be with both [parties] at the same time! [. . .] People excuse Ibsen since he comes from "simple people". He needs it for his self-esteem. Well, well!' Brandes agreed with Bjørnson that Ibsen was 'cautious, tender towards his laboriously hard-earned reputation and will be unwilling to risk it by supporting efforts which are not popular among "the educated"'.[52] He found rich comedy in Ibsen's lust for orders: 'The poet of *Brand*, hungering for an honour such as being a Knight of the Dannebrog'.

By the turn of the decade, the literary-political positions were polarised even further. Denmark and Norway had parallel, ongoing power struggles between the governments and parliamentary majorities fighting for a parliamentary system of government. In Norway, the final stage of this struggle was initiated in 1880, leading to courts of impeachment against all the members of government and the eventual call on the leader of the opposition, Johan Sverdrup, to form a government of the Left party in 1884. This process dragged on for much longer in Denmark, but the political issues, the chronology of electoral mobilisation, and the alliances were more or less the same.[53] In both countries, the political Left had a

[49] V. Pingel, Letter to G. Brandes, 24 December 1877, ibid. (Copenhagen: Gyldendal, 1940), vol. 3, 266.
[50] J.P. Jacobsen, Letter to G. Brandes, 12 February 1878, ibid. 135–36.
[51] Bjørnson, Letter to G. Brandes, 10 June 1878, ibid. (Copenhagen: Gyldendal, 1939), vol. 4, 57–8.
[52] G. Brandes, Letter to Bjørnson, 24 June 1878, ibid. 65.
[53] René Karpantschof & Flemming Mikkelsen, 'Folkelige protestbølger og demokrati i Danmark seet i et internationalt perspektiv 1700–2000', in Nils Rune Langeland (ed.), *Politisk kompetanse* (Oslo: Pax, 2014), 117–29.

predominantly agrarian following which in cultural and religious matters stood removed from the urban radicalism represented by the Brandes brothers and the 'new literature'. What held the groups together was their common opposition to the conservative governments and the demand for cabinet ministers accountable to parliament. The polarisation of the political struggle led in 1879 to more or less formal alliances between the political Left and what in the course of this year came to be known as 'the Literary Left'. In Norway, this alliance was already personified in Bjørnson. In Denmark, it was formalised in an agreement between the agrarian leader Christen Berg on the one side and Edvard Brandes and Viggo Hørup on the other. Edvard Brandes was to run as a liberal candidate for parliament in Copenhagen, and he and Hørup gained access to Berg's newspaper *Morgenbladet*, and thereby to a much wider audience than they previously had been able to reach. The political cleavages which split the state thereby contributed to the polarisation of every aspect of culture in the two countries. The political situation was different in Sweden, but a similar grouping emerged there with the 'young Sweden' and the 'eighties' generation of authors ('åttitalisterna'). These developments were, we should note, contrary to what took place in Germany at the time. There, Bismarck cut his ties to the national-liberals and blocked any step towards parliamentary rule at exactly the time when the balance of power tipped the other way in Norway.

It took another two plays before Ibsen had restored his relations to Bjørnson and Brandes. The relationship to Brandes did not deteriorate like the relationship to Bjørnson, but it is remarkable that during the absolutely central phase of Ibsen's new development, from the summer of 1877 and until 1882, there was no correspondence and no meetings between them, especially since Brandes was now living in Germany.[54] As late as October 1879, less than two months before the publication of *A Doll's House*, Brandes wrote to Paul Heyse that Ibsen 'in recent years has been courting the arch-conservatives'.[55] For those most familiar with his authorship, Ibsen's masterpieces of social drama were far from being expected events.

---

[54] Ibsen's last letter to Brandes was written 1 August 1876, and in June 1877 Brandes visited him in Munich before deciding to move to Berlin.
[55] G. Brandes, Letter to P. Heyse, 29 October 1879, *Correspondance*, vol. 3, 200.

4

Nora's Exit

Ibsen reinvented himself as a dramatic author in the context of the literary-political dynamics in Scandinavia by the late 1870s and early 1880s. These dynamics, known as the Modern Breakthrough, have the characteristics of an emerging literary field, opposing 'old' to 'young', 'free art' to 'bourgeois demand', and indicating that the producers were now capable of asserting their own norms and standards on literary production. When Ibsen entered into this dynamic, he was not simply subdued by it; he gave it an extra, powerful momentum. This also brought him into a precarious position, however, and no sooner had he joined the Literary Left before he started working to escape the restrictions imposed upon him by this new literary-political logic.

Where Did Nora's Exit Come From?

Nora's exit in *A Doll's House* is a decisive turning point, both in Ibsen's career and, as it happened, in the history of modern drama. Not that Nora was the first to leave, not even in Scandinavian literature. In Bjørnson's 1877 novel *Magnhild*, partly inspired by *Madame Bovary*, the main character leaves her husband,[1] and Ibsen had himself anticipated Nora in his most socially affirmative play, *The League of Youth*. There he created the character Selma who is outraged at being excluded from serious matters by her husband: 'You dressed me up like a doll. You played with me as you might play with a child [...] Now I don't want any of your troubles. I'm leaving you!'[2] She does not leave, but Brandes, who otherwise had many objections to *The League of Youth*, singled out Selma as the only interesting minor character in the play. He regretted her marginal part because she

---

[1] Per Amdam, *Bjørnstjerne Bjørnson* (Oslo: Gyldendal, 1993), 437.
[2] Quoted in Robin Young, 'Ibsen and Comedy', in James W. McFarlane (ed.), *The Cambridge Companion to Ibsen* (Cambridge: Cambridge University Press, 1994), 64.

was 'a new character and it would be possible to write an entire drama about her relationship to her family'.[3] Selma can be used, as Robin Young does, to argue as to how a 'sceptical, ironic cast of mind' – the satirical mode – goes through the different stages of Ibsen's authorship, and at the same time 'how great was the distance Ibsen had to travel' from the *The League of Youth* to the later cycle of contemporary plays[4]; we would even say from *Pillars of the Community* to *A Doll's House*. So how did Ibsen arrive at the uncompromising finale of *A Doll's House*, where the institution and values of the family are not being reconfirmed, as in *Pillars of the Community*, but utterly shaken?

It would be impossible to give a 'complete' account of how the play came about, and the way experiences, intellectual impulses and changing possibilities are being converted in the creative act will in any case never be fully accessible.[5] Even so, we can with some confidence assert that certain personal and second-hand experiences fed into its composition. So did the growing attention given to the 'social question' of women's status.

As is well known, Ibsen availed himself of elements from the novelist Laura Kieler's life story in his new play: a secret loan to finance a trip to Italy for the sake of her husband's health, and rumours about an attempt at counterfeiting. As a young writer, Kieler had visited Ibsen in Dresden in 1871 and he had supported her. In 1876 the Kieler family visited the Ibsens in Munich on their return from Italy, and Laura revealed to Susanna that she had secretly taken a loan to finance the trip and that their stay in the south had helped her husband recover. When she later got into financial trouble, she begged Ibsen to recommend a manuscript of hers to his publisher Hegel. Ibsen's negative answer – he thought it far from ready for publication – ended, it seems, with her entering into but not completing a forgery. When it was all revealed, her husband was sympathetic at first, but under pressure from his family he demanded divorce, her baby was taken from her, and she was sent to a psychiatric institution. The story circulated widely in literary circles, rumours having it that she had forged a bill to finance her consumption of luxuries. When

---

[3] Quoted in Vigdis Ystad, *Innledning til De unges Forbund: Utgivelse: Mottagelse av utgaven*, www.ibsen.uio.no/skuespill.

[4] Young, 'Ibsen and comedy', 65. Ståle Dingstad too argues for the centrality of comedy to Ibsen's modern drama, *Den smilende Ibsen*, 95. This is a valuable corrective, but Ibsen's long-term effort to achieve something like 'tragic seriousness' in his contemporary prose plays almost disappears in Dingstad's account.

[5] A comprehensive account of the play's genesis is given in Vigdis Ystad, *Innledning til* Et Dukkehjem: *Bakgrunn*, www.ibsen.uio.no/skuespill.

A Doll's House was published, it was immediately assumed that Ibsen had based the plot on the Kieler story.[6]

Ibsen was informed of what had happened to Laura by her husband, and a couple of times he even asked Hegel for more information.[7] On 19 October 1878 he wrote the first known draft of the play, called 'Notes for the tragedy of modern times' ('Optegnelser til nutids-tragedien'). It contains passages sharply opposing the world of men and the world of women:

> There are two kinds of moral law, two kinds of conscience, one in man and a completely different one in woman. They do not understand each other; but in matters of practical living the woman is judged by man's law, as if she were not a woman but a man. [...] A woman cannot be herself in contemporary society, it is an exclusively male society [...]. She has committed a crime, and she is proud of it; because she did it for love of her husband [...]. Depressed and confused by her faith in authority, she loses faith in her moral right and ability to bring up her children.[8]

This is the first time Ibsen conceives of something like 'tragic' seriousness in a contemporary realist prose play. The dramatic conflict, at this stage, is based on an essentialist conception of separate and irreconcilable gender spheres.

Other personal experiences also contributed to Ibsen involving himself in questions of women's rights. By the autumn of 1878 he once more went to Rome, where the family stayed until the spring, before moving southwards to Amalfi where he completed *A Doll's House* during the summer of 1879. In Rome, he became embroiled in a heated struggle in the Scandinavian Society. In January 1879, he proposed engaging a woman as the new librarian – an old acquaintance of his from Bergen had come to Rome and could do with a part-time position. He also proposed changing the Society's laws so that women gained the right to vote. His proposals did not obtain a sufficient majority, however, and Ibsen was furious, refusing to speak to his opponents afterwards. At a later gala evening, Ibsen turned up again, apparently in good spirits. During the evening he rose to his feet, captured everyone's attention and gave a passionate speech, castigating the audience for their ignorance and outdated opinions, and particularly turning on the women among them who had 'thrown his gift into the

---

[6] See, e.g., J.P. Jacobsen to E. Brandes, 30 December 1879, *G. og E. Brandes brevveksling*, vol. 2, 344.
[7] See Ibsen, Letters to L. Kieler, 26 March 1878, and to F.V. Hegel, 2 August and 8 October 1878, with comments.
[8] Quoted and trans. in McFarlane (ed.), *The Oxford Ibsen* (London: Oxford University Press, 1961), vol. 5, 436–37.

mud' and schemed against him. A countess even fainted, according to one of Ibsen's enthusiastic young supporters, the playwright Gunnar Heiberg. It was as though, writes Heiberg retrospectively, 'he were clarifying his own secret thoughts', as though 'his spirit were scouring the darkness in search of his immediate spiritual goal, his play – as though he were personally living out his theories, incarnating his characters. And when he was done, he went out into the hall, took his overcoat, and walked home. Calm and silent.'[9] It was, Heiberg suggests, as if Ibsen were rehearsing the last act of *A Doll's House*.

The Danish author J.P. Jacobsen, another young Ibsen supporter in Rome at the time, wrote to Georg Brandes after *A Doll's House* had been published in December: 'The play makes me understand Ibsen's behaviour in Rome on the issue of women's right to vote [. . .] in which I, by the way, as was only reasonable, followed him through thick and thin. How delightfully insolent he was towards his opponents!'[10] The old literary celebrity Ibsen had managed to command the support of the young generation.

In Rome Jacobsen worked on his novel *Niels Lyhne* (1880), later considered one of the precursors of the modernist European novel,[11] and praised by Ibsen upon its publication.[12] Gunnar Heiberg would soon become a new leading playwright, critic and theatre director. 1879 was the year not only of *A Doll's House*, but also of August Strindberg's breakthrough novel *The Red Room* and Alexander Kielland's successful debut with a collection of short stories. The new authors sought support from the Brandes brothers, who encouraged them and called on them to take up leading positions. While Edvard incited Strindberg,[13] Georg took care of Kielland and wrote to him in June 1879: 'The two old ones [Bjørnson and Ibsen] are laboriously working to get loose; show that you have a lead. The old ones could not write a Norwegian novel; write one, or a longer short story; the old ones cannot do that either. In short, the field is wide open.'[14] In August he continued: 'Your danger would be to be

---

[9] Gunnar Heiberg, *Salt og sukker* (1924), quoted and trans. in Meyer, *Ibsen*, 471.

[10] J.P. Jacobsen, Letter to G. Brandes, 30 December 1879, *G. og E. Brandes brevveksling*, vol. 2, 344.

[11] For example, Theodor Adorno, 'The Position of the Narrator in the Contemporary Novel', *Notes to Literature*, ed. Rolf Tiedemann, trans. Shierry Weber Nicholsen (New York: Columbia University Press, 1991), vol. 1, 32.

[12] Ibsen, Letter to F.V. Hegel, 16 January 1881, with comment.

[13] See E. Brandes, Letter to A. Strindberg, 14 August 1880, Georg Brandes & Edvard Brandes, *Georg og Edv. Brandes brevveksling med nordiske forfattere og videnskabsmænd*, ed. Morten Borup (Copenhagen: Gyldendal, 1939), vol. 6, 8–9.

[14] G. Brandes, Letter to A.L. Kielland, 22 June 1879, ibid., vol. 4, 256.

accepted by the ruling philistinism'.[15] Brandes urged Kielland to avoid what had happened to Ibsen: 'What is incredible in this respect has of course happened with Ibsen in Norway, who, as cutting as he is and was, has been appropriated and has let himself be appropriated. Be an artist completely!'

The strength of the emerging literary field can be measured by the fact that it exerted influence on the most prominent of all Scandinavian authors. With *A Doll's House* Ibsen once again made himself into a contemporary Scandinavian author, and his own positioning became infused with the field's oppositional logic, which he also gendered. In his heated rhetoric in the Scandinavian Society in Rome, he associated women with youth and with 'true artists', commonly opposed to the men with their 'little ambitions, and little thoughts, little scruples and little fears'.[16] He welcomed the ladies to the meetings, 'so that they, together with the young, may see to it that power is placed in true, and truly artistic, hands'.

The Social Question

A Doll's House is not only a new move towards the 'truly artistic'; it also marks a 'social turn' in Ibsen's authorship. The interest in and attention to 'the social' was generally on the increase in the last part of the nineteenth century. From the 1830s and '40s governments all over Europe systematically started mapping the social world. 'The social' was commonly defined in opposition to politics, and 'the social question' widely used as synonymous with the 'labour question'. But the social was also the sphere of women: family, health, welfare. In Norway, Eilert Sundt's 1850s and '60s studies of poverty, travellers, literacy, marriage patterns, mortality, building traditions and more were pioneering. These studies aimed at uncovering statistical regularities that could guide government regulations and reforms. The social had, in this conception of it, neither direct political representation nor independent agency. It was a sphere of duties, not of rights.[17]

At first sight, Ibsen seems to fit well into this reasoning. From the end of the 1870s he repeatedly held up the social as an alternative to politics, in

[15] G. Brandes, Letter to Kielland, 20 August 1879, ibid. 263.
[16] 'Forslaget om bibliothekaren' (1879), www.ibsen.uio.no/sakprosa, quoted and trans. in Meyer, *Ibsen*, 469–70.
[17] Denise Riley, *'Am I That Name?'* (Houndmills and London: Macmillan, 1988), 44–66; Joan Wallach Scott, *Only Paradoxes to Offer* (Cambridge, Mass.: Harvard University Press, 1996), 67, 93, 114–15.

seeming continuity with his earlier antipolitics. His first draft of *A Doll's House* was, as we have just seen, based on the common conception of essential social difference, not on the political concept of equality. On closer inspection, though, Ibsen's use of 'the social' took on a turn distinctly different from the conservative defence of separate spheres; in fact, he must be credited for having delivered a major blow to that ideology.

That blow was first and foremost made through *A Doll's House*.[18] What the play demonstrated was that there was no such thing as a social sphere of female duties existing above and beyond law and politics. When Nora's actions, dictated by what she takes to be her duties as wife, are deemed illegal, she wakes up from her 'doll life' to realise that it is politics and law that circumscribe her duties: 'And I now hear, too, that the laws are otherwise than I'd imagined.'[19]

This social turn meant that Ibsen faced contemporary society in a more direct way than he had done so far. Up until now, he had needed to detach himself from 'society', and he had achieved this through moving abroad, and by rhetorical, poetic distance, or by historical distance: 'I shall have to find salvation in remoteness of subject', he wrote in 1870; 'That is when I intend to begin *Emperor Julian*.'[20] As John Northam observes, Ibsen's earlier contemporary heroes had stood more or less outside society. Falk in *Love's Comedy* is a student and therefore not yet directly involved in the social structure he condemns. Brand is to an extent woven into his community, but 'his small parish can serve only as an emblem of real modern existence'.[21] Nora Helmer and Helene Alving are fully socialised individuals, living ordinary, although privileged middle-class lives with ordinary responsibilities in ordinary families. This move demanded, and made possible, a departure from the abstract problems of vocation and sacrifice in the service of absolutes, and a reformulation of the problems of meaning, purpose, and fulfilment in far more concrete, social and everyday terms.

There is an only apparently paradoxical link, then, between increased literary autonomy and a more direct immersion in 'the social'. As long as society exerted a direct pressure that distance through emigration seemed

---

[18] Joan Templeton: '*A Doll House* is the greatest literary argument against the notion of the "two spheres"', *Ibsen's Women* (Cambridge: Cambridge University Press, 1997), 137.

[19] Ibsen, *A Doll's House*, trans. Deborah Dawkin & Erik Skuggevik, in *A Doll's House and Other Plays*, ed. Tore Rem (London: Penguin, 2016), 185.

[20] Ibsen, Letter to P. Hansen, 28 October 1870, *Letters and Speeches*, 103.

[21] John Northam, *Ibsen* (Cambridge: Cambridge University Press, 1973), 109.

to be the primary way of overcoming, Ibsen's contemporary heroes had been outsiders. With a growing autonomy from society, in the sense that literature itself took over as the major field of influence, Ibsen could let his heroes be fully embedded in contemporary social institutions. Autonomy did not produce a more 'detached' literature; the result was rather the opposite. But the change of subject, to the family of contemporary society, at the same time gave Ibsen a new means of obtaining distance: he would choose female heroines.

Ibsen had used major female characters in his early historical plays, but when turning to contemporary society, women had largely played more marginal parts. All the works from *Brand* to *Pillars of the Community* have male protagonists. Only with Lona Hessel of *Pillars* is there again a prominent female character, and in the next two plays women are centre stage. One reason for Ibsen's attraction to bourgeois women seems to have been a spontaneous identification with their subordinate social position: bourgeois writers and bourgeois women both belonged to 'the dominated among the dominant'.[22] This social affinity resonates through Ibsen's audacious speech in the Scandinavian Society in Rome. The other reason, we will suggest, was literary and dramatic. The literary advantage of the female perspective was that it enabled him to enter into the core institution of bourgeois life with the distancing perspective of the dominated part and the experience of failed love. This provided Ibsen with a conflictual perspective on contemporary institutions essential to his dramatic imagination.

The social turn also forced Ibsen to concretise his 'politics'. As already noted, it might at first seem that the social only became another means with which he could discount politics, in continuity with his former antipolitics. But there is more to it than this. In 1879, it was Bjørnson's turn to approach Ibsen, trying to enrol him behind a demand for a 'clean' national flag; a flag stripped of the signs of the union with Sweden. Ibsen turned him down, however, stating that he was totally opposed to the proposal and that there was far too much concern with symbols, theories and ideas. He regretted that the Norwegian parliament, more than sixty years after it was established, acted as if it was still a constituent assembly. The letter indicates that Ibsen did not show much concern for the constitutional question that was on top of the national agenda at the time, the fight for parliamentary rule. But this time he at least advocated a concern with 'practical matters' as an alternative: 'There is only one issue in Norway that is worth fighting for now, and that is the introduction of an up-to-date public education system.'[23]

In 1882 the last phase of the constitutional struggle started, with Bjørnson touring the country as the main agitator on the liberal side. Meanwhile Ibsen had published his next, highly controversial play *Ghosts*, and Bjørnson intervened to defend his colleague. Bjørnson's intervention finally brought the two together again and Ibsen wrote to say that he had followed Bjørnson's campaign closely. But he again asked: 'is it a good thing that politics should so completely take precedence over social problems?'[24] Ibsen claimed that Norway was out of tune with the rest of Europe in this respect and he himself thought that 'where progress is concerned, it is more imperative to liberate people than institutions'. At the same time he acknowledged Bjørnson's 'powerful gift for politics' while 'I have not even a gift for citizenship; I am without any talent in that direction. Therefore it is just as natural for you to put yourself at the head of things as it is for me to remain outside.'

Here, Ibsen is still pursuing the social/political distinction in a relatively straightforward manner. Two years later, however, he was happy to support a social-political reform. For the first time, he responded positively to being enrolled by Bjørnson, who invited Ibsen to support a bill proposing to give separate property rights to married women. When Ibsen now, at the same time, continued to push the social/political opposition, he ended with what seems like highly idiosyncratic conclusions. He did not have high hopes for the reform, he told Bjørnson, as long as the political vote was a privilege just for men. He thought peasant landowners at home were no more liberal minded than the ultramontane agrarian population of Tyrol, where he spent his summers. Therefore he was not optimistic about an extension of suffrage either. 'Such things are not given away by their possessors; they must be fought for', he noted, adding:

> If I could have my way at home, then all the unprivileged should unite and form a strong, resolute, progressive party, whose program would include nothing but practical and productive reforms – a very wide extension of the suffrage, the statutory improvement of the position of woman, the emancipation of national education from all kinds of medievalism, etc. I would give theoretical political questions a long rest; they are not of much consequence.[25]

---

[23] Ibsen, Letter to Bjørnson, 12 July 1879, *Letters and Speeches*, 178.
[24] Ibsen, Letter to Bjørnson, 4 August 1882, ibid. 209.
[25] Ibsen, Letter to Bjørnson, 23 March 1884, ibid. 228–29.

On his visit to Norway the following year, Ibsen gave the well-known speech in Trondheim where he stated that Norway still had a long way to go towards 'real liberty'. He doubted that the present democracy was capable of solving these problems:

> An element of *nobility* must enter into our national life, our administration, our representative bodies, and our press. Of course I am not thinking of a nobility of *birth*, nor of that of *wealth*, nor that of *knowledge*, neither of that of *ability* or talent. I am thinking of a nobility of character, of a nobility of will and spirit. [. . .] This nobility [. . .] will come to us from two sources. It will come to us from two groups that have not as yet been irreparably harmed by party pressure. It will come to us from our women and from our workingmen. The reshaping of social conditions now under way in Europe is concerned chiefly with the future position of the workingmen and of woman. This is what I hope for and what I wait for. It is what I intend to work for and what I shall work for all my whole life so far as I am able.[26]

This is as close as we get to Ibsen the 'socialist' in his domestic contexts. It is a socialism of a very peculiar kind, one demanding democracy in the name of nobility.

This paradox resulted from Ibsen pursuing the social/political dichotomy all the way to declaring extended suffrage a 'social' and not a 'political' reform. His negative conception of politics and 'institutional' questions identified such concerns as 'purely' constitutional matters, 'state affairs' in the narrowest sense. There is a logical continuity to this reasoning. But Ibsen's embrace of the social as an alternative at the same time gave his antipolitics a distinctly new character in the 1880s. In his disparate logic, he mobilised the social against the political while at the same time wanting to give the social a political voice and independent agency. This brought him to a position in the middle of the 1880s that in some respects comes across as the extreme opposite of his antimass rhetoric from ten years earlier.

Ibsen's involvement in social issues also raises questions about how we read *A Doll's House*. If Nora's conflict could be solved by social reforms, then the play would hardly qualify as a 'tragedy': 'More pliant divorce laws could not alter the fate of Agamemnon', as George Steiner has put it.[27] In this austere, metaphysical view, reformable problems are by definition not tragic; they are simply problems to be solved. More liberal than Steiner on the matter, *A Doll's House* may fit more easily under the Hegelian definition of tragedy as staging a conflict between competing rights: here the duty towards

---

[26] 'Speech to the Workingmen of Trondhjem' (1885), ibid. 249.
[27] George Steiner, *The Death of Tragedy* (London: Faber & Faber, 1961), 8.

the children and the duties towards oneself. When Ibsen originally conceived the play as a tragedy, however, it was most probably because he intended Nora, in her confusion and despair, to carry out the suicide that she only contemplates in the finished play. From a feminist perspective, it is one of the great merits of the play that Ibsen avoided that kind of tragedy. Had Nora been another Agnes of *Brand* or Solveig of *Peer Gynt*, *A Doll's House* would have been another tragedy of female sacrifice and self-sacrifice – exactly the reason why feminism has generally been hostile to tragedy.[28] Nora's exit instead made Ibsen's drama a play about female agency.

But what happens with the play when it moves into an age when women *do* have choices and when they *can* walk away? Has not the play then lost its relevance, confirming Steiner's point after all? The fact that *A Doll's House* continues to be one of the most frequently performed plays worldwide runs counter to such an assessment and indicates that it probes deeper than 'purely' political issues. Sexual conflicts have not gone away, even though the terms of their articulation have changed. Following the social/political question we have explored so far, we will suggest that another reason for its continuing relevance has to do with the way Ibsen perceived a conflict between political equality and social difference and how he negotiated this conflict in *A Doll's House*.

It could seem that from the first draft to the final version Ibsen moved from the social conception of separate spheres and gender complementarity towards the political conception of liberal individualism and equality. His draft, as we have seen, is based on the first kind of reasoning, while in the final version a key part of the concluding dialogue seems to evoke equality pure and simple:

NORA: What, then, do you count as my most sacred duties?
HELMER: And I really need to tell you that! Aren't they the duties to your
    husband and your children?
NORA: I have other equally sacred duties.
HELMER: You do not. What duties could *they* be?
NORA: The duties to myself.
HELMER: You are first and foremost a wife and mother.
NORA: I don't believe that any more. I believe I am first and foremost a human
    being, I, just as much as you – or at least, that I must try to become one.[29]

---

[28] Rita Felski, 'Introduction', in Rita Felski (ed.), *Rethinking Tragedy* (Baltimore: Johns Hopkins University Press, 2008), 17.
[29] Ibsen, *A Doll's House*, 188.

In the draft, we have noted, the basis for claiming equality is the essential difference between male and female; in the final dialogue, it seems to be sameness. But this becomes more complicated as soon as we ask what being 'a human being' would mean? Nora hardly wants to be *like* her husband, her claim must be on a more abstract level. But nor does she want to be his kind of 'individual'. Throughout the play, it has been demonstrated that what defines Thorvald Helmer's sense of being a responsible, mature individual is his difference from his childish, helpless, ignorant wife. Nora to some extent accepts that identity: her exit is based on it. She takes on her husband's description of herself as a 'child' and makes it the primary argument for declaring that she can no longer take the responsibility for raising her children. To become 'a human being' seems for her, at that moment, incompatible with remaining a woman: that is, in her case, wife and mother. Even so, we would not expect the outcome of her 'growing up' to be an 'individual' defined by its opposition to everything 'female'. Could being a human being really turn out to be incompatible with being wife and mother? Nora says that she has to find out who is right, she herself or 'society', but everything suggests that she, even at the end of the play, identifies with and is willing to defend what she has done as a 'woman'. She might claim that she does not want to be a 'woman' as patriarchal society defines 'woman', as daughter, wife and mother. But those are the positions and those are the experiences from which she is speaking. It seems impossible for Nora to transcend femininity and sexual difference in order to become a full 'human being' without evoking that difference.[30]

The meeting between abstract individualism and social, sexual, racial, religious difference is a continuing source of paradox. We would not argue that this is what the play is all about, but we will suggest that approaching the play from such a perspective is in accordance with Ibsen's own struggle to negotiate between the political and the social. Ibsen tried to keep, as we have repeatedly seen, distance from being a citizen, seeing in this term only the abstract, homogenised, political individual, while he saw the social as the source of difference and true individuality. In *A Doll's House*, he was able to explore these kinds of contradictions in ways that proved productive, compelling and of continuous relevance. One of the merits of the play is precisely the fact that Ibsen does not do away with the paradox, siding either with equality or with difference, but keeps it open.

---

[30] This reading draws on Scott, *Paradoxes*, 1–11, 171–75.

With *A Doll's House* we can again observe how far Ibsen had moved in a decade. During the beginning of the 1870s, Ibsen had been unreceptive to feminist concerns, as advocated for example by the pioneering feminist writer Camilla Collett, even though he had created a character like Selma Bratsberg in *The League of Youth* in 1869. Collett stayed with the Ibsen family in Dresden in 1872 and Susanna proved very attentive to her ideas, while Collett, in a letter to her son, described Ibsen as 'from top to bottom an egotist and despot and not least as a man towards women. [. . .] Imagine our confrontation, Alf!'[31] In 1877, Collett criticised Ibsen's female characters, particularly in *Brand* and *Peer Gynt*, in her *From the Camp of the Silent* (*Fra de stummes Leir*).[32] Georg Brandes, generally presented as the vanguard of everything progressive, had a trajectory in these matters almost opposite to Ibsen's. He translated John Stuart Mill's *On the Subjection of Women* as early as 1869, but ended in a heated polemic with Collett in the late 1880s, after he had accused her of starting the 'gender war' in Scandinavia. In the meantime, Ibsen and Collett had grown much closer. For all Brandes's admiration of *A Doll's House*, its most 'feminist' dimensions went beyond his imagination. His main objection was the ending, which he found 'impossible': 'The lover is missing. No woman travels to the countryside in order to attend to her own inner improvement.'[33]

German Setback

Ibsen oversaw the production of *A Doll's House* in Munich, and prided himself on all the attention and discussion aroused by the play. Different reports indicate that the first two acts met with universal approval, while the third provoked starkly opposed responses in the audience.[34] Overall, though, while *A Doll's House* was a huge success in Scandinavia, it must be considered as yet another blow to Ibsen's German ambitions, both as book and as theatre.

To avoid a repetition of what had happened with *Pillars of the Community*, a theatre success of no economic advantage to the author, Ibsen this time allied himself with one of the 'pirates', Wilhelm Lange. Lange received sheets for *A Doll's House* from Copenhagen as soon as they were ready, and the German translation came out as 'Einzig autorisierte deutsche Ausgabe' in the cheap Reclam Universal-Bibliothek series, almost

---

[31] Quoted in Ellisiv Steen, *Den lange strid* (Oslo: Gyldendal, 1954), 154–55.   [32] Ibid. 229.
[33] G. Brandes, Letter to E. Brandes, [December 1879], *G. og E. Brandes brevveksling*, vol. 2, 58–59.
[34] See comment to Ibsen, Letter to G. Groeben, 21 March 1880.

at the same time as the original Copenhagen edition. The deal was that they shared theatre incomes and this time Ibsen earned a considerable amount. But new troubles soon arose. Reclam sent their book to Scandinavia, where many potential readers were competent readers of German. Costing the equivalent of 0, 18 *kroner*, the Reclam edition competed with an original costing 2, 25 *kroner*, more than twelve times as much. Ibsen was informed that one Copenhagen bookshop alone had sold 600–800 copies of the German *Nora*.[35] And even worse: when German theatre directors wanted another ending to the play, Ibsen realised that he had no means to prevent them, and preferred to make one himself. In this alternative, Thorvald forces Nora to have a last look at her sleeping children, making Nora realise that she is not capable of leaving them motherless after all.[36]

Georg Brandes witnessed the Berlin premiere of *A Doll's House* and wrote an illuminating report on the event, basically arguing that a 'masterpiece', as he called the play without any hesitation, does not make its way all by itself, but that its recognition is highly dependent on contingent circumstances, and in particular on the relative strength between languages and literatures.[37] He emphasised the expectations and literary competence of the audience, the name and status of the author, the prestige of the author's originating culture, and the efforts put into the production.

The first major obstacle for a play like *A Doll's House*, he thought, was that the Berlin audience expected to be entertained and had been thoroughly corrupted by Sardou, while Ibsen's play was nothing but serious. Neither did the author's name command any respect in Berlin, according to Brandes, in spite of the success of *Pillars of the Community* a few years earlier: 'He is known by few and you can see from the theatre bill that he is foreign and does not belong to a nation whose culture one admires.'[38]

The lack of copyright only enhanced the negligence and disrespect, Brandes continued: 'The respect for Nordic literature at German theatres is of the kind which one in this world has for what can be acquired for free.'[39] Wanting to secure a new play by Dumas, he explained, a Viennese theatre director would write a humble letter to the author, negotiate a price

[35] Ibsen, Letter to H.E. Berner, 18 February 1882.
[36] Ibsen, Letter to the Editor of *Nationaltidende*, 17 february 1880, *Letters and Speeches*, 183–84.
[37] Georg Brandes, '"*Et Dukkehjem*" i Berlin', *Udvalgte skrifter*, ed. Sven Møller Kristensen (Copenhagen: Tiderne Skifter, 1987), vol. 8, 24–30.
[38] Ibid. 28. Dingstad argues that Emil Jonas's radical domestication might have been the most important reason for the success of *Pillars*, *Smilende*, 167–77.
[39] Brandes, '"*Dukkehjem*" i Berlin', 26.

before he had seen a line, send an advance payment of 30,000–40,000 francs and promise a share of the box office revenue in addition. To make sure that he had his expenses covered, he would then put all his efforts into making a successful production, sparing nothing on the stage design, sending the leading actors to study the Paris production, and holding up to 70 rehearsals. Ibsen's play, in contrast to such procedures, had cost the director 20 *Pfennig*, the price of the Reclam edition, and it had been rehearsed three or four times. Adding to these difficulties were the facts that no one in Berlin, as opposed to in Scandinavia, had read the play before seeing it, and that the actress Hedwig Niemann-Raabe was incapable of performing the transformation of Nora in the final act. Finally, Brandes could not avoid putting at least some blame on Ibsen, for an ending that was more logically than psychologically consistent.[40] Fortunately, Brandes somewhat cynically concluded, the great majority of the audience had long since given up Ibsen's 'claim of the ideal', and would marvel at that fact that 'there still exists a man who treats two people's life together so seriously and solemnly'.[41]

Ibsen's return to Italy in 1880 indicates his disillusionment with Germany at this stage. After staying in Italy from September 1878 until October 1879, the Ibsen family first went back to Munich where Sigurd studied law at the university. Upon their return to Munich, Ibsen wrote from Rome that 'for various reasons I wish to get into closer contact again with German literary life. Here one is too entirely out of touch with the movements of the day.'[42] In the summer of 1880, Sigurd went with his mother to Norway to inquire about whether he could continue his studies there. This plan failed when Sigurd was not exempted from the obligatory preparatory courses of the university. Eventually they decided to move back to Rome once more, where Sigurd continued his law degree and where his parents stayed for the next five years.

Moving back to Italy meant, in other words, yet another winding down of his German ambitions and, consequently, once again a stronger orientation towards Scandinavia. In 1881, we know of only three German theatres that put on *A Doll's House*. No German performance of the play is registered in 1883, 1884 and 1885, and Berlin brought no Ibsen play whatsoever between 1881 and 1886.[43] In Munich, there was no new Ibsen play until 1889, when *Ein Volksfeind* premiered,[44] and Ibsen terminated

---

[40] Ibid. 28–29.   [41] Ibid. 30.   [42] Ibsen, Letter to M. Grønvold, 9 March 1879, *Letters of*, 318.
[43] Wolfgang Pasche, *Skandinavische Dramatik in Deutschland* (Basel: Helbing & Lichtenhahn, 1979), 191.
[44] Hans Wagner, *200 Jahre Münchener Theaterchronik 1750–1950* (München: Wissenschaftlicher Verlag Robert Lerche, 1958), 30–44.

his membership in the German society for dramatic authors in 1884. In the meantime, as we have noted, his home market had become legally homogenised and integrated.

Advance and Retreat: From *Ghosts* to *An Enemy of the People*

With his next play, *Ghosts*, Ibsen radically challenged what it was appropriate to put on display in the theatre, and even the book publication caused an outcry. Ibsen was nevertheless not totally prepared for the hostile reactions to *Ghosts* and he was particularly upset by negative criticism in some liberal papers – while at the same time seemingly enjoying the fact that his old disrespect for 'liberals' was being confirmed.[45] This time, however, he did not resort to accusations of 'Scandinavian backwardness'. He noted that the play had caused violent reactions in Scandinavia, and from that experience, he drew the conclusion that it would be impossible on German stages.[46] He did not send *Ghosts* or *An Enemy of the People* to Emma Klingenfeld in Munich, up until now his preferred translator, later explaining that he thought 'that these pieces deal with problems which I did not imagine likely to be of so much interest to you'.[47] He feared that she might feel receiving his latest plays as an invitation to do something she would rather abstain from, and his instinct was probably right. Klingenfeld too belonged to the circle of Paul Heyse. In 1878 and 1879, before and after Ibsen's stay in Italy, Ibsen and Heyse met almost daily in Munich.[48] Heyse was enthusiastic about Ibsen up until *A Doll's House*, but with *Ghosts* it was full stop. Heyse found the play disgusting and *An Enemy of the People* even worse: just plain boring, he claimed.[49]

With *Ghosts*, Ibsen consolidated his literary hegemony in Scandinavia; this much is clear from contemporary reactions in the literary world. Georg Brandes could not quite comprehend why Ibsen had abandoned his 'relative position of cautiousness' but thought it might be 'in order not to lose his advanced position'.[50] He did not particularly like *Ghosts*, however; 'we need works which will persuade and conquer', he wrote to

---

[45] Ibsen, Letter to G. Brandes, 3 January 1882, *Letters and Speeches*, 198.
[46] Ibsen, Letter to L. Passarge, 22 December 1881, ibid. 197.
[47] Ibsen, Letter to E. Klingenfeld, 4 July 1883, *Letters of*, 372.
[48] P. Heyse, Letters to G. Brandes, 4 October 1878 and 12 December 1879, G. Brandes, *Correspondance*, vol. 3, 188, 206.
[49] Heyse, Letters to G. Brandes, 24 December 1881, 15 January 1882, and 23 December 1882, ibid. 247, 252, 265–66; see also comment to Ibsen, Letter to E. Klingenfeld, 4 July 1883.
[50] G. Brandes, Letter to V. Pingel, 28 January 1882, *G. og E. Brandes brevveksling*, vol. 3, 344.

Bjørnson, 'not that provoke and frighten'.[51] But *Ghosts* was useful to him because it 'undoubtedly places Ibsen in the ranks of those among whom one has for so long refused to see him'. Brandes told Bjørnson that Ibsen 'after 5 years' silence' had sent him a letter thanking him for his review; 'It pleased me since I have always thought highly of him and from the old days owe him much encouragement.' Brandes even welcomed the attacks on Ibsen: 'It is pure grist to our mill.'[52] After Ibsen so distinctly had 'shown his true colours, there is not in the two countries a single writer with talent enough to fit on a nail, who does not belong to us. Much has been gained.' The Dane openly admitted that his positive review was dictated by 'sound literary politics', not by aesthetic opinion.[53] He had no interest in 'this eternal nonsense about wives leaving their husbands', but it was wise to support Ibsen: 'our entire literature has become one gang: Bjørnson, Ibsen, Kjelland [sic], Elster, the Brandes brothers and the other Danes'.[54]

Around this time Ibsen himself started adopting a rhetoric of moving boundaries. *Ghosts* might in several respects have been 'rather daring', he wrote to a Danish journalist; 'But it seemed to me that now was the time when some boundary posts had to be moved. And for that undertaking an older writer like myself was more fitted than the many younger authors who might desire to do something of the same nature.'[55] The passage indicates how Ibsen consciously had confronted the challenge from the younger generation.

After *Ghosts* Kielland wrote that this 'amassing of horrors' interested him 'less for its own sake than for the insight it gives me into this fine, cautious, decorated, slightly snobby person, who like Nora has always had a secret desire to say "bloody hell!" in the midst of all this niceness'.[56] He wondered where Ibsen had gained the courage suddenly to 'find himself air for such a wild attack'. Part of the answer might in fact lie with Kielland himself. In April 1881, Kielland's novel *Arbeidsfolk* (*Workers*) caused an uproar. The conservative *Morgenbladet* called it 'the syphilitic novel'. The liberal press too thought Kielland had gone 'too far', and to Kielland's great

[51] G. Brandes, Letter to Bjørnson, 22 January 1882, ibid., vol. 4, 147–48.
[52] G. Brandes, Letter to S. Schandorph, 22 January 1882, ibid., vol. 3, 209.
[53] G. Brandes, Letter to Kielland, 26 February 1882, ibid. vol. 4, 338.
[54] G. Brandes, Letter to Ernst Brandes, 14 January 1882, *Breve til Forældrene 1872–1904*, ed. Torben Nielsen (Copenhagen: Reitzel, 1994), vol. 2, 94.
[55] Ibsen, Letter to O. Borchsenius, 28 January 1882, *Letters and Speeches*, 203.
[56] Kielland, Letter to G. Brandes, 12 January 1882, *G. og E. Brandes brevveksling*, vol. 4, 337.

disappointment, even Brandes expressed a similar view.[57] There is little
doubt that Ibsen had been thinking about the material that became *Ghosts*
before this, at least since the summer of 1880.[58] But it is equally clear that
he was working on something else in the winter of 1880–81, and that it
was only in June 1881 that he started writing *Ghosts*. The controversy
around Kielland's novel is likely to have contributed to his putting the one
work aside in favour of the new play 'that forced itself upon me now with
such urgency that I could not let it alone', as he wrote to Hegel in June.[59]

Georg Brandes thought that the new books by Kielland and other
young authors had led Ibsen to miscalculate public opinion, thinking that
'the climate in the Nordic countries was more conducive for a work such as
his last one than it has proven itself to be, and the next time he will make a
better battle plan'.[60] Kielland for his part immediately realised that Ibsen's
Ghosts had created a broader scope for young authors.[61] It is quite clear
that Ibsen's 'comeback' during these years had a profound impact on
Scandinavian literature, particularly the Danish-Norwegian, giving the
whole field a higher degree of autonomy. Ibsen's conservative Danish
publisher would never have accepted something like *Ghosts* from any of
his young authors. Hegel still set limits, for example when rejecting the
naturalist novelist Amalie Skram's depiction of female sexuality in *Con-
stance Ring*, with the author's gender as a major reason.[62] In spite of this,
he became the publisher of most of the literature of the Modern
Breakthrough. It was in this respect Brandes publicly acknowledged Ibsen
for having 'risked all of his patiently and slowly won authority, his
goodwill among the public, almost his entire bourgeois reputation'.[63]
Ghosts might not, in spite of its enormous significance, be his most perfect
drama, Brandes thought, 'but it is the most noble deed of his literary life'.
In Sweden the young generation did not have a corresponding literary
authority to back them, and for that reason not a corresponding publisher
either. During the 1880s, Strindberg and others had trouble finding
publishers for anything that could be suspected of raising controversy.[64]

[57] Tore Rem, *Forfatterens strategier* (Oslo: Universitetsforlaget, 2002), 192–94.
[58] See comment to Ibsen, Letter to Sigurd Ibsen, 3 September 1880.
[59] Ibsen, Letter to F.V. Hegel, 18 June 1881, *Letters and Speeches*, 195.
[60] G. Brandes, Letter to V. Pingel, 28 January 1882, *G. og E. Brandes brevveksling*, vol. 3, 344.
[61] Kielland, Letter to G. Brandes, 12 January 1882, ibid., vol. 4, 337.
[62] Tveterås, *Norske*, 305–10.
[63] Quoted in Jørgen Knudsen, *Georg Brandes* (Copenhagen: Gyldendal, 1988), 250.
[64] Thomas von Vegesack, 'Sweden', in Derek Jones (ed.), *Censorship* (London: Fitzroy Dearborn, 2001), vol. 4, 2355.

Around the time of *Ghosts,* there is, as noted, a distinctive turn in Ibsen's poetics. His rhetoric of distance now became temporalised. 'The minority is always right', he wrote in his first letter to Brandes for almost six years: 'I mean that minority which leads the van and pushes on to points the majority has not yet reached. I mean: that man is right who has allied himself most closely with the future.'[65] A year later, after *An Enemy of the People,* he continued in the same vein, now with reference to the hero of his new play. In ten years, he wrote in another letter to Brandes, the majority might have reached the standpoint held by Dr Stockmann at the public meeting: 'But during those ten years the doctor will not have been standing still; he will still be at least ten years ahead of the majority. The majority, the mass, the mob will never catch up with him.'[66] It is one of the many ironies of *An Enemy of the People* that it was written as a means with which to close the gap that had opened between Ibsen and his audience with *Ghosts.*

The usual assumption about *An Enemy of the People* is almost the opposite: that it reflects Ibsen's fury over the reception of *Ghosts,* in the liberal press generally and particularly in Arne Garborg's negative review in *Dagbladet.* Edvard and Georg Brandes were the first to resort to this interpretation and it has enjoyed a permanent circulation since then. Some of that controversy of course went into the play.[67] But as already indicated, the play that became *An Enemy of the People* had been in preparation before Ibsen started to write *Ghosts.*[68] Just before *Ghosts* was published, Ibsen wrote to Hegel: 'I am already busy with plans for a new comedy in four acts, a work which I had in mind before, but which I laid aside because *Ghosts* forced itself on me and demanded all my attention.'[69] This 'comedy' must be *An Enemy of the People,* and despite all the controversy around *Ghosts* Ibsen stuck to the plan of striking a 'light' tone in his next play. In March 1882, he wrote to Hegel: 'It will be a very peaceable play this time, one which may safely be read by the state councilors and the merchants and their ladies; and the theaters will not have to recoil in horror from it.'[70]

---

[65] Ibsen, Letter to G. Brandes, 3 January 1882, *Letters and Speeches,* 199.

[66] Ibsen, Letter to G. Brandes, 12 June 1883, ibid. 220.

[67] See comment to Ibsen, Letter to H.E. Berner, 18 February 1882.

[68] Lorentz Dietrichson, who met Ibsen regularly at this time, countered the usual assumption in his 1896 memoirs, claiming that 'the ideas [which Ibsen] expresses in *An Enemy of the People* were completely ready in him already in the spring of 1881 and were aired in nearly all the conversations we had at that time', *Svundne,* vol. 1, 362.

[69] Ibsen, Letter to F.V. Hegel, 23 November 1881, *Letters and Speeches,* 196.

[70] Ibsen, Letter to F.V. Hegel, 16 March 1882, ibid. 206.

While entertaining avant-garde rhetoric in his letters to Brandes, Ibsen struck a distinctly different tone in letters to other recipients, like the Swedish Sophie Adlersparre. He completely agreed with her, he wrote, that he 'dare not go further than *Ghosts*. I myself have felt that the general conscience in our countries will not permit it, nor do I feel any urge to go further. A writer dare not alienate himself so far from his people that there is no longer any understanding between them and him.'[71]

Brandes was probably right when he conjectured that Ibsen had miscalculated his audience with *Ghosts*. Ibsen initially thought that all the sensation around the play would only spur the sales, as he had experienced it before. But this time Hegel was at first forced to take back quite a number of books as returns from booksellers and dreaded to tell Ibsen about it.[72] At the same time it should be noted that the first edition of *Ghosts* was a record high 10,000 copies. The setback was thus more about the continuous increase in the size of first editions stopping up and levelling out than it was about a setback in the book market.[73] Ibsen did experience economic losses with *Ghosts* but these mostly came from the theatres rejecting the play. Ibsen had no interest in losing and permanently alienating a major part of his audience and his new affiliation with the Literary Left was in this respect a problem. Brandes wrote to a German recipient in 1882 that he had founded a 'school of literature' and that Ibsen and Bjørnson had joined him.[74] Ibsen did not want to be associated with a literary school or party, but nor could he risk his newly-won literary position. It was this complex situation that he managed to renegotiate with *An Enemy of the People*.

For quite some time, Ibsen was uncertain as to what generic title he would use, 'whether I should call it a comedy or a straight drama. It has many of the characteristics of comedy but it also has a serious theme'.[75] In the end, he simply opted for 'play' ('skuespil'). During the row over *Ghosts* he had emphasised, in a letter that was also made public, that 'there is not in the whole book a single opinion, a single utterance, that can be laid to the account of the author. [...] in none of my other plays is the author such an outsider, so entirely absent as in this one'.[76] In *An Enemy of the People* Ibsen explicitly did the opposite; he deliberately made Stockmann

---

[71] Ibsen, Letter to S. Adlersparre, 24 June 1882, ibid. 208.
[72] Kielland, Letter to G. Brandes, 12 January 1882, *G. og E. Brandes brevveksling*, vol. 4, 336–37.
[73] We thank Maria Purtoft for drawing our attention to this fact.
[74] G. Brandes, Letter to A. Fitger, 16 and 22 May [1882], *Correspondance*, vol. 3, 330.
[75] Ibsen, Letter to F.V. Hegel, 21 June 1882, *Letters and speeches*, 207.
[76] Ibsen, Letter to S. Schandorph, 6 January 1882, ibid. 200–1.

into a mouthpiece. He wrote to Hegel that 'Dr. Stockmann and I got on so very well together; we agree on so many subjects. But the doctor is more muddle-headed than I am; and moreover he has other peculiarities that permit him to say things which would not be taken so well if I myself said them.'[77] When the play was out, he told Brandes that it had amused him 'to recall many of the scattered and sketchy utterances in my letters to you'.[78] These mainly belong to Stockmann's interrupted speech in the fourth act.[79]

The mouthpiece character of Stockmann, with the *Ghosts* controversy as the immediate context, afforded a range of conflicting readings. Jonas Lie wrote that Stockmann had made a 'great' and 'tragic' impression on him. He had himself only lately come to embrace Ibsen's great idea, '[t]he declaration of the liberty of individuality'.[80] The leading Swedish idealist critic Carl David af Wirsén praised Ibsen's technical mastery, as he always did. But *Ghosts* shaped all his subsequent reading: with that play Ibsen had 'openly joined the party which will tear down the foundations of every orderly society'.[81] Later, as secretary of The Swedish Academy's Nobel committee, he saw to it that Ibsen never was awarded its literature prize. With *An Enemy of the People* Wirsén regretted that it was 'the friends of Brandes' that seemed to be Ibsen's 'model of a healthy, unprejudiced minority'.[82] But the Brandes brothers for their part saw it the other way round. Edvard Brandes had become a liberal member of parliament in 1880 and took *An Enemy of the People* to be a reactionary attack on the principle of majority rule, and that just because of some stupid newspaper articles.[83] Georg Brandes too had to distance himself from 'the message' of Ibsen's play in the speech he gave on his return to Denmark early in 1882 (Figure 4.1).[84]

The 'serious' side of the play was, in other words, taken very seriously. That Stockmann's statement about the minority always being right was not a statement on and from the inside of politics, but followed from Ibsen

[77] Ibsen, Letter to F.V. Hegel, 9 September 1882, ibid. 210.
[78] Ibsen, Letter to G. Brandes, 21 September 1882, ibid. 211.
[79] For example, more or less straight quotations from letters to F. Gjertsen, 21 March 1872 and G. Brandes, 4 April 1872.
[80] J. Lie, Letter to Ibsen, 1 December 1882, NLN, Letter coll. 200.
[81] [Carl David af Wirsén], 'Henrik Ibsen: Gengangere', *Post-och Inrikes Tidningar*, no. 1, 2 January 1882.
[82] [Carl David af Wirsén], 'Henrik Ibsen: En Folkefiende', *Post-och Inrikes Tidningar*, no. 289 and 290, 12 and 13 December 1882.
[83] Edvard Brandes, 'Henrik Ibsen: "En Folkefjende"', *Morgenbladet* (Copenhagen), no. 285, 7 December 1882.
[84] Jørgen Knudsen, *Georg Brandes* (Copenhagen: Gyldendal, 1994), 43.

Figure 4.1 'Henrik Ibsen as disciplinarian' (December 1882).
At the top Stensgaard in *The League of Youth* is beaten, to the delight of the Right, in the middle Bernick of *Pillars of the Community* is beaten, to the delight of the Left, and at the bottom both sides are beaten by Ibsen in the shape of Dr. Stockmann.

opposing the principle of 'individuality' to the homogenising and levelling effects of politics, did not generally come across. The many ways in which he created a distance between himself and Stockmann were also down-played, and have largely been so ever since. Importantly, Ibsen gave the conflict a class dimension, the Stockmann brothers being civil servants and editor Hovstad coming from 'poor folk'. The liberal Hovstad reveals himself as completely unprincipled and is the one who gets the harshest treatment in the play. In his letter to director Hans Schrøder during rehearsals at Christiania Theater, Ibsen was remarkably specific as to Hovstad's social background, far more so than in the play-text. He explained that Hovstad had grown up in miserable and poor circum-stances, and been exposed to all kinds of trials as a child and young man. This, Ibsen insisted, had to be reflected in his bodily appearance, in his stooping posture and insecure movements.[85] In the play-text, Hovstad only says that 'I descend from simple farming stock'.[86] It seems that Ibsen, at least in performance, wanted to address the effects of poverty just as much as political opportunism.

Stockmann's social arrogance is repeatedly underlined already in the play-text and also enhanced by Ibsen's use of comical degrading through the use of gender oppositions. Stockmann is the one who takes care of 'society' while his wife Katrine is the narrow-minded 'woman': 'all the men here in this town are nothing but old women – just like you; they only ever think about their families, not about society'.[87] Even so, Katrine is the sensible, moderating and down-to-earth type, caring for what they shall live from even though she supports her husband. Stockmann's arrogance culminates in his incapacity to learn the name of their maid. Four times he calls on her without remembering her name, until finally he just calls her 'that girl who's always got soot on her nose'.[88] When the mob rips a hole in Stockmann's trousers, he declares: 'People should never wear their best trousers when they're out fighting for truth and freedom'.[89] But it doesn't matter, he says to Katrine, 'you can always patch them up for me'. We understand that Stockmann's fight for truth and liberty rests on his capacity to command female labour to attend to practical matters. Stockmann is already prefiguring Gregers Werle of *The Wild Duck*, the apostle of truth who cannot make a fire without sooting the whole room.

---

[85] Ibsen, Letter to H. Schrøder, 13 December 1882.
[86] Ibsen, *An Enemy of the People*, in *A Doll's House*, 341.   [87] Ibid., 325.   [88] Ibid., 356.
[89] Ibid., 348.

Reading *An Enemy of the People* together with Ibsen's other 'speech acts' at the time, it is hard not to appreciate its character of self-irony and self-parody. When Stockmann asks Hovstad if it is not the editors who rule the press, the printer Aslaksen answers: 'No, it's the subscribers, Doctor.'[90] Ibsen was not less concerned about his 'subscribers' than the pathetic couple Hovstad and Aslaksen. Neither was he less worried than Katrine about the household economy. And 'the general conscience in our countries' that would not 'permit' him to go further, evoked in the letter to Adlersparre, is this not exactly 'that damned solid, liberal majority' that Stockman holds to be 'the most dangerous enemies to truth and freedom'?

One of the peculiar strengths of literature is that it can have it both ways. *An Enemy of the People* could stand out as another heroic, uncompromising statement on individuality – while openly intended to get state counsellors and merchants back in the theatre. The play declared that the strongest man is the one who stands alone – while restoring the family solidarity that had been totally undermined by *A Doll's House* and *Ghosts*. The play could make the 'market disappear',[91] declaring total disrespect for 'demand', while at the same time actively trying to restore Ibsen's public relations.

An Enemy of the People terminates a short cycle in Ibsen's literature, and it inaugurates a new turn. It must be considered one of many contributions to the eventual dissolution of the Scandinavian Literary Left. The last blow to Brandes's ambitions of holding together a progressive literary party came by the end of 1883 when Holger Drachmann changed sides and joined the 'national' campaign against Brandes and the 'Europeans'. At the same time, the political alliance in Denmark between radicals and agrarians broke down. Georg Brandes's biographer describes the literary and political setbacks by the end of 1883 as a disaster.[92] Ibsen, however, welcomed what was happening. 'I see from the papers that a literary civil war has broken out in Copenhagen, and that severe fighting is going on', he wrote to Hegel in December 1883.[93] 'I, for my part, see no great misfortune in a disruption of the literary Left. I believe that the many highly gifted authors who belong to it will work better each for himself, without any side glances at a common programme.'

[90] Ibid., 324.   [91] Bourdieu, *Rules*, 81.   [92] Knudsen, *Brandes: Symbolet*, 36, 184.
[93] Ibsen, Letter to F.V. Hegel, 27 December 1883, *Letters of*, 376.

5

The Sphinx

The avant-garde rhetoric adopted by Ibsen in the early 1880s, and the reading of *An Enemy of the People* as a polemical response to the reception of *Ghosts*, have decisively shaped the general image of Ibsen's relation to his domestic audience. In *Det moderna genombrottet i Nordens litteratur* (*The Modern Breakthrough in Nordic Literature*) (1947/1974), often considered the 'classic' account of the subject and repeatedly evoked up till this day,[1] Gunnar Ahlström paints a gloomy picture of the conditions at the time. While liberalism was triumphing on the continent, he claims, time stood still in the north, and the institutions of traditional Christianity retained their power. When, inspired by Georg Brandes, the new literature eventually managed to begin to make itself noticed, it was met with massive hostility and was soon thoroughly suppressed. Most of what posterity has considered the great achievements of the period, Ahlström contends, was welcomed with disapproval and animosity in its own time. When the matter was put to the test, it became all too evident that there was no harmony between the authors and their domestic public. In Ibsen this reversal found its strongest expressions in the dramatist's depiction of society as an infected public bath in *An Enemy of the People*, and in the pessimistic message of *The Wild Duck* that people were not ready to hear the truth and ought rather to be left in peace with their ignorant 'life-lies'.[2]

In another prominent account written from within the Brandesian 'cultural-radical' tradition and dealing with the Modern Breakthrough in a Danish perspective, Sven Møller Kristensen holds the 'congenial' audience of this new literature to be infinitesimal, consisting of perhaps just around 200 people.[3] Even though acknowledging the 'great modern

[1] David Gedin, *Fältets herrar* (Stockholm: Brutus Östling, 2004), 27; Rønning, *Umulige*, 378.
[2] Gunnar Ahlström, *Det moderna genombrottet i Nordens litteratur* [1947] (Stockholm: Rabén & Sjögren, 1973), 9–11, 65, 209–19, 257–83.
[3] Sven Møller Kristensen, *Digteren og samfundet i Danmark i det 19. århundrede, Naturalismen* [1945] (Copenhagen: Munksgaard, 1970), vol. 2, 185.

Norwegians' to be a major power in the Danish book market,[4] his main
picture is of a literature being imported prematurely from 'advanced'
Europe to backward Denmark and meeting a massive national-liberal
'storm' ('uvejr'):

> While the Modern Breakthrough according to the usual European and
> literary-historical time scheme comes belatedly to Denmark, which is what
> Brandes suggested, one must from a sociological point of view think that it
> comes around 20 years too early. Many of the struggles of modern Danish
> literature and its quarrels with the public can probably be explained by way
> of this hypothesis.[5]

We have already seen other versions of this narrative,[6] and we have also
seen that such rhetoric permeated correspondence and public polemics and
that it was constitutive of how the world of literature was imagined at the
time. But this narrative is incompatible with available evidence of how
Ibsen in particular was received. Such evidence does not conform to the
picture of hostility and isolation, quite the contrary.

Income

Basic measures of Ibsen's standing in Scandinavia is provided by the
records of his income, his book sales and the success of his plays in the
theatres, all of which can be reconstructed in some detail. Ibsen's finances
are extraordinarily well documented for the key part of his career. In 1870,
in Dresden, Ibsen started keeping an account book where he made entries
for every payment received. He opened a new such book in 1890 in
Munich which he kept until he was hit by his first stroke in the spring
of 1901. His spending is not specified, unfortunately, but it is possible to
reconstruct the main components of the income side of his economy
during the last three decades of the century (Appendix, Figure A.1).[7]

The mere existence of these account books, with all their meticulous
and accurate entries, is persuasive testimony to the importance of authorship as business and to the great attention the playwright paid to the
commercial side of his career. What they document is that after he left the
theatre in the middle of the 1860s, Ibsen's home market soon provided

---

[4] Ibid. 166.   [5] Ibid. 205, see also 200.
[6] Yet another example, extreme but widely circulated, is Egon Friedell, *Vår tids kulturhistorie* [Cultural
History of the Modern Age; orig. German edn. 1927–31] (Oslo: Aschehoug, 1959), vol. 3, 488–89.
[7] Based on Henrik Ibsen, Regnskapsbøker 1870–1901. 2 vols., NLN, Ms. fol. 3222. The expenses are
not specified and can only, with some accuracy, be divided into consumption and investment, see
Narve Fulsås, *Innledning til brevene: Økonomi*, www.ibsen.uio.no/brev.

him with an astonishingly wide and attentive audience, both as book and theatre author. Ibsen's contention in his first plea for a state grant that it was impossible to live solely from one's writings in Norway, was soon to be proven wrong. Already by 1870 we can see (Appendix, Figure A.1), with the sole exception of 1872, that the state grant makes up just a small part of Ibsen's income and that its economic significance becomes ever more marginal. In 1871, the year in which Ibsen published *Poems*, he asked the Gyldendal director Hegel for the first time to invest part of the royalty in bonds. By 1877, the returns from these investments were higher than the state stipend. The accumulated value of his securities was 45,000 kroner by 1880, 107,000 kroner by 1890, and 260,000 by 1900.

A few comparative figures should bring out how well he did. The top salary for a professor was 6000 kroner, a cabinet minister was paid 12,000 kroner, and the prime minister 20,000. Ibsen's average annual income in the 1870s was 10,700. In other words: in the late 1870s, when he began the cycle of contemporary drama, Ibsen had already left the professors behind in terms of income. He was closer to a member of the cabinet and clearly a well-established author, financially as in other respects. The Modern Breakthrough did not interrupt this ascending curve; in the 1880s Ibsen's annual average income rose further to 17,550 kroner; Ibsen was approaching a prime ministerial level, while still receiving 93 per cent of his earnings from his Scandinavian home market. In the 1880s, the theatre income slightly outweighs book income, making up 36.6 per cent of the total as against 34.4 per cent for book royalties. A main reason for this is the Scandinavian mutual agreements on copyright; the rise is to a large part due to an increase in payments from Denmark and Sweden.

The general pattern in Ibsen's economy is that book royalties represent the most significant income in the years when a new drama is published, while, since Ibsen from the late 1870s always published new plays quite late in the year, the theatre earnings are harvested during the following year. As a dramatic author it was Ibsen's privilege to have two markets. But it is also worth underlining the fact that he chose to restrict himself almost exclusively to these two markets. He turned down all proposals to have his plays serialised, avoiding this wherever he could control it, insisting on the book format as his only way of addressing the reading public. He also declined nearly all offers to write for journals or newspapers, and he never went on reading or lecturing tours. There were many different ways in which Scandinavian authors could make money during these last few decades of the nineteenth century, but Ibsen focused solely on producing dramatic literature.

Ibsen's colleagues in Scandinavia held him to be the financially most successful among them.[8] In terms of print runs, which we will soon consider more closely, his contemporaries Bjørnstjerne Bjørnson, Jonas Lie and Alexander Kielland were not far behind. Bjørnson wrote both novels and drama, and even Lie and Kielland, although primarily novelists, tried their luck in the theatre market. All of these writers regularly suffered financial troubles even though publishing more than Ibsen, and it seems that their problems had more to do with the expense side than with the income side of their economies. Lie had lost a fortune on forest speculations in the 1850s and is said to have entered a career as author in order to pay back his debt. Kielland had a costly lifestyle, and Bjørnson bought the estate of Aulestad which became a drain on his budget, in addition to having rather expensive children. Ibsen had much stricter control on his spending. In the 1880s his household expenses were around 10,000 *kroner* annually, increasing to 15,000 to 20,000 *kroner* in the 1890s. In the 1880s, the expenses covered two to three months in a summer resort, most often in southern Italy or later in Tyrolean Gossensass. Sigurd was Henrik and Susanna's only child and they never owned a house or a flat, for a long time even almost no furniture. Neither did Ibsen have any talent for conspicuous consumption or for expensive entertaining. In contrast to most writers, Ibsen would use his publisher more for investment business than for advances.

Books

Ibsen's considerable income from Gyldendal was the combined result of large print runs and expensive books. The rapid increase in print runs around this time in Scandinavia fits into the general European pattern. In France in the 1840s, a best-selling author like Victor Hugo appeared in editions of 5,000 copies. In the 1870s the cheapest editions of Jules Verne reached 30,000.[9] The naturalist novel initiated a new wave, and Zola's *L'Assommoir* (1877), which the publisher had hoped to sell in a print run of 5,000–6,000, had in 1882 reached more than 100,000 copies. Zola's *Nana* (1880) sold 90,000 in its first year and had reached 182,000 by the turn of the century. The success of the naturalist novel led to a tremendous

---

[8] For example, Bjørnson, Letter to J. Lie, September 1884, in Bjørnson, *Artikler og taler*, ed. Chr. Collin & H. Eitrem (Kristiania: Gyldendal, 1913), vol. 2, 344

[9] Martyn Lyons, *A History of Reading and Writing in the Western World* (Basingstoke: Palgrave Macmillan 2010), 141.

expansion in French publishing business from the 1870s and into the 1890s, when a long-lasting crisis set in.[10]

Bjørnson's peasant tales soon appeared in several editions; when Gyldendal bought *Synnøve Solbakken*, the Danish publisher's first edition (1866) was already the fifth since the tale's first publication in Norway in 1857. A relatively rapid expansion occurred in the Scandinavian countries from this point. Hegel thought he was taking a risk by ordering 3,000 copies of Bjørnson's novel *The Fisher Maiden* in 1868, but it soon went to 7000. This was a commercial success without precedent in Danish-Norwegian publishing.[11] As for Ibsen, he reached editions of 10,000 by the end of the 1870s, which is an impressive number by almost any comparison (Appendix, Figure A.2). The average Norwegian edition has been estimated to 800 copies before 1873, rising to 1,000 for the rest of the century.[12] Few European authors, if any, could compare with Zola. Alexander Kielland wrote from Paris in 1888 that he thought no more than twenty French authors sold more than 5,000–6,000, and that only Zola broke the 10,000 barrier.[13] Not least are the print runs of the early Scandinavian Ibsen editions astonishing by today's international standards. Only exceptionally will 'upmarket' novels, poetry or drama sell ten or twenty thousand copies in the first year after publication.[14]

The peculiar thing about Ibsen's print runs is that they were so high despite the fact that the books were so expensive. A standard Ibsen book cost around 3 *kroner* unbound and 4–4, 75 *kroner* bound. A male manual labourer would have to spend more than a day's payment for the unbound book, and almost two days' payment for the bound. An experienced seamstress would have to spend almost two days' payment for the unbound and nearly half a week's payment for the bound. The mass sale of such expensive books seems to be particular to Scandinavia. In 1875, Ibsen wrote to Hegel that 'among literary people the material quality of Danish books ['de danske Bøgers Udstyr'] is generally admired down here, and it is regularly said that you far too rarely see anything similar in Germany'.[15] In Germany at the time, books existed in two main kinds, either as costly luxury editions for conspicuous consumption or as cheap

---

[10] Robert F. Byrnes, 'The French Publishing Industry and Its Crisis in the 1890s', *The Journal of Modern History*, vol. 23, no. 3 (1951), 232–35.
[11] Tveterås, *Norske*, 121.   [12] Tveterås, *Bokens*, 80.
[13] Alexander L. Kielland, *Brev 1869–1906*, ed. Johs. Lunde (Oslo: Gyldendal, 1978), vol. 2, 237.
[14] Gisèle Sapiro, 'Translation and the Field of Publishing', *Translation Studies*, vol. 1, no. 2 (2008), 160.
[15] Ibsen, Letter to F.V. Hegel, 31 December 1875.

mass editions without material value, destined to be read to pieces.[16] Gyldendal books had, in comparison, good paper quality, spacious pages and solid binding. Gyldendal paid authors per sheet (sixteen in-octavo book pages) per thousand copies, and Kielland was notorious for pushing Gyldendal to print a minimum amount of text per page.[17] In Paris, he could not but notice that Zola's latest book cost almost the same as his own, while having ten times as much text.

To reach high sales on the continent, book prices generally had to be low. Reclam's Universal-Bibliothek, established in 1867 after the German classics of the late eighteenth and early nineteenth century had moved out into the public domain, was one of the most successful series for mass consumption, publishing a mixture of entertaining, classical and educational literature. The first title of the series was *Faust* and the Universal-Bibliothek brought a majority of Ibsen's plays to the German reading audience. The price of Reclam books remained the same right up to World War I: 20 *Pfennig* (0, 18 *kroner*).

In the Nordic countries, there was simply no cheap version of Ibsen available. Gyldendal did not follow the practice of for example Ibsen's English publisher William Heinemann, who issued new editions on a descending price scale. Heinemann would start with an edition in 'small 4to, with Portrait' for 5 shillings (4, 50 kroner), equivalent in price to the Gyldendal bound edition, followed by a 'popular edition' for 1 shilling. With Gyldendal, every edition, apart from the choice between bound and unbound, looked and cost the same. It was only after the arrival of the new director Peter Nansen in 1896 that a different policy was adopted with the first collected edition of Ibsen's work. Nansen later claimed that he even had to fight with the Gyldendal veteran August Larsen to have his plans for this edition of Ibsen accepted. Why should they sell Ibsen cheap, Larsen asked, when the expensive books sold so well?[18]

Increased print runs was a general European phenomenon during these decades, and the causes are probably more or less the same. These include a general growth in populations, rapid urbanisation, industrialised communications, growing literacy, an extended public sphere and an expansion in social groups identified as middle class by virtue of their education. In the Scandinavia of the 1860s, when Ibsen wrote *Brand* and *Peer Gynt*, he had addressed what seems to be a relatively well-defined and restricted

[16] Reinhard Wittmann, *Geschichte des deutschen Buchhandels* (München: C.H. Beck, 1999), 270–71.
[17] Rem, *Forfatterens*, 168–69.
[18] Peter Nansen, *Mine 20 Aar i Gyldendal* ([Copenhagen]: L. Levison Jun. [1918]), 19.

readership with a university educated core. This group was in itself expanding, as indicated in the doubling of the number of students at the university from the 1860s to the 1880s,[19] while now forming just a part of a more heterogeneous and anonymous 'mass' readership.

Little is known about these new and expanded readerships, whether to their gender composition or even their distribution between the Scandinavian countries. In 1892, Ibsen wrote to the Swedish author Gustaf af Geijerstam, who had translated *Peer Gynt* into Swedish for the stage, that he was absolutely against the translation being published: 'My new books are being printed at [Hegel's] in 10,000 copies, but if he had to fear competition through Swedish translations, I would have to be prepared for the fact that the number of copies of my books would hereafter be reduced with at least 1500–2000.'[20] This, whether it was just a qualified guess or based on information from Gyldendal, might suggest that 15–20 per cent of an edition was sold in Sweden and Finland. While Ibsen's Scandinavian policy of not allowing translations into Swedish reserved the market for Gyldendal, it probably restricted his overall readership in Sweden. Swedish readers in general preferred reading Danish-Norwegian authors in translation.[21]

Nowhere in the correspondence between Ibsen and Gyldendal is there any hint as to how the rest of the print run was distributed between Norway and Denmark. When *Little Eyolf* was published in 1894, a newspaper reported from Copenhagen that according to advance orders from bookshops, the demand seemed to be higher in Denmark than in Norway.[22] We do not know whether this case is representative, however, or even whether it holds for this particular play.

One important feature can be established, though, namely that Ibsen's Scandinavian literary market was already surprisingly integrated and synchronised by the end of the 1870s, in the sense that the new literature reached the remotest provincial towns with almost no time lag from the capitals. As early as on the release of *Peer Gynt* in 1867, there had been regrets in Bergen that the book had arrived late and Hegel heard reports of annoyed customers grumbling about Danish publishers neglecting Norwegian readers while making profit on Norwegian authors. Hegel was very sensitive to such criticism and gradually developed a sophisticated,

[19] *Historisk statistikk 1968* (Oslo: Statistisk sentralbyrå, 1969), 611.
[20] Ibsen, Letter to G. af Geijerstam, 29 March 1892.   [21] Rem, *Forfatterens*, 110–11.
[22] Asbjørn Aarseth, *Innledning til Lille Eyolf: Utgivelse: Mottagelse av utgaven*, www.ibsen.uio.no/skuespill.

extensive apparatus to secure that Ibsen books were on sale all over Scandinavia on more or less the same day.[23] This involved sending book cases to the west and northern coast of Norway some days before those heading for Kristiania, as well as keeping the Copenhagen book shops waiting until publication date.

The debate and attention caused by *A Doll's House* therefore took place all over Scandinavia. The most extended newspaper exchange seems to have taken place in Tromsø, in the far north of Norway, with between 5,000 and 6,000 inhabitants at the time. Early in January 1880, just a month after *A Doll's House* had been published, a correspondent in the local *Tromsøposten* explained why Nora had to leave her family, provoking a response from a defender of the inviolable duties of motherhood. The debate continued well into March with multicolumn contributions over 14 issues. In the middle of May that same year a professional touring company visited Tromsø with *A Doll's House* – it was the first time a professional company had been that far north. The venue was over-crowded, the papers reported, 'because here too everyone wanted to see brought to life on stage the characters that were already so familiar to them from reading.'[24] The company continued all the way up to Hammerfest, where it gave four performances. Among the plays presented were a couple of Danish farces and an operetta by Scribe. The newspapers complained about a rather meagre attendance on the whole, with one exception, namely *A Doll's House*, which filled the venue.[25]

Such reports indicate that Ibsen's new plays mobilised new groups of readers, including in the provinces. A couple of weeks after the publication of *A Doll's House* Hegel informed Ibsen that the book had found 'Buyers also in other places that do not otherwise distinguish themselves in terms of literary interests, e.g., Saxkjøbing, Skjelskov, Ringkjøbing, Veile, Grenaa, Middelfart etc., where they have sold from 11 to 35 copies in each place; quite a rare thing!'[26] The expansion of the readership in this period must be one reason why Hegel almost systematically underesti-mated Ibsen's market potential. With *Brand, Peer Gynt,* and *Emperor and Galilean* he had immediately had to order new editions. With *Pillars of the Community* and *A Doll's House* the gap between supply and demand even

[23] Tveterås, *Norske*, 200–1, 397.
[24] Anon.: ['Paa Theatret opførtes Mandag . . . '], *Tromsø Stiftstidende*, no. 41, 20 May 1880.
[25] Thoralf Berg, 'Teater og underholdning i Tromsø, Hammerfest og Vadsø', in Claes Rosenqvist (ed.): *Artister i norr* (Umeå: Kungl. Skytteanska Samfundet, 2008), 355.
[26] F.V. Hegel, Letter to Ibsen, 20 December 1879, NLN, Letter coll. 200.

widened, until it stabilised with first editions around 10,000 copies in the 1880s (Appendix, Figure A.2).

A basic conclusion that can be drawn from this is that 'modern' literature in Scandinavia evolved together with an expanded circle of readers, not ahead of it. To the extent that there was a mismatch between supply and demand, it rather consisted in Hegel underestimating the demand. Quite contrary to the story of rupture and alienation between the modern Scandinavian authors and their home public, there thus emerges a picture of mutual dependence. The remarkable rise of Norwegian literature in this period, the preconditions for its move into world literature, can be seen as a joint product of an extraordinary generation of authors on the supply side and a receptive and growing readership on the demand side. The new literature met an immediate response and attention at home, not a delayed one – and certainly not only after it had first been acknowledged abroad.

Secrecy and Launching Fever

Since attention and interest could be taken for granted, Ibsen and Hegel adopted a strategy of growing secrecy around new publications. This concerned not least the titles of Ibsen's new works. With *Ghosts* (1881) the author gave Hegel the title by the end of September. Shortly afterwards he wrote that he was anxious that the manuscript should not fall into the wrong hands, but felt that the title and the news of the publication might well be made known.[27] With *An Enemy of the People* (1882) Hegel was informed of the title in June. This time Ibsen wanted only the news of a new play to be published, not the title.[28] After the theatres had rejected *Ghosts*, he would not even send his new play to the theatres; he wanted them to come asking for it.[29] With *The Wild Duck* the secrecy escalated. This time the playwright did not even reveal the title to his publisher until the letter he sent with the complete print manuscript on 2 September 1884. To the rest of the world the title was kept secret until the day of publication. By the middle of the 1880s, Ibsen publications had become media events.

The Wild Duck appeared on 11 November in both Copenhagen and Kristiania. The Danish *Nationaltidende* reported from the Norwegian capital that the book had arrived between noon and one o'clock and that

---

[27] Ibsen, Letters to F.V. Hegel, 30 September and 16 October 1881.
[28] Ibsen, Letter to F.V. Hegel, 21 June 1882.   [29] Ibsen, Letter to F.V. Hegel, 13 September 1882.

it was on sale in the bookshops at a little past two.[30] Albert Cammermeyer
and a couple of other booksellers had asked for five copies to be sent to
them by mail beforehand, but Hegel was inflexible. That would only
create confusion, he answered, and it would be in everyone's interest that
no copies were sent out in advance.[31] The literary reporters worked full
steam, and that same afternoon *Morgenbladet*, *Aftenposten*, and *Christiania
Intelligentssedler* carried full summaries of the play's plot.[32] Ibsen was not at
all pleased with this particular kind of interest, interfering as it did both
with the reader's curiosity and with professional criticism. On the occasion
of *Hedda Gabler* he published a letter in the Danish *Berlingske Tidende*
requesting Nordic newspapers not to report on the plot and content,
leaving it to be dealt with in the context of serious criticism.[33]

Excitement accompanied every new publication. When *The Lady from
the Sea* appeared in 1888, *Verdens Gang* wrote on 30 November that the
new Ibsen book had been expected in Kristiania two days earlier, in the
morning, but that it had not arrived until the previous day around noon:
'The book was in great demand in all the bookshops, and down on the
customs quay yesterday morning, the city's book dealers were virtually
coming to blows over who was to have his crates unloaded first.'[34] The
paper proudly established that it was the only one in town 'that had found
itself able, thanks to its Copenhagen telegram connection, to convey to the
public any information about this work, awaited with such excitement.'

At this time, Gyldendal did not have any principal commissioning agent
or delivery depot in Kristiania. In order to take delivery of an Ibsen book,
therefore, all the booksellers had their own teams of dockers on the
quayside. Ibsen tended to publish his books in November-December,
when there was often ice, bad weather or fog, and the booksellers' emis-
saries might have to stand for hours waiting for the Danish steamer Baldur,
always the one to carry the Gyldendal cargo. A few editors and literary
critics were also often on hand. These people kept themselves informed
about how far up the fjord the ship had come, and when it had passed
Drøbak, a couple of hours' journey from Kristiania, they called the shops.

Once the ship had docked, the burning issue became the location of the
crates in the hold, high or low, together or scattered. In the case of new

[30] *Dansk Nationaltidende* quoted in Johan Irgens Hansen, 'Det literære Reportervæsen', *Dagbladet*,
no. 405, 18 November 1884.
[31] Vilhelm Haffner, *Albert Cammermeyer* (Oslo: Cammermeyer, 1948), 128–29.
[32] Hansen, 'Reportervæsen'; Halvorsen, *Forfatter-Lexikon*, vol. 3, 76.
[33] Ibsen, Letter to *Berlingske Tidende*, 7 December 1890.
[34] Anon., '[Note on "Fruen fra Havet"]', *Verdens Gang*, no. 282, 30 November 1888.

books by Ibsen or Bjørnson, a firm might have ordered as many as a thousand copies, and they could not pass through customs until all the ordered goods had been gathered together. Once that had been done it was all clear, as no customs duty was due. What mattered was getting through customs first and getting up to the shop as quickly as possible. There the booksellers had lists ready of the customers who were to receive the book on approval. Address labels had been completed and arranged in the order of the carriers' routes. But the title was usually missing until the book arrived, and the price always. Delivery could not begin until the invoice had been found and the numbers checked. This could be done more quickly if the invoice was mailed in advance, but because of the secrecy around the titles, the invoice only arrived with the goods.[35]

When the prices had been entered and the copies counted, the race to the customers began. It was not unusual for a single family to receive several copies for inspection. Women with an interest in literature invited their lady friends to sessions of reading aloud. Customers who had ordered in advance waited impatiently. The literary historian Francis Bull has written about the first publication event he could remember, the arrival of *John Gabriel Borkman* in 1896. On the day of publication his father Edvard Bull, who later became Ibsen's doctor, was walking restlessly up and down, waiting for the delivery boy from Cammermeyer's bookshop: 'When it came, not only my mother, but also my brother Edvard, who was 15 years old, were taken into the house's holy of holies, the office, where on ordinary days we were never allowed to stay, and where my father read the play aloud.'[36] Such excitement among customers and competition among bookshops are not unusual for the time. What is extraordinary, however, is that they concerned a serious playwright.

Theatre

This impression of Ibsen's remarkable position by the 1880s is confirmed if we move from book to theatre. Ibsen's theatre incomes were more or less on a level with his book incomes. This might sound like a trivial point, given that Ibsen was a dramatic author, but it is not at all what we would expect from usual assumptions about Ibsen belonging to the theatre avant-garde, assumptions to which we will return (see Chapter 8). Looking at

---

[35] Haffner, *Cammermeyer*, 126–29; Johan Grundt Tanum and Sverre Schetelig, *Den norske bokhandlerforening* (Oslo: Foreningen, 1926), 54–7.
[36] Francis Bull, *Tradisjoner og minner* (Oslo: Gyldendal, 1945), 190–91.

first-season productions of Ibsen plays at Christiania Theater (Appendix, Figure A.3),[37] which becomes synchronised with Ibsen's book history only from *A Doll's House* onwards,[38] we see that from 1870 Ibsen was one of the theatre's most popular authors. *The League of Youth* (1869/70), *Peer Gynt* (1875/76), *Pillars of the Community* (1878/79), *A Doll's House* (1879/80), and *The Wild Duck* (1884/85) were all the best attended productions in their premier seasons, while many of the others were number two or three. During Christiania Theater's time of existence, between 1827 and 1899, *The League of Youth* was the play most frequently put on, with a total of 122 performances. A vaudeville by the Danish actress-author Johanne Luise Heiberg (*En Søndag paa Amager*) achieved the same number, while a play by her husband Johan Ludvig Heiberg (*Elverhøi*) came in as number three. The two next on the most played list were Ibsen's *The Vikings at Helgeland* and Bjørnson's *Maria Stuart in Scotland*, with 100 performances each.[39] If we take into account the number of years in which the different plays were available up until 1899, *A Doll's House*, performed 73 times since 1880, was almost as popular as *The League of Youth*.

It should be stressed that Christiania Theater was a purely commercial enterprise, in a city with only 100,000 inhabitants in 1875, growing to 250,000 by the turn of the century. Several attempts were made to obtain a state grant for the theatre, but to no avail. Accordingly, the repertory had to be varied, always containing popular German and Danish farces and proven Boulevard staple by Augier, Sardou, Dumas *fils* and their like. It would also contain the classics of the English Renaissance, French (and Danish) classicism, and German romanticism. In some periods the theatre would also put on opera. In this particular and significant sense Scandinavian theatre was indeed 'backward': it was weakly differentiated. There was no pure commercial sector directly opposed to an experimental sector, with institutions for the classics and the recognised contemporary drama in the middle.[40] In Scandinavia, all was middle: Shakespeare and Schönthan, Goethe and Bjørnson, Holberg and Scribe, Ibsen and Sardou side by side – and Ibsen competing well with all of them, even the blockbusters from Paris.

Three points concerning Ibsen on the contemporary Scandinavian stage deserve emphasis. First: *A Doll's House* was not just an instant but also an

---

[37] Based on Anker, *Christiania Theater's*.

[38] When *Pillars of the Community* was published Ibsen was angry at the change in management and did not submit the play. It was performed at Christiania Theatre with a year's delay.

[39] T. Blanc, *Henrik Ibsen og Christiania Theater 1850–1899* (Christiania: J. Dybwad, 1906), 30.

[40] Bourdieu, *Rules*, 161–62.

anticipated success on Scandinavian stages. Ibsen's publisher Hegel was a cautious, Christian man, head of the Danish Bible Society, and definitely no radical. He very rarely interfered in literary matters where Ibsen was concerned, but after having read the sheets of *A Doll's House*, he could not resist commenting that 'I would only have wanted a different ending'.[41] Even so, he immediately predicted that the play would be a success in the theatre. The head of The Royal Theatre in Copenhagen, Edvard Fallesen, had at this time still not given up trying to force Ibsen and Hegel to postpone book publication until after the premiere in the theatre. Hegel told Ibsen to overlook Fallesen's threats of not accepting the play if it already had been printed, since Fallesen 'clearly sees that he here has a play which will bring the theatre a substantial income'.[42] Neither are there any indications that Scandinavian theatre directors considered changing the ending – which was the case almost everywhere else in Europe and in the US when the play was first introduced. It was just as successful with its original ending in Copenhagen as it was in Kristiania. The Royal Theatre in Copenhagen put all its efforts into the production and managed to stage the world premiere of *A Doll's House* as early as 21 December 1879, a month before the first night in Kristiania. The premiere in Copenhagen yielded a record income and the play was regularly taken up again. By 1898, it had been performed 66 times – and the audience capacity of the Royal Theatre in Copenhagen was around three times that of Christiania Theater. In fact, only two other new works were more successful on the main Danish stage: the national 'fairy-tale comedy' ('eventyrkomedie') *Once upon a time* ('Der var engang') by Holger Drachmann (141) and the opera *Mignon* by Ambroise Thomas (67).[43] Comparing this success to Brandes's report from Berlin and Ibsen being forced to write an alternative ending for one of the German productions, it is reasonable to ask whether *A Doll's House* would have been written at all if Ibsen had succeeded in becoming 'a German author' in the late 1870s.

The second point relates to the one play that is missing from these performance statistics: *Ghosts* (1881). It is the great exception in the domestic reception of Ibsen, but it has miraculously been transformed into the general rule. The decisions not to accept this play, then, has had an enormous symbolic significance. Ibsen himself helped initiate the

[41] F.V. Hegel, Letter to Ibsen, 8 November 1879, NLN, Letter coll. 200.
[42] F.V. Hegel, Letter to Ibsen, 12 November 1879, ibid.
[43] Arthur Aumont, 'Henrik Ibsen paa danske Teatre', in Gerhard Gran (ed.), *Henrik Ibsen* (Bergen: John Grieg, 1898), 273, 276.

mystification. When the turmoil was at its most intense, he wrote to Hegel that he was 'not the least disturbed by the violence of the reviewers and all the crazy nonsense written about *Ghosts*. I was prepared for it.'[44] He claimed that the outcry had been just as great when *Love's Comedy* appeared, just as *Peer Gynt*, *Pillars of the Community* and *A Doll's House* had also been reviled: 'The cry will die away this time as it did before.'

The reason why things have been turned upside down in later accounts must be related to how the dynamics of an inverted economy guides the perception of 'autonomous' literature. *Ghosts* suits this perception; Ibsen as one of the commercially most successful authors of his time does not. *Ghosts* caused the playwright financial loss, but for exactly that reason it earned him an invaluable fund of symbolic, literary capital and the priceless reputation of being an uncompromising, if not persecuted author.

The decisions not to stage *Ghosts* in the main theatres in Copenhagen and Kristiania also tend to obscure the fact that it was not prohibited to perform the play in public in the Scandinavian countries as it was in Germany, until 1896, and in the UK, until 1914. The Swedish actor-director August Lindberg was the first to bring *Ghosts* to the stage in Europe. The premiere took place in the August of 1883 and Lindberg went on to perform *Ghosts* to much acclaim in Sweden, Denmark and Norway. No one tried to stop him and his success made the Royal Theatre in Stockholm put on the play in the same year, largely as a result of continuous pressure from its leading actress Elise Hwasser. When the director of Christiania Theater, Hans Schrøder, stood by his decision not to produce *Ghosts*, he caused recurrent demonstrations against him and the board throughout the 1880s. Alongside Lindberg there were a couple of other touring companies also playing *Ghosts* in Scandinavia and even crossing the border to Germany. A rather conservative estimate suggests that something like 50,000 spectators saw *Ghosts* in 1883.[45]

Lindberg, it should furthermore be noted, was no Scandinavian avant-garde director, even though August Strindberg tried to make him one. In 1887, Strindberg suggested that they together form a 'Swedish Theatre', performing only new Strindberg plays. He appealed to Lindberg's patriotism: 'You can't stick to Ibsen for long, because he probably won't write much more, and his genre is his specialty and on the decline – You ought to read the Germans about *Rosmersholm*! He to himself, and we for us!'[46]

---

[44] Ibsen, Letter to F.V. Hegel, 2 January 1882, *Letters and Speeches*, 197.

[45] Ståle Dingstad, 'Ibsen and the Modern Breakthrough – The Earliest Productions of *The Pillars of Society*, *A Doll's House*, and *Ghosts*', *Ibsen Studies*, 16 (2016), 127.

[46] Quoted in Per Lindberg, *August Lindberg* (Stockholm: Natur och kultur, 1943), 206.

But Lindberg had to tour with an eclectic repertoire if he was to make a living from the theatre, and realised that this would be 'an experiment, not a professional theatre'.[47] On his so called 'second tour' (1888–90) Lindberg's repertoire was composed of plays by Ibsen (*Love's Comedy, A Doll's House, Ghosts, The Wild Duck*), Bjørnson, Strindberg and other new Scandinavian playwrights, accompanied by *Hamlet, The Winter's Tale* and *Faust*, the popular Swedish history drama *The Wedding at Ulvåsa* (*Brölloppet på Ulvåsa*), French comedy as well as operettas in the summer season.[48] Lindberg's repertoire was thus characterised by the blending of the high and the low, the literary and the entertaining, the classic and the contemporary.

Our third point on Ibsen and the theatre concerns the variations we can observe in the overall pattern of economic success. The substantial incomes Ibsen had from the theatre show that he had strong economic motives for avoiding a repetition of *Ghosts*. *Ghosts* caused a sharp fall in incomes after a decade with more or less constant growth – in fact, 1882 ended up providing him with the second lowest income in the last two decades of his career. It is reasonable to speculate that this was part of the reason why *An Enemy of the People* came out just a year after *Ghosts*, and we have seen that Ibsen with this play explicitly intended to win back his former theatre audience. During Ibsen's whole career at Gyldendal, *An Enemy of the People* is the only example besides *Peer Gynt* (1867) of Ibsen issuing two new plays within just a year's time. It is also a remarkable fact that Ibsen claimed an acceptance fee of 4,000 *kroner* for *An Enemy of the People* from Christiania Theater, while for the preceding *A Doll's House* and the following *The Wild Duck* his demand was 2,500 *kroner*. It is as if he presumed that he was entitled to some kind of compensation for the economic 'losses' that the theatre had inflicted upon him by rejecting *Ghosts*, and might even suggest that Ibsen considered himself a kind of house dramatist who deserved a predictable and regular return.

'Ibsen' vs. Ibsen

Ibsen's literary and economic standing helps explain a rare incidence of Hegel forcefully interfering in the author's literary plans, and that in a counterintuitive way. In 1880, the year after the publication of *A Doll's House*, Ibsen suggested to his publisher that he write a short book of 160 to 200 pages containing information 'on the inner and outer conditions

---

[47] Ibid. 208.   [48] Ibid. 296–97.

under which each of my works was created'.[49] He would not go into interpretations, he assured Hegel, and he would observe the utmost discretion, leaving 'the field wide open for all sorts of conjectures'. He would simply describe the circumstances and conditions under which he had written in Bergen, Kristiania and Rome.

Hegel's response was unequivocally negative. Ibsen had referred to the preface he had written to the new edition of *Catiline* (1875) and Hegel admitted that such information could be useful in a case like that: an early work later rewritten by 'the fully evolved poet'. But apart from such instances it would just be 'a notice of a half-private nature', interesting only because of the name 'Henrik Ibsen'. It was something that really ought to occur only once:

> Repetitions would weaken the impression and when they are being stretched out to cover a whole series of works, they would probably strike the reading world as rather anedoctal, something which should be avoided at any cost. – Your works stand each on its own as clear, characteristic wholenesses, whose meanings should not be associated with such small asides that unconsciously will work their way into the readers' consciousness and later bring a new and disturbing element into their appropriations, since the wholeness and the fragments will no longer harmonise. It is quite a different matter, it seems to me, if you ever wanted to write an 'aus meinem Leben' [from my life], in which such fragments would then be put neatly into their places in the series and thus cease being fragments. But I think it would be wise to postpone such a work for a while yet. If you go the other way and let out private matters, the audience may easily become conceited and create a new basis of negotiation over your future works, with which you might not be well served.[50]

Neither Ibsen nor Hegel used the word 'autobiography' and Hegel explicitly stated that such a work would be welcome – but only in due time: when life itself could be conceived of as a 'whole'.

Ibsen did not quite give up the plan, however, and by the end of 1881 he mentioned it once more, now as a possible journal article.[51] After the controversy around *Ghosts*, Hegel too returned to the project, and this time was even more decisively against it. Ibsen had just written letters on the *Ghosts* controversy which he intended to have published, and he had been encouraged by 'my Copenhagen friends', to 'give a distinct and complete explanation of my position.'[52] Hegel wrote that he stood by

---

[49] Ibsen, Letter to F.V. Hegel, 31 May 1880, *Letters and Speeches*, 185–86.
[50] F.V. Hegel, Draft to Letter to Ibsen, 6 June 1880, RDL, NKS 3742, 4°, II, 'Fr. Hegels Concepter'.
[51] Ibsen, Letter to O. Skavlan, 12 November 1881.
[52] Ibsen, Letter to F.V. Hegel, 16 March 1882, *Letters and Speeches*, 206.

his earlier opinion on the plan for 'an account of your authorship'. He had only been confirmed in this by Ibsen's recent correspondence on the controversy around *Ghosts*, he said, 'and so unconditionally that I would wish that there after your death – may it be far off – will exist no papers in that line.' He wanted to make clear to Ibsen that whatever he wrote, a drama or a letter, he was a public person whose most ordinary remarks immediately became public property:

> Your works stand as a series of statues in a gallery and should, like real statues, keep the beholder at a certain distance. Were the statues to climb down from their pedestals and engage with the audience, they would only suffer, because the audience has always and will always be forward and, furthermore, rarely turn up with clean hands. Every one of your works, after all, speaks for itself and says, as clearly and penetratingly as is possible, what it has to say; and I believe, or, more precisely, I am absolutely certain, that you should not let on about this topic to anyone because this will later, unnoticeably drag you down into the petty polemics of everyday life, which would hinder you from keeping the lines sharp and clean.[53]

Ibsen's intentions are hard to figure out. He had for a long time advocated 'distance' as a main precondition for authorship and the necessity of staying above petty concerns and controversies. Realising how *A Doll's House* had changed his literary-political identity, he may have wanted to reassert unity and coherence to his production through constituting a biographical narrative. Hegel, on the contrary, seems to have thought that the best way of preserving unity was to keep 'Ibsen' as abstract as possible, a principle of origin, unity and autonomy which ought not be confused with the biographical Ibsen, but kept as elevated as ancient statues. There was no need to build up the author: Ibsen's name was already so powerful that it was rather a question of defending 'Ibsen' from Ibsen.

Hegel's intervention contributed towards increasing the symbolic capital already accumulated in the author's name and to bolster the aura of remoteness and isolation that came to be associated with Ibsen for the remainder of his life. 'Do like Ibsen!', wrote Strindberg to Bjørnson in 1884; 'Place yourself in a corner like some other Moses on the mount and speak only one word once a year, and speak cunningly so that no one understands what you are saying, because then the people will be down on their faces worshipping the Sphinx' (Figure 5.1).[54] It was this distanced

[53] F.V. Hegel, Letter to Ibsen, 16 February 1882, NLN, Letter coll. 200.
[54] Strindberg, Letter to Bjørnson, 4 May 1884, *Bjørnstjerne Bjørnsons brevveksling med svenske 1858–1909*, ed. Øyvind Anker, Francis Bull & Örjan Lindberger (Oslo: Gyldendal, 1961), vol. 2, 184.

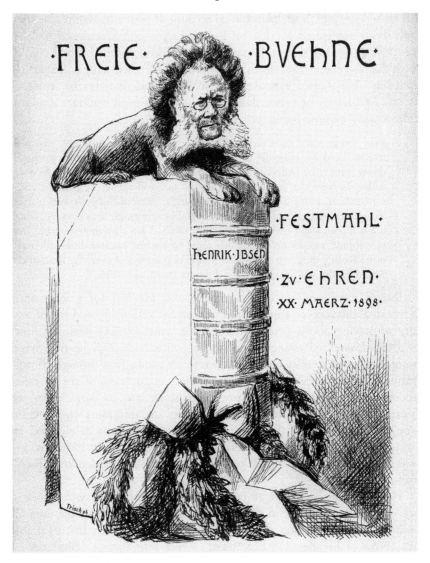

Figure 5.1   Ibsen as Sphinx. The Sphinx image followed Ibsen across Europe.

sovereignty several modernist writers came to admire in Ibsen, taking him
as a model for their own authorial role. The young James Joyce hailed the
old master's 'lofty impersonal power' and, in his letter to Ibsen in 1901,
found inspiration in how Ibsen in 'absolute indifference to public canons

of art, friends and shibboleths [...] walked in the light of your inward heroism.'[55] Rainer Maria Rilke, in *The Notebooks of Malte Laurids Brigge* (1910), called Ibsen 'You, the most lonely, the one set aside'.

'The Double Rupture': *The Wild Duck*

The Wild Duck (1884) initiates a new stage in Ibsen's authorship and it is accompanied by another adjustment of poetics. After having used avant-garde rhetoric for a couple of years, Ibsen left it behind after *An Enemy of the People* and explained his intention in yet a new way. About *The Wild Duck*, he wrote to Hegel: '[...] this new play occupies a position by itself among my dramatic works, its plan and method differing in several respects from my former ones.'[56] He thought it 'might perhaps entice some of our young dramatists into new paths, which I think is desirable', and that it had rewarding roles for actors but 'the study and representation of these characters will not be an easy task.' Concerning *Rosmersholm* (1886), he told Hegel that he had no interest in the German translation being speeded up since he did not intend to have 'this difficult play performed in the better German theatres as early as this coming winter.'[57] With the next play, *The Lady from the Sea* (1888), he once again signalled a new turn: 'It is of course in many ways a new direction I have chosen this time around.'[58] In one letter, he observed that the indeterminacy of 'the Stranger' was vital. No one was supposed to know what or who he was, or his name: 'This uncertainty about him is the essential element in the method I have deliberately chosen.'[59]

From *The Wild Duck* on, Ibsen seems no longer to have seen himself as moving moral boundaries or venturing into the future ahead of the majority. He no longer measured distance in terms of temporal distance to 'society' but in terms of exploring new artistic possibilities. At the same time he underlined that his new works were 'difficult' and 'challenging'. And they were indeed experienced as such by readers and critics, without this new level of difficulty seriously affecting demand in his home market.

If *A Doll's House* is Ibsen's rejection of 'bourgeois' art, then we might see *The Wild Duck* as the second step in what Bourdieu calls 'the double

---

[55] Joyce, Letter to Ibsen, March 1901, *Letters of James Joyce*, ed. Stuart Gilbert (London: Faber and Faber, 1957), vol. 1, 52.

[56] Ibsen, Letter to F.V. Hegel, 2 September 1883, *Letters and Speeches*, 237.

[57] Ibsen, Letter to F.V. Hegel, 6 November 1886.

[58] Ibsen, Letter to J. Hegel, 26 September 1888.

[59] Ibsen, Letter to J. Hoffory, 14 February 1889, *Letters and Speeches*, 275.

rupture', the rejection of 'social' art.[60] We saw that in the transition to the
contemporary drama the opposition between 'bourgeois' and 'free' art
informed the agents' perception, but also that Ibsen was able to transcend
this logic. After having broken away from Brandes's 'school' of social art,
Ibsen obtained a position from which he could dictate his own laws and
which allowed him to maximise his economic, social and literary capital at
one and the same time.

References to the recent literary turmoil in Scandinavia went directly
into Ibsen's preparations for *The Wild Duck*. In notes that seem to be
connected with this play, there is a reference to Holger Drachmann, once
associated with the Literary Left, and to his changing of sides: 'Many a
doctrinaire agitator gradually grows into becoming his own grandfather.
(Drachmann e.g.).'[61] And there are several references to Alexander
Kielland, the foremost representative of literature as social criticism. Ibsen
did not know Kielland but inferred from his social origins that he must be
rich and thus able to keep a purely aesthetic relation to life's problems:
'The sybarite A.K. enjoys an aesthetic indignation with poverty and
misery. He enjoys his visits to the wretched schoolmate, without being
clearly conscious of it', and in the same vein: 'A.K.-d: Lying full and
cushioned up in a soft bed, hearing the rain splashing and thinking of
troublesome journeys in storms and the cold – it is a great pleasure.'[62]

In another note we find among the characters 'The rich old shipping
magnate and businessman. A libertine in silence', and then there is 'His
son, the rich social writer. Widower; champion of the rights of the poor;
takes it as sport.' The note says that the son, 'A.K.', has no objection to his
father marrying 'Mrs. M'. Such a marriage would hinder possible scandals
with the maids and force his father to divide the estate with his son. A.K.
would himself gladly have married Mrs. M, but then there would be no
sharing of the fortune and 'it is not good if the capital stays for too long in
old people's hands. 400,000 kroner with a man of 34 are more productive
than a million with an oldie in his 60s.'[63] Kielland was born in 1849: the
age is spot on.

It was no doubt notes like these that Hegel hoped there would be none
of among Ibsen's papers. One of the things Ibsen is doing here, however, is
negatively defining his conception of writing. 'A.K.' is depicted as an easy-
going big spender with a purely 'aesthetic' interest in social problems. At

[60] Bourdieu, *Rules*, 77–81.
[61] Ibsen, [*Vildanden*] – NBO Ms. 4° 1674, www.ibsen.uio.no/skuespill/Vildanden.   [62] Ibid.
[63] Ibsen, [*Vildanden*] – NBO Ms. 8° 1944, ibid.

the same time, in letters, Ibsen complained that Kielland 'is far too productive, as here he is again with a new novel; it will be his third book within a short year.'[64] Kielland, then, was both too productive and too much of a man about town. In both ways, he came to represent the opposite of Ibsen's conception of authorship as nothing but regular, laborious, serious work.

A long time had passed since Ibsen's Roman poetic frenzy, when *Brand* and *Peer Gynt*, works of verse, had come about like 'the effect of wine' ('vinrus').[65] In the early 1870s Ibsen already looked upon his mode of composition in his first Roman period as undisciplined, calling the style of *Peer Gynt* 'wild and formless, written recklessly'.[66] The following drama, *The League of Youth* (1869), was his decisive shift to prose drama. It was also his first play written in Germany, 'a community that is well ordered to the point of boredom.'[67] In the year after *The League of Youth* Ibsen opened his first account book, that paramount technology not just for keeping the economy under control, but also for heightening overall precision, respect for facts and attention to order and clarity. In 1883, he declared that he had hardly written a single line of verse for seven or eight years, 'devoting myself exclusively to the very much more difficult art of writing the straightforward, plain language spoken in real life.'[68] Ibsen is, in other words, a supreme example of the intimate connection between prose, work and the growing regularity of private life, which Franco Moretti's identifies in *The Bourgeois*.[69]

When Ibsen describes the emergence of his works in the 1880s, it is all about steady and slow work of thinking, followed by careful writing and rewriting in several versions, usually three, and not least about a regular, unbreakable daily rhythm.[70] Work spread out to every segment of the schedule. The long time he took over dressing, the extensive walks, the regular café visits – it was all work. Ibsen was annoyed that people would think that he sat in the cafés just drinking his pint of beer: 'the truth is that I am working and bodying forth in the sweat of my face. I imagine how my characters round themselves off, I see them from the front and from behind etc.'[71] He did not complain, however. While work had replaced

[64] Ibsen, Letter to F.V. Hegel, 4 March 1881.
[65] Ibsen, Letter to P. Hansen, 28 October 1870, *Letters and Speeches*, 102.
[66] Ibsen, Letter to E. Gosse, 30 April 1872, *Letters and Speeches*, 124.
[67] Ibsen, Letter to P. Hansen, 28 October 1870, ibid. 103.
[68] Ibsen, Letter to L. Wolf, 25 May 1883, *Letters and Speeches*, 218.
[69] Franco Moretti, *The Bourgeois* (London: Verso, 2013), 18, 32, 80, 84.
[70] Jæger, 'Opptegnelser', 156–60.
[71] John Paulsen, *Mine erindringer* (Copenhagen: Gyldendal, 1900), 183.

inspiration, it had only heightened pleasure and a sense of satisfaction. In 1890, he stated that it was only late in life that he had learnt to love work and had understood the happiness it gave: 'But when I learned that lesson, I learned it thoroughly.'[72] When finishing *The Wild Duck* in 1884 he wrote to Sigurd: 'I am very happy when I work on this play. I keep putting in more and more details all the time; and I hate to part with it.'[73] By the 1880s, a thoroughly regulated bourgeois life was not just reconcilable, but perfectly compatible with the demands of authorship.[74]

The preliminary notes containing the reference to 'the rich social writer' do not bear directly on the final play text of *The Wild Duck*. A lot was changed. But they point towards how certain fantasies about Kielland, thought of as a well-off writer of 'social literature', fed into what eventually became the truth fanatic Gregers Werle. There were obviously home-grown sources for Gregers as well: he can be seen as Brand reduced to a bourgeois format, just as Hjalmar Ekdal may be considered a re-use of Peer Gynt. But the references to Kielland indicate how consciously *The Wild Duck* was conceived as a departure from social art and from the unqualified blessings of exposing the truth, in that respect also representing a self-critical and even meta-theatrical turn. The setting of the play itself under-mines a simple idea of realism. Much of the action takes place in a photographic studio, a stage within the stage where pictures of reality are being staged, directed and retouched.[75] Hjalmar Ekdal, 'photographer' according to the character list, but more occupied with the work of retouching, is the one blindest to reality.

While in one sense departing from social art, *The Wild Duck* might also be considered a new twist to the social turn, with Ibsen now entering into the social unconscious. *A Doll's House*, *Ghosts* and *An Enemy of the People* had all been about individuals in opposition to society. Ibsen had not made this a purely external conflict, at least not in the first two plays. In the cases of Nora and Mrs. Alving the social had also been inside them in the form of duties, norms, beliefs, conventions, conscience – 'ghosts' – and the conflicts between individual and society must therefore also be seen

---

[72] Ibsen, Letter to K. Hals, 30 October 1890, *Letters and Speeches*, 294.

[73] Ibsen, Letter to Sigurd Ibsen, 27 August 1884, ibid. 235.

[74] Cf. Flaubert's famous statement in his letter to Gertrude Tennant, [25 December] 1876: 'soyez réglé dans votre vie et ordinaire comme un bourgeois, afin d'être violent et original dans vos œuvres', *Correspondance 1871–1877*, in *Œuvres complètes de Gustave Flaubert* (Paris: Club de l'Honnête Homme, 1975), vol. 15, 516.

[75] Peter Larsen, *Ibsen og fotografene* (Oslo: Universitetsforlaget, 2013), 213–14. On the meta-theatrical character of *The Wild Duck*, see particularly Moi, *Ibsen and Birth*, 248–68.

as an internal and internalised conflict. But the heroines of these plays had been able to confront, identify and express the experiences that had shaped them and the conflicts they faced; they had been able to confront the social with a relatively uncorrupted self and a conception of 'natural life'. They had also been able to reveal and recognise the truth about their past and present condition, even, as in the case of Mrs. Alving, the unpleasant truth about her own involvement in killing the 'natural' happiness in her late husband.[76] And even though the recognition in her case came too late, she had been able to identify and describe the moments of crisis and to articulate responses to them, right up to her last, chaotic stuttering 'No; no; no! – Yes! – No; no!'

The social reality of *The Wild Duck* is as hostile as in the foregoing plays, but it does not end in a heroic confrontation with reality. For this reason, Hedvig might be seen as the first truly tragic hero or heroine of Ibsen's contemporary prose plays. Hedvig is unable to comprehend the intricacies of her family situation, the demands of her father and the role assigned to her by Gregers. Hedvig is, in John Northam's apt words, 'the first of Ibsen's inarticulate poets of living.'[77] She dies in silence because she has no means of expressing the passionate conviction and the inscrutable logic that makes her kill herself to win back her father's love. She is clearly handicapped by her young age, but the Ibsen heroines who follow are no more capable of articulating what drives them and what happens to them.

This holds particularly true for Hedda Gabler. With Hedda Gabler, wrote Ibsen in a preliminary note, 'there is a deep poetry at bottom'.[78] She certainly has a kind of 'heroic', transgressing aspiration, but in her case 'society', what she tries to oppose and break loose from, has penetrated so deeply into her personality that her actions and her language 'are all turned into fragmentary vagueness [. . .] a poet rendered almost inarticulate and incomprehensible by her inner contradictions.'[79] If a distinguishing trait of tragedy is 'an uncanny unravelling of the distinction between agency and fate, internal volition and the pressure of external circumstance',[80] *Hedda Gabler* is certainly a modern tragedy.

About *Hedda Gabler* Ibsen said that he wanted to 'depict human beings, human emotions and human destinies, upon a groundwork of certain of the social conditions and principles of the present day.'[81] The way Ibsen

---

[76] Bjørn Hemmer, 'Ibsen and the realistic problem drama', in McFarlane, *Companion*, 85–87.
[77] Northam, *Ibsen*, 146.
[78] Ibsen, Hedda Gabler – NBO Ms. 8° 2638, www.ibsen.uio.no/skuespill.
[79] Northam, *Ibsen*, 181.   [80] Felski, 'Introduction', 11.
[81] Ibsen, Letter to M. Prozor, 4 December 1890, *Letters and Speeches*, 297.

contextualised social conditions in *Hedda Gabler* made him transcend, we might say, a primarily repressive and 'negative' concept of social power. In this play, social power is no longer mainly external, a force restricting the self from the outside through law, morality, conventions or people like Thorvald Helmer, pastor Manders and Peter Stockmann. Social power is shown in its 'positive' and productive capacity to produce a habitus that generally disposes the self to her 'right place' in society. It is for that reason that Hedda Gabler's sense of schism from the world is so inarticulate, so deeply internalised and even unattractive. Her desperate longing for freedom seems inseparable from her brutality, destructiveness and manipulations. She is a bourgeois snob suffocated by *embourgeoisement*. Ibsen struck an extremely delicate balance here between showing the prosaic normality of society while even so confronting it with a marginal and inarticulate 'poetic' aspiration and sense of 'style'. If Flaubert in *Madame Bovary* showed the complete, homogenising triumph of bourgeois prose,[82] then *Hedda Gabler* might be seen to uphold a sense of poetic opposition and transgression, although bleak and desperate. Emma Bovary and Anna Karenina, argues Joan Templeton, committed suicide 'in keeping with the normative assumption that women live for love, men for themselves'; Hedda destroys herself not because she has failed to satisfy that norm, 'but because she refuses to.'[83]

Rosmersholm and the Transformation of Politics

In Ibsen's first 'social' plays, politics and politicians had disappeared. Before this, both had usually been there, as a natural part of the environment of the social class he depicted. His first contemporary play, *Norma* (1851), was, as already noted, a parody on parliamentary debates. *Love's Comedy* contained both a politician and numerous references to contemporary political issues and so did *The League of Youth*. In *Pillars of the Community* there are no politicians, but there is a political issue that is important to the action, the decision made about the new railway line.

A *Doll's House* initiates both a radical reduction of characters and a contraction of the social universe. In *The League of Youth* there are eighteen characters, in *Pillars of the Community* there are 19, and in both of them working-class people appear in the immediate environment. *A Doll's House* has eight characters, plus the children, who may be physically dispensed with in production, and in the Helmer family sphere both commoners and

---

[82] Moretti, *Bourgeois*, 98–100.   [83] Templeton, *Ibsen's Women*, 230–31.

politics seem far away. *Ghosts* reduces the number of characters even further, to five, and from then on, with the exception of *An Enemy of the People*, Ibsen always stuck to between six and eight.

A comparison of the stage settings is revealing. In the first act of *Pillars of the Community* we have 'A spacious garden-room in Consul Bernick's house' where 'a number of ladies are gathered'; in the second we have 'A comfortably and tastefully, though not expensively, furnished room.' From the consul's garden-room, we see through the garden and out onto a street with 'small, brightly painted wooden houses.' If there is a view at all to the outside world from the Helmer living room in *A Doll's House*, we hear or see nothing of it. And although Helmer obviously belongs to the dominant class, being a bank director, he seems to have no connection with politics or any aspiration in that direction.

This contraction of the social universe in Ibsen's plays maps onto the overall expansion of the bourgeois lifestyle in the late nineteenth century, centred on the house and the garden, the home and the family. In opposition to the country houses and mansions of the aristocracy and the great merchants, where power was displayed and where private life was inseparable from public life, the bourgeois house accommodated a private and privatised way of living.[84]

In *Rosmersholm* (1886), the play which followed *The Wild Duck*, politics once more enters the action. It had been in the background also in *An Enemy of the People*, but rather in Ibsen's old satirical mode, even through the recirculation of a couple of characters from *The League of Youth*, Aslaksen and Steensgaard. In *Rosmersholm* politics reappears in a tragic mode, very differently from the way politics had been represented in the earlier plays. The change indicates that the 'exodus' of the bourgeoisie, in the words of Eric Hobsbawm, was also 'a certain abdication of the bourgeoisie from its role as a ruling class.'[85] With the emergence of mass democracy and the professionalisation of politics, political power had to be fought for and new paths to power were opened up. In this sense, the play responded to recent changes in Norway, changes and controversies that clearly were part of the contexts from which *Rosmersholm* emerged.

When sending the print manuscript to Hegel in the autumn of 1886, Ibsen wrote that '[t]his play should be considered a fruit of studies and observations which I had occasion to undertake during last summer's stay

[84] E.J. Hobsbawm, *The Age of Empire 1875–1914* (London: Cardinal, 1989), 165–68.
[85] Ibid. 167.

in Norway'.[86] As related in Chapter 3, the political conflict in Norway culminated in 1884, when the King finally had to give in to the demand for parliamentary rule and appointed the leader of the newly founded Left (liberal) party, Johan Sverdrup, as new Prime Minister.

Ibsen followed the debates in Norway closely and although he had now lived outside Norway for twenty years, he knew many of its main participants. While finishing *The Wild Duck* in Gossensass in the summer of 1884, he was visited by Emil Stang, his lawyer in the suit against the printer Jensen. Stang's father Frederik Stang had for many years been prime minister, but he had been forced to retire in 1880. When Emil Stang visited Ibsen, his father had just died and he had also experienced the demise of what has later been called 'the civil servant state'. On his return to Norway, it became Emil Stang's task to lead the conservatives into the age of competitive party politics.[87] Just after meeting Stang, Ibsen had his reunion with Bjørnson, another major political player during these years, in Schwaz in Tyrol, their first meeting in over twenty years. When Sigurd and Susanna Ibsen visited Norway at the same time, Sigurd was received by Prime Minister Sverdrup. The realisation of how personally close Ibsen still was to the conflicting parties, again highlights how intimate the social space of Norwegian political and cultural life was at the time.

When Ibsen himself went to Norway in the following year, 1885, he immediately found himself involved in heated controversies. On 10 June, he attended the debate in the Storting about a state grant for Kielland. The issue was the first to blow open the internal antagonisms in the coalition which had overthrown the civil servant government. In matters of culture and religion, there was a deep divide among the coalition parties. Ibsen's acquaintances were this time distinctly different from what they had been in 1874. He did not visit his conservative friends from the 'erudite Holland' circle, but met one of them, the historian L.L. Daae, coincidentally at a hotel in Trondheim.[88] Daae had been one of the leading campaigners for the conservatives in the decisive 1882 election and was once more campaigning.[89] Most spectacular, however, was Ibsen's confrontation with Lorentz Dietrichson, caused by rivalries in the student society and Dietrichson's position there as one of the leaders on the

---

[86] Ibsen, Letter to F.V. Hegel, 2 October 1886.
[87] See Ibsen, Letter to Susanna Ibsen, 19 August 1884, with comment.
[88] See comment to Ibsen, Letter to F.V. Hegel, 11 July 1885.
[89] Daae is said to have thought that headmaster Kroll in *Rosmersholm* was modelled on him and he was never reconciled with Ibsen, Ludvig Ludvigsen Daae, *Professor, Dr. Ludvig Daaes erindringer og opptegnelser om sin samtid*, ed. Nic Knudtzon (Oslo: Novus, 2003), 440.

conservative side. Ibsen attacked his old friend both publicly and privately and sparked a prolonged battle in the student world of Kristiania.[90]

In the case of Dietrichson Ibsen certainly did not shy away from conflict, but the intensity of these conflicts clearly shook him. Earlier that year he had once more entertained the idea of moving back to Norway. In April 1885, he wrote to Hegel from Rome that he considered staying in Germany for one year, 'where I could attend to a great many literary matters better than I can down here,'[91] and that 'lately I have begun to think seriously about buying a little villa, or, rather, a small country house, in the neighbourhood of Kristiania – on the fjord – where I could live in seclusion and give myself entirely to my work.' The year before he had even enquired with a leading architect about what a house near Kristiania would cost him.[92] The experiences he underwent on his visit in 1885, being immediately drawn into political turmoil, were probably one reason why he chose to remain in Germany through the 1880s.

But these experiences also became raw material for drama. After having finished *Rosmersholm*, Ibsen wrote to Brandes that the impressions had disturbed him for a long time, and 'not until I had come to a distinct understanding of my experiences and had drawn my conclusions could I think of transforming my thoughts into a work of fiction.'[93] Never, he asserted, had he felt so estranged from his Norwegian compatriots: 'Never have I been more repelled. Never more disgusted. [. . .] It was a bad hour for progress in Norway when Johan Sverdrup came into "power" – and was muzzled and handcuffed.' In the beginning of the 1870s, Ibsen had thought of Sverdrup as a dangerous revolutionary threat to social and political order.[94] His 'disgust' with Norway had then been articulated from a position to the right of the conservative government, while it was now being articulated from a position to the left of the liberal government.

It is by no means clear what 'distinct understanding' Ibsen had come to, however. *Rosmersholm* baffled critics when it was published and the play has ever since been regarded as among his most enigmatic. The main character, Johannes Rosmer, is a husband who has lost his wife, a clergyman who has lost his faith, and he belongs to a class that has lost its political power. In the

[90] Ibsen, Letters to L. Dietrichson, [6 October] 1885, Det Norske Studentersamfund, 23 October 1885 (*Letters and Speeches*, 251–256), F.S. Lund, 8 November 1885, and C. Snoilsky, 14 February 1886 (ibid. 258), with comments.
[91] Ibsen, Letter to F.V. Hegel, 25 April 1885, *Letters and Speeches*, 248.
[92] Adolf Schirmer, Letter to Ibsen, 16 July 1884, NLN, Letter coll. 200.
[93] Ibsen, Letter to G. Brandes, 10 November 1886, *Letters and Speeches*, 259–60.
[94] Ibsen, Letter to J.H. Thoresen, 21 November 1870, ibid. 104.

'spacious, old-fashioned and comfortable' living room at Rosmersholm 'the walls are hung with past and recent portraits of clergymen, officers and officials in their robes and uniforms',[95] the class that had governed Norway until 1884. Rosmer has left their conservative beliefs and decided to go into politics on the side of 'the young'. He wants to 'create a true democracy.'[96] The true task of democracy, he explains to the conservative Kroll, is 'to make all my countrymen noblemen', which is achieved 'by liberating their minds and purifying their wills'.[97] This is almost word for word what Ibsen had said in Trondheim in 1885. One way into the historically and politically motivated complexities of the play is to ask why Ibsen chose to let this character represent his own programme.

Rosmer's idealism fails completely in the encounter with the harsh realities of politics. But is the play just a new turn in Ibsen's criticism of politics? Politics and politicians are certainly not represented with sympathy, but Rosmer's failure has as much to do with himself and his programme as it has to do with politics. It soon becomes evident that Rosmer does not have that basic 'noble' quality of self-assurance and natural ruling instinct. It had been the prerogative of his class to rule, but that time is now over. Instead, political power has to be conquered, but Rosmer shuns struggle and controversy. His political vision is that 'peace and happiness and conciliation' must replace struggle, and he criticises Kroll 'for how violently you had been carrying on at the public meetings' and 'all the uncharitable speeches you made there.'[98] Kroll's confrontational style is what has made Rosmer decide to 'stand forth'.

As soon as Rosmer has announced his decision, however, he becomes guilt-ridden and loses faith in his powers. He feels guilt for the death of his wife Beate, Kroll's sister, who had been mentally disturbed, but it also turns out that Rosmer probably was as impotent in his marriage as he is in his politics, as scared of his wife's sexual desire as he is of her brother's 'violent' rhetoric. His idea of true love is 'calm, happy, serene contentment.'[99] It is a definition that Rebecca West, who loves Rosmer, is deeply uncomfortable with. When Rebecca eventually adapts to 'the Rosmer philosophy of life', she says that it 'ennobles', but at the same time 'kills happiness'.[100]

Rosmer mistakes the basic codes of both love and politics. He wants love without desire and politics without force. Ibsen certainly shows the

[95] Ibsen, *Rosmersholm*, in *An Enemy of the People, The Wild Duck, Rosmersholm*, trans. James W. McFarlane (Oxford: Oxford University Press, 1999), 223.
[96] Ibid. 244.   [97] Ibid.   [98] Ibid. 245–46.   [99] Ibid. 281.   [100] Ibid. 301.

destructive potential of both – in Kroll's fanaticism, Mortensgaard's cynicism and Rebecca's willingness to commit crimes for her love. But even though they have a destructive potential, eliminating these forces would mean eliminating what constitutes love and politics in the first place.

Is the play 'a pessimistic analysis of the condition of politics and love in modernity', as Toril Moi claims?[101] Pessimistic it certainly is, but at the same time it seems to accept the inevitable reality of functional differentiation. With the fall of the civil servant state, 'Politics was politicised';[102] it was no longer a class privilege for the officials but a professionalised struggle for power in a voters' market. Modern, competitive mass politics has no place for 'literary politicians' like Rosmer, shying away from struggle and the search for power in favour of ennoblement of character.[103]

Functional differentiation was explicitly negotiated in the series of heated controversies over the borders between literature, politics, morality, religion and law during these years. Literary issues actually became major public and political issues in all Scandinavian countries, and represented major challenges to the cohesion of the Left. In Denmark Herman Bang was convicted for his novel *Haabløse Slægter* in 1880, while in Sweden legal action was taken against Strindberg for *Giftas* in 1884. In Norway the novel *Fra Kristiania-Bohêmen* by Hans Jæger (a relative of Ibsen's later biographer Henrik Jæger) was confiscated by the new Sverdrup government in 1885. Hans Jæger was arrested, charged, and later convicted for blasphemy and for 'offending public decency'. In 1886 Christian Krogh's *Albertine*, a novel about prostitution, was also confiscated by the new Left government, but this time to much more protest.

Ibsen had little sympathy with his persecuted colleagues.[104] In 1887, he wrote to his commissioner in Kristiania that Jæger's 'crude book' had been sent to him and 'I sort of read it through.'[105] He did not know *Albertine* and did not bother to get acquainted with it: 'It is, by the way, impossible that all of this literary boorishness can be more than a passing bewilderment. But at least it shows clearly enough that our people are still not even near to being ready for the ideas of freedom.' Ibsen, in other words, did not feel the lawsuits as a threat to literary autonomy, but rather that his country's authors had an immature notion of 'freedom'.

Controversies over literature and other cultural matters now resulted in a divide within the Norwegian Left, between 'radicals' and 'moderates'.

---

[101] Moi, *Ibsen and Birth*, 291.   [102] Stråth, *Union*, 564.   [103] Rønning, *Umulige*, 210, 217.
[104] Hans Jæger was not supported by Brandes, Bjørnson or Kielland either.
[105] Ibsen, Letter to N. Lund, 4 March 1887.

Ibsen did not join either side and dissociated himself from the widely shared intellectual 'disappointment' with Sverdrup. By the end of 1888, he wrote to Georg Brandes that 'I cannot say that the political development has been a disappointment to me. What has happened is exactly what I expected.'[106] The problem was, he thought, that the leaders of 'our party of the Left' completely lacked experience and consequently had been 'cherishing the most unreasonable illusions. They imagined that a leader of the Opposition would and could remain the same after he got into power.' Political power would, in other words, necessarily mean retreat from principled idealism, but now Ibsen stated this more as a matter of fact than as a cause of hostility.

Here Ibsen was in accordance with his son, in the service of the Swedish-Norwegian Foreign Office and communicating his observations of domestic politics from Washington and New York. Writing to his parents, Sigurd thought the radical Left in Norway stood in danger of becoming a 'literary clique', while the liberal paper *Verdens Gang* seemed to live in an atmosphere of '"impressionism" and "naturalism", which was not healthy for a practical politician.'[107] He agreed that Sverdrup was a power-seeking opportunist, but the writer 'ought not to be too strict with the politician', Sigurd thought. The writer created his own characters while the politician not only had to work with living people with their own will; they were his lord and master. To the writer's son, the controversies over literature at this time was not just about the government interfering with literature, regrettable as it was, it was about literature being unable to comprehend the nature of democratic politics.

Accepting politics as not just an enemy, but a separate sphere of modern society, allowed Ibsen to move from militant antipolitics – and in 1885 militant engagement for a while – to a more indifferent attitude. After 1888, politics disappears almost completely from his letters, as it again does from his plays. To the extent that politics is mentioned at all in letters in the 1890s, it is from the perspective of an interested spectator. The great irony of it all is that from the end of the 1890s, Sigurd Ibsen became a key player in the struggle with Sweden over the arrangement of the diplomatic and foreign service, precisely the kind of 'unproductive' and 'theoretical' political question his father had thundered against a couple of decades earlier.

---

[106] Ibsen, Letter to G. Brandes, 30 October 1888, *Letters and Speeches*, 272.
[107] Sigurd Ibsen, Letter to Susanna Ibsen, 31 January 1887, NLN, Letter coll. 200.

Canonisation

At the end of the 1880s Ibsen was still, after *A Doll's House* and *Ghosts*, 'morally' controversial in Norway. Conservative readers and critics would disagree with what they took to be his 'ideas' and many would find his later works difficult and confusing. But they tended to distinguish sharply between regrettable 'content' and literary quality. Ibsen's literary mastery was generally beyond question and he commanded an unprecedented respect. One sign of the status he enjoyed across party lines is the special issue published by the leading conservative newspaper *Aftenposten* on the occasion of his sixtieth anniversary in 1888. Including lexical articles on Ibsen's biography, on editions, theatre performances, translations and secondary literature, the special issue represents a strong exercise in canonisation. *Aftenposten* even made more out of the celebrations than the liberal newspapers, who now confidently considered Ibsen their own.

Aftenposten's lead article was not signed, but it was written by one of its critics, Bredo Morgenstierne. He used the opportunity to question the notion, often advocated by the author himself, of Ibsen having been wronged by his fellow countrymen. Morgenstierne claimed that Ibsen, on the contrary, had met with critical approval right from his debut, and that he now was at a stage which every 'genius' would enter and which was bound to create controversy: Ibsen had now confronted the most basic questions of life, questions of concern to religion. Contrary to Tolstoy, Morgenstierne argued, Ibsen had, with *Ghosts* as a turning point, moved towards a denial of Christianity with all its consequences for moral and social teaching. But Ibsen could hardly complain that those critics at home who had 'painstakingly weighed the new moral lessons of his plays – to the extent that they can be ascertained – and found them too light, have omitted in our criticism to treat him with the reverence owing to one of the country's greatest men.'[108] To a leading conservative critic like Morgenstierne, Ibsen was in the domain of the universal. The playwright immediately welcomed what he took to be a conciliatory gesture from the conservative side. He later thanked Morgenstierne personally, adding: 'When I come to Christiania again – if such a thing ever happens – I shall seek admission into the circle in which I feel that I am most at home.'[109]

---

[108] Quoted in a comment to Ibsen, Letter to A. Schibsted, 27 March 1888.
[109] Ibsen, Letter to B. Morgenstierne, 21 November 1888, *Letters of*, 423.

There were some voices expressing more fundamental criticism. The other conservative paper, *Morgenbladet*, did not mention the anniversary. The critic Johan Vibe, who had replaced Ibsen's favourite Ludvig Josephson as director at Christiania Theater in the years 1877–1879 and caused Ibsen's short boycott of the theatre, sounded a criticism which anticipates a major theme of the British reception in particular, as well as of later theatre scholarship. In an article in a conservative periodical in 1887, Vibe claimed that Ibsen had violated the basic laws of drama, criticising him for the large role played by the past in most of his plays: 'The main action is often over *before* the play begins. [. . .] Much more is often *told* about the past than what is *happening* in the now [. . .]. Playwrights of the first rank rarely or never proceed like this.'[110] Ibsen had stuck to the rules in *The League of Youth* and *An Enemy of the People*, which Vibe accordingly held to be Ibsen's best plays. His true form, however, was verse, in which he had created three definite masterpieces: *Brand, Peer Gynt* and *Love's Comedy*. It was unfortunate that Europe had only learnt to know his 'problem plays', plays which had received immediate attention but not been able to stay in the repertoire. Posterity would not count Ibsen among its great dramatists, Vibe predicted, and his prose plays would probably not survive him for long.[111]

Vibe's was clearly a minority position, however. Most conservative critics and readers seem to have shared Morgenstierne's positive assessment of Ibsen's literary qualities, and his position as an author who created and declared his own laws was acknowledged on both sides. When *Rosmersholm* was published, Edvard Brandes completely abstained from a political reading: 'What is to be commended if this is not to be praised! [. . .] He is, furthermore, always ten times as good as the others.'[112] In 1889, Georg Brandes wrote that Ibsen had never compromised with the 'thoughtless masses' and had 'never for the sake of popularity lowered his demands on himself and on art.'[113] Even *Morgenbladet* would soon follow general opinion. In 1893, the paper printed a series of articles on the literature of the 1880s, criticising most of it for being politicised ephemera. Ibsen was the exception, dealing as he did with problems of a different order.[114]

---

[110] Johan Vibe, 'Henrik Ibsen som Forfatter af Nutidsdramaer', *Vidar* (1887), 482.
[111] Ibid. 481, 501–502.
[112] E. Brandes, Letter to G. Brandes [November 1886?], *G. og E. Brandes brevveksling*, vol. 2, 141.
[113] G. Brandes, 'Henrik Ibsen', *Verdens Gang*, no. 184, 6 August 1889.
[114] Haffner, *Cammermeyer*, 172–74.

Literature in Small Nations

Ibsen's generation of Norwegian authors profited from and contributed to a strong sense of national progress in the last decades of the nineteenth century. The extraordinary position Ibsen achieved in his home market evokes the often-quoted remarks of Franz Kafka on the advantages of writing in a small, peripheral language. Among the general benefits of literature, Kafka mentions 'the pride which a nation gains from a literature of its own and the support it is afforded in the face of a hostile surrounding world' and 'the acknowledgement of literary events as objects of political solicitude'. Comparing the large German literature with the small Yiddish and Czech ones, Kafka noted that such effects could also be produced by relatively restricted literatures. In small nations there would certainly be fewer experts in literary history, but literature would be less a concern of literary history than of the people: 'What in great literature goes on down below, constituting a not indispensable cellar of the structure, here takes place in the full light of day, what is there a matter of passing interest for a few, here absorbs everyone no less than a matter of life and death.'[115]

The Norwegian novelist Jonas Lie, while staying in Stuttgart in 1879, made the same point in comparing the interest in literature and the position of authors in Germany and the Scandinavian countries. He felt that Germany's

> popular ['folkelige'] life and education [...] lie fifty years *behind* our life in the Nordic countries. Here in Southern Germany one – and I'm not even speaking of women – knows not one's own poets and writers; nor do these enjoy much civil recognition apart from rank and titles. [...] everywhere they have excellent *experts* and *books*; but the *wife* doesn't read what her husband writes, the *people* don't [read] what their first-rate men write, – that is *the general picture*. Authors like Paul Lindau, Vischer, Lübke etc etc cannot live solely off their authorship, and that a poet should live off his pen is quite inconceivable to them, but [it is] even more incomprehensible that he would want to be that or an artist if he were able to acquire a permanently salaried and honored public position – look, there you see reality, the spirit governing everything, and compare that to our blessed country back home![116]

---

[115] Franz Kafka, *Diaries, 1910–1923*, ed. Max Brod, trans. Joseph Kresh, Martin Greenberg & Hannah Arendt (New York: Schocken Books, 1976), 148–50.

[116] Jonas Lie, Letter to Olivia Hansen, 11 June 1879, *Brev 1851–1908*, ed. Anne Grete Holm-Olsen (Oslo: Novus, 2009), vol. 1, 478–79.

In 1888, Alexander Kielland wrote from Paris: 'in my opinion there is no nation today where as many books are being read as in Scandinavia.'[117]

From the opposite angle, Knut Hamsun lends support to this verdict. Fighting the old in order to create a space for himself, Hamsun in the 1890s attacked what he held to be a peculiarly Norwegian 'overrating of poets and poetry', including the frenzy around book launches:

> We follow these books through their genesis, we know the day on which they are being printed, we run towards them on the quay and watch them arrive, we write notices in the papers about Baldur being delayed with the books out there on the fjord . . . There certainly is no other people on earth who behave like this because of books.[118]

Without this intense interest in literature, some of which was no doubt created by a small-nation effect, it would be hard to explain how it was possible to live from authorship in such a small linguistic community as the Scandinavian, or to explain why authors were being put on the state budget. In Norway, this effect was heightened by the sense of inferiority in the face of the old hegemonic powers of Denmark and Sweden. This rivalry, and the role played by literary prestige in compensating for an inherited disadvantage, must be part of the explanation why the Norwegian branch of the Modern Breakthrough is characterised by overall much higher book sales than the Danish one. For example, in 1882, J.P. Jacobsen's *Mindre fortællinger (Mogens og andre noveller)* was issued in a 3,000 copies edition, while Holger Drachmann's *Vildt og tæmmet* had been issued in 2,500 copies the year before,[119] doing at least some justice to Møller Kristensen's dismissal of the popular success of Danish authors. While questioning the dubious retrospective national exclusion of the Norwegian authors from the Danish literature, these Danish author's editions were far behind the 5,000–10,000 editions of Ibsen, Bjørnson, Lie and Kielland, and they can hardly be accounted for by resorting to differences in literary quality. With Bjørnson, Ibsen, Lie and Kielland advancing to become the foremost authors of a Copenhagen publisher, and eventually gaining international fame, literature became one of Norway's strongest claims to gaining a respected position among nations.

---

[117] Kielland, Letter to Jacob Hegel, 9 February 1888, *Brev*, vol. 2, 237.
[118] Knut Hamsun, 'Mot overvurdering av diktere og diktning', *Samlede verker*, ed. Lars Frode Larsen (Oslo: Gyldendal 2009), vol. 25, 149.
[119] RDL, Gyldendals Arkiv, A7, forlagskladder, bind D and J-L; we thank Maria Purtoft for this reference.

But the national stake in a literature of the periphery also had a reverse side. It intensified controversy and aggravated hostility, and it made literature more vulnerable to political and national pressure. Small conditions created a claustrophobic atmosphere and Ibsen clearly needed social distance to enjoy a form of literary freedom. At first he had no intention of staying abroad as long as he did, but on his return to Norway in 1874 and 1885 he was immediately back in the centre of attention and conflict. Living abroad offered him a double privilege, the privilege of the indifference of his immediate surroundings and of a growing interest in his literature at home. Ibsen, then, did not flee Norway and stay abroad because of provincial conservatism, indifference and hostility; we might rather say that he 'fled' because of an excess of interest in and an exceptionally strong commitment to literature.

6

European Breakthrough

From 1887, extra-Nordic income became a noticeable and growing contribution to Ibsen's earnings (Appendix, Figure A.1). At first, they came primarily from German theatres and reflect his breakthrough on the German stage at this time. In both German and English Ibsen had existed as translated book for a long time already, but in neither country had this yielded him profit nor established his name. In Germany, many of the translations had been initiated by the playwright himself. It was only when Ibsen, from the middle of the 1880s, was firmly appropriated by local agents as a vehicle for their own struggles to change existing aesthetic norms and hierarchies that his European career took off. These agents had different and partly conflicting agendas, but one major issue was the perceived distance that existed between literature and theatre. Ibsen was an asset in their struggle both to promote the 'literary theatre' and to revive national drama.

Early German Efforts

In 1899, Ibsen claimed that 'it is against my inclination to contribute to the distribution of my works'.[1] This was hardly an accurate reconstruction of his own dissemination history. The first book by Ibsen to be translated and published was *Brand*, which appeared in German in Kassel in 1872. It has always been a mystery how the otherwise unknown travelling salesman P.F. Siebold came to take the role of translator, but a letter published only in 2010 suggests that it was the result of an initiative taken by Ibsen himself.[2] For the launching of *Brand* Ibsen also asked his friend Lorentz Dietrichson to write a biography. He wanted nothing of the narrative of

---

[1] Ibsen, Letter to D. Grønvold, 14 October 1899.
[2] Ibsen, Letter to H. Thaulow 16 May 1866, see also Letters to P.F. Siebold, 14 January and 3 February 1870, with comments.

controversy he otherwise cultivated but 'information as to my position in Scandinavian literature, my personal circumstances, etc. [...] write as favourably as your conscience will permit'.[3] Siebold translated the biography and published it in *Illustrierte Zeitung* in March 1870. He had to wait another two years to get *Brand* out, however.

Later on, as we have seen, Ibsen financed and supervised translations by Emma Klingenfeld in Munich, namely of *Nordische Heerfahrt* (1876), *Die Herrin von Oestrot* (1877) and *Stützen der Gesellschaft* (1878). In the meantime, others had been active as well. By 1882, when Ibsen wrote to apply for an increase in the state grant on the ground that lack of protection caused him financial loss abroad, he could already list eight verse and prose dramas that had been published in fourteen different German versions by eight different translators and seven different publishers, of which Ibsen had a stake in just four.[4] As for the theatre, we have already learnt that Ibsen's first appearance on a German stage took place in 1876 when the Meininger Hoftheater brought *Die Kronprätendenten* to Berlin and *Nordische Heerfahrt* was performed in Munich, followed by the many *Stützen der Gesellschaft* productions in 1878 and the not very successful *Puppenheim*, or *Nora*, productions of 1880.

Imperial Appropriations

Outside Germany Ibsen was dependent on mediators completely beyond his control. Some of the first ones fit into an empire model, with mediators appropriating foreign literature and plays in ways which served to reassess the centrality of their own, hegemonic literatures. In France, Philarète Chasles (1798–1873), who in 1870 planned to give lectures in Paris on the new, Norwegian literature, is an example. To Chasles, who was a professor of 'northern' literatures and languages at Collége de France and regularly informed journal readers of literary news from England and other countries, France was the self-evident centre of literature and civilisation: 'What Europe is to the rest of the world, France is to Europe; everything reverberates toward her, everything ends with her'.[5]

Ibsen was asked to send Chasles materials for his planned lectures: 'This is of course very flattering', he wrote to his brother-in-law, 'but also takes up a lot of time'.[6] The idea for these lectures probably came up during

---

[3] Ibsen, Letter to L. Dietrichson, 28 May 1869, *Letters and Speeches*, 80.
[4] Ibsen, Letter to H.E. Berner, 18 February 1882, with comments.
[5] Quoted in Damrosch, *What Is?*, 9.   [6] Ibsen, Letter to J.H. Thoresen, 8 March 1870.

Georg Brandes's stay in Paris that summer, where he met Chasles regularly.[7] They came to nothing in the end, probably both because of the Franco-Prussian war that autumn and Chasles's advanced age. Ten years later, in 1880, Ibsen was elected foreign member of Société des gens de lettres de France, together with Andreas Munch, Bjørnstjerne Bjørnson and Jonas Lie, but the circumstances around the election are not known.[8] Neither had it any conceivable effects on his standing in France. There were three minor articles on Ibsen in French between 1873 and 1882, all of them by female authors.[9] It was only towards the end of the 1880s, largely under the impression of what happened in Germany, that Ibsen became known in France.

In the English context, Edmund Gosse (1849–1928) is another example of the imperial mediator. Contrary to Chasles, Gosse had no position in the literary world when he became acquainted with Ibsen, but had set out to search the periphery for resources which he could use to advance his position in the hierarchy of the metropolitan centre. Gosse wanted a career in literature and was advised to 'choose something out of the way, Scandinavian literature for example'.[10] In the summer of 1871 the twenty-two-year old Gosse travelled to Norway, returning with a copy of Ibsen's *Digte* (Poems). He immediately went on to undertake an intensive study of the Danish language and when he felt able to understand Ibsen's written Dano-Norwegian, wrote an unsigned review for the *Spectator*, published on 3 March 1872, called 'Ibsen's New Poems'. This was the first time Ibsen's name found its way into print in English – although, and this was to be proleptic of Gosse's further career in inexactness, the poet was named 'Henrick Ibsen'.

Gosse promptly sent his first Ibsen article off to the playwright in Germany, and received a glowing response. 'Several editions of my works are being prepared here in Germany', Ibsen told Gosse; 'Having my works presented to the English reading public is, however, the matter of chief importance to me'.[11] Ibsen had the impression that Gosse was launching a major translation programme, but was disappointed. During the 1870s,

---

[7] Georg Brandes, *Breve til Forældrene 1872–1904*, ed. Morten Borup & Torben Nielsen (Copenhagen: Reitzel, 1978), vol. 3, 56.

[8] See Ibsen, Letter to Sigurd Ibsen, 8 August 1880, with comment.

[9] Kela Nyholm, 'Henrik Ibsen paa den franske scene', *Ibsenårbok 1957–59*, 10–11; Kirsten Shepherd-Barr, *Ibsen and Early Modernist Theatre, 1890–1900* (Westport, Conn.: Greenwood Press 1997), 17–18.

[10] See Elias Bredsdorff (ed.), *Sir Edmund Gosse's Correspondence with Scandinavian Writers* (Copenhagen: Gyldendal, 1960), 2; Gosse's 'autobiographical sketch' for *Ny Illustreret Tidende*, reprinted in ibid. 82–5; Ann Thwaite, *Edmund Gosse* (London: Secker & Warburg, 1984), 107.

[11] Ibsen, Letter to E. Gosse, 2 April 1872, *Letters and Speeches*, 119.

Gosse translated several poems and even the entire *Love's Comedy*, only to experience the frustration of not being able to interest a single publisher in the latter.

Ibsen's first English mediator nevertheless continued to promote his discovery. From 1872 till February 1879, he wrote around twenty notes, essays and reviews on Ibsen alone, plus many more on other Scandinavian topics and writers. His first more substantial piece was an attempt at accommodating the Norwegian writer to the centre. Having worked his way through *Love's Comedy*, *Brand* and *Peer Gynt*, Gosse in 1873 posed the question in *Fortnightly Review*: 'Where shall we look for a young great poet among continental nations'?[12] Gosse could find none, the answer lay to the north: 'It is my firm belief that in the Norwegian, Henrik Ibsen, the representative of a land unknown in the literary annals of Europe, such a poet is found'. Gosse stressed Ibsen's status as poet and his universal qualities, and the claim, strengthened by the allusions to 'world poet' and *Weltliteratur*, was that a new Goethe had arrived from the periphery. Even when Gosse belatedly would turn his attention to the modern prose plays, he continued to refer to Ibsen as 'the Poet', generally avoiding the more hum-drum 'playwright'.

The Ibsen-Gosse correspondence gives evidence of one particularly significant lost opportunity. In November 1880, Ibsen granted Gosse the rights to translate and produce *A Doll's House*, and added: 'How this play is being received in England will interest me to a high degree'.[13] But by 1879 this by now thirty-year-old English critic had reached his aim of achieving expert status on Northern literature.[14] Gosse was beginning to acquire an extensive network in his own literary field and was ready to move on to greater things, namely English literature.[15]

Pillars of the Community was the last play to receive Gosse's public homage in Britain until *The Lady from the Sea* nearly ten years later. There are no extant letters between Ibsen and Gosse in the period from November 1880 to January 1889, but Gyldendal must have continued sending him new Ibsen publications.[16] In March 1882, a little more than three months after *Ghosts* had been published in Copenhagen, Gosse communicated his

[12] E. Gosse, 'Ibsen, the Norwegian Satirist', *Fortnightly Review*, vol. 19 (January 1–June 1 1873), 74.
[13] Ibsen, Letter to E. Gosse, 26 November 1880.
[14] See T.H. Ward, 'Review of Studies in the Literature of Northern Europe', *The Academy*, vol. 15, 10 May 1879, 294.
[15] John Gross, *The Rise and Fall of the Man of Letters* (London: Weidenfeld and Nicolson, 1969), 177; see also Bredsdorff, *Gosse's Correspondence*, 11.
[16] See ibid. 40–1.

response to Georg Brandes. The 'play itself' had torn his 'nerves to pieces', Gosse declared, 'It is one of the most powerful pieces ever written'.[17] This seemingly awed reaction, if no doubt coloured by Gosse's aim to please the addressee, was not accompanied, however, by a need to communicate the play's power to a larger public or to report on the sensations created in Scandinavia and Germany by the new Ibsen plays of the 1880s.

Ibsen appeared on the English stage for the first time with *Quicksands* in 1880, a heavily adapted version of *Pillars of the Community*. *A Doll's House* appeared next in 1884, under the title *Breaking a Butterfly* and also adapted beyond recognition. Excepting these versions, up until 1889 the English Ibsen only appeared on the page. The first complete translation of an Ibsen play was Catherine Ray's *Emperor and Galilean* (1876), with Ray stressing the point that Ibsen was 'a poet without a tendency', and with an appeal to 'the educated classes'.[18]

Radical Appropriations

Henrietta Frances Lord's *Nora: A Play*, published 1882 and referring to one 'Henry Ibsen' both on its title page and in the introduction, must be counted as the first translation into English of one of the playwright's modern prose dramas.[19] While never achieving wide distribution or much of a critical reception, Lord's was a strong reading of the political Ibsen. In sharp contrast to Ray, she presented Ibsen as a propagandist and more particularly as a 'Woman's Poet'.[20] Lord went on to translate *Ghosts*, which was serialised in the socialist magazine *To-Day* from January to March 1885, about four years after the play's original publication.

The space of reception of translated works, argues Gisèle Sapiro, is structured by the two oppositions politicised/depoliticised and universal/ particular.[21] Nowhere were these oppositions as strongly articulated as in

[17] Gosse, Letter to G. Brandes, 11 March 1882, *Correspondance de Georg Brandes*, ed. Paul Krüger (Copenhagen: Rosenkilde & Bagger, 1956), vol. 2: *L'Angleterre et la Russie*, 96; see also Olav Lausund, 'Edmund Gosse', in Inga-Stina Ewbank, Olav Lausund & Bjørn Tysdahl (eds.), *Anglo-Scandinavian Cross-Currents* (Norwich: Norvik Press, 1999), 139–58.

[18] Ray, 'Henrik Ibsen', in *The Emperor and Galilean*, trans. Catherine Ray (London: Samuel Tinsley, 1876), iii. Little is known about Ray, see Narve Fulsås, *Biografisk leksikon til Ibsens brev – med tidstavle* (Oslo: Centre for Ibsen Studies, 2013). The impact of this translation seems to have been minimal. There were reviews in the *Examiner*, the *Athenaeum* and the *Academy*. Bredsdorff thinks all three may have been written by Gosse, *Gosse's Correspondence*, 37.

[19] Mrs. Lord's edition claims that 'The Rights of Translation and Reproduction are Reserved', but there is no extant Ibsen letter confirming this.

[20] H.F. Lord, 'Life of Henrik Ibsen', in *Nora* (London: Griffith and Farran, 1882), vii, xiii–xxiv.

[21] Sapiro, 'Translation', 163.

the Englishing of Ibsen. To some degree, these oppositions framed a chronological sequence, 'politicised' and 'topical' Ibsen replacing Gosse's 'world poet', while at the same time polarising Ibsen in a way that constituted a major challenge for some of his most important mediators. Lord's translations addressed a socialist-feminist audience hardly found at home, making radical appropriations of Ibsen in order to affect *transformations* of the existing aesthetic, social and political order. Ibsen's socialist-feminist following sought confrontation, distinction and rupture, and in their way, they contributed to making the 'Ibsen battles' in Britain from 1889 until 1893 so heated. At that time, they had been active for some years already, taking over where Gosse broke off and making the 1880s the decade of the 'socialist Ibsen'. Ian Britain, in the most comprehensive article on the topic, remarks on 'the peculiar concentration' of interest in the 'New Drama' and Ibsen among those belonging to 'the literary fringe of the Fabian Society and other reform and revolutionary organisations'.[22] The 1880s saw the emergence in Britain of a number of socialist political parties and working groups, with the more middle-class-based, gradualist and parliamentarian Fabian Society, formed in 1884, particularly well represented among Ibsenites.[23]

We would suggest that this part of Ibsen's early English-language reception demonstrates the vulnerability and openness of translated literature, and not least of that originating in small cultures and being appropriated in cultural centres. The mechanisms at play are not just matters of a general domestication (or exoticisation), but also of literature being used for idealist reasons and ideological purposes. What is clear is that the British Ibsen for a while became almost inextricably associated with socialism, in spite of the fact that this was, as we have seen, far from his political meanings in a Scandinavian context.

Within these circles, the earliest signs of Ibsen's arrival can be found around 1884. Olive Schreiner, the South African author often hailed as the first New Woman writer, noted in her journal on 9 March 1884 that 'I love Nora by Ibsen', and, in a letter to Havelock Ellis at the end of the month, recommended Ibsen's *Nora*, calling it 'a most wonderful little work [...] It shows some sides of a woman's nature that are not often spoken of, and that some people do not believe exist – but they do'.[24]

[22] Ian Britain, 'A Transplanted *Doll's House*', in Ian Donaldson (ed.), *Transformations in Modern European Drama* (London: Macmillan, 1983), 24.
[23] See Yvonne Kapp, *Eleanor Marx* (London: Lawrence & Wishart, 1976), vol. 2, 248
[24] Note quoted in ibid. 101; Schreiner, Letter to Havelock Ellis, 28 March 1884, in *Olive Schreiner: Letters 1871–9*, ed. Richard Rive (Oxford: Oxford University Press, 1987), 36.

A few months later, Ellis and Schreiner spent a holiday with Eleanor Marx, Karl Marx' youngest daughter, and Edward Aveling, her common-law husband. By this time Aveling, probably because of his connections with the journal *To-Day*, was able to share the manuscript of Henrietta Frances Lord's translation of *Ghosts* with the others. Marx and Aveling even seem to have encountered Ibsen before Schreiner. Marx would probably have been made aware of Ibsen through her German connections, and Aveling also refers to German translations around this time.[25]

Aveling's earliest known public involvement in the Ibsen cause was an intervention on behalf of *A Doll's House* on the occasion of the adaptation *Breaking a Butterfly*. The playwrights Henry Arthur Jones and Henry Herman had Anglicised the characters and setting and created an entirely new and harmonious ending.[26] Aveling lamented that 'rarely has an opportunity, at once literary and dramatic, been so unhappily thrown away', claiming that Ibsen was born to be 'the woman's poet', and that he was a writer wanting to 'aid in the revolutionising'.[27]

A part of the history of early socialist reception is of a semi-private character, consisting of readings and hastily rehearsed amateur performances. Towards the end of 1885 and at the beginning of 1886 Marx sent out letters to a circle of acquaintances. She wanted to organise a reading of *A Doll's House* and had invited 'only people who we know do love and understand Ibsen already, or those who will love and understand him, and who in turn will go on preaching him to others [. . .] just a few people worth reading Nora to'.[28] Such a performance would have a greater impact than solitary reading, she thought, while consciously wanting to build a small and committed following for Ibsen.[29]

When this little amateur performance took place in a flat in London's Great Russell Street on 15 January 1886, Eleanor played Nora, Aveling Thorvald Helmer, May Morris Mrs. Linde, with George Bernard Shaw taking the part of Krogstad. Each of these had already achieved or was about to achieve prominence as socialists and supporters of women's emancipation.[30] Marx, Aveling and Shaw all went on to play central parts in the Ibsen campaign. Shaw later called this 'the first performance of *A Doll's House* in England, on a first floor of a Bloomsbury lodging house',

---

[25] See Edward Aveling, '"Nora" and "Breaking a Butterfly"', *To-Day*, vol. 1 (Jan–Jun 1884), 475.

[26] Henry Arthur Jones & Henry Herman, *Breaking a Butterfly*, BL, Lord Chamberlain's Collection, 53271.

[27] Aveling, 'Nora', 473–74.

[28] Eleanor Marx, Letter to Havelock Ellis, January 1886, quoted in Britain, 'Transplanted', 46.

[29] E. Marx, Letter to H. Ellis, December 1885, quoted in ibid. 46.   [30] Britain, 'Transplanted', 17.

noting that he at this time had 'a very vague notion of what it was all about'.[31] Sally Ledger hails it as 'heralding the emergence of "Ibsenism"' in terms of the political and cultural formation associated with Ibsen in the years that followed.[32]

Eleanor Marx's early work to make Ibsen known to her circle of friends and acquaintances was followed by translations of what she called *An Enemy of Society* (1888) and *The Lady from the Sea* (1890), and she also began work on *The Wild Duck*.[33] For the translation of *The Lady from the Sea*, Marx asked the Norwegian Hans Lien Brækstad to contact Ibsen in order to have his authorisation, which she thought would be invaluable for the sale; 'It may please him to know a daughter of Karl Marx has translated two of his works – & hopes to do others', she noted.[34] Ibsen's response is not known, but *The Lady from the Sea* appeared with 'the Author's Permission'.

Marx was a capable linguist who had translated *Madame Bovary* in 1886, and it seems that Havelock Ellis commissioned her translation of *An Enemy of the People* as early as 1885.[35] After this, Marx must have started teaching herself Norwegian, although her translation was at least in part based on German Ibsen translations. She struggled to finish *An Enemy*, however, calling her translation 'literary hackwork', and she also seems to have been among the socialists who found this play's strong concern with individualism puzzling or even troubling.[36]

Along with the construction of a socialist Ibsen, the association with the figure of the New Woman became the most powerfully marked feature of his reception in English from the middle of the 1880s, and this is also the area of Ibsen's British reception which has been most extensively covered. A large number of Ibsen's followers were women and they often, like Marx, worked for emancipation, politically and culturally. The appearance of Lord's *Nora* established the connection, and in 1884 Havelock Ellis's article 'Women and Socialism' brought in Ibsen's 'Nora'.[37] Conservative

---

[31] G.B. Shaw, 'An Aside', in Lillah McCarthy, *Myself and My Friends* (London: T. Butterworth, 1933), 3.

[32] Sally Ledger, 'Eleanor Marx and Henrik Ibsen', in John Stokes (ed.), *Eleanor Marx (1855–1898)* (Aldershot: Ashgate, 2000), 53.

[33] E. Marx, Letter to H.L. Brækstad, 8 May 1890 and 16 May 1890, NLN, H.L. Brækstad Collection, Letter coll. 17.

[34] Eleanor Marx, Letter to H.L. Brækstad, 10 April 1889, ibid.

[35] See Ruth Brandon, *The New Women and the Old Men* (London: Secker & Warburg, 1990), 96.

[36] See E. Marx, Letter to her sister Laura Lafargue, 25 June 1888, quoted in Kapp, *Eleanor Marx*, vol. 2, 248.

[37] H. Ellis, 'Women and Socialism', *To-Day*, vol. 2 (July–Dec 1884), 351–63.

critics would later inherit such labels, habitually referring to 'the socialistic Nora' and 'the Socialist prophet of the North', while puzzled, moderate observers simply would note 'Ibsen's socialism and peculiar ideas'.[38]

A Doll's House was to play a particularly important part in these circles. After the premiere of the play at the Novelty Theatre in London in 1889, *Justice*, the newspaper of the Social Democratic Federation, in an article tellingly entitled 'A Play with a Purpose', declared unequivocally that this was a play 'which no socialist should miss'.[39] In the end, however, Ibsen's links to female emancipation became his foremost and most enduring political association in Britain. 'Excepting Queen Victoria, Ibsen's heroine [Nora] was probably the most famous woman in late Victorian Britain, within literary and intellectual circles at least', Peter Keating observes.[40]

The Separation of Literature and Drama

Arguably, the most important mediators and those contributing most decisively to creating Ibsen's massive European breakthrough by the end of the 1880s, were agents primarily intent on reforming the theatre and revive the literary drama. They could be socialists and radicals, but their main priorities were in general artistic and literary. According to the theatre historian Erika Fischer-Lichte, '[a]s the nineteenth century progressed, the situation in theatre across Europe grew more and more desolate. By about 1880, the literary level of theatre had reached an all-time low'.[41] There might be an in-built avant-garde prejudice to such an assessment. Much theatre scholarship in recent decades has aimed at rehabilitating melodrama and providing nuance to the general image of the theatre as a debased, commercial institution of pure entertainment.[42] Even so, there can be no doubt that Fischer-Lichte's verdict corresponds to that of key agents at the time. An often-quoted example is Émile Zola's theatre criticism of the late 1870s, lamenting that French theatre lagged at

---

[38] Clement Scott, 'A Doll's House', *The Theatre*, 1 July 1889, N.S., 21; [Anon.], 'Ibsen', *The Weekly Dispatch*, 9 June 1889, in VAM, William Archer Collection, GB 71 THM/368/3, Box 2: Press cuttings; [Anon.], 'Notes', *The Playgoers' Review*, vol. 1, 1 January 1891, 25.

[39] [Anon.], 'A Play with a Purpose', *Justice*, 22 June 1889, 1.

[40] Peter Keating, *The Haunted Study* (London: Secker & Warburg, 1989), 167.

[41] Erika Fischer-Lichte, *History of European Drama and Theatre*, trans. Jo Riley (London and New York: Routledge, 2002), 244.

[42] This turn may be said to have begun with Peter Brooks's revaluation of melodrama in *The Melodramatic Imagination* (London: Yale University Press, 1976). Some representative publications within theatre studies are Jacky Bratton et al. (ed.), *Melodrama* (London: BFI Publishing, 1994), Elaine Hadley, *Melodramatic Tactics* (Stanford: Stanford University Press, 1998), and Sos Eltis, *Acts of Desire* (Oxford: Oxford University Press, 2013).

least thirty years behind the French novel. Balzac, stated Zola, had long ago introduced truthfulness, the study of everyday reality and the spirit of objective analysis in the novel, and the time was more than ripe for a corresponding revolution in the theatre: 'The domain of the novel is crowded; the domain of the theatre is free'.[43] This would require a return to tragedy, Zola argued, because of its 'simplicity of action' and unique psychological and physiological study of character.[44] The challenge was to do great things with subjects and characters that it had become customary to consider small, to realise that 'there is more poetry in the little apartment of a bourgeois than in all the empty, worm-eaten palaces of history'.[45] In Britain, the Irish novelist George Moore, one of the literary drama's most bookish advocates, observed in 1889 that 'no first-rate man of letters now writes for the stage' and went on to dissect the works of all the leading English dramatists.[46]

The distance between literature and theatre was such that some of Ibsen's keenest British admirers were sceptical as to whether he would ever be possible on their stages. When Gosse had introduced Ibsen to the English audience, it was most definitely as literature, his sole experience of Ibsen being as a reader. After reading *Ghosts*, he could not 'conceive that Ibsen can get this tragedy acted on any boards: it would actually kill an audience'.[47] It was only when he returned to the Ibsen fray in January 1889 that Gosse revealed a consciousness of formerly having spoken of Ibsen only from the literary side. The source of this sudden awareness was William Archer, who had given a series of lectures at the Royal Institution during the spring of 1888, in which he, according to an evidently surprised Gosse, 'spoke in a very interesting manner of Ibsen as an acting dramatist'.[48]

Archer, however, who became Ibsen's most important and trusted intermediary in Britain, would himself well into the 1890s express severe doubts as to Ibsen's chances of ever succeeding on the British stage. Confident that the dramatist's reputation would continue to grow for 'all students of literature in general', Archer worried not only about their commercial viability, but also that the plays were so topical as to be

---

[43] Émile Zola, 'From *Naturalism in the Theatre*' [1878], in Eric Bentley (ed.), *The Theory of the Modern Stage* [1968] (Harmondsworth: Penguin, 1976), 367.
[44] Ibid. 366.   [45] Ibid. 365.
[46] George Moore, 'Our Dramatists and Their Literature', *Fortnightly Review*, vol. 52 (November 1889), 620–32.
[47] Gosse, Letter to G. Brandes, 11 March 1882, *Correspondance*, vol. 2, 96.
[48] Gosse, 'Ibsen's Social Dramas', *Fortnightly Review*, vol. 45, 1 January 1889, in Michael Egan (ed.), *Ibsen* (London: Routledge & Kegan Paul, 1972), 93.

antiquated before the British public was ready for them.[49] But it was also a
matter of native traditions for domestication. Responding to the critics of
Breaking a Butterfly, Archer pessimistically concluded that 'Ibsen on the
English stage is impossible. He must be trivialized'.[50] Some months ago,
he concluded, he had seen a performance of 'the even more extraordinary
drama of *Ghosts*'. Archer had spent the summer in Norway,[51] so he is
probably referring to August Lindberg's *Ghost*-tour in Sweden, Denmark
and Norway from late summer 1883: 'It proved to me the possibility of
modern tragedy in the deepest sense of the word; but it also proved the
impossibility of modern tragedy on the English stage'.[52]

The German Meiningen theatre is generally considered a pioneering
company in the realignment of literature and theatre. Their basic principle
was to 'reproduce an overall image of poetry'. This principle meant being
'true to the work', entailing that the poet's text should not be cut, if
possible, that the actor was subordinate to the poetry, and that costumes
and set should derive from the poetry.[53] The Meiningen theatre made a
name for themselves not least by historically and textually 'truthful'
productions of Shakespeare, and they were also among the first to pick
up the new, Norwegian historical drama. In 1874 and 1875 they played
Bjørnson's *Zwischen den Schlachten* (*Mellem Slagene*) when visiting Berlin,
followed, as related earlier, by Ibsen's *Die Kronprätendenten* in 1876. None
of these productions was an immediate success, however.[54]

Moving to contemporary drama, texts of a comparable standard to the
classic repertoire were hard to find, and even more: contemporary drama
hardly existed as literature in Britain. In June 1889, just before what was to
become the breakthrough production of *A Doll's House*, Henry James
pronounced judgment on the state of contemporary English drama. As
his starting point for the dramatic dialogue 'After the Play', James took the
London performances by André Antoine's Thèâtre Libre and let his
mouthpiece Mr. Dorriforth present a number of reasons why 'the sun of

---

[49] 'Ibsen and English Criticism', *Fortnightly Review*, 1 July 1889, in Egan, *Ibsen*, 123. As late as 1893,
Archer would rather *The Master Builder* remained only in book form, because he feared its
performance would not be understood by the Great British Public, see Charles Archer, *William
Archer* (London: Allen & Unwin, 1931), 198.

[50] William Archer, '*Breaking a Butterfly* (*A Doll's House*)', *Theatre*, vol. 3, 1 April 1884, in Egan, *Ibsen*,
72.

[51] Peter Whitebrook, *William Archer* (London: Methuen, 1993), 46.   [52] Archer, '*Breaking*', 72.

[53] Fischer-Lichte, *History*, 244–45.

[54] Max Grube, *Geschichte der Meininger* (Berlin: Deutsche Verlags-Anstalt Stuttgart, 1926), 80, 85,
93.

the drama has set'.[55] These included the dramatists' lack of literary skill, the preponderance of puerile adaptations from the French, the excessive concern with scenery and stage effects, bad acting and the tyranny of the box office and the long runs. James also went on to voice a very specific concern, letting Dorriforth note about the contemporary drama that 'to begin with, you can't find it – there's no text'.[56] The withholding of British plays from the book market was presented as one of the clearest signs of the theatre's moribund state.

The State of the Printed Play: Britain

In trying to map the possible 'competitive advantages' of Ibsen's 'backward' Scandinavian conditions of production, the state of the printed play sticks out as one of the most important issues. The distance between Scandinavia and 'Europe' in this respect might have been the widest with regard to Britain. With the exceptions of W.S. Gilbert's and Tom Taylor's collected works, there had been a complete dearth in the publication of plays in Britain since James Sheridan Knowles and Edward Bulwer-Lytton in the early 1840s, and the habit of reading contemporary plays had been moribund for almost all of the nineteenth century. In 1891 *The National Observer*, albeit with its usual tendency towards hyperbole, claimed that it was 'a *genre* which died a century ago'.[57] Instead, manuscripts were printed in a limited number of copies in acting editions issued by Lacy's (later French's), Dicks' and other publishers, not catering for ordinary readers but the amateur and provincial market, presenting texts cluttered with technical abbreviations. In Scandinavia, as we have seen, Ibsen had never existed in two versions: the technical apparatus was always an integral part of the literary expression of his dramatic texts.

As to the reasons why play publication had gone out of fashion in Victorian Britain, Daniel Barrett has pointed to the rise of the novel, the changing nature of the drama, the proliferation of acting editions, and the concern with copyright and performance rights.[58] In Britain the commercial theatres could

[55] Henry James, 'After the Play', *New Review*, vol. 1 (June 1889), 42.

[56] Ibid. 40. James also returns to this point in the preface to *What Maisie Knew*, see Leon Edel, 'Foreword', *The Complete Plays of Henry James* (Philadelphia: Lippincott, 1949), 9.

[57] 'Drama for the Study', *National Observer*, vol. 6, 12 September 1891, 434.

[58] Daniel Barrett, 'Play Publication, Readers, and the "Decline" of Victorian Drama', *Book History*, vol. 2 (1999), 173–87. For a more recent and extensive discussion of the relationship between book and stage, see W.B. Worthen, *Print and Poetics and Modern Drama* (Cambridge: Cambridge University Press, 2005).

offer very lucrative fees, while the printed play provided no source of income and even, because of the lack of protection in America, exposed the playwright to potential loss.[59]

Bibliographical evidence reveals the difference between Ibsen's Scandinavian publishing context and the British one. In the main Danish bibliography, *Dansk Bogfortegnelse*, imaginative literature is listed under 'poetical writing in verse and free form', comprising three main categories: 'lyrical and epical poems', 'dramatic poems', and 'novels and stories'. 'Dramatic poems' contains nothing but 'plays', listed after their national origin. From his very first publication at Gyldendal, *Brand* (1866), and up until his last, *When We Dead Awaken* (1899), Ibsen is to be found under 'Danish plays', the only alteration being that in the 1890s the category was renamed 'Danish and Norwegian plays'. Native plays were by far the largest grouping under 'Dramatic poems'. Measured by individual authors listed under each of three main categories, 'plays' was the smallest but most rapidly expanding genre. In 1859–68, there were 130 (lyrical) poets listed, 53 playwrights and 190 novelists. In 1881–92, the number of poets had grown to 177, playwrights to 140 and novelists to 306.

When the first influential English-language translations of Ibsen appeared in the late 1880s, the British trade journals operated with a category called 'Poetry and Drama'. These lists were almost completely dominated by poetry, with only a sprinkling of classical drama. When the first successful Ibsen publication, *The Pillars of Society, and Other Plays*, was published in 1888, it was typically the only play by a contemporary playwright listed under this category in *The Bookseller*, and with rare exceptions Ibsen's plays continued to have this special status until 1891. The title of Alan Monkhouse's *Books and Plays*, issued with the Bodley Head in 1893, gives testimony to the dichotomous relationship between stage and literature. Since the trade did not operate with a separate category for the printed contemporary play, it is difficult to provide hard statistical evidence of the dearth in English dramatic literature upon Ibsen's arrival. But when *The Bookseller* supplied its statistics for the entire literary production of 1889, it gave the number of published works in Britain at 7737, and of these only 231 books were in the category of

---

[59] Cf. 'A Dramatist' [Jerome K. Jerome], *Playwriting* (London: The Stage Office, 1888): 'Anything beyond a one-act piece, however, it is not safe to have published, because, under the American copyright laws, a play, published over here in book form, can be sneaked and performed over there for nothing', 81. One-act pieces were not a problem since they were rarely used in America; cf. also Martin Puchner, *Stage Fright* (London: Johns Hopkins University Press, 2002), 21.

'Poetry and Drama', as many as 117 being new editions and reprints.[60] Whereas new editions and reprints made up 18.3 per cent of the total production of books, they made up as much as 50.6 per cent of this category. This fact does not of course rule out the existence of contemporary plays, but the available data reveal an extremely low output. Simon Eliot has studied the trends and patterns in British publishing between 1800–1919 by analysing the figures from *The Bookseller* and *The Publisher's Circular* in detail and his figures imply that 'Poetry and Drama' was at its lowest ebb in the 1880s, even indicating a 'collapse'.[61] From the decade of the 1870s to the 1880s this category had declined from 6.5 per cent to 2.9 per cent of the total output and Eliot notes that the 'traditional' genres seem to have been 'squeezed by the more popular forms of fiction' during this decade. Whereas the super-category 'Literature' was composed of 'roughly, 68 per cent "Fiction", etc. and 32 per cent "Poetry and Drama"' between the years 1814–46, 'Poetry and Drama' only constituted 10 per cent of 'Literature' in *The Publisher's Circular*'s figures for the 1870s and 1880s. In such a publishing context the arrival of a printed, readable, contemporary play was a highly conspicuous phenomenon.

German Breakthrough

To many people of the theatre the separation of stage and page was as it should be; to them the 'literary', 'new' or 'intellectual' drama, as it was variously called, meant the end of theatre. '*[T]o a real dramatist*', wrote Sydney Grundy in 1914, '*it matters no more how his drama reads than how a hen crows.* "Literature", is the cant, "literature" is the curse of our theatrical day and generation'.[62] In the 1890s, such a view was representative of conservative criticism. The foreign practitioners of the new drama were to Robert Buchanan, one of Ibsen's fiercest critics, '[t]he dismal throng of literary undertakers', destroying the fairy tale, illusion and imagination that had been the virtues of English drama, replacing these with a barren intellectuality.[63]

---

[60] *Bookseller*, vol. 1, 9 January 1890, 7. These are the figures after American, Colonial and Foreign books have been excluded. The statistics are admittedly incomplete and, being based on *The Bookseller*'s own lists, probably exclude a number of provincial booksellers.

[61] Simon Eliot, *Some Patterns and Trends in British Publishing 1800–1919* (London: The Bibliographical Society, 1994), 50.

[62] Sydney Grundy, *The Play of the Future by a Playwright of the Past* (London: French, 1914), 8–9.

[63] Robert Buchanan, 'The Dismal Throng', in *The Complete Poetical Works* (London: Chatto & Windus, 1901), vol. 2, 399.

Publishers more or less held the same view. This is true even for Germany, in spite of the popularity of some contemporary playwrights and the *bildungsbürgerliche* practice of arranging drama recitations. In 1874, the *Magazin für den deutschen Buchhandel* stated that 'whoever wants to put a German publisher in a chilly mood, will offer him a collection of plays. The German public now, only from a somewhat different point of view, completely agree with their aestheticians, thinking that the drama is for the stage, not for reading'.[64] One of the major impacts Ibsen's drama had when it started travelling outside Scandinavia was precisely to change such notions.

The fight to promote Ibsen – often accompanied by Bjørnson – in order to realign literature and theatre, first took hold in Germany, and Germany became the main transit centre for Ibsen's dissemination to continental Europe. After rather unsuccessful efforts at self-promotion in the 1870s, Ibsen was, as has been noted, from the middle of the 1880s taken up by local protagonists with their own agendas, while Berlin took over as the main centre of activity. Both in the theatre and in the book market *Ghosts* came to play a particularly important part in the German Ibsen campaign.

A German 'theatre opposition' took shape around 1880. As early as 1878, the brothers Heinrich and Julius Hart in Berlin had pointed to the innovative contributions of Bjørnson, Ibsen and Turgenev, and they continued their campaign for a new theatre in *Kritische Waffengänge* (1882–1884) and *Berliner Monatshefte für Literatur, Kritik und Theater* (1885).[65] They asked for a 'reborn' German theatre, national and modern at the same time, committed to the now and the truth. They pointed to Ibsen, Bjørnson and with some reservations Zola as examples.[66] In 1884 Otto Brahm, soon to become one of Ibsen's most important German theatre mediators, wrote his first articles on Ibsen. Brahm related the success of August Lindberg's Scandinavian tour with *Ghosts* and, although partly critical of the play, he called for a German theatre that dared put it on.[67]

Gespenster arrived on the German book market in January 1884, translated by Marie von Borch, whom Ibsen did not know at the time, and

[64] Quoted in Reinhard Wittmann, *Buchmarkt und Lektüre im 18. und 19. Jahrhundert* (Tübingen: Max Niemeyer, 1982), 149.
[65] James W. McFarlane, 'Berlin and the Rise of Modernism', in Malcolm Bradbury & James W. McFarlane (eds.), *Modernism* (London: Penguin, 1991), 107–8.
[66] Manfred Brauneck, *Die Welt als Bühne* (Stuttgart: Metzler, 1999), vol. 3, 659–60.
[67] Otto Brahm, *Kritische Schriften* (Berlin: S. Fischer, 1915), vol. 1, 73–81. For a recent discussion of Brahm's role, see Magnus Qvistgaard, *Pioneering Ibsen's Drama*. Unpublished doctoral dissertation (European University Institute, Florence, 2015), 118–22, 152–54.

published in Reclam's Universal-Bibliothek. A first edition of 3,000 copies was soon followed by another of the same size. After this, however, there was a two-year halt in German Ibsen publications, until April 1886 when Reclam published *Gedichte* translated by Ludwig Passarge. This collection of poetry was followed in November by a new 3000-copy edition of *Gespenster* and from then on new titles and editions followed in rapid succession.[68]

The upsurge in book sales was closely related to the stage history of *Ghosts*. The Munich naturalists were the first in line. In 1885 naturalism found organised expression in Munich with Michael Georg Conrad's periodical *Die Gesellschaft*. The naturalists made Paul Heyse the foremost representative of everything they wanted to transcend, while Richard Wagner, Friedrich Nietzsche, Émile Zola and Ibsen represented what art ought to be in the modern world.[69] The author Felix Philippi and the Munich naturalists, with Ibsen's consent, organised a staging of *Ghosts* at the Stadttheater in Augsburg on 14 April 1886. Ibsen attended the event, called a 'general rehearsal'.[70]

The Meiningen Hoftheater followed after Augsburg on 21 December 1886, also with Ibsen present.[71] Being run by the duke himself, the Meiningen theatre could ignore censorship at home, but they gave in to police pressure to drop *Gespenster* from their touring programme after just one performance outside Meiningen. Having returned from Meiningen, Ibsen immediately travelled northwards again to attend what came to be considered the theatre event of the year, the production of *Gespenster* at the Residenz-Theater in Berlin on 9 January 1887.[72] To avoid censorship, the performance was this time organised for invited guests only, but the police turned down an application for further performances. Ibsen wrote to Hegel that he would have preferred to stay at home, but 'I can hardly refuse to put in an appearance, especially since *Ghosts* has become a hot literary and dramatic subject in Germany'.[73]

From this point, book sales took off. Three new editions of *Gespenster* were published in 1887 in a total of 15,000 copies. At the same time new

---

[68] Keel, 'Reclam', 133–35; Friedrich Pfäfflin and Ingrid Kussmaul, *S. Fischer, Verlag, von der Gründung bis zur Rückkehr aus dem Exil* (Marbach: Deutsche Schillergesellschaft, 1985), 66–7.

[69] Peter Jelavich, *Munich and Theatrical Modernism* (Cambridge, Mass.: Harvard University Press, 1985), 26–33.

[70] Sabine Fleischhacker, 'Ibsen im Lichte der Münchener Presse (1876–1891)', *Ibsenårbok 1983/84*, 122–25.

[71] See Ibsen, Letter to Susanna Ibsen, 21 December 1886, with comments.

[72] See Ibsen, Letter to F. Hegel, 5 January 1887, with comment.

[73] Ibsen, Letter to F. Hegel, 5 January 1887, *Letters and Speeches*, 263.

titles followed each other closely, together with new editions of older publications.[74] By the end of 1890 Reclam's *Gespenster* had reached a print run of almost 70,000 copies.[75] At that time Ibsen was represented with sixteen titles in all in Reclam's Universal-Bibliothek, printed in a total of 494,000 copies.[76] Such a cheap series did not allow for royalties, but, as we will return to in the next chapter, Reclam was important to Ibsen since the theatres often used the Reclam editions. In 1890, Reclam, wanting to stay on good terms with Ibsen, even allowed him a 'voluntary' royalty of 1,000 *Mark* (889 *kroner*).

While Reclam made Ibsen a cheap bestseller, the new Berlin publisher Samuel Fischer accommodated him to a more restricted reading audience, without exactly being elitist. After moving his business to Berlin in 1887, Fischer started off with a translation of Ibsen's latest play *Rosmersholm*. It was followed by *Die Frau vom Meere* in a new series called *Nordische Bibliothek* in December 1888, just a week after the Copenhagen publication of the original. *The Lady from the Sea* was soon also published by Reclam, in a different translation. With *Hedda Gabler* Fischer paid Ibsen for early delivery of sheets, but again Reclam soon followed with their own version. Like Reclam, Fischer wanted to distribute what he took to be high-quality literature as widely as possible, but in different formats. Fischer's edition of *Die Frau vom Meere* in his Nordische Bibliothek series cost 1 *Mark* 50 *Pfennig* (1, 34 *kroner*), as compared to Reclam's standard 20 *Pfennig* editions.[77]

Just as Ibsen existed in different circuits in the German book market, he also made it in different types of German theatres. In 1889, he was for the first time taken up by the Königliches Schauspielhaus in Berlin, where *Die Frau vom Meere* was performed on 4 March 1889. The event took place during the so-called Ibsen Week, with the author once more visiting the German capital.[78] The performance was considered a test of Ibsen's position. Otto Brahm wrote that it was not just about one play, but about 'Ibsen's significance for the German contemporary stage'.[79] Both the so-called 'Ibsen congregation' and its opponents made their presence loudly felt during the performance, and it seems to have ended without critical consensus.[80]

Later that year the Freie Bühne opened its activities in Berlin with *Gespenster* at the Lessing-Theater 29 September. Freie Bühne was

---

[74] Pfäfflin & Kusmaul, *S. Fischer*, 65–7.   [75] Keel, 'Reclam', 134–45.   [76] Ibid. 136.
[77] Ibid. 139.   [78] See Ibsen, Letter to Susanna Ibsen, 5 March [1889], with comments.
[79] Brahm, *Kritische*, vol. 1, 233.
[80] [Anon.], '"Fruen fra Havet" paa det kgl. Theater i Berlin', *Aftenposten*, no. 148, 9 March 1889.

modelled on André Antoine's Théâtre Libre in Paris, and was headed by Brahm. At this time *Ghosts* was already about to become canonised avant-garde in Germany. Theodor Fontane, who distanced himself from the 'theses' of the play while admiring Ibsen's literary mastery, welcomed *Ghosts* as the opening performance since it had already passed the ordeal.[81]

In retrospect, we may conclude that neither *Pillars of the Community* in 1878 nor *A Doll's House* in 1880 resulted in a definitive breakthrough for Ibsen in Germany. Not that he was unknown by the middle of the 1880s, but it was only with *Ghosts* in 1887 that his work was firmly established, both as book and as theatre, in German-speaking Europe.

By the time of Ibsen's sixtieth birthday, he had definitely come out of the obscurity of his Dresden days. In Munich he was celebrated by the literary community, including Paul Heyse and Emma Klingenfeld, the latter bringing out her new translation *Das Fest auf Solhaug* in parchment binding. Public events had even been planned other places in Germany, but the death of Emperor William I shortly before the birthday cast a damper on celebrations. Georg Brandes wrote to Paul Heyse and asked if it was really true that Ibsen made such a deep impression on German youth as reported in Nordic papers: 'When I lived in Germany, he was little known. I find it hard to imagine such a huge change'.[82]

From Germany to France

What happened in Germany seems to a large extent to have influenced the French reception.[83] The first major and positive introduction of Ibsen in French, written by Jacques Saint-Cère for *Revue d'art dramatique*, was published in 1887. It was based on Saint-Cère's experiences from working as Paul Lindau's secretary in Germany.[84] But Ibsen's most important translator in France came to be Count Moritz Prozor. As secretary with the Russian legation in Stockholm, Prozor was taken by August Lindberg's performance of *Ghosts* there in 1883, and after moving to Bern, he and his Swedish wife translated *Ghosts* and *A Doll's House*. After a part of *A Doll's House* (*La Maison de Poupée*) and the complete *Ghosts* (*Les Revenants*) had been published in *La Revue Indépendante*, Albert Savin in Paris published

---

[81] Theodor Fontane, *Sämtliche Werke* (München: Nymphenburger Verlagshandlung, 1964), vol. 22, no. 2, 691, 705.

[82] G. Brandes, Letter to P. Heyse, 20 April 1888, *Correspondance*, vol. 3, 299

[83] It was also vital to Ibsen's Italian reception, see Giuliano d'Amico, *Domesticating Ibsen for Italy* (Bari: Edizioni di Pagina, 2013).

[84] Nyholm, 'Ibsen paa den franske', 11.

them in one volume in 1889, entitled *Henrik Ibsen: Théâtre*. The sale seems to have been very modest, but the leading critic Jules Lemaître wrote a series of articles on the plays in *Journal des Débats*. At this time, from the middle of the 1880s to the middle of the 1890s, there was a wave of interest in foreign literature, particularly the Russian and the Scandinavian, and Tolstoy and *le snobisme ibsènisme* were formative components of the so-called cosmopolitan movement.[85] The main thrust of Lemaître's criticism was assimilationist, however. Ibsen was not as original as often claimed, he thought. Reading a foreign author, he often experienced an immediate 'shiver of joy and excitement', but on second thoughts 'that which I have loved most in them is that in which they are like us. I have travelled enough. I shut and close my door and again become a Latin man and Frenchman'.[86]

Ibsen was pleased to be translated to French. In 1889, he thanked Prozor for helping him 'extend my field of operations to that great and inaccessible city, Paris, or what in matters literary is the same thing – to France'.[87] Their common friend, the Swedish poet Carl Snoilsky, wrote to Ibsen in 1889 hoping that his success in Germany would be followed by just as triumphant an entry on the French stage, 'the hallmark of an artist's world reputation'.[88] Strindberg was consumed by the idea of 'conquering Paris',[89] but Ibsen does not seem to have shared this Paris-centred view. In letters to Snoilsky, Prozor complained more than once that it was impossible to cooperate with Ibsen, who ignored his letters, neglected interest from theatres and put Prozor in delicate situations.[90] Prozor also complained about French protectionism and Paris being anything but the unprejudiced world capital of literature: 'In France, literature considers itself to be a national industry which wants to be protected and, for that purpose, deploys a whole army of customs officers in the form of critics'.[91]

As theatre, Ibsen was introduced in France by André Antoine and the naturalist avant-garde. It seems that Antoine became aware of Ibsen in 1888, after talking to actors from the Meiningen theatre, and he read an unpublished translation of *Ghosts* that he received with an introductory

[85] Shepherd-Barr, *Ibsen and Early*, 8–9.   [86] Quoted in Nyholm, 'Ibsen paa den franske', 13.
[87] Ibsen, Letter to M. Prozor, 25 October 1889, *Letters and Speeches*, 283.
[88] C. Snoilsky, Letter to Ibsen, 22 October 1889, NLN, Ms. 4° 2590, 311.
[89] Stellan Ahlström, *Strindbergs erövring av Paris* (Stockholm: Almqvist & Wiksell, 1956).
[90] M. Prozor, Letters to C. Snoilsky, 22 January 1892, 11 March 1892, 14 August 1899, NLS, The Carl Snoilsky Collection, Ep. S. 39:14–15.
[91] M. Prozor, Letter to C. Snoilsky, 22 December 1892 and 9 January 1893, ibid., Ep. S. 39:15. Many thanks to Terence Cave for suggesting this translation.

letter from Zola.[92] Antoine was not happy with the translation and he did not like Prozor's either. When he put up *Les Revenants* at his Théâtre Libre in May 1889, he had the play translated once again. Ibsen, having first conceded exclusive rights to Prozor, now allowed Antoine to use the new translation, and it all caused an unpleasant row.[93] Prozor thought it would not at all be in Ibsen's interest to be associated with 'ce charlatan d'Antoine'.[94] Anyway, Antoine's efforts meant that Ibsen was introduced in the leading, 'literary' sector of the theatre, although not at all as massively as in Germany and not as much as literature as in both Germany and Britain.

Prozor's complaints about French nationalism seem to have been widely shared by Scandinavians. To Scandinavian authors, Germany was generally the first stop on their way to Europe and the German market was held to be the most open to cultural imports from the north. In 1888, in a series of articles on Ibsen in Germany, the journalist and critic Johan Irgens Hansen wrote that it was probably the Germans who would make Ibsen's theatre into an object of academic criticism, in ways similar to what had happened as a result of the German veneration of Shakespeare. Germany was the most universal of the great nations, he thought: 'They don't shrug things off as easily as the French, nor are they as darkly ignorant of everything foreign as them, and they have through their entire cultural position a mission as the great interpreter of our shared European culture'.[95] This is very much in accord with Goethe's belief that translation was one of the ways in which Germany in particular would contribute to world literature: 'whoever knows and studies German inhabits the market place where all nations offer their products'.[96]

Faithful Translators: William Archer

Via the transnational network of socialism, Germany's mediating role also extended to Britain. However, the British Ibsen campaign was very much a bilateral affair with its own history. Ibsen's most important English mediator came to be William Archer, working both as translator, theatre critic and as consultant and partly organiser of a number of the most important

---

[92] Nyholm, 'Ibsen paa den franske', 26.
[93] See Ibsen, Letters to M. Prozor, 17 April 1890, A. Antoine, [April 1890], R. Darzens, 6 May 1890 and C. Snoilsky, 29 June 1890, with comments.
[94] M. Prozor, Letter to C. Snoilsky, 22 January 1892, NLS, The Carl Snoilsky Collection, Ep. S. 39:15.
[95] Johan Irgens Hansen, 'Ibsen i Tyskland IV', *Dagbladet*, no. 95, 28 March 1888.
[96] Quoted in Puchner, 'Goethe, Marx, Ibsen', 34.

theatre productions. Contrary to Gosse, Archer already had a position as influential theatre critic when he entered into the most decisive phase of his Ibsen campaign by the late 1880s. Also, contrary to Gosse, Archer, being fluent in Norwegian, was well acquainted with Ibsen's source culture. Archer could be termed a 'faithful translator', a mediator with profound linguistic and cultural competence of both contexts of origin and contexts of appropriation and committed to doing justice to them both. He was close to many of Ibsen's socialist followers, like Bernard Shaw, and he had a strong agenda of his own: to revive the native drama and create a 'national' theatre released from commercial pressure and capable of giving priority to artistic considerations. But Archer was more a reformist than a revolutionary, intent on winning followers and keeping Ibsen at a distance from factional interests and what we have termed 'radical appropriations'. He always stressed the 'almost Protean' quality of Ibsen's multifaceted dramatic art, arguing, in direct confrontations with the socialists, and not least Shaw, that '[t]here never was a less systematic thinker'.[97] Archer's stubborn integrity involved admitting weaknesses in Ibsen's plays and he frequently irritated and bewildered Ibsen's most zealous supporters.

Archer had discovered Ibsen without the aid of Gosse.[98] His grandfather and uncle's family had settled in Norway, he had gone there for many summer holidays, had spoken Norwegian fluently as a child and picked it up again in his teens. He came across Ibsen in 1873, when as a boy of 17 he spent the summer with his uncle. His first appearance as an Ibsen man was not as a 'faithful translator', however, but rather as an adaptor in accordance with the prevailing norms of British theatre. In 1878, he received Ibsen's new play 'hot off the press' and soon produced a translation entitled *The Supports of Society*.[99] He could not find a publisher, and the translation lay fallow until it appeared on the London stage in adapted form, as *Quicksands; or The Pillars of Society*, produced by Mr. W.H. Vernon for a single matinee performance at the Gaiety Theatre on 15 December 1880. A Danish correspondent reported that an enthusiastic audience called loudly for the author, 'a request which was readily met, without any reserve or trace of embarrassment by Mr. Archer, the English translator'.[100] In the British context it was not at all exceptional that the translator-adaptor took the original author's place.

---

[97] W. Archer, 'Mr. Archer Protests', *The National Observer*, vol. 8, 17 September 1892, 456.
[98] W. Archer, Letter to Gosse, 23 March 1898, Brotherton Library, quoted in Whitebrook, *William Archer*, 18.
[99] See C. Archer, *William Archer*, 72.   [100] Quoted in Egan, *Ibsen*, 55.

In the autumn of 1881, Archer went to Rome where he managed to see Ibsen just before the publication of *Ghosts*, and the two met on a number of occasions while the controversy around this play raged in Scandinavia.[101] Archer thought that the play was great, but that it was 'too ghastly and hasn't enough action'.[102] He also disagreed with Ibsen's attack on marriage.[103] Archer's personal acquaintance with Ibsen, renewed during a meeting in northern Denmark in the summer of 1887, nevertheless gave him the playwright's confidence and established a privileged connection which was to be enjoyed by no other British middleman.

Archer's intimate knowledge of Ibsen's works and his philological competence would gradually lead to respect even from hostile critics, and he was, furthermore, able to report about a 'real' Scandinavian Ibsen to which the great majority of British readers and audiences did not have access. Archer's authority was strengthened through his regular references to nuances in the original, to not-yet-translated plays and to performances he had witnessed in Kristiania and Copenhagen.

Alongside Archer worked a mediator of a more obscure kind, the already mentioned Hans Lien Brækstad. Brækstad, who is rarely mentioned in studies of Ibsen's early English-language reception, had worked in Liverpool in his youth, and, after a spell as bookseller in Trondheim (it was he who had recommended and sold Ibsen's *Poems* to Gosse), moved to London in 1877, making his living as a journalist and literary agent. Brækstad was a freethinker who became associated with British socialist circles. He also soon became intimately involved in many of the early efforts on Ibsen's behalf, conducting an extensive correspondence with both Scandinavian and British writers, and functioning as advisor to almost everyone engaged in the front lines of the Ibsen campaign. Brækstad seems to have done everything from advising on translations, to organising Gosse's trips to Scandinavia, with recommendations to many men of letters, to finding a Norwegian-looking stove for the Novelty production of *A Doll's House*.[104] Apart from his linguistic competence, Brækstad was able to offer access to an extensive network of Scandinavian

[101] See Archer's own report, written from his diary notes in 1906, 'Ibsen as I Knew Him', *The Monthly Review*, vol. 23 (June 1906), 1–19.
[102] W. Archer, Letter to Charles Archer, 5 March 1882, in C. Archer, *William Archer*, 54.
[103] W. Archer, Letter to H.L. Brækstad, 28 December 1881, NLN, H.L. Brækstad Collection, Letter coll. 17.
[104] For the last of these, see W. Archer, Letter to Brækstad, 28 May 1889, NLN, H.L. Brækstad Collection, Letter coll. 17.

contacts, and he was kept informed about literary news, not least through close contact with Gyldendal.

A sign of the trust Brækstad had gained, as a kind of necessary mediator of a second order, is that after five years in London it was he who dealt with the placing of Archer's first collection of dramatic criticism, *English Dramatists of To-day* (1882), an important early statement of a new, more serious dramatic criticism and a call for a renewal of the theatre.[105] In *English Dramatists of To-day* Archer for the first time launched the idea of an endowed theatre. Such a theatre did not have to be endowed by the state; the important thing was that it was raised above 'the necessity of being always and immediately a remunerative speculation'.[106] Archer returned to the idea with a more formal call in 1889, during the first major British Ibsen year, in an article in the *Fortnightly Review* called 'A Plea for an Endowed Theatre'. Here he envisaged a theatre that would be committed both to the classics and to innovatory drama. He returned to this topic on numerous occasions, in parallel with his work for Ibsen and the renewal of the native drama.[107]

Walter Scott: Educational Literature for the People

William Archer's early appearance as a translator-adaptor represented the norm. Far more striking is the fact that when he started an ambitious publishing programme on Ibsen's behalf from 1888 onwards, he changed his approach radically, opting for fidelity and scholarly attentiveness to the original texts. After the early and uncoordinated attempts at launching Ibsen on the British reading public, it was the Newcastle-based Walter Scott who was to become Ibsen's main publisher in the crucial years around his British breakthrough. Archer, who in 1882 had expressed grave doubts about whether Ibsenian metaphysics would be acceptable to London publishers, had found a solution in provincial Newcastle, bringing his own translation *The Pillars of Society*, a revised translation of Lord's *Ghosts*, and Eleanor Marx's *An Enemy of Society* to Scott's series of cheap reprints. The general editor of the series, Ernest Rhys, was instrumental to the enterprise, but it is not clear whether the publication was initiated by him, by Havelock Ellis, who wrote the introduction, or by Archer. Archer,

---

[105] See C. Archer, *William Archer*, 111.

[106] W. Archer, *English Dramatists of To-day* (London: Sampson Low, Marston, Searle, & Rivington, 1882), 17.

[107] For example, W. Archer, 'On the Need for an Endowed Theatre', *The Theatrical 'World' of 1896* (London: Scott, 1897), xi–lviii.

however, had been peddling his *The Pillars of Society* with English publishers since 1878.

An inconspicuous advertisement in the *Bookseller* of 4 August 1888 thus heralded a significant moment in the history of Ibsen's reception in Britain. The readers of the trade journal were informed that in Walter Scott's 'Camelot Series' there would appear on August 25, 'The Pillars of Society, and other Plays. By Henrik Ibsen. With an Introduction by Havelock Ellis'.[108] The series, they were told in capital letters, would be 'In SHILLING MONTHLY VOLUMES'. The book was attractively produced in red (or blue) morocco, and in the April 1889 issue of the *Universal Review*, Arthur Symons greeted it as 'a literary event', and 'one of the most truly notable books published in England for some time past'.[109]

The omission of the play which had already established itself as the central Ibsen drama for his most energetic British supporters did not go unnoticed: Eleanor Marx strongly felt that the first well-produced volume of three of Ibsen's plays ought to have contained *A Doll's House*.[110] The selection not only reflected Archer's early infatuation with *Pillars of the Community*, but also perhaps his ambivalence towards *A Doll's House*.

When Rhys had asked Gosse to write the general introduction to the Camelot Series, the latter is supposed to have replied that he would not work for 'your Tyneside publishers, of whom nobody has heard'.[111] From 1883, however, Walter Scott had built up a solid business that was beginning to receive notice in the publishing world. The Camelot Series represented a courageous, progressive and smart business move. Rhys appears to have written the prospectus, expressing a brave hope of forming 'A Complete Prose Library for the People', a series of books that would 'contest not ineffectually the critical suffrages of the democratic shilling'.[112] Scott would offer the reader cheap books, but 'without the reproach which cheapness usually implies, comprising volumes of shapely form, well printed, [and] well bound'.[113] In his introduction to the first volume of the series, Rhys referred to how Caxton's printing revolution had led to 'the popular approach to letters' and went on to hail '*The Democracy*'! as the 'shape that stands ominously at the gates of Academe

---

[108] Advertisement, *The Bookseller*, 4 August 1888, 864.
[109] Arthur Symons, 'Henrik Ibsen', *Universal Review* (April 1889), 567.
[110] E. Marx, Letter to Havelock Ellis, quoted in Ellis, 'Eleanor Marx – II', 33–41 and to her sister Laura Lafargue, quoted in Kapp, *Eleanor Marx*, vol. 2, 249.
[111] Quoted in John R. Turner, 'The Camelot Series, Everyman's Library, and Ernest Rhys', *Publishing History*, 31 (1992), 31. The series began publication in February 1886.
[112] Quoted in ibid.   [113] Ibid.

demanding irregular entrance'.[114] Attacking cultural elitism, Rhys strategically softened his near-revolutionary rhetoric by admitting the necessity of creating a popular approach to elevated literature. Camelot was intended as self-improvement for the working classes, and that at a very affordable price.

Havelock Ellis's long preface to the Camelot Ibsen volume began by claiming that the Scandinavian countries had now taken Germany's literary position at the beginning of the century. For 'almost the first time' Ibsen was here 'adequately presented to the English reader', and this was an Ibsen who, Ellis claimed, was the most important European figure to emerge 'in the Teutonic world of art since Goethe'.[115] The whole tone of this essay treats Ibsen with the same respect as the classics in the Camelot repertoire. Ellis's assertions may seem close to the ones first forwarded by Gosse fifteen years earlier, but with an important difference: they invoked the author of *Ghosts*, and only secondarily the author of *Brand* and *Peer Gynt*. Ellis carefully detached Ibsen from 'the aristocratic school of Carlyle', presenting him as a champion of democracy: 'Ibsen is at one with the American'.[116]

The truly distinguishing feature of Ibsen's arrival in this company, in a series which has later been hailed as a forerunner of Everyman's Library, was that he was not an English or World Classic of fiction or poetry, but a contemporary foreign playwright. Here was, for the first time in many decades, the contemporary play in print; it was, furthermore, cheap and it sold well.[117] By the end of 1893 the one-shilling volume of the three plays published five years earlier had sold 14,367 copies.[118] By the end of 1892, Scott had sold 16,834 copies of the five-volume series, at three and sixpence each. This amounted to a total of 31,000 volumes issued by Scott alone, most of them containing several plays, so that, Archer noted, 'we are well within the mark in estimating that one hundred thousand prose dramas by Ibsen have been bought by the English-speaking public in

---

[114] *Malory's History of King Arthur and the Quest for the Holy Grail* [Le Morte d'Arthur], ed. Ernest Rhys (London: Walter Scott, 1886), v, viii.
[115] 'Preface', in Ibsen, *The Pillars of Society, and Other Plays*, ed. Havelock Ellis (London: Scott, 1888), ix, vii (extract in Egan, *Ibsen*, 73–7).
[116] Ibid. xx.
[117] By November 1889, Scott had been so encouraged by the sales of the Camelot Ibsen that he let Archer go ahead with an ambitious multi-volume series of *Ibsen's Prose Dramas*. By 1891, five volumes containing fourteen plays had been published. A text at the back of the first volume announced that Ibsen's name had been 'made famous by the production of *A Doll's House*' throughout 'the English-speaking world', and that this publishing enterprise constituted the first 'uniform and authoritative edition in English'.
[118] W. Archer, 'The Mausoleum of Ibsen', in Egan, *Ibsen*, 307.

the course of the past four years. Is there a parallel in the history of publishing for such a result in the case of translated plays?'[119] The publishing historian John R. Turner's claim that 'Scott introduced Ibsen to the English-speaking world' is not too large, if this concerted and professional publishing programme is seen against the background of the weak and largely obscure publishing attempts which preceded *The Pillars of Society, and Other Plays*.[120]

By publishing the successful *Fabian Essays in Socialism* in 1889, Scott also created particular intellectual contexts into which Ibsen's plays would be read. When George Bernard Shaw's *The Quintessence of Ibsenism* was added to Scott's list in 1891, it meant yet another confirmation of British associations between Ibsen and socialism. The early English Ibsen thus became associated with socialism not just because of literary middlemen, or his audiences, but through this publishing house, its democratic ambitions and marketing strategies.

Ibsen Actresses

Ibsen's breakthrough in English was not just literary, but as much a result of a handful of high profile theatre productions around the turn of the decade. When it comes to his rapid canonisation during the 1890s, it must to a large degree be attributed to the new level of attention generated in the theatre. The massive attacks, spurred by the appearance of his most controversial pieces on the stage, may have been more important than the degree of innovation they represented in terms of acting and production. They meant that Ibsen became one of the most written about authors in the British press in the years following 1889.

This does not mean that he did not help cause changes in the theatre. One of the key factors of Ibsen's success was his strong appeal to the acting profession and to actresses in particular.[121] It took the efforts of a handful of dedicated performers – Janet Achurch, Elizabeth Robins and Marion Lea – to show the theatrical potential of Ibsen on the British stage. When Robins spoke on 'Ibsen and the Actress' on the occasion of Ibsen's centenary in 1928, she began by describing the momentous experience of seeing Achurch as Nora at The Novelty in 1889. Robins stressed 'the

---

[119] Ibid. 308
[120] John R. Turner, *The Walter Scott Publishing Company* (Pittsburgh, Pa: University of Pittsburgh Press, 1997), xiv.
[121] See, e.g., Simon Williams, 'Ibsen and the Theatre 1877–1900', in McFarlane, *Companion*, 172–79.

unstagey' effect of the production, noting that her colleague wore 'the clothes of Ibsen's Nora, almost shabby, with a touch of prettiness', thus breaking with the convention of invariably coming on in new clothes.[122] With the minor exception of the 'theatricalism' of the Tarantella scene, Robins found that this was 'the most satisfyingly *done* modern play' she had 'ever seen', thus, albeit at a distance of almost forty years, distinguishing between performance and play-text.[123]

The sense of a momentous occasion, an intellectual turning point, and one particularly associated with the so-called woman question, is also captured in another retrospective account from the opening night, by the women's rights activist Edith Lees:

> How well I remember, after the first performance of Ibsen's drama in London, with Janet Achurch as Nora, when a few of us collected outside the theatre breathless with excitement. Olive Schreiner was there and Dolly Radford the poetess, Dr. Alice Corthorn, Honor Brooke (Stopford Brooke's eldest daughter), Mrs. Holman Hunt and Eleanor Marx. We were restive and impetuous and almost savage in our arguments. This was either the end of the world or the beginning of a new world for women. [. . .] I remember that I was literally prostrate with excitement because of the new revelation.[124]

The play was produced by Achurch's husband Charles Charrington, who also played Dr. Rank, and this production was the first time the British Ibsen was not exposed to heavy domestication.

The run at the Novelty was extended to twenty-four days, and the Charringtons lost only 70 pounds of the salary they had mortgaged as security. But in order to finance the production they had agreed to a tour of Australia and New Zealand, where *A Doll's House* would be performed almost weekly over a two-year period, and the London run was therefore broken off prematurely.[125]

With hindsight, the production of *A Doll's House* came to be seen as a watershed. It ensured a new and nation-wide attention to Ibsen, and was deemed an artistic success. While some critics rejected the performance as a failure, a large number of 'moderates' responded enthusiastically to the

---

[122] Elizabeth Robins, *Ibsen and the Actress* (Edinburgh: Neill, 1928), 9; see also Tracy C. Davis, *Actresses as Working Women* (London: Routledge, 1991) and Joel H. Kaplan and Sheila Stowell, *Theatre and Fashion* (Cambridge: Cambridge University Press, 1994).

[123] Robins, *Ibsen and Actress*, 13.

[124] Edith Lees Ellis, *Stories and Essays* (Berkeley Heights: Free Spirit Press, 1924), 128; Katherine Lyon Mix adds that in addition to these, 'feminists like E. Nesbit and Mona Caird were much impressed' with this production, *A Study in Yellow* (London: Constable, 1960), 10.

[125] Eileen Hoare, 'A Doll House in Australia', *The Ibsen Society of America*, www.ibsensociety.liu.edu/conferencepapers/adollhouse.pdf.

experience, as did the audience. *The Sunday Times*, generally sceptical of Ibsen, applauded the acting and noted that the production was 'a very interesting experiment', while at the same time suspending some of its judgment with reference to the special kind of audience present on the first night.[126] Arthur Bingham Walkley, the 'Spectator' of the *Star*, was 'wild with delight' and saw the 'beginning of a dramatic revolution'.[127] His emphasis was on the fact that 'the great intellectual movement of the day has at length reached the theatre'. *A Doll's House*, Walkley noted, differed 'not merely in degree, but wholly in kind from any play seen in England before last night'. In the same line, Arthur Symons called Achurch's performance something not generally associated with the stage, 'an intellectual achievement'.[128]

The American Elizabeth Robins's breakthrough as Ibsen performer came with *Hedda Gabler* at the Vaudeville in 1891. Her performance of the title role became one of the sensations of the London season, and perhaps the greatest Ibsen success in the theatre of the 1890s. Although Justin Huntly McCarthy had secured the rights to do an adaptation of *Hedda*, still believing that Ibsen would not succeed on the British stage without substantial domestication, Robins and her fellow American Marion Lea managed to secure the acting rights. They failed to find a manager, however, and Lea went on to suggest that the two co-produce the play themselves.[129]

While Lea and Robins clearly wanted to stay closer to Archer's more faithful approach to Ibsen, this did not mean that the book text simply became the stage text. The two actresses set to work altering 'Ibsen's English dress', after which Archer accepted and rejected their suggestions.[130] The result, according to Robins, was 'a very speakable, very playable version', 'more faithful – to Ibsen'. Joanne E. Gates, having examined Robins' promptbooks, claims that the changes made 'amounted to a complete retranslation'.[131] This Ibsen venture, while differentiating

---

[126] [Anon.], notice, *Sunday Times*, 9 June 1889, in VAM, William Archer Collection, GB 71 THM/368/3, Box 2: Press cuttings.

[127] Arthur Bingham Walkley, 'A Doll's House: Henrik Ibsen in English', *The Star*, 8 June 1889, newspaper cutting, ibid.

[128] Symons, 'Ibsen on the Stage', *The Scottish Art Review*, vol. 2 (1889), 40.

[129] This decision may have been influenced by the publisher's reputed infatuation with Elizabeth Robins, but Heinemann also knew the promotional value of this and other theatre projects, see John St. John, *William Heinemann* (London: Heinemann, 1990), 120. See also Shepherd-Barr, *Ibsen and Early*, 91.

[130] Robins, *Ibsen and Actress*, 17.

[131] Joanne E. Gates, 'Elizabeth Robins and the 1891 Production of *Hedda Gabler*', *Modern Drama*, vol. 28, no. 4 (December 1985), 611.

between Ibsen on page and stage, nevertheless radically broke with the general tendency to evince 'indifference toward the script'.[132]

The success of *Hedda Gabler* at the Vaudeville Theatre, where the play ran from 20 April to 1 June 1891, an extraordinary five weeks in Ibsenist terms, was clearly also indebted to a new and more serious approach to rehearsals. Robins noted that few plays on the London stage had been 'rehearsed longer and more carefully'.[133] In addition to this came an unusual emphasis on ensemble work.[134] As to her own interpretation of the leading role, Robins claims never to have been tempted 'to try to make [Hedda] what is conventionally known as "sympathetic".'[135] The result seems to have been an uncharacteristically ambiguous Victorian stage figure, equally attractive and repellent; Shaw described a Hedda made 'sympathetically unsympathetic'.[136]

The result of this production, which seems to have appealed particularly to the aesthetes and decadents of the British *fin de siècle*, was that Ibsen won new and influential friends in Britain, with Henry James, who now wrote his 'On the Occasion of *Hedda Gabler*', as the most public convert. Oscar Wilde and his circle were present, as were both Thomas Hardy and George Meredith. Even those who did not like the play seemed to 'admire the acting'.[137] From this point it clearly also became more difficult to write Ibsen off as a propagandist or didacticist.

Robins was later to assert that 'no dramatist has ever meant so much to the women of the stage as Henrik Ibsen'.[138] In spite of the commitment of many of these central theatrical mediators to socialism and women's emancipation, it is worth heeding their assertions that their primary concern was with the theatrical challenge Ibsen presented.[139] Robins even claimed that what Ibsen offered 'had nothing to do with the New Woman; it had everything to do with our particular business – with the art of acting'.[140] Ibsen's challenge was associated both with certain constrictions, such as his detailed stage directions and the displacement of traditional

---

[132] Gay Gibson Cima, *Performing Women* (London: Cornell University Press, 1993), 25.

[133] Robins, *Ibsen and Actress*, 17–18.   [134] Ibid. 34.   [135] Ibid. 20–1.

[136] Shaw, Letter to E. Robins, 20 April 1891, in *Bernard Shaw: Collected Letters, 1874–1897*, ed. Dan H. Laurence (New York: Dodd Mead, 1965), vol. 1, 292.

[137] O.E. [Oliver Elton], '*The Master Builder*', in *The Manchester Stage, 1880–1900* (London: Constable, 1900), 197. For a comprehensive assessment of Ibsen's influence on Wilde, see Kerry Powell, *Oscar Wilde and the Theatre of the 1890s* (Cambridge: Cambridge University Press, 1990).

[138] Robins, *Ibsen and Actress*, 55.

[139] For a further discussion, see Jan McDonald, 'The Actors' Contributions', *Scandinavica*, vol. 15 (1976), 2.

[140] Robins, *Ibsen and Actress*, 31; see also Penny Farfan, 'From "Hedda Gabler" to "Votes for Women"', *Theatre Journal*, vol. 48 (March 1996), 60.

plots, and with a new freedom. The latter was exercised in the interpretation of his complex psychology, dialogue, and subtexts, and in his rejection of an easily decodable emotional relationship with stock characters, plus a general openness, reinforced by Ibsen's own poetics of reticence.[141] Robins wrote about her choice of 'points' with reference to 'those that Ibsen had left me not merely to make, but to find'.[142] More than any other playwright, she argued, Ibsen collaborated with his actors in activating the actor's imagination so as to make him or her a fellow-creator.[143]

The role of female actors in prompting Ibsen in the theatre was important far beyond the London stage. Actresses were instrumental in bringing Ibsen on stage also in Scandinavia and other parts of Europe. Furthermore, Julie Holledge and her collaborators have shown that a number of actress-managers were responsible for the first global expansion of *A Doll's House* as performance. Achurch's world tour is the most well-known, but she had a series of followers. In the twenty-five-year span before the war, at least fourteen major international touring productions in eleven European languages travelled to thirty-five countries over five continents, with German and English as the dominant languages.[144]

Ghosts and the Independent Theatre

Alongside Robins' and Lea's *Hedda Gabler*, the Vaudeville Theatre had already brought another Ibsen success at this time with the production of *Rosmersholm* in February 1891, with Florence Farr starring as Rebecca West. This spring also saw perhaps the most disastrous of all early Ibsen productions in Britain, the Marx-Avelings' *The Lady from the Sea* at Terry's Theatre in May 1891, generally considered a gift to the anti-Ibsenites.[145]

---

[141] Many thanks to Sos Eltis for her contribution to this argument.

[142] Robins, *Ibsen and Actress*, 48.

[143] Ibid. 52–4. See also Gail Marshall's analysis of 'Ibsen's gift to the actress', which allowed 'her to exceed the possibilities of the spectacular stage, and the constraints, moral, intellectual and creative, embodied in the sculptural metaphor previously applied to her', *Actresses on the Victorian Stage* (Cambridge: Cambridge University Press, 1998), 141; Chima sees these productions as breakthroughs in 'psychological acting' and more generally refers to the emergence of 'critical actors' who, through a new devotion to text and rehearsal, responded to the complexity and interpretive openness of Ibsen's art, *Performing*, 35.

[144] Julie Holledge, Jonathan Bollen, Frode Helland & Joanne Tompkins, *A Global Doll's House* (London: Palgrave, 2016), 25–27.

[145] See, e.g., 'Spectator' [A.B. Walkley], 'The Lady from the Sea', *The Star*, [May 1891?], and [Anon.], notice, 'Terry's Theatre', *Echo*, [May 1891?], in VAM, William Archer Collection, GB 71 THM/ 368/3, Box 2: Press cuttings. See also Justin Huntly McCarthy, 'The Lady from the Sea', *The Hawk*, 19 May 1891.

In between these productions came one of the great successes by scandal of theatre history: *Ghosts* at The Royalty Theatre on 13 March 1891.

A few weeks before it was reported that *Ghosts* had been read aloud by Edward Aveling in front of an invited audience in the Playgoers' Club. On hearing of the event, *The Era* challenged the censor: 'The followers of "the master" who would invite ladies to a reading of *Ghosts* and a discussion thereon would stick at nothing'.[146] To the defenders of Victorian morality this reading demonstrated that the Ibsenites were ignoring every call for decency.[147]

The case of *Ghosts* illustrates how the unprecedented fact of a contemporary play existing as book challenged and potentially undermined a main rationale behind the censorship institution. British theatre censorship was based on the distinction between private reading and public performance and was concerned only with the latter. Aveling's reading of *Ghosts* demonstrated that Victorian reading practices were not always as private as the censorship argument would have it. Furthermore, with the book already out, the verdict of the censors could be checked and the play would still be there. In the mid-1880s Edward Pigott, the Examiner of Plays, had claimed that the essence of his office and its great advantage to the stage, was that 'it is preventive, and, above all, secret; if authors whose plays are rejected choose to advertise themselves and their rejected plays in the hopes of getting other orders for similar pieces, that is their affair, not mine'.[148] This was a vital point in contemporary defences of the administration of the theatre censorship: the unlicensed play simply disappeared, it did not necessarily become public knowledge. Most often it would be in the interest of managers and playwrights alike simply to hush it up and try again in order to retain a good working relationship with The Lord Chamberlain's office. As for the censor, it meant that he would continue his work at his own discretion. With *Ghosts*, however, every reader was able to check for himself whether the censor had come to the right conclusion. The printed text of *Ghosts* was a privileged pretext or paratextual category in relation to that which was not officially allowed to exist: *Ghosts* as performance.

[146] [Anon.], notice, 'Theatrical Gossip', *Era*, 28 February 1891, in Egan, *Ibsen*, 170.
[147] James Raven et al. (eds.), *The Practice and Representation of Reading in England* (Cambridge: Cambridge University Press, 1996), 2. A critic attacked the play, but preferred Aveling's reading to a performance, 'so long as young girls continue to be the chief ornaments of English theatres', *Saturday Review*, 14 February 1891, in Egan, *Ibsen*, 157.
[148] William Archer, 'The Censorship', *The Theatrical 'World' of 1895* (London: Scott, 1896), 72.

The Royalty performance of *Ghosts* was produced by the newly founded Independent Theatre headed by J.T. Grein. Grein was yet another outsider central to Ibsen's cause in England, together with the Scot Archer, the Irishmen Shaw and George Moore, and the Americans Marion Lea and Elizabeth Robins. The child of Anglo-Dutch and German parents, Grein had arrived in London to work as a bank clerk in 1885, at the age of 23. Keen on introducing a more intellectual drama to Britain, in November 1889, he had published an appeal for the foundation of a British Théâtre Libre, supported by William Archer, Henry James and Thomas Hardy.[149] Both Moore and Symons had witnessed the Théâtre Libre's performance of *Ghosts* in Paris in June 1890, after which the latter came up with a very particular suggestion: 'it is possible that the Lord Chamberlain might have but little desire to license a play which is not even an adaptation from the French. But a Théâtre Libre could be improvised for the occasion, and *Ghosts* in this way at least, performed – privately'.[150] Grein toyed with calling the new theatre both the British Théâtre Libre and the Free Theatre, but these were abandoned on Archer's advice, the result being the Independent Theatre.

As a play with which to test the possibilities and licence of British theatre, *Ghosts* was an ideal choice for an opening production. Grein saw it as 'a manifesto', asking whether it did not express his policy of 'a play that has a literary and artistic rather than a commercial value'?[151] When he first inquired about the possibilities of a licence for *Ghosts*, Grein is supposed to have received a clear answer from The Lord Chamberlain's Comptroller, Sir Spencer Ponsonby Fane: 'Do not come to me with Ibsen'.[152] On learning that they would not be granted a licence for *Ghosts*, the forming of a society that charged a membership fee, rather than having the spectators pay at the door, became the only option available.[153] The demand was great, with 3,000 applications being submitted for the 657 seats at the Royalty Theatre.[154]

---

[149] Quoted in James Woodfield, *English Theatre in Transition 1881–1914* (London: Croom Helm, 1984), 40; See also Michael Orme, *J.T. Grein* (London: Murray, 1936), 13.

[150] Arthur Symons (*The Pall Mall Gazette*, 5 June 1890), quoted in John Stokes, *Resistible Theatres* (London: Paul Elck, 1972), 135–36.

[151] J.T. Grein, 'The Independent Theatre', *Black and White*, 14 March 1891; see Stokes, *Resistible*, 138.

[152] Quoted in Nicholas de Jongh, *Politics, Prudery & Perversions* (London: Methuen, 2000), 29.

[153] This loophole had hardly been exploited before. John Russel Stephens points to a predecessor of the well-known performance of *The Cenci*, namely Sydney Grundy's censored play *The Novel Reader*, performed privately under the title *May and December* in 1882, *The Censorship of English Drama, 1824–1901* (Cambridge: Cambridge University Press, 1980), 138.

[154] See Jean Chothia, *English Drama of the Early Modern Period, 1890–1940* (London: Longman, 1996), 25.

Kate Santley, manager of the tenant-less Royalty Theatre, made several enquiries with the Lord Chamberlain's Office before the first night. Like other managers, Santley was dependent on the censor's goodwill, and she awaited the censor's 'commands'.[155] The Lord Chamberlain's papers at the Public Record Office also reveal that Clement Scott was actively lobbying the office as soon as the plans for the production had become public knowledge. 'How far can the Independent Theatre people go in opening at Royalty and playing Ibsen's *Ghosts* without a Lord Chamberlain's license'?, he wondered three days before the performance.[156] The pressure on the Lord Chamberlain was thus exercised both in public and behind the scenes. In a draft of an explanatory letter to the Privy's Purse written the day after the first performance, the examiner comments that *Ghosts*, 'though harmless in language is suggestive of an *unwholesome* state of things, and would certainly not be licensed by The Lord Chamberlain'.[157] 'Mr. Ibsen', the letter continued, 'is a Danish writer who has attained a reputation of late as a realistic writer after the manner of Zola: His works being dramatic instead of novelistic'. The conclusion was, however, that, because of the private nature of the performance, the censor had 'no power to interfere'.

Cecil Raleigh, a specialist in the production of melodrama, had been put in charge of the production of *Ghosts*, and Archer this time played a smaller part. It was thus perhaps inevitable that the stage-management, in Archer's judgment, was 'inartistic and stagey', not adhering to the wish Ibsen had expressly stated in his correspondence with Grein, to be 'true to nature'.[158] The production was not on the whole innovative in formal terms.[159] Grein seems as a rule not even to have attended rehearsals, but the very simplicity or minimalism of this semi-amateur production, combined with its artistic seriousness and ambition, in itself represented a novelty.

[155] Kate Santley, Letter to The Lord Chamberlain's Office, 7 March 1891, PRO, Lord Chamberlain's Papers I/564 (1891). In September Santley again had underhand communication with the censor regarding the next Independent Theatre production.
[156] C. Scott, Letter to Sir Spencer Ponsonby Fane, 10 March 1891, ibid.
[157] The Lord Chamberlain, Draft of Letter to the Privy's Purse, 14 March 1891, PRO, Lord Chamberlain's Papers I/565 (1891). Looking back at the Ibsen debates in 1911, C.E. Montague suggested that there had been only two main categories in English dramatic criticism, 'wholesomeness' and 'unwholesomeness', C.E. Montague, *Dramatic Values* (London: Methuen, 1911), 247–48.
[158] See *Playgoers' Review*, 15 April 1891, 131–32; and Sara Jan, 'Naturalism in the Theatre', in Ewbank, Lausund & Tysdahl, *Anglo-Scandinavian*, 171.
[159] Grein had, in the unmerciful judgment of his biographer, 'no theory about the new naturalistic drama, although he was in favour of it, being in favour of anything new', N.H.G. Schoonderwoerd, *J.T. Grein: Ambassador of The Theatre 1862–1935* (Assen: Van Gorcum, 1963), 99.

The furore that followed the London premiere in the end generated around 500 articles and notices.[160] *The Daily Telegraph*'s editorial called the play 'a dirty act done publicly'.[161] The production was criticised for its use of a 'surreptitious' and 'semi-private stage', and the writer, unquestionably Clement Scott, doubted whether the production was technically 'outside the Act of Parliament governing this department of public morals'.[162] It had been intimated to Grein on the first evening that there would possibly be a question in Parliament the next day, and the consideration of a prosecution under Lord Campbell's Act, the Obscene Publications Act of 1857, but the critic of *The Daily News*, Moy Thomas, apparently informed Grein that the Member in question had been asked by the Home Office to desist, as 'Downing Street was afraid to make England the laughing-stock of Europe' due to the general political ignorance as to who this Henrik Ibsen was.[163]

Sir Spencer Ponsonby Fane had a meeting with officials in the Home Office few days after the performance of *Ghosts*, and an internal memo from the meeting describes the play as 'disgusting in idea though containing nothing coarse or indecent in words'.[164] But the Lord Chamberlain raised the issue of whether it was 'advisable to exercise a quasi arbitrary power to prevent such performances' in the future.

No Ibsen reception seems to have been as strongly polarised as the British one, and most of all in the years 1889–91. William Archer's most effective polemical counter-attacks in the face of the massive hostility of conservative criticism took the form of two essays, 'Ghosts and Gibberings' (1891) and, two years later, 'The Mausoleum of Ibsen', the first acquiring an additional impact by being recycled in George Bernard Shaw's *The Quintessence of Ibsenism*.[165] In 'Ghosts and Gibberings' Archer listed a great many examples of the violent attacks on Ibsen, and laconically noted that he was compiling a book on the model of Wagner's Schimpf-Lexicon.[166] He was anxious, he claimed, to make it a complete 'Baedeker to Billingsgate' and planned on giving it the title 'Ibsenoclasts: or, an

---

[160] See Chothia, *English*, 25.

[161] [Clement Scott], Editorial comment on *Ghosts*, *Daily Telegraph*, 14 March 1891, in Egan, *Ibsen*, 190.

[162] Ibid. 189.   [163] See Orme, *J. T. Grein*, 86.

[164] Internal memo from Ponsonby Fane, 16 March 1891, PRO, Lord Chamberlain's Papers I/ 564 (1891).

[165] W. Archer, 'Ghosts and Gibberings', *Pall Mall Gazette*, 8 April 1891, in Egan, *Ibsen*, 209–14 and 'Mausoleum', ibid. 304–12. A similar but less well-known response was presented by William Alison, 'Ghosts and the Reptile Press', *Playgoers' Review*, vol. I, 15 April 1891, 125–32.

[166] Archer, 'Ghosts and Gibberings', 211.

Anthology of Abuse'. The fact that Archer brought out both the extremity and extent of the critical responses, in itself seems to have had something of a sobering effect, and even some of Ibsen's most hostile critics evinced a degree of embarrassment.[167] When the Scot returned to the topic of Ibsenoclasm in 1893, he was already able to adopt something of a triumphalist tone, confronting the anti-Ibsenites with earlier statements about the Norwegian's imminent demise.

The early English-language Ibsen became an Ibsen quite different from the Scandinavian one. Part of the reason, in addition to a number of new, local contexts, no doubt lay in another mechanism connected with the import of literature: the changed order in which the plays were introduced. It was clearly significant that his breakthrough in Britain came with *A Doll's House* and *Ghosts*, not with *Brand* and *Peer Gynt*. While Ibsen at home was first solidly established as a poet, and even as a politically conservative writer, Ibsen abroad could be written off as unpoetic and didactic, and even associated with socialism. For the British Ibsen, however, the 1891 *Ghosts* was a key moment and one that became, with hindsight, a fortunate provocation. It led to a new level of attention for Ibsen and the new drama, and strengthened the dynamic relationship between Ibsen on stage and page, also leading to an increased interest in Ibsen as reading matter.

[167] See Egan, 'Introduction', in Egan, *Ibsen*, 2.

7

Copyright and Circulation

Moving Home

In 1891, after twenty-seven years in Italy and Germany, Ibsen moved back to Norway. The reasons for his decision are not evident, and the move came about rather accidentally. It seems, however, that his own European breakthrough was a motivating factor when Ibsen eventually decided to settle in Norway. His rising star had resulted in more and more invitations, more travelling and in him becoming a more and more public and also controversial person. This all made it increasingly difficult to keep that distance to political and literary conflicts that living abroad had provided him with in the first place. By the end of 1890 Georg Brandes wrote to Paul Heyse: 'Strange that Ibsen after the many years leading a quiet life in Germany and after long since having entered Elysium in Scandinavia ["Norden"], has suddenly become a controversial figure ["Kampfigur"] with you, the old man.'[1] Ibsen's European position was now such that Norway again might offer him a more secluded and tranquil environment.

During Ibsen's last spring in Munich he made a triumphant but rather exhausting trip to Vienna and Budapest in April. Invitations also started coming from London and Paris. Then came controversy. The world premiere of *Hedda Gabler* in Munich 31 January 1891, with Ibsen present, turned into a heated confrontation between the different factions of the audience. In May, Ibsen publicly denied news that he had accepted becoming honorary president of the newly formed Freie Bühne in Munich.[2] At its first meeting, one of the organisers parodied the poems of Heyse and other stalwarts of Munich's official culture, causing protests from some of those in attendance.[3] Ibsen and Heyse had long since drifted apart personally. '[Ibsen] I see most rarely and only in the street,' Heyse

---

[1] G. Brandes, Letter to P. Heyse, 14 February 1890, *Correspondance*, vol. 3, 314.
[2] See Ibsen, Letter to *Münchener neueste Nachrichten*, 15 May 1891, with comments.
[3] Jelavich, *Munich*, 34.

wrote to Georg Brandes in 1888, 'where we with resigned respect greet each other like two people who have nothing to say [to each other].'[4] But Ibsen would never participate in or be associated with any public disapproval of other authors.

There are other episodes illustrating this consistent effort to maintain a detached position. When Ibsen went to Berlin for the so-called Ibsen-Woche in March 1889, a party was held for him at Hotel Kaiserhof, initiated by the Freie Bühne leaders Brahm and Schlenther, and which also included Paul Lindau among the guests. Lindau had adapted Sardou, Augier and Dumas *fils* for the German stage and used them as models for his own successful plays in the 1870s.[5] He was one of the foremost representatives of the French hegemony these circles wanted to fight. Lindau, whom Ibsen had known for a long time, had not initially been invited to the Kaiserhof party, but when Ibsen learnt that he was not included, he was upset and made Brahm and Schlenther make him a late invitation. According to Lindau, Ibsen took an almost demonstrable note of his presence there.[6] A Danish journalist reported that among those attending the parties organised for Ibsen in 1889, were also people like Johannes Brahms, Bismarck's personal physician Ernst Schwenninger, the law professor Rudolf von Gneist, count von Ratibor, the Norwegian painter Hans Gude, and the author Theodor Fontane – 'in order to give an impression of how different those circles are, in which there is now interest in the Norwegian writer'.[7] This was, it seems, exactly the image Ibsen wanted to convey.

Sometimes Ibsen's balancing act was delicate and demanding. In August 1890, the *Daily Chronicle* published an article on 'Ibsen and socialism', claiming that Ibsen had told the journalist that he had never been a member of the social democratic party and that he was surprised to experience that he was used as propaganda for social democratic dogmas. Ibsen immediately wrote to Brækstad in London and to the leading social democrat Georg von Vollmar in Munich, explaining that the article was highly misleading. His sole intention, he declared, had been to express surprise that his own efforts at depicting human characters and human destinies at certain points had coincided with the results of socialist studies. As to party membership, his main point was that he belonged to no party

---

[4] Heyse, Letter to G. Brandes, 2 January 1888, in G. Brandes, *Correspondance*, vol. 3, 295.
[5] 'Lindau, Paul', *Neue Deutsche Biographie* (Berlin: Duncker & Humblot 1953–).
[6] Paul Lindau, *Nur Erinnerungen* (Stuttgart & Berlin: Cotta, 1916–1917), vol. 2, 377–79.
[7] Ove Rode, 'Ibsen-Ugen i Berlin', *Politiken*, nos. 76 and 77, 17 and 18 March 1889, quoted in comment to Ibsen, Letter to Susanna Ibsen, 5 March [1889].

at all. This was 'what I would like to have clarified to my British friends and those like-minded with me'.[8] He hoped the letter would be published in British papers and from there find its way to Germany.[9]

At other times, Ibsen's display of his independence was more provocative. In 1887, when passing through Copenhagen, Ibsen made Georg Brandes furious when he declined his invitation to the radical Progress Club (Fremskridtsklubben) only to accept an invitation to a students' union with a clear conservative identity (Studenterforeningen).[10] But Ibsen's conspicuous display of his social respectability would also cause puzzlement. When he met admirers in Vienna in April 1891, one of the organisers, Engelbert Pernerstorfer, later representing the social democrats in parliament and one of the founders of Wiener Freie Volksbühne (1906), asked Ibsen why he carried his royal orders in such a company. The playwright answered that it was in order to stay moderate when invited to long-lasting parties with the young, an answer which was well received.[11]

When Ibsen a couple of months later decided to visit Norway, it was not his initial intention to move 'home'. After returning from a tourist trip to the North Cape, the main purpose of his visit, he at first only decided to stay in Kristiania for the winter. He had not for a long time felt as good as this summer, he told his publisher, but he would, of course, not live in Kristiana all year round.[12] In 1892 he still envisioned a future involving extensive travel.[13] As it turned out, Kristiania became his permanent and all-year residence for the rest of his life. The only exception is the Scandinavian tour on the occasion of his seventieth birthday in 1898. Susanna, on the other hand, who had always been the one wanting to move home, now found the Norwegian winters hard to bear and went southwards every autumn.

Kristiania had grown into a city since Ibsen last lived there. An urban novel like Knut Hamsun's *Hunger* (1890), with its anonymous protagonist, would have been unthinkable in the 1860s. Not that Ibsen himself could enjoy anonymity; he was now the greatest celebrity living in the Norwegian capital (Figure 7.1). But staring eyes no longer seemed to bother him and he was largely beyond political controversies. 'Since my return last year', he wrote to Gyldendal's director Jacob Hegel in 1892,

---

[8] Ibsen, Letter to H.L. Brækstad, 18 August 1890.   [9] Ibsen, Letter to G.Vollmar, 22 August 1890.
[10] See Ibsen, Letter to Studenterforeningens Seniorat, 1 October 1887, with comments.
[11] Max Burckhard, 'Begegnungen mit Ibsen', *Neue Freie Presse*, no. 15007, 3 June 1906, 12–13.
[12] Ibsen, Letter to J. Hegel, 5 September 1891.   [13] Ibsen, Letter to M. Prozor, 7 May 1892.

Ibsen og de engelske Turister.

Paa „*Kurland*" de flirer og flaner
og engelsk det pludrer de au;
saa møder de *Ibsen* og glaner,
saa Gamlingen næsten bli'r flau.

(*Fredriksborg-Revyen.*)

Figure 7.1   Ibsen surrounded by English tourists on Karl Johan street, 1898.

'I have been in the fortunate position of knowing and experiencing daily that both the Right and the Left are in favour of me'.[14]

Throughout the 1890s Ibsen repeatedly stated that he felt at ease in Kristiania and that he would work well there.[15] There are three major exceptions, all of them from 1897 and one addressed to Bjørnson: 'I must say Norway is a difficult country to belong to'.[16] This and the other similar remarks were made when Sigurd Ibsen, now Bjørnson's son-in-law, was

---

[14] Ibsen, Letter to J. Hegel, 5 July 1892.
[15] Ibsen, Letters to J. Elias, 1 November 1892, J. Hegel, 18 September 1893, J. Hegel, 25 July 1894, Susanna Ibsen, 26 January 1895, J. Hegel, 17 August 1895, Sigurd Ibsen, 30 May 1897, and Susanna Ibsen, 2 July 1897.
[16] Ibsen, Letter to Bjørnson, 15 June 1897, *Letters and Speeches*, 326; see also Letters to G. Brandes, 3 June 1897, and M. Prozor, 5 December 1897.

not found competent for a full professorship in sociology at the university. But these highly situated utterances have most often been removed from that context and made into canonised quotations as yet more evidence of Ibsen's troubled relationship with Norway.[17]

Ibsen did face generational controversy, however. Among his first experiences on his return to Norway was Hamsun's series of lectures in Kristiania in October 1891. With unheard-of polemical impertinence, the younger writer attacked the old quartet, Ibsen, Bjørnson, Lie and Kielland, in order to pave the way for a new literature. The 'old ones' had never treated modern, composite human beings and disharmonious souls, he claimed. Ibsen had only written about characters with one or two typical traits, representing concepts and ideas rather than modern life. At a time when Ibsen had written plays like *Rosmersholm* and *Hedda Gabler*, later hailed as anticipating modern psychology, Hamsun regarded drama as a crude genre which in itself excluded a penetrating, complex psychology.[18]

Ibsen attended the first two of Hamsun's three lectures.[19] Although clearly annoyed with Hamsun, he was not at all insensitive to the generational struggle. On the contrary, he responded in his own way, making it a central motif in his first play after his return to Norway, *The Master Builder* (1892).

The Late Plays

The four plays Ibsen wrote after his return – *The Master Builder* (1892), *Little Eyolf* (1894), *John Gabriel Borkman* (1896), and *When We Dead Awaken* (1899) – are often treated as a distinct group, 'the late plays'. In the perspective we have pursued, they may be seen as a last rearticulation of Ibsen's poetics by framing his authorship in terms of internal intertextuality, self-reflexivity and interpretive complexity.

Firstly, the last plays are almost stripped of references to contemporary settings and topical issues. Such references had gradually diminished throughout the 1880s and disappear almost completely in these last plays.[20] This tendency could only be stimulated by the plays now being

---

[17] Most notably in the series of quotations moulded into the pavement along Karl Johans gate and Henrik Ibsens gate in Oslo in 2006, in connection with the centenary of his death.

[18] Knut Hamsun, *Paa turné*, ed. Tore Hamsun (Oslo: Gyldendal, 1971), 15–37.

[19] Lars Frode Larsen, *Tilværelsens Udlænding* (Oslo: Schibsted, 2002), 148.

[20] Measured, for example, by the number of 'historical' comments, mostly written by Narve Fulsås, on the plays in the latest critical edition. Taking a liberal definition of 'historical' comments (titles, politics, communications, technology, law, currency etc.) the number of such comments is around

written not just for a Scandinavian audience, but also for a Europe-wide constituency. At the same time, the letters become briefer and more and more business-like and they have practically nothing to tell us about authorial intentions or the circumstances of production. This has partly to do with the change in the leadership of Gyldendal. When F.V. Hegel died in 1887, his son Jacob took over, and Ibsen never developed the same confidential relationship to Jacob as he had had to his father. And if Christiania Theater wanted advice on productions, they could now seek up the author in person.

Secondly, the last plays are characterised by their self-reflexive and 'meta-Ibsenesque' qualities. By 1890, Ibsen had written a series of plays creating an illusion of reality, with individuals in quest of selfhood, and in conflict with society: 'The last four works', states Inga-Stina Ewbank, 'in a number of ways, play with these expectations, both fulfilling and subverting them'.[21] This tendency included a return to the mythical geography of Ibsen's early literature, with its oppositions between the inwards/downwards and the outwards/upwards movements. In the last plays this whole mythology is reproduced, set in play and questioned. Like The Lady from the Sea, the last plays break out again from the bourgeois parlour to use outdoor settings. In a seemingly realist way these settings represent the basically vertical dimension of Ibsen's metaphorical landscape and the spiritual landscape of his protagonists. Alfred Allmers in Little Eyolf comes down from the mountain heights to experience his son drowning in the fjord and sinking to the bottom, after which the action of the play freezes. Halvard Solness (The Master Builder), John Gabriel Borkman and Arnold Rubek (When We Dead Awaken) all climb to their deaths, the last play even reintroducing the avalanche from Brand.

These landscapes are only seemingly realist; they are just as much the mental creations of the protagonists. In none of them is there any straight-forward movement from illusion to reality, but rather an intensification of private myths and concluding images that are doubly exposed. In the last scene of The Master Builder, Hilde Wangel sees her hero triumphing; the other onlookers see a man with vertigo falling into the quarry and smashing his head.[22] In When We Dead Awaken Rubek and Irene realise that their ascent is towards death, but their rhetoric presents it as a choice of life.[23]

20–30 for the plays from The League of Youth up until An Enemy of the People and down to around five for the plays of the 1890s.
[21] Inga-Stina Ewbank, 'The last plays', in McFarlane, Companion, 130.   [22] Ibid. 131, 133.
[23] Charles S. Lyons, Henrik Ibsen (Carbondale and Edwardsville: Southern Illinois University Press, 1972), 153.

Thirdly, the last plays present themselves as devastating self-examinations by 'artists' looking back on their achievements and failures, if in 'artists' we include the philosophically inclined Allmers and the creative capitalist Borkman. They all live bourgeois lives, and they are all males. Particularly in the two last plays, however, the women's viewpoint is given priority over those of the men. In privileging the female voice, this last group of plays, in a reversal of *Brand*, seem to question vocation from the perspective of 'life'. Borkman and Rubek have both destroyed the lives of women by using them for their own purposes and the language of vocation and authenticity now sounds more like self-serving tautologies. Solness will not give a young man a chance because 'I am the way I *am*, after all! And I can hardly change my nature, can I?'[24] Borkman has speculated with the bank's funds 'because I was who I was [...] and no one else'.[25] Even so, the female perspective is not an innocent and unambiguous one, and the female characters are being as ruthlessly questioned as the male ones. Solness is haunted by the notion that he is responsible for the fire that killed their twin sons, thereby also ruining the life of his wife Aline. But according to what Aline tells Hilde, this is a complete misapprehension. She herself contributed to their deaths, and she mourns the loss of her childhood home and her dolls more than she mourns the loss of her children. The twin sisters Gunhild Borkman and Ella Rentheim have both been crushed by Borkman, but Ibsen seems less interested in Borkman's abuse of them than he is in 'the women's continuing absorption in their victimization'.[26] Irene in *When We Dead Awaken* cannot forgive Rubek for having sacrificed sexuality to art, but reveals that she might have killed him had he touched her. Rubek's sacrifice, it turned out, was devastating also to himself, both to his life and to his art, but the play hardly suggests that everything would have been well if only they had married. *Little Eyolf* seemingly ends on an optimistic note, but it has also been interpreted as the darkest play of all in this last cycle.[27]

Fourthly, Ibsen's last plays demanded more than ever of their readers and theatre audiences, and particularly in the theatre he was not met with unequivocal enthusiasm. Even some of his most ardent admirers were put

---

[24] Ibsen, *The Master Builder*, in *The Master Builder and Other Plays*, trans. Barbara J. Haveland & Anne-Marie Stanton-Ife, ed. Tore Rem (London: Penguin, 2014), 11.
[25] Ibsen, *John Gabriel Borkman*, in ibid. 208.   [26] Templeton, *Ibsen's Women*, 292.
[27] Ewbank, 'Last plays', 147; McFarlane, *Ibsen and Meaning*, 338; Frode Helland, *Melankoliens spill* (Oslo: Universitetsforlaget, 2000), 243–92.

off. William Archer found *When We Dead Awaken* 'a sad fiasco', not at all a dramatic summation but 'a mere hash up of fifty-year-old ideas ... utterly without dramatic fibre'. He and Elizabeth Robins decided not to stage it.[28] The way Ibsen resisted interpretation generally enhanced his literary prestige, however. Somewhat surprisingly, Georg Brandes ended up engaging more directly with Ibsen in the 1890s than he had done in the preceding decade. He had actually not written proper reviews of any of the new plays from *Pillars of the Community* (1877) to *The Lady from the Sea* (1888). But from *Hedda Gabler* onwards he reviewed them all extensively upon publication.[29] A very young James Joyce wrote a completely enthusiastic review essay on Ibsen's last play, declaring *When We Dead Awaken* to 'rank with the greatest of the author's work – if, indeed, it be not the greatest'.[30] Writing to Ibsen in 1901, as '[y]our work on earth draws to a close and you are near the silence', Joyce claimed to be representing the young: 'As one of the young generation for whom you have spoken I give you greeting.'[31] This was, we may note, ten years after the much older Knut Hamsun had deemed both Ibsen and his chosen genre as being hopelessly out of date.

With the meta-Ibsenesque character of the last plays Ibsen performed a final, retrospective enclosure on his corpus which decisively shaped later scholarship. These plays contributed to uniting this disparate textual body into a coherent and autonomous whole, transforming historical contingency into teleology. The playwright made the point explicitly in one of his few statements on his authorial intentions in the 1890s, the preface to the Gyldendal edition of his collected works. There he noted that new readers 'lack awareness of the mutual connections between the plays': 'Only by grasping and comprehending my entire production as a continuous and coherent whole will the reader be able to receive the precise impression I sought to convey in the individual parts of it.'[32] He appealed to the readers not to skip anything and to read the plays 'in the order in which I wrote them'.

At the same time he once more came back to his autobiographical project of old. On the occasion of his seventieth birthday in 1898 he said

---

[28] Quoted in Whitebrook, *William Archer*, 209.
[29] Per Dahl, 'Georg Brandes' fire indtryk', Jørgen Dines Johansen, Atle Kittang and Astrid Sæther (eds.), *Ibsen og Brandes* (Oslo: Gyldendal, 2006), 52–4.
[30] James Joyce, 'Ibsen's New Drama', *Fortnightly Review*, 1 April 1900, in Egan, *Ibsen*, 391.
[31] Joyce, Letter to Ibsen, March 1901, *Selected Letters of James Joyce*, ed. Richard Ellmann (London: Faber & Faber, 1975), 6–8.
[32] Ibsen, 'To the Reader', March 1898, *Letters and Speeches*, 330.

that he now really intended to write a book 'that will link my life and my writings together into an explanatory whole'.[33] This was precisely the timing and the kind of book Hegel had advocated in the early 1880s, a book that would only have been 'fragments' twenty years earlier. Whether the plan was serious or not is hard to say. Just a couple of months after his birthday Ibsen wrote to Julius Elias, engaged in preparing Ibsen's collected works in German for Fischer: 'I have never thought of completing my so-called "Memoirs" in the near future.'[34]

The idea of unity and coherence nevertheless had clear effects. Ibsen criticism in the 1890s had already developed in that direction, characterised by a constant search for inner connections, and thereby contributing to giving literary studies in Norway a distinct professional and academic identity.[35] The unity and coherence of Ibsen's corpus seem ever since to have been a basic assumption, also by those most suspicious of taking authorial intentions at face value.[36] The collected works published around the turn of the century, concluding with a series of self-reflexive plays, terminated a creative achievement that already in the author's own time could be conceived of as a de-historicised and self-sufficient unity.

The Scandinavian Market in the 1890s

Although his plays became more demanding and even bewildering, Ibsen's standing in his home market remained unshaken. This holds in particular for book sales. After having settled for first editions of 10,000 copies by the beginning of the 1880s, a new level was reached by the second half of the 1890s (Appendix, Figure A.2). With *Little Eyolf*, Gyldendal had to print two extra editions of 2,000 and 1,250 copies in the course of the first five months, reaching a total of 13,250. With *John Gabriel Borkman* the first edition was increased to 12,000, but a new edition of 3,000 copies had to be issued the same month. *When We Dead Awaken* was also printed in a first edition of 12,000, immediately followed by a new edition of 2,000 (Figure 7.2).

In the theatre, the picture is more nuanced. At Christiania Theater, attendance to new Ibsen plays went slightly down in the 1890s. In general, there is a noticeable co-variation between theatre attendance and the mood

---

[33] Ibsen, 'Speech at the Banquet in Christiania', 23 March 1898, ibid. 331–32.
[34] Ibsen, Letter to J. Elias, 29 May 1898.   [35] See de Figueiredo, *Masken*, 450.
[36] For example, Atle Kittang: 'there is a far stronger inner connection in his authorship than the traditional literary-historical categorisations count on', *Ibsens heroisme* (Oslo: Gyldendal, 2002), 27.

Figure 7.2   'Ever higher!' ['Stadigvæk højere op!'] (early 1895).
From a modest start – the first plays represented here are *The Vikings at Helgeland*
(*Hærmændene*) and *The Pretenders* (*Kongsemnerne*) – Ibsen advances continuously, with one
exception: *Ghosts* (*Gjengangere*). With *Little Eyolf* he has reached such heights that he is no
longer visible. © Olaf Gulbransson / BONO, Oslo 2016.

of the new plays (Appendix, Figure A.3). *Rosmersholm* (1886–1887) marks
a low point in the performance statistics for the last two decades. *Rosmersholm*'s novel-like quality was a challenge to theatre conventions, it baffled
the critics and it was anything but uplifting. The Royal Theatre in
Copenhagen ended up not accepting the play for production while at
Christiania Theater *Rosmersholm* had, in Ibsen terms, a relatively short run
of ten performances during its first season. In addition, Ibsen had for once
accepted profit-sharing payment, 10 per cent of gross income, while
1887 was also one of few years without a new edition of one of his older
books. This all resulted in 1887 being Ibsen's lowest income year in the
period 1875–1900 (Appendix, Figure A.1).

The next play, *The Lady from the Sea* (1888), with a seemingly happy
ending, caused a new peak on the attendance curve, while *Hedda Gabler* and

The Master Builder brought attendance down again. With *Little Eyolf* (1894), again with a seemingly optimistic conclusion, Ibsen experienced a new box office success. The overall pattern was the same in Copenhagen. Arthur Aumont has pointed out that in Copenhagen this pattern also more generally affected the interest in Ibsen, so that average seasonal incomes from new performances of *A Doll's House* in the Royal Theatre in Copenhagen show the same ups and downs.[37] It would, of course, be too reductive to claim that Ibsen simply let economic motives direct his writing, but he did take theatre attendance into account, he paid considerable attention to the business side of his authorship, and he was extremely pleased to note the positive reception of *Little Eyolf* and all the money it provided him with for new investments.[38] The economic context of Ibsen's authorship has been almost completely neglected in Ibsen scholarship, but the author himself did not ignore it. He did not let it dictate his artistic decisions, but it is reasonable to assume that economy played some part when he from time to time seemed to meet more idealistic expectations and deviated from his usual pattern since *The Wild Duck*, namely to end with the death of his protagonists.

One major qualification needs to be made of this argument, however: The co-variation between 'happy endings' and overall Ibsen interest that Aumont observed in Copenhagen is not to be found in Kristiania. *Hedda Gabler* and *The Master Builder* seem to indicate an overall downward trend but on closer inspection, the opposite is true.[39] While *Hedda Gabler* achieved seventeen performances in its first season, *A Doll's House* was also taken up again and performed sixteen times. Three other Ibsen plays were performed three to four nights each, and the season 1890/91 ended up being the strongest Ibsen season that far, with a total of forty-four performances. The next season *Peer Gynt* was played thirty-five times and with four other Ibsen plays on the bill the total went up to fifty-five. This culminated during the first season of *The Master Builder* (1892/93) when six Ibsen plays were on the bill, two of which were as popular as the new one. The most popular was *Love's Comedy* (21) followed by *Peer Gynt* (15) and the new play, *The Master Builder* (15). In addition came *Hedda Gabler* (8), *A Doll's House* (2), and *The Wild Duck* (1), a total of sixty-two Ibsen performances. In other words, in 1892/93 Ibsen was on the bill every fourth night.[40] All in all the 1890s was by far Ibsen's best decade at Christiania Theater.

[37] Aumont, 'Ibsen paa danske', 277.
[38] Ibsen, Letters to Susanna Ibsen, 20 December 1894 and 6 February 1895.
[39] See Blanc, *Ibsen og Christiania Theater*, 72–3.
[40] For the total number of performances, see Trine Næss, *Christiania Theater forteller sin historie 1877–1899* (Oslo: Novus, 2005), 79.

Copyright, Circulation and Synchronisation

In the rest of Europe, Ibsen's dissemination history was strongly influenced by the transitory stage of copyright. A European convention had been put in place in 1886, but the Scandinavian countries decided to stay outside. The awareness of being translation and import cultures formed the Scandinavian debate about international copyright. It was the major export powers that pushed for extending authors' rights to encompass protection against unauthorised translation. The Scandinavian countries did not become signatories to the Berne Convention of 1886 because it had a paragraph that secured a ten-year protection against unauthorised translation. In Scandinavia, this paragraph was generally considered a hindrance to a partaking of the overall development of culture. Ibsen shared this attitude. In 1881 he wrote that 'as a good Norwegian' he could not even wish that Norway should become a party to the convention already existing because it would greatly increase the cost of foreign scientific or literary works: 'And this would be equivalent to obstructing a great number of those streams of enlightenment that now flow into Norway gratis.'[41] He immediately added that 'gratis' meant free for the state, but not for himself and Bjørnson. It was they who bore the cost of this privilege, he claimed, and they ought therefore to be compensated by a rise in the state grant.

Since it was now obviously possible to live from authorship in Norway, this was a convenient way of reframing the argument for state grants to authors and even ask that they be increased. Ibsen's appeals became part of the parliamentary discussions on these matters, but did not in the end result in changes. The most noteworthy point about Ibsen's initiative is perhaps that he, despite expanding markets, still asked for state sponsorship. State intervention could be seen as a necessary compensation for an unsustainable market and for the lack of inherited family fortunes in an initial stage of literary development. But this was not Ibsen's view. Though generally hostile to the expansion of state power, he consistently fought for extended state commitment in matters concerning authors, literature and the theatre.

Ibsen did not touch on the fact that in his case, it was Denmark's position that mattered, and he probably did not fully realise it. He thought that when Norway actually did join the Berne Convention in 1896, as the

---

[41] Ibsen, Letter to H.E. Berner, 27 March 1881, *Letters and Speeches*, 193. See also Ibsen, Letters to J. Sverdrup 4 February 1877 and H.E. Berner, 18 February 1882.

first Nordic country, his situation had changed and that he would be protected. However, he was far from alone in not being in full command of these matters. In the complex context of copyright legislation, it seems that pretending to have intellectual property rights often was effective in itself – either because of naivety, ignorance, or business code. Most important for Ibsen's financial interests in the 1890s was his commercial potential. He had become 'hot property',[42] and competition among publishers secured him some revenue from the European markets even though Denmark did not join the Berne Convention until 1903. To protect their own interests, publishers had to be first in their respective markets. In order to achieve that, they paid for delivery of sheets to the translators as soon as they were ready from the Copenhagen print shops. This was the mechanism behind one of the conspicuous publishing phenomena of the 1890s: the simultaneous publication of new Ibsen plays in several European capitals.

In many respects, Ibsen's British and continental publishing history differs from his Scandinavian. In Scandinavia, he was all until the turn of the century issued by one publisher and in one version only, while elsewhere he existed in different publishing circuits and different formats. Neither does his publishing history conform to the standard pattern for 'high literature'. If literary recognition is opposed to commercial success, then there will be a delay before literary value can be converted into economic value. Being confident that symbolic recognition by literary authorities will eventually result in canonisation, inclusion in anthologies, textbooks and so on, it is not economically irrational to invest in a new, 'small scale' author, but reaping profits will be a long-term process.[43] Ibsen deviated from this pattern all from the start: in his Scandinavian home market, he was 'modern', 'high' and profitable at the same time. Moving to the rest of Europe the accumulation cycle was to some extent reversed, Ibsen being introduced as cheap 'classic' before he started to move upwards towards more exclusive circuits. In Germany, the second translation of *Brand* was, according to Ibsen, published in 1874 in Bremen in Kühtmann's Bibliothek ausländischer Klassiker.[44] Reclam gave similar connotations, and in Britain, as we have seen, Walter Scott introduced Ibsen as educational literature for the people.

With the synchronisation of Ibsen publishing in the 1890s, the situation in many ways changed. Ibsen was now taken up by more 'upmarket'

---

[42] See Tore Rem, 'Hot Property', http://ibsen.nb.no/id/98024.   [43] Sapiro, 'Translation', 155.
[44] Ibsen, Letter to H.E. Berner, 18 February 1882.

Henrik Ibsen

bragte i Dag Kl. 11.35' sit Manuskript paa Posten

(Telegr. til Ritz Bureau)

Figure 7.3   'Today, at 11.35 am, Henrik Ibsen brought his manuscript to the
post office', 1892.

publishers, but given his preexisting publishing history, this caused conflicts. His move to new publishers also initiated a new accumulation cycle,
culminating in collected works by the turn of the century. With this
ultimate canonisation gesture, Ibsen had moved full circle, in an ascending
spiral.

Germany: Fischer vs. Reclam and Langen

By the 1890s Ibsen's interests in Germany was concentrated in Berlin,
where Julius Elias became his foremost mediator. Elias was a middleman
comparable to Archer, although with a lower profile and not involved in as
many areas of Ibsen interest. As son of a banker, he was a man of independent means who chose a Scandinavian subject for his dissertation and spent
part of his study years in Copenhagen. Elias had two cultural agendas in
Germany: to promote Scandinavian literature, particularly Ibsen and
Bjørnson, and to promote the new French painting.[45] He founded, edited
and ran *Jahresberichte für neuere deutsche Literaturgeschichte* (1892–1925)

[45] 'Elias, Julius', *Neue deutsche Biographie* (Berlin: Duncker & Humblot, 1953).

and was a leading critic of the antimodernist art policy of the Academy director Anton von Werner. He corresponded with Monet, Pissarro, Cézanne and other French painters and is credited for having discovered the talent of Käthe Kollwitz. Elias became acquainted with Ibsen in Munich and became Ibsen's Berlin middleman in the 1890s. He was involved in the most important publications of the 1890s and took the initiative to Ibsen's *Sämtliche Werke* in German.

Since Samuel Fischer now tried to gain control, every new German Ibsen publication of the 1890s was conflict-ridden, introduced new ways of manipulating copyright, and made Ibsen more and more expensive. As noted, Fischer's *Die Frau vom Meere* and *Hedda Gabler* had been followed by Reclam editions of the same plays, but in different translations. Ibsen had not received any payments from Fischer during the 1880s, but Fischer had to pay 300 *Mark* for early deliveries of sheets to *Hedda Gabler*. By the start of his Nordische Bibliothek in 1888, Fischer had announced that he intended to bring authorised translations only, and he needed to stay on good terms with Ibsen. By paying, he could be the first on the market, which was important to Ibsen as well since it improved the chances that the German theatres would use the authorised versions. For this purpose, Fischer printed extra copies that were distributed by the theatre agency Felix Bloch Erben. Ibsen entered new contracts with this agency for every new play.

Reclam's editions were a threat to this strategy as they were cheaper for the theatres, but at the same time, they enabled Ibsen to reach a very wide reading audience, which meant he did not want to exclude them.[46] On the publication of *Hedda Gabler*, Ibsen used the lack of copyright to encourage rivalry between Fischer and Reclam.[47] He welcomed the competition since it forced Fischer to hurry up and to abandon his first plan of publishing a part of the new play in a journal.[48] He even signalled that for the future he would let Reclam publish the authorised versions.[49] Fischer did not give in, however, but the competition enabled Ibsen to dictate better terms. For *The Master Builder* royalty was doubled to 600 *Mark*, twenty-five theatre copies should be provided without extra costs and Reclam should be allowed to issue the same translation as soon as Fischer's book was out.[50] *Baumeister Solness* was published by Fischer on 12 December 1892 and by

[46] Ibsen, Letter to A. Larsen, 4 January 1891.
[47] Ibsen, Letters to J. Elias, 17 December 1890 and to Ph. Reclam jun., 2 December 1890.
[48] Ibsen, Letter to J. Elias, 18 December 1890.
[49] Ibsen, Letter to Ph. Reclam jun., 20 December 1890.
[50] Ibsen, Letters to J. Elias, 1, 7 and 18 November and 3 December 1892.

Reclam in January 1893. Both editions had 'Deutsch von Sigurd Ibsen' on their title pages. In this way, Ibsen blocked a rushed and unauthorised version by Reclam but he could not prevent two other translations being published in 1893.[51]

Sigurd Ibsen, who had broken off his diplomatic career and did not have a regular occupation for some years, continued to translate *Little Eyolf* and *John Gabriel Borkman* into German. With *Little Eyolf*, Fischer opted for exclusive rights in the German market, paying Ibsen 1,000 *Mark*. Ibsen again wanted a parallel Reclam edition, but had to back down. *Klein Eyolf* was issued simultaneously with the Copenhagen edition, and on its title page, it was called 'deutsche Original-Ausgabe'.[52] No translator was given, thereby blurring the distinction between original and translation, in an effort to obtain the full protection of the Berne Convention and forcing Reclam to wait with their edition. The strict legality of the tactic was contested but not openly challenged either by Reclam or other publishers. Reclam actually offered Ibsen a payment of 500 *Mark* for the right to issue the authorised version a month after Fischer, a sum which, given the extremely low price of 20 *Pfennig* per book, would correspond to a 50,000 copies edition.[53] Fischer's strategy probably contributed to making *Little Eyolf* one of Ibsen's least widely spread books in German. The size of Fischer's Ibsen edition is not known, but some of the remaining copies have '2.–9. Auflage' on their covers, while 'Auflage' by Fischer always meant 1,000 copies.[54] In comparison, *Hedda Gabler* by Reclam had been printed in 80,000 copies by 1900 and *Baumeister Solness* in 70,000.[55]

When *John Gabriel Borkman* appeared, matters again turned more complicated when a new rival publisher, Albert Langen, entered the scene. Langen's entry is a striking illustration of how important Scandinavian literature had become to German publishers in a short time. Langen had become acquainted with Knut Hamsun in Paris, and after Fischer turned down Hamsun's *Mysteries*, Langen started his publishing house in Paris and Cologne, moving to Munich in 1895. He went for contemporary Scandinavian and French authors, among his German ones were Heinrich Mann and Rilke. In 1896, the year *Borkman* was issued, Langen married Bjørnson's daughter Dagny, the sister of Sigurd Ibsen's wife Bergliot. Sigurd seems to have played a part when Langen managed to snatch *John*

---

[51] Pfäfflin & Kusmaul, *S. Fischer*, 67.   [52] Ibsen, *Klein Eyolf* (Berlin: S. Fischer Verlag, 1895).
[53] Pfäfflin & Kusmaul, *S. Fischer*, 60.
[54] Hjalmar Pettersen, *Skrifter af Henrik Ibsen* (Kristiania: [s.n.] 1922), vol. 2, 37; Peter de Mendelssohn, *S. Fischer und sein Verlag* (Frankfurt am Main: S. Fischer, 1970), 64.
[55] Keel, 'Reclam', 139.

Gabriel Borkman from under Fischer's nose, paying 5,000 *Mark*, five times Fischer's price for *Little Eyolf*.[56] Langen also published the first German translation of *Catiline* this year. As for his new play, Ibsen informed Elias that Fischer's offer was quite unacceptable, particularly as he now thought he was protected after Norway had joined the Berne Convention.[57] Langen for his part seems not to have been informed about Fischer's prices since at first he was not certain that he had offered more than his rival.[58] As with *Little Eyolf*, Langen gave no translator on *John Gabriel Borkman*'s title page.

According to Elias, it was in this situation that he conceived the plan of a collected works. It was intended as a counter-strategy to 'rescue' Ibsen from being exploited by 'all kinds of dubious publishers' and from '[Wilhelm] Lange and [Ernst] Brausewetter's paper crackling ['papirknitrende'] German'.[59] Fischer hesitated because of the cost of securing all the copyrights and arranging several new translations, but was tempted by the idea of coming out with such a project even before Gyldendal. Ibsen gave his approval to Elias, actually at the same time as he sold *Borkman* to Langen.[60] It seems that Ibsen even gave Langen hopes for *When We Dead Awaken*, and there was an intense fight between the two publishers over the play, which Fischer eventually won.[61] Furthermore, the copyright issue was again put to the test as another publisher, probably Reclam, announced their own collected works, including *John Gabriel Borkman*, and yet another publisher came up with a competing edition of *Little Eyolf*. This might more generally reflect German impatience with Denmark. At the international publishers' congress in 1901, a German contribution thought that Danish and Swedish authors ought not to be protected as long as these countries did not join Berne.[62]

Fischer tried to push Gyldendal to open an office in Kristiania, but to no avail. The original *Når vi døde vågner* was published with a title page saying: 'København. / Gyldendalske Boghandels Forlag (F. Hegel & Søn). / Berlin. / S. Fischer. / 1899'. The German edition, *Wenn wir Toten erwachen*, was translated by the author Christian Morgenstern. Morgenstern had translated Strindberg from French in 1897, before being offered to translate Ibsen. He started in Berlin with *Das Fest auf Solhaug*,

[56] See Helga Abret & Aldo Keel, *Im Zeichen des Simplicissimus* (München: Knaur, 1992), 163.
[57] Ibsen, Letter to J. Elias, 1 November 1896.   [58] Abret & Keel, *Zeichen*, 164.
[59] Mendelssohn, *S. Fischer*, 236–37.   [60] Ibsen, Letter to J. Elias, 1 November 1896.
[61] Mendelssohn, *S. Fischer*, 246.
[62] Fritz Schwartz, 'Die Ausdehnung des internationalen Urheberrechtsschutzes', *Vorbericht. IV. Internationaler Verleger-Kongress zu Leipzig vom 10.–13. Juni 1901* (Leipzig: Brockhaus, 1901), 63.

before moving to Norway in 1898–1899 where he continued with *Komö-die der Liebe, Wenn wir Toten erwachen, Brand, Peer Gynt, Catilina* and the poems. In 1897 Ibsen received 9,000 *Mark* (8,000 *kroner*) from Fischer for the German edition of all his works published until then, and an additional 5,000 *Mark* (4,444 *kroner*), the price introduced by Langen, for *When We Dead Awaken* in 1899.

It later became part of Fischer's strategy to go after authors with a potential not just for writing a series of books, but for becoming a *Gesamtausgabe*. With new authors, he wanted long-term contracts. In 1911 he wrote that authors who published soon here, soon there made it difficult for readers and booksellers 'to get an overview of his oeuvre and for publishers to stabilise his works in the market'.[63] His efforts to consolidate authorships eventually manifested themselves in his representative editions of collected works. *Henrik Ibsens sämtliche Werke*, dedicated to a contemporary, foreign author, initiated this activity. It turned out to be successful in economic terms too, particularly after Fischer in 1907 launched a 'popular edition' in five volumes. The first edition was printed in 20,000 copies, and by the end of World War I this edition had reached 70,000.[64] At the same time, Ibsen came in constantly new editions by Reclam, reaching a total of 4, 5 million copies by 1917. This made him Reclam's most sold foreign author, ahead of Shakespeare.[65]

Britain: From Scott to Heinemann

In Britain, Ibsen in the 1890s moved from Scott to the London publisher William Heinemann and here too the change caused controversy, with Archer and Gosse as main adversaries. Gosse had now re-entered the British Ibsen scene as Heinemann's literary adviser. By Christmas 1890 Heinemann advertised 'A New Play. By Henrik Ibsen' which would be 'issued by special arrangement with the author, and will be Copyright'.[66] In the same number of the *Bookseller*, under Walter Scott's 'New Books', was an advertisement for volume five of *Ibsen's Prose Dramas*, with the information that 'a special interest is attached to this Volume, as it will contain Ibsen's latest drama'.[67]

---

[63] S. Fischer, 'Der Verleger und der Büchermarkt', in *S.F.V. Das XXVte Jahr* (Berlin: S. Fischer, 1911), 26.
[64] Mendelssohn, *S. Fischer*, 90–1, 247–48.   [65] Keel, 'Reclam', 145.
[66] *The Christmas Bookseller*, December 1890, 200.   [67] Ibid. 124.

Ibsen himself contributed to this confusion, it seems, by promising too much to both parties or by being misinformed. William Archer published a fierce attack on Gosse and Heinemann, called 'A Translator-Traitor: Mr. Edmund Gosse and Henrik Ibsen'. He felt betrayed by Gosse after having waived his advantage as Ibsen's main translator in order to let Gosse publish a separate edition of *Hedda Gabler* with Heinemann. His condition had been that this would not impede Scott in completing his edition of the prose plays. Now Gosse asserted 'a monopoly in the play', and Archer felt it opportune to expose Gosse's 'sadly imperfect' Norwegian, as well as the 'cruel injustice' done to Henrik Ibsen. '"Hedda Gabler" is one of the very worst translations on record', Archer stated:

> To find a parallel for Mr. Gosse's conduct in this matter, I need go no further than the play itself. Yet the parallel is not exact. It was by chance, not through an act of courtesy, that Hedda became possessed of Lövborg's manuscript; and having become possessed of it, she did not deface it, stultify and publish it – and then claim copyright. She did a much less cruel thing – she only burned it.[68]

In presenting a long list of Gosse's blunders, Archer did much to demonstrate that his reaction was justified, at least as to the quality of the translation.

Heinemann intervened publicly and took responsibility for the issue of copyright, then going on the counter-attack. He suggested that Archer had used his knowledge of the fact that Ibsen was unprotected by the Berne Convention to take the play illegally, while he, on the contrary, 'copyrighted the book with Mr. Ibsen's consent, and under a contract granting me the full rights appertaining to copyright'.[69] Heinemann was, in short, accusing Ibsen's main British translator of piracy, or, technically, of availing himself of the unprotected Ibsen's works for free. It was easy for Archer to counter:

> In June 1890 I entered into an agreement with Henrik Ibsen under which I secured the privilege of translating 'Hedda Gabler' from the proof sheets and publishing my translation simultaneously with the appearance of the original in Copenhagen. This Mr. Heinemann knows, for both Ibsen and I have told him so.[70]

---

[68] W. Archer, 'A Translator-Traitor', *Pall Mall Gazette*, 23 January 1891. Archer's greater linguistic competence led to several confrontations with Gosse, the first already in 1879.

[69] From W. Heinemann, *Pall Mall Gazette*, 24 January 1891, VAM, William Archer Collection, GB 71 THM/368/3, Box 2: Press cuttings.

[70] From W. Archer, *Pall Mall Gazette*, 3 February 1891, ibid.

Apart from its effective use of Ibsen as guarantor, the letter reveals that Archer was not aware of the possibility of securing copyright. Heinemann was ahead of the game – by rather too much.

Heinemann was already an adept strategist in the literary marketplace. He was looking for names to get his firm off to a good start, and by this time Ibsen was coveted property, both symbolically and commercially. To manipulate the copyright laws, Heinemann adopted another strategy than Fischer. He realised that publishing Ibsen's new works in the original language in Britain, before the publication in Copenhagen, would mean that subsequent translations would be safe from pirates. In fact, if Ibsen's work was first published in its original language in a country that had signed the Berne Convention, both the work itself and later translations would be covered. Heinemann had acted swiftly, and offered Ibsen the generous fee of £150 if he would authorise a translation of his new play.[71] Both the money and the promise of copyright must have appealed to Ibsen and Gyldendal.

Ibsen had been hesitant when first contacted by Gosse in October 1889. To Gyldendal's clerk August Larsen, he expressed his debt to Archer and felt inclined not to commit himself until he had heard from him.[72] When Archer voluntarily ceded Scott's first rights to Gosse, Ibsen must have assumed that he had only ceded first rights to Heinemann, after Archer granted Gosse this privilege.[73] Unbound copies were rushed over from Gyldendal in Copenhagen, and on 11 December 1890, five days before the Danish-Norwegian edition was published in Copenhagen, Heinemann published six copies of what was technically the first edition of *Hedda Gabler* under its own imprint and thus secured the exclusive rights to publish the work in England.[74] Gosse's translation followed on 20 January 1891. The scheme was clever, but Heinemann had not bargained with Archer's response. Gosse, who had suffered serious academic damage after Churton Collins's exposure of the many glaring scholarly faults in his book

---

[71] In his eagerness to create a good list, Heinemann seems to have treated his authors generously around this time, see Keating, *Haunted*, 20. But part of his cost in relation to Ibsen was recouped through sale of the American rights, £40 according to a Letter from W. Archer to H.L. Brækstad, undated [January 1891?], NLN, H.L. Brækstad Collection, Letter coll. 17, Ms. 4° 3017.

[72] Ibsen, Letter to August Larsen, 13 October 1889.

[73] Larsen had misconstrued Ibsen's meaning, thinking that he wanted to give Gosse 'Eneret' (sole or exclusive rights), and that Archer was out of the picture, A. Larsen, Letter to H.L. Brækstad, 16 Feb. 1891, NLN, H.L. Brækstad Collection, Letter coll. 17, Ms. 4° 3017.

[74] Some historians refer to twelve copies, but several of those involved refer to six copies, and even after the event. *The Master Builder* was certainly printed in twelve copies, however, see Turner, *Scott: Bibliography*, 117 and Bredsdorff, *Gosse's Correspondence*, 44; as was *Little Eyolf*, see below.

From Shakespeare to Pope in October 1885, was again publicly humiliated. It became more than evident that his early championing of Ibsen, and his more recent activity as editor both of British and American editions, were not based on philological competence. One friend, Henry James, reported to another, Robert Louis Stevenson, that Gosse had 'a genius for inaccuracy', and that he might just, again, have 'been almost saved by the extravagant malevolence [...] of the critic'.[75]

After Gosse, with assistance from H.L. Brækstad, had revised his translation, Heinemann ended up publishing *Hedda Gabler* in four differently priced editions. Archer was eventually allowed to include his own translation of *Hedda Gabler* in the fifth volume of *Ibsen's Prose Dramas*, out in late August 1891, a small footnote on the contents page acknowledging Heinemann's good will.

Other publishers also entered the scene at this time, challenging Scott's control of Ibsen. Frances Lord's translation of *Ghosts*, which had previously only appeared in a magazine version, had come out already in 1888. Lord's *Nora* (1882) was published in a revised edition (*Nora: or, A Doll's House*) with Griffith, Farran, Okeden & Welsh in 1890, and the same firm added Louis N. Parker's translation of *Rosmersholm* to their list in the same year, in a 'very limited edition' dedicated to the actress Alma Murray.[76] There was also William Wilson's translation of *Brand*, published with Methuen in 1891. Wilson congratulated Archer on the Scott editions of the prose dramas, while thinking that 'the three historical dramas' were more important.[77]

Unwin was the other significant rival for Ibsen around this time. Since Scott's list soon came to include improved translations of Lord's plays, Unwin was to offer the most interesting other Ibsen publications on the market. He had published an *édition de luxe* of Archer's translation of *A Doll's House* (1889) and a year later issued Eleanor Marx's translation of *The Lady from the Sea* in its Cameo Series. The first of these was a costly publication of Archer's translation for the Novelty production, with a print

---

[75] Henry James, Letter to Robert Louis Stevenson, 18 February 1891, *Henry James: Letters*, ed. Leon Edel (London: Macmillan, 1980), vol. 3, 338. The episode was widely noted, see, e.g., Thomas Hardy, Letter to Emma Lavinia Hardy, [24 Jan 1891], *The Collected Letters of Thomas Hardy*, ed. Richard Little Purdy & Michael Millgate (Oxford: Clarendon, 1978–88), vol. 1, 227.

[76] Parker later claimed that *Rosmersholm* had become 'an obsession' and that it was 'the only useful lesson in playwriting I ever had', *Several of My Lives* (London: Chapman and Hall, 1928), 148; There is no sign that Parker and his publisher had received Ibsen's authorisation. Charles Archer's translation of *Rosmersholm* appeared with Scott in 1891.

[77] 'Preface', in *Brand*, trans. by William Wilson [1891] (London: Methuen, 1894), ix. This play also advertised 'All rights reserved'.

run of 115 copies only, not meant to threaten Archer's translation projects with Scott. Walter Crane may have overestimated the book's importance when he thought that this introduced 'the souvenir book' as a valid commercial proposition, but it certainly created precedents for the play as luxury item in the 1890s, something on which someone like Oscar Wilde was to capitalise.[78] Ibsen expressed his tremendous gratification for the 'wonderful and expensive' edition, and reported the admiration of visitors with an eye to 'works of art within the typographical area'.[79] Unwin's second initiative was widely advertised, and could have proved a greater challenge to Scott's hold on Ibsen. *The Lady from the Sea* is generally held to have been a more successful translation than Marx's earlier attempt with *An Enemy of the People*, but at 3s 6d it was considerably more expensive than Scott's editions.[80] After having signed the contract with Unwin, Marx asked Bræksted to attain Ibsen's authorisation, both for moral and commercial reasons, and Gosse's preface, written before the *Hedda Gabler* affair, was to act as guarantor.[81] The play was advertised as having 'Frontispiece, Portrait and Autograph of the Author', thus also drawing on the author's authority.[82] But, perhaps because of Heinemann's brazen arrival on the scene, it was to be the last of Unwin's Ibsen titles.

The publication of *Hedda Gabler* was not an auspicious start, but it is a testament to Heinemann's business acumen that he still managed to become Ibsen's new British publisher. It is likely that Scott could or would not compete with the financial terms Heinemann was willing to offer Ibsen, and this no doubt helped persuade Archer to change sides. In this way, it was Heinemann who became the British beneficiary and maintainer of the new simultaneity of Ibsen's European fame. From *Hedda Gabler* onwards Ibsen's books carried information that translations in English, French, German, Hungarian, Italian and so on would be printed simultaneously with the original. Through the 1890s, each new Heinemann Ibsen was eagerly awaited as a publishing phenomenon.

---

[78] Walter Crane, *An Artist's Reminiscences* (London: Macmillan, 1907), 335.

[79] Ibsen, Letter to William Archer, 3 November 1889.

[80] See Ledger, 'Eleanor Marx and Ibsen', 64.

[81] E. Marx, Letter to H.L. Bræksted, 10 April 1889, NLN, H.L. Bræksted Collection, Letter coll. 17, Ms. 4o 3017. A later letter shows that Bræksted had promised to contact Ibsen, and that Unwin insisted on the author's permission. He was even unsure as to whether he could publish the book legally without it, Marx, Letter to Bræksted, 17 May 1889, ibid.

[82] *Publishers' Circular*, 6 December 1889 (Christmas number), 1740; *The Christmas Bookseller*, 1889 (Sep–Dec), 269.

Already on 27 September 1892, *The Pall Mall Gazette*, in which the battle over *Hedda Gabler* had taken place, speculated that 'Ibsen's new play will probably be translated, wholly or in part, by Mr. Edmund Gosse, and will be issued by Mr. Heinemann in this country simultaneously with its publication on the Continent'.[83] When *The Master Builder* appeared as a co-translation, by Gosse and Archer, reviewers gleefully noted that the breach was healed, 'that there is now no anti-pope in the English branch of the Ibsenite church'.[84] Charles Archer confirms that the settlement came about 'amicably', and stresses its significance in leading his brother into the firm with which he would complete the monumental *Collected Works* after the turn of the century.[85]

In spite of the fact that Heinemann was now Ibsen's main publisher, and that Gosse was Heinemann's man, Ibsen continued to go via Archer with his book news in later years. When the next play, *Little Eyolf*, was ready, Ibsen encouraged Archer to contact Gosse and Heinemann, in order to avoid 'uncomfortable competition'.[86] When the deal with Heinemann was done, this time with Archer as sole translator, Ibsen thanked him for 'your arrangement with Mr. Heinemann'.[87] Heinemann continued his manipulation of copyright; in order to secure performance rights, he also began to arrange for the new plays to be technically 'produced' in public, what Shaw called 'stagerighting'.[88] The plays that he was to attain exclusive copyright for, and publish in separate volumes after *Hedda Gabler*, were the *Master Builder* (1893), *Little Eyolf* (1895), *John Gabriel Borkman* (1897), and *When We Dead Awaken* (1900).

There are, however, traces of Ibsen's mistrust in Heinemann and Gosse in their later relations. These surface in a dispute over copyright procedures in relation to *When We Dead Awaken*. Heinemann had complained that Gyldendal had not been able to follow their promised schedule, that this would scupper his chances of securing American copyright, and that he would therefore only offer half the promised fee unless the publication was

---

[83] 'Theatrical Notes', *Pall Mall Gazette*, 27 September 1892.
[84] '*The Master Builder*', *Saturday Review*, vol. 75, 4 March 1893, 241. Sales were good, if we are to believe Edmund Gosse: 'It makes one smile to record that this "tiresome" and "uninteresting" drama has had a reception from the public such as no recent printed play has approached,' 'Bibliographical Note' in *The Master Builder*, New [second] edition (London: Heinemann, 1892), xi. This note documents that an edition of twelve copies of 'the Danish original' was published in London, due to 'excite the passions of the bibliophile' of the future, ibid. v.
[85] C. Archer, *William Archer*, 174.   [86] Ibsen, Letter to W. Archer, 24 October 1894.
[87] Ibsen, Letter to W. Archer, 5 November 1894.
[88] Twelve copies of the original text were published on 6 December 1892, and a special matinée performance was arranged at the Theatre Royal, Haymarket on 7 December 1892 at 10 o'clock.

delayed.[89] Ibsen was furious: 'I will not receive *half* a fee from Mr. Heinemann. I will, however, present him with the *entire* fee, which he can keep on the condition that I for the future will be spared any association with him.'[90] Ibsen wanted a new contract, however, be it with Heinemann or another publisher; the important thing was that the publication date was not delayed.[91] Archer at this stage in fact contacted both Grant Richards and Duckworth on Ibsen's behalf, two of Heinemann's competitors as publishers of contemporary plays. Duckworth was greatly interested, but away, and could not make an offer until the following week, and by then Heinemann had made a new offer of £120 which Ibsen accepted. When he had the book in hand, Ibsen reported that he was pleased with its 'noble' appearance and that he had 'read – or spelt my way through a review by Mr. James Joyce in *Fortnightly Review*, which is very well disposed and for which I really would want to thank the author if I had but mastered the language'.[92] Archer did it for him.

The change from Scott to Heinemann inevitably had an influence on how Ibsen was perceived by British readers. Like Samuel Fischer, Heinemann was a new house when it acquired Ibsen, only in its second year. It came to represent a new and dynamic generation of publishers in the British 1890s, defining itself in opposition to large established houses like Macmillan's. William Heinemann was a reasonably wealthy cosmopolitan Englishman, born of an English mother and with a naturalised German father. He had spent much of his youth and early adulthood on the continent, spoke fluent German, French and Italian, was well-informed about the cultural life of continental Europe, and had developed an extensive network there.[93] These were rare strengths in the British publishing scene, and Heinemann set out to utilise them already from the outset of his business venture, after he had learnt the trade at Trübner's.[94] Ibsen and the other foreign titles became an important part of the new firm's positioning in the market. Whereas the old established houses had let insularity and stolidness keep them away from much contemporary foreign

---

[89] See Ibsen, Letter to W. Archer, 16 December 1899, with comments.   [90] Ibid.

[91] Ibsen, Letters to A. Larsen, 11 November 1899 and to W. Archer, 8 January, 28 January and 16 April 1900; W. Archer, Letter to Ibsen, 20 January 1900, BL, William Archer Correspondence, Add. MS. 45, 292.

[92] Ibsen, Letter to W. Archer, 16 April 1900.

[93] In a report from London's literary life, Georg Brandes in 1896 described Heinemann as 'a good fortune for a foreign writer in London', and with an amazing network in the literary world, 'Indtryk fra London', *Tilskueren*, vol. 3 (June 1896), 430.

[94] See 'Trade news', *The Bookseller*, vol. 1, 9 January 1890, 5.

literature, Heinemann quickly achieved a distinct profile as perhaps the foremost channel for new continental literature into Britain.

Heinemann's Ibsen first had company in the 'International Library', a series of foreign novels edited by Edmund Gosse. It had begun with Bjørnson's *In God's Way*, and soon received acclaim for issuing new translations every month by writers such as Guy de Maupassant, Juan Valera and Ivan Goncharov. Such associations were quite different from Scott, dominated as that list had been by cheap reprints of the classics. Ibsen's plays were now surrounded by contemporary foreign literature, and the 'International Library' became 'one of the cornerstones' of what was to become Heinemann's huge success as a publisher of literature in translation.[95]

Some critics noted the radical qualities of this modern foreign fiction, while Gosse saw the translations as 'a series of spiritual Baedekers or Murrays', thus invoking two hallowed middle-class institutions. The formulation of the aim of the International Library was on the whole pitched to the moderately liberal middle-class reader. Adverse criticism of the realism of much of this literature was inevitable, but while Heinemann must have thought that greater moral leverage was necessary in judging foreign works, he was also well aware of how negative criticism could hurt business.[96] To this international profile should be added, of course, that Ibsen helped Heinemann become a leading publisher of both native and foreign drama, his native list beginning with the works of Arthur W. Pinero in the autumn of 1891.[97]

Heinemann's profile differed from Scott's in his emphasis on weightier, scholarly work, thus signalling a different intended readership. In a pamphlet in Heinemann's honour published just after his death, Chalmers Roberts noted that Heinemann had a great 'abhorrence of the banalities of literature for the multitude'.[98] Heinemann did not as a rule pander to the popular reader. This will no doubt have led to a shift in the make-up of Ibsen's readership, and it may have contributed to an increase in cultural status and his gradual canonisation during the 1890s.

---

[95] St John, *Heinemann*, 16.

[96] See a rather tough attack on William Heinemann in a review of Louis Couperus' *Footsteps of Fate*, 'Paulo-post Ibscene', *National Observer*, vol. 6 (July 1891), 200.

[97] *Hedda Gabler* came to introduce a series of foreign drama; an announcement in the *Publisher's Circular* points out that Tolstoy's *The Fruits of Enlightenment* will be 'uniform with "Hedda Gabler"', New Series, vol. 2, 1 August 1891, 104.

[98] [Chalmer Roberts], *William Heinemann*, by the Editor of the World's Work, Printed for Private Circulation [1920], 3.

Ibsen's move from Scott to Heinemann was not a clean break, however. Scott still kept his rights of the works he had already published and continued to reissue Ibsen both in volumes of one and three plays throughout the'90s. His last Ibsen editions, of *A Doll's House, Peer Gynt and Rosmersholm*, came as late as 1911–1913.[99] Archer continued to work for Scott as well as for Heinemann, and helped Scott publish a revised edition of separate plays in 1906, the year in which the *Collected Works* began to appear with Heinemann.[100] There were agreements made between the two publishers, they even co-operated in some respects, and it was one of these agreements that enabled Heinemann to bring out the *Collected Works*.[101] In a reflection of the different pricing policies, and thus the different readerships, of the two publishers, Heinemann made Scott undertake 'not to reduce the price of your edition as long as the price per volume of my edition is higher than yours'.[102] Heinemann's advantage was, as Shaw put it in a letter to another publisher, that he could fetch 'the rent of Ibsen's unique European position'.[103] With Scott, it was Ibsen the Norwegian; with Heinemann, it was Ibsen the European.

In the years that followed, Heinemann adopted a policy similar to that of Scott's in putting forth a number of titles in some way or other connected with Ibsen. But Heinemann's policy was more liberal. He chose, e.g., to include both parodic and critical attacks on Ibsen, such as *Punch's Pocket Ibsen* by F. Anstey (1894), and Max Nordau's *Degeneration* (1895), which portrayed Ibsen as a true 'graphomaniac' and devoted twice as much space to him as to any other artist.[104] The Norwegian-American critic and writer Hjalmar H. Boyesen's *A Commentary on the Works of Henrik Ibsen* (1894) followed in the vein of serious Ibsen criticism; already in 1890 Heinemann had published Henrik Jæger's *The Life of Henrik Ibsen*. Heinemann built a generously varied Ibsen list, on the principle that all titles would benefit from such a dialogue, not least the translations.

---

[99] See Turner, 'Scott and "Camelot"', 41. By this time, a new rival in the cheap market had arrived, run by Scott's old editor, Ernest Rhys: between 1910 and 1915 Dent published twelve of Ibsen's plays in its Everyman's Library, Ibsen being the first author to appear in its category of 'Poetry and Drama'.

[100] J. Turner, 'A History of the Walter Scott Publishing House', unpublished doctoral thesis (University of Wales, Aberystwyth, 1995), 124.

[101] Heinemann seems to have paid £120 for the right to print a revised version of the translations Archer had made for Scott.

[102] Heinemann, Letter to Frederick Crowest [Scott's general manager], 24 July 1905, see Turner, 'History of Scott', 122–23.

[103] Shaw, Letter to Grant Richards, 25 September 1897, quoted in Richards, *Author Hunting* (London: Hamish Hamilton, 1934), 131.

[104] See T. Carlo Matos, *Ibsen's Foreign Contagion* (Bethesda: Academia Press, 2012), 167.

Overall, Ibsen's and Archer's move from Scott to Heinemann was more than just a practical matter. In terms of the perception of Ibsen, it involved a move from province to metropolis, from being associated with cheap reprints of classics to being linked with innovative foreign literature, and it also meant that the target readership would be different. At the same time, Ibsen's works continued their life with Scott; they were not restricted to the upmarket circuit catered for by Heinemann.

This double-circuit existence in both German and English is one of the results of the transitory stage of copyright regulating Ibsen's European dissemination. Had Denmark joined the Berne Convention from the outset, Ibsen's existence at home and abroad would probably have been more similar. In Scandinavia Ibsen and Gyldendal used copyright to restrict circulation, by issuing only expensive editions and by denying translations to Swedish. His market standing was such that both Ibsen and his publisher could afford it, but it is highly probable that another price and translation policy would have widened the readership even more, unquestionably so in Sweden. The general Scandinavian 'mass' potential is indicated by the astonishing print runs achieved by 'cheap' Ibsen in German and English. Conversely, with a copyright convention encompassing Scandinavia, a cheap Ibsen would probably not have existed in German and English. Heinemann would most likely have published Ibsen on a descending price scale, but probably not with the same 'mass reading' profile as Ibsen was given by Scott and by Reclam. In this way, the state of the development of copyright seems to have contributed to Ibsen moving more unrestrictedly and reaching a wider reading audience than he would have as a protected book, thus confirming William St Clair's argument about the paramount importance of intellectual property to the access to reading.[105] Although it meant economic losses short term, the lack of protection was an advantage to Ibsen in gaining his status as world drama.

Income

Ibsen earned almost nothing from translated books in the 1880s. His income here consists mainly of small sums from his commissioner Th. Ackermann in Munich. This changed in the next decade. In 1890, he entered the 'voluntary' royalty from Reclam and the first payments from

---

[105] William St Clair, *The Reading Nation in the Romantic Period* (Cambridge: Cambridge University Press, 2004).

Scott and from Fischer, and in this decade, income from translated books, primarily German and English, became regular and quite substantial.

In the theatre, he had received some income from Germany and Austria as early as the 1880s; they make up the greater part of his extra-Nordic earnings during this decade (Appendix, Figure A.1). In the 1890s, these became considerable. Extra-Nordic theatre income was now on the same level as his theatre income from the Scandinavian home market, and continued to come primarily from Germany and Austria. The largest amount came through the agency Felix Bloch Erben, the rest from the Burgtheater in Vienna and the royal theatres in Munich, all with which Ibsen had separate agreements. The income from Burgtheater alone was equal to what he received from The Royal Theatre in Copenhagen and almost as much as that from Christiania Theater.

The income from British theatres were much lower and came mostly from the first half of the 1890s, a clear indication that Ibsen was not at this time commercially viable on stage (Appendix, Figure A.4). His French theatre income is also low, if quite regular throughout the decade. Ibsen became a member of the Société des auteurs et compositeurs dramatiques, probably in 1890. It was a contested issue whether this association would allow foreigners membership and even more whether it would be able to represent the interests of foreign authors.[106] But the Société was highly effective and even succeeded in collecting royalties for playwrights who were long since out of copyright.[107] Whether this was important in Ibsen's case is more doubtful, however. More significant is probably the fact that Ibsen was primarily performed by directors in the independent sector who could not afford to alienate him.

Turning to Ibsen's total earnings in the 1890s, we see from Figure A.1 (Appendix) that the ascent of the income curve gets steeper in the last decade of the century. 1898 has been left out of the figure because it blows up the scale. That year, in which he celebrated his seventieth birthday, Ibsen entered a payment of 75,000 *kroner* from Gyldendal for the right to publish 15,000 copies of his collected works. If we include that sum, the average annual income in the eleven-year period 1890–1900 is almost 38,500 *kroner*, nearly twice the salary of the head of government and more than six times the maximum salary for a professor. And even though extra-Nordic

---

[106] Narve Fulsås, *Innledning til brevene: Forfatterrett og utgivelsespolitikk – 1890-årene: Traktater: Frankrike og Italia*; www.ibsen.uio.no/brev.

[107] Hemmings, *Theatre Industry*, 239.

income now weighed a lot more than in the preceding decade, Scandinavian earnings still accounted for 75 per cent of the total.

Ibsen seems to have been highly successful by Norwegian standards, but his biographer Michael Meyer found these standards highly misleading. According to Meyer, Anthony Trollope could make up to £4,500 a year (almost 82,000 *kroner*), although he did not specify whether this includes the salary from Trollope's position in the post office. John Ruskin earned £4,000 (74,000 *kroner*) in book royalties alone, Meyer notes, while George Eliot in 1862 turned down an offer of £10,000 for the copyright to *Romola*. Examples like these, he concludes, make Ibsen's Gyldendal incomes 'pathetically little' in comparison: 'Yet so humble was the rate of earning in Norway that the myth that he was a rich man has survived there to this day.'[108]

Is this a reasonable assessment if we see Ibsen's earnings in a wider European context? What about the authors of the other 'peripheral' literature that affected the European markets at this time, the Russian? Few Russian writers were professionals. Tolstoy and Turgenev were landowners, and Goncharov was a wealthy government official. Dostoyevsky was the writer who was most dependent on authorial incomes, but he, too, had a paternal inheritance which started him off.[109] In the 'semi-peripheral' literary power Germany, the social position of authors was more middle class, but there too authorship was generally a part-time business. Theodor Fontane never managed to live off his literary authorship alone; he took work as a journalist and theatre critic. Wilhelm Raabe wrote incessantly for the press, while Theodor Storm and Gottfried Keller held positions in the civil service. Ibsen had no contact with any of these writers, but his acquaintance in Munich, Paul Heyse, was one of the most celebrated German authors of the time and in 1911 the Nobel Prize winner in literature. Heyse entertained the cultural elite in Munich and celebrities visiting the Bavarian capital in his grand villa, but there was a glaring contrast between his sovereign *Dichterfürst* image and the harsh productivity claims to which he was subjected. The 'almost indecently productive epigone' Heyse, as Thomas Mann called him, left behind around 150 short stories, eight novels, more than sixty dramas, numerous poems and five volumes of translations. His career was accompanied by recurrent nervous breakdowns.[110]

[108] Meyer, *Ibsen*, 404.
[109] William Mills Todd III, 'The Ruse of the Russian Novel', in Franco Moretti (ed.), *The Novel* (Princeton, NJ: Princeton University Press, 2006), vol. 1, 404–5.
[110] Sigrid von Moisy, *Paul Heyse* (München: C.H. Beck, 1981), 100; Wittmann, *Buchmarkt*, 170; Wittmann, *Geschichte*, 281.

Finally, what did comparable authors' incomes look like in the hegemonic literatures of France and England? Émile Zola belonged to the very exclusive group of French authors with incomes of 50,000–100,000 francs a year, equivalent to about 35,000–70,000 *kroner*. That placed him on a level with the highest echelons of the bourgeoisie.[111] In British literature, Robert Louis Stevenson topped the list of high earners towards the end of the century. After his success with *The Strange Case of Dr Jekyll and Mr Hyde* in 1886 and until his death in 1894, Stevenson made £4,000–5,000 a year, equalling 75,000–90,000 *kroner*.[112] Oscar Wilde made good money for a short while from early 1893 until his first trial in the spring of 1895, when several of his plays were being produced simultaneously in Britain and the US. He probably made a total of £10,000 during these years, equivalent to 60,000 *kroner* annually if we consider it a full three-year period.[113] At the 'bottom' end of the income scale of major authors, we find someone like George Gissing, who famously depicted the hardships of literary work in his *New Grub Street* (1891), and who claimed never to have earned more than £300 a year (5,000 *kroner*).[114]

Comparing these incomes with those of Ibsen, we can see that Ibsen's four best years in the 1890s lie within Zola's range. Stevenson's income was more than double Ibsen's annual average in the 1890s, and Wilde too was well ahead of him for a brief time. At the same time, Ibsen earned almost eight times as much as Gissing at his best. And more importantly: we need to make corrections for the very considerable variations in the size of the respective markets. By the turn of the century the British Isles had around 40 million inhabitants, the US had 76 million. There were almost 40 million French speakers in France alone. Norway and Denmark, the core countries of Ibsen's home market, both had just above 2 million inhabitants, Sweden around 5 million.

This comparative point was made at the time, in an article entitled 'Some Figures' in the *Festschrift* to Ibsen on the occasion of his seventieth birthday in 1898. The anonymous author, probably the new Gyldendal director Peter Nansen, thought that Ibsen could stand comparison even with Zola. Taking into consideration the much lower populations of

---

[111] Christophe Charle, 'Le champ de la production littéraire', Henri-Jean Martin & Roger Chartier (eds.), *Histoire de l'édition française* (Paris: Fayard/Cercle de la Librairie, 1985), vol. 3, 158, 160.

[112] Patrick Leary & Andrew Nash, 'Authorship', in David McKitterich (ed.), *The Cambridge History of the Book in Britain* (Cambridge: Cambridge University Press, 2009), vol. 6, 212.

[113] Josephine M. Guy & Ian Small, *Oscar Wilde's Profession* (Oxford: Oxford University Press, 2000), 133–34.

[114] Leary & Nash, 'Authorship', 212.

Norway and Denmark, he argued, Ibsen was 'undoubtedly the most read writer in the world, relatively speaking'.[115] The 15,000 copies edition of *John Gabriel Borkman* in countries with 4–5 million inhabitants, he continued, was in fact a step ahead of the Zola editions of 100,000, in the almost ten times as densely populated France, without counting the wider, Francophone reading world.

It is hard to dismiss this assessment. Taking into account the nature of Ibsen's literature, his modest rhythm of production, his very limited home market and the lack of protection outside Scandinavia, we can hardly avoid the conclusion that Meyer got it fundamentally wrong. Ibsen had a rather phenomenal income from his authorship.

[115] Anonymous, 'Nogle Tal', in Gran, *Festskrift*, 245.

8

The Many Ibsens

The simultaneous publications of the 1890s to some extent synchronised the Ibsen phenomenon across the European world. At the same time, however, a more striking and important characteristic of 'Ibsen' by the turn of the century is that he existed in such a multitude of cultural circuits and temporalities: he was classic and contemporary, avant-garde and bestseller, popular and elitist, old and young, poet and revolutionary, national and cosmopolitan. In some languages, his position in the theatre corresponded to his position in literature, while in others there was a huge discrepancy between Ibsen as book and Ibsen as performance. 'Ibsen' was not at all one phenomenon.

The diversity of Ibsen's early reception has tended to be overshadowed by the modernist narrative of Ibsen the avant-gardist. This narrative has particularly come to dominate the field of theatre history. Eric Bentley, the critic, playwright and influential theatre historian, writes that the 1880s saw a great renewal of the culture of the theatre, and that the renewal is generally attributed to 'Ibsen and Ibsenism'. But this renewal was not at all popular, Bentley insists: 'The new plays were most often performed privately, on special occasions only, before literary clubs, on Sunday evenings. Very few enjoyed even a short commercial run; many were given single performances.'[1] The Ibsen scholar Brian Johnston underscores that a major function of Ibsen's drama was to divide the world of theatre into two markets: 'The Ibsen phenomenon was the confirmation that theater and drama now joined the other arts and literatures of the modern world in addressing separate, and often mutually hostile mainstream and minority publics.'[2] This narrative has a limited applicability, however, and should

---

[1] Eric Bentley, *The Playwright as Thinker* [1946] (Minneapolis: University of Minnesota Press, 2010), 130–31.
[2] Brian Johnston, 'The Ibsen Phenomenon', *Ibsen Studies*, vol. 6, no. 1 (2006), 9. See also for example Archibald Henderson, *The Changing Drama* (New York: Henry Holt and Co., 1914), 250; Stokes, *Resistible*, 3; Chothia, *English*, 2.

not be taken as a general truth, not even for theatre history. It captures one essential feature of Ibsen's existence in English and French but it is completely inadequate for Scandinavia and Germany, and consequently it is also incapable of accounting for how such a dramatic authorship could emerge in the first place. Furthermore, it conceals the fact that Ibsen had a dual existence in English, which again makes it different from the French Ibsen.

Scandinavian and German Mainstream

Theatre statistics confirm the information given by Ibsen's income figures: his main theatre market was Scandinavia and German-speaking Europe. Of sixty-eight Ibsen productions registered in the year 1900, forty-one were in German and thirteen in Scandinavian languages. There were just two in English, a New York production of *The Master Builder* and a Stage Society production of *The League of Youth* in London. There were none in French.[3]

In Scandinavia, the 1899/1900 season was the opening season of the new Nationaltheatret, with Bjørnstjerne Bjørnson's son Bjørn Bjørnson as director. The new theatre was very much a monument to the extraordinary achievements of Bjørnson and Ibsen. The huge statues of the two outside the entrance were unveiled on the opening day, and the opening productions were dedicated to Holberg, Ibsen (*An Enemy of the People*) and Bjørnson (*Sigurd Jorsalfar*). During its first season, Nationaltheatret also produced *When We Dead Awaken*, *Ghosts*, for the first time at the leading theatre of the capital, and *Peer Gynt*.

Ibsen himself never wanted to be too closely associated with a literary theatre movement catering for a highly select audience. Instead, he was always committed to the idea of a national theatre: a theatre that, with the support of the state, would be able to let artistic priorities go ahead of commercial ones, without thereby addressing only the self-styled cultural elite. Contrary to what might have been expected, Ibsen did not engage in the antimass rhetoric of the late nineteenth century, seeing the theatre as an instrument of cultural and social distinction. Instead, in the Norwegian context, he would refer to the theatre as a force for creating a collective identity: 'Nowadays the task of the theatre is this: not simply to work as an art institution, but also to serve as an institution which owns a unifying

---

[3] *Repertoardatabase*, http://ibsen.nb.no (accessed in 2014; transferred to https://ibsenstage.hf.uio.no in 2017).

power and ability.'[4] The campaign for a new theatre in Kristiania, finally brought to a conclusion with the foundation of Nationaltheatret, is among the few causes in which he engaged himself in public.[5]

At this time Ibsen's collected works by Gyldendal, called 'Folkeudgave' ('popular edition'), was also well under way. The first volume was out in 1898, the ninth in 1900, while a tenth supplement volume with previously unpublished plays (*The Burial Mound* and *Olaf Liljekrans*), the last play (*When We Dead Awaken*), articles, speeches and selected poems came in 1902. Each volume had extended bibliographical information.[6] Advertisements for the collected works drew attention to the fact that with the new 'popular edition' it would be possible to get a play for around 1/3 of the old price. Ibsen himself by this stage welcomed the idea of a cheap edition: 'I have already long wished for such a one in order to secure my collected works a distribution in classes of society that the more expensive editions have difficulties reaching.'[7] With a print run of 15,000 for each volume of these collected works, the publisher too made good money.

In terms of Ibsen as book, Germany was even, as we have noted, just ahead of Scandinavia. Fischer's *Sämtliche Werke* programme was, if we trust Julius Elias, the first of its kind to be conceived, and it started in the same year as Gyldendal's, 1898. Fischer's edition contained ten volumes and was finished in 1904. Elias and Paul Schlenther wrote the general preface, while every volume had introductions by Georg Brandes or Schlenther. Like the Danish edition, it contained prose articles ('Prosa-schriften') and speeches (in vol. 1, published only in 1903). Unlike the Danish edition, however, the tenth volume, published in 1904, was something quite new: a volume of Ibsen letters edited, introduced and annotated by Elias and Halvdan Koht.

Taking the figures of the year 1900 as indications of Ibsen's standing in the German theatre world, they show that not only was Ibsen played a lot, but he was also all over, both in terms of German-speaking countries and cities and in terms of institutions. Ibsen was performed in every sector, in *Hoftheater, Stadttheater, Volkstheater* and more 'experimental' or 'literary' theatres. The Ibsen campaigners did not stay locked within the independent sector, with activists from the Freie Bühne, like Brahm and Schlenther,

---

[4] Ibsen, Letter to Laura Gundersen, [March/April 1888].
[5] Ibsen, [Speech at Christiania Theater's celebrations], *Samlede verker* (Oslo: Gyldendal 1930), vol. 15, 426–28.
[6] Henrik Ibsen, *Samlede værker*, 10 vols. (Copenhagen: Gyldendal, 1898–1902), with bibliographical information by J.B. Halvorsen (vols. 1–7), Sten Konow (vols. 8–9) and Halvdan Koht (vol. 10).
[7] Ibsen, Letter to J. Hegel, 16 January 1898.

moving on to become leading directors of more established institutions. In 1894, Brahm took over the direction of Deutsches Theater, already one of the leading 'art' scenes in Berlin, where he every season put on Ibsen.[8] Throughout the 1890s he was criticised for his subdued, psychological style, but after moving to the Lessing-Theater, he experienced a second successful period, with Gerhard Hauptmann and Ibsen as his two most frequently performed authors. Schlenther in 1898 went directly from being head of the Freie Bühne to taking over Vienna's Burgtheater. He regularly produced Ibsen, while disappointing the 'moderns' by not bringing a single play of Arthur Schnitzler. When also receiving criticism from the conservative side, he stepped down in 1910.[9]

France: With the Cosmopolitans

In a comparative outlook in 1898, the Danish author Sven Lange thought that Ibsen's prominent position as both book and theatre in Germany betrayed a difference in importance: 'In Germany, the reading of Ibsen is far more important than the performances, since he is so very poorly played nearly everywhere.'[10] In France, on the contrary, he thought that Ibsen's literary significance was non-existent: 'In Paris, Ibsen exists only on the stage.'[11] Although exaggerated, Ibsen did figure more prominently as theatre than as literature in France, and even more: as theatre, he remained a minority interest. His plays rarely reached outside Paris, and in Paris they stayed largely in the experimental sector where Ibsen from the start had been appropriated as an asset in the struggle for avant-garde hegemony. André Antoine and his Théâtre Libre followed up the introduction of *Les Revenants* (*Ghosts*) in May 1890 with *Le Canard Sauvage* (*The Wild Duck*) in 1891. Naturalism was already in decline at that time, and Moritz Prozor was not at all happy that Ibsen was introduced by Antoine, in whose company, he claimed, Ibsen would appear as a 'morally depraved curiosity'.[12] By the beginning of 1893, Prozor thought Ibsen had made a significant advance in France with *The Master Builder*, and he put faith in the literary turnaround: 'the symbolist movement which is so strong at the moment may help him survive'.[13] Prozor was proven right in the sense that Ibsen was now taken over by Antoine's rival Aurélien Lugné-Poë and his

[8] See Fulsås, *Biografisk* and *Neue Deutsche Biographie.*   [9] Ibid.
[10] Sven Lange, 'Henrik Ibsen og det unge Europa. Spredte Indtryk', in Gran, *Festskrift*, 231.
[11] Ibid. 227.   [12] M. Prozor, Letter to C. Snoilsky, 22 January 1892, NLS, Ep. S. 39:15.
[13] M. Prozor, Letter to C. Snoilsky, 9 January 1893, ibid.

Théâtre de l'Oeuvre. He was made into a brand of Symbolist theatre and a major vehicle in Lugné-Poë's effort at creating an identity in opposition to naturalism. Of just above twenty Ibsen productions in Paris in the 1890s, Lugné-Poë was involved in fifteen.[14]

In the hands of Lugné-Poë, Ibsen became the object of very peculiar experiments, by some considered 'one of the most bizarre chapters in theatrical history'.[15] The actors moved in a dreamlike manner, and although the intention was to be pure 'instruments' of the poet and the text, not to play roles or deliver lines, the style of performance caught as much attention as the textual content.[16] Ibsen was obviously slightly anxious about what was going on. The Danish author Herman Bang participated in some of the productions and helped temper the style somewhat.[17] Bang himself thought that *Rosmersholm* and *Un Ennemi du Peuple* in the 1893/94 season represented a theatrical breakthrough for Ibsen in Paris.[18]

Ibsen made only a couple of entries into the sector of the Boulevard theatre. In 1891, *Hedda Gabler* was played at the Théâtre Vaudeville, and, more importantly, in 1894, *A Doll's House* was played there with the star performer Réjane as Nora. The production was a box office success, and was hailed as a triumph in Norway.[19] That same year, *Solness le Constructeur* at the Théâtre de l'Oeuvre was also enthusiastically received. In addition, there were many adaptations. Some did well, while also illustrating that only an illicit love affair could make Nora plausible, while the idea of her leaving her children to attain full self-realisation was impossible to an average French theatre audience.[20]

By the middle of the 1890s, however, the general climate became less favourable, with xenophobia and nationalism on the rise. From 1895 the literary field crystallised into a sharp opposition between 'nationals' and 'cosmopolitans', and the climate of acceptance of foreign works began 'to change to one of hostility'.[21] In 1896, Jules Lemaître published 'De

---

[14] *Repertoardatabase*, http://ibsen.nb.no. (accessed in 2014; transferred to https://ibsenstage.hf.uio.no in 2017).

[15] Joan Templeton, 'Antoine versus Lugné-Poë', in Maria Deppermann et al. (eds.), *Ibsen im europäischen Spannungsfeld zwischen Naturalismus und Symbolismus* (Frankfurt aM: Peter Lang 1998), 75.

[16] de Figueiredo, *Masken*, 442; Shepherd-Barr, *Ibsen and Early*, 157–58.

[17] Nyholm, 'Ibsen paa den franske', 38–45.

[18] Herman Bang, 'De norske skuespil i Paris', *Nyt Tidsskrift*, 1893–94, 322.

[19] Nyholm, 'Ibsen paa den franske', 51–7.

[20] Kirsten Shepherd-Barr, 'Ibsen in France from Breakthrough to Renewal', *Ibsen Studies*, vol. 12, no. 1 (2012), 64–5.

[21] Shepherd-Barr, *Ibsen and Early*, 163; Blaise Wilfert-Portal, 'Une nouvelle géopolitique intellectuelle', in *La Vie intellectuelle en France* ed. Christophe Charle & Laurent Jeanpierre (Paris: Le Seuil, 2016), vol. 1, 561–63.

Figure 8.1 Trade cards with Ibsen portraits.
By the turn of the century Ibsen was such a celebrity that he was used for commercial
purposes across Europe. Here he is on a collection of *trade cards*: advertising cards
formed as visiting cards and particularly widespread in the last decades of the
nineteenth century. They brought commercial information at the back, while also
being cards to be traded among collectors. At the left he figures as no. 82 in a series of
modern authors placed in cigarette packets from Ogden's Guinea Gold Cigarettes,
issued 1894–1907. In the middle, his portrait is used by the French magazine chain
Felix Potin, in a collection issued 1898–1908. The right card is from the Portuguese
soap firm Claus & Schweder's series *Clebridades* (Peter Larsen: *Ibsen og fotografene.*
1800-tallets visuelle kultur, Oslo: Universitetsforlaget, 2013, 147–50). In Germany, *Der
Zeitgeist* commented on Ibsen's celebrity status and the commercial uses of him already
in 1891: 'Ibsen, Ibsen überall! / Da geht nichts mehr drüber! / Auf dem ganzen
Erdenball / Herrscht das Ibsen-Fieber! / Alle Welt wird Ibsen-toll, / Wenn auch wider
Willen, / denn die ganze Luft ist voll / Ibsen-Ruhm-Bacillen! /Keine Rettung! Überall
/ Kunden Ibsens Namen, / Preisend mit Posaunenschall, / Moden und Reclamen. /
Auf Cigarren, Damenschmuck, / Torten, Miedern, Schlipsen, / Prangt das Wort in
gold'nem Druck: / Ibsen! A la Ibsen!' (quoted in Mentz Schulerud: *Ibsen-bilder*, Oslo:
Gyldendal, 1978, 121).

l'influence récente des littératures du nord', attacking George Eliot, Tolstoy,
Gerhart Hauptmann and particularly the Scandinavians: Ibsen, Bjørnson and
Strindberg. There was nothing new about these authors, he now asserted even
more strongly, they had taken all their ideas from France. Reducing Ibsen to a
few main notions related to the value of love and truth, he declared that
Ibsen's ideas, 'tout entier', were taken from Dumas *fils*.[22] The death of Dumas

[22] Shepherd-Barr, *Ibsen and Early*, 163–64.

that same year became an occasion for hailing a return to the national literary heritage. By the end of 1897, *John Gabriel Borkman* at Théâtre de l'Oeuvre was again well received, but a month later the success of Édmond Rostand's *Cyrano de Bergerac* reinvigorated cultural nationalism.[23]

After the turn of the century and until the World War I Ibsen continued to stay in the same circuit, mostly through Lugné-Poë, while Théâtre Antoine also picked him up again. Overall, only twelve productions are registered in this period. Theatre scholars have characterised the state of French theatre in the first two decades of the century as 'an almost unparalleled low point' and without any native playwright comparable to Ibsen, Strindberg or Chekov.[24] A renewal came only after the war, when Lugné-Poë, who long ago had abandoned his 'symbolist' style, also experienced a belated success with Ibsen. The decade 1919–1929 saw a veritable resurrection of Ibsen plays and now Ibsen had become a playwright Lugné-Poë put on when he needed money. In 1921, Ibsen was also finally accepted at Comédie Française with a production of *An Enemy of the People*.[25]

The 'national' opposition to 'foreign' literature took such hold in the course of the 1890s that the literary avant-garde was completely marginalised.[26] While the poet Stephane Mallarmé payed unqualified tribute, Zola's attitude shifted with the political currents. When Georg Brandes went on the counterattack in 1897, claiming that Ibsen owed nothing to supposedly French models and that French critics were ignorant of foreign literature, Zola sided with Lemaître's opinion that the French had nothing new to learn from Bjørnson, Ibsen and Tolstoy.[27] The Dreyfus affair changed his view once more. In 1898, after Zola's 'J'Accuse' article, *Un Ennemi du Peuple* was staged as a manifestation of the artistic community's support.[28]

Book incomes from France remained insignificant. This seems to reflect small print runs and low sales, supporting Lange's verdict some of the way. In France, there was nothing comparable either to Fischer and Heinemann or to Reclam and Scott. Ibsen's first book publisher, Albert Savine, had a highly eclectic profile,[29] and to some extent Ibsen moved 'upwards' in the course of the decade. *La Nouvelle Revue* published *The Master Builder*,

[23] Nyholm, 'Ibsen paa den franske', 69–72.   [24] See Shepherd-Barr, 'Ibsen in France', 68.
[25] Templeton, 'Antoine versus Lugné-Poe', 81. Shepherd-Barr, on the other hand, questions whether there ever was a 'breakthrough' for Ibsen in France, depicting a 'decline' in the middle decades of the century, 1930s–1970s, and a 'renewal' only in 1981 with a much acclaimed *Peer Gynt* production and a later 'spate of new translations', 'Ibsen in France', 71–3.
[26] Wilfert-Portal, 'Une Nouvelle', 588–90.   [27] Shepherd-Barr, 'Ibsen in France', 61.
[28] Shepherd-Barr, *Ibsen and Early*, 164–65.
[29] René Pierre Colin, 'Un éditeur naturaliste. Albert Savine (1859–1927)', *Les Cahiers naturalistes*, vol. 46, no. 74, 2000, 263–70. On Savin's Ibsen publications, see Fulsås, *Biografisk*.

under the title *Halvard Solness*, and *Le Petit Eyolf*, while *John Gabriel Borkman* and *Quand Nous Nous Réveillerons d'Entre les Morts* were published by *La Revue de Paris*. *La Nouvelle Revue* was founded in the 1880s by people connected to Leon Gambetta and with close ties to the '*grande presse*' and the political field. *La Revue de Paris* aimed at an intellectual, 'elite' audience and André Gide as well as Marcel Proust would offer their manuscripts there.[30] It took a moderate, mildly 'dreyfusard' position in the Dreyfus affair and aimed at reconciling the opposing poles. Both journals belonged to the 'cosmopolitan' side of the literary opposition; not to the avant-garde, but to those favouring literary import to the extent that it served to reconsider the centrality of French literature.[31]

A complete works programme was carried out also in France, albeit belatedly compared to the German and English undertakings. A translation programme was commenced by P.G. la Chesnais in 1914. The war interrupted the progress, and it was completed only in 1930.[32] In republican France, Ibsen was long perceived as morally suspect for the general public. The Republic operated a state controlled supervision of popular reading, and Ibsen was not among authors considered suitable for French public libraries. The Commission des bibliothèques populaires, which was set up by the government in 1882 to recommend books for the new popular lending libraries, put on their not-recommended list authors and titles from Herodotus and Macchiavelli's *Le Prince* to Ibsen, Zola, Oscar Wilde and Thomas Hardy. In 1893, even a book on Norwegian theatre was found not recommendable.[33] In Scandinavia, similar efforts usually took the form of lists of recommended reading.

Britain: Classic Literature, Independent Theatre

As we have seen, Ibsen's existence in English was characterised by a still prevailing theatre-literature divide. In 1901, *The Academy* would take the dichotomous existence of Ibsen in Britain as a given. With a new and revised edition of Walter Scott's *Ibsen's Prose Dramas* as its starting point,

---

[30] Jean-Yves Mollier, 'La revue dans le système éditorial', in Jacqueline Pluet-Despatin, Michel Leymarie & Jean-Yves Mollier (eds.), *La Belle Époque des revues 1880–1914* (Paris: Éditions de L'Imec, 2002), 45; Thomas Loué, 'Un modèle matriciel: les revues de culture générale', ibid. 62.

[31] We are grateful to Blaise Wilfert-Portal for sharing his expertise on French literary journals.

[32] Shepherd-Barr, 'Ibsen in France', 58

[33] Martyn Lyons, *Le Triomphe du livre* (Paris: Promodis, 1987), 182–83. We thank the author for this reference.

the journal noted that 'Ibsen is the supreme pariah of the English stage, while by English bookmen he is honored beyond any other living dramatist, native or foreign.'[34] Around the same time, *The Speaker* noted that 'Ibsen may not be a popular classic, or an uncontested classic; but a classic he undoubtedly is.'[35] The critic thought there had been a change in the attitude of translators, from treating Ibsen as 'a very brilliant contemporary playwright' to treating him 'with the reverence due to a classic'.

Heinemann and Archer was not far behind Scandinavia and Germany, although they waited to the year of Ibsen's death before launching their *Collected Works* in twelve volumes, appearing as it did between 1906 and 1912. Archer was general editor, also translating most of the plays as well as providing introductions to the various volumes. Such an unusual venture, a contemporary foreign playwright's collected works in English, and even containing a critical apparatus, was rare and represented a monumental affirmation of Ibsen's English-language canonisation. Ibsen's works, Archer stated in his 'General Preface', 'have taken a practically uncontested place in world-literature', and he went on to describe the sensation of waiting for each new Ibsen play.[36] His Ibsen was not, the translator and editor added, 'the man of ideas or doctrines', but 'Ibsen the pure poet, the creator of men and women, the searcher of hearts, the weaver of strange webs of destiny.' The edition included a volume called *From Ibsen's Workshop*, containing 'notes, scenarios, and drafts of the modern plays'.[37] *The Academy*, formerly sceptical of Ibsen, welcomed the books with the observation that England now would have 'what Scandinavia and Germany have had for some time', and went on to compare Ibsen with Shakespeare as a 'pure dramatist', and in his complexity, his need to be expounded upon.[38] In another assessment, it added that Ibsen was no preacher, but a poet of the subtle and unspoken, the 'first' and 'supreme example' of someone 'making great tragic stuff out of the minute study of common life'.[39] Heinemann's *Collected Works* became the standard edition

---

[34] [Anon.], 'Ibsen in England', *The Academy*, vol. 60, 23 March 1901, 244.

[35] 'The Revised Translation of Ibsen', *The Speaker*, 20 April 1901, 59.

[36] W. Archer, 'General Preface', in *The Collected Works of Henrik Ibsen* (London: W. Heinemann, 1908), vol. 1, xi, xiv–xv.

[37] Ibsen, *From Ibsen's Workshop*, trans. A.G. Chater and ed. William Archer (London: Heinemann, 1912), vol. 12.

[38] [Anon.], 'Great in Little', *The Academy*, 23 March 1907, 289. It would have taken time for this investment to repay itself in economic terms. A draft letter from H.L. Brækstad to the Norwegian writer Hans E. Kinck quotes Heinemann as saying that he still has not recovered expenses for his Ibsen and Bjørnson editions, 19 March 1911, NLN, H.L. Brækstad Collection, Letter coll. 17, Ms. 4° 3017.

[39] [Anon.], 'Ibsen', *The Academy*, 21 March 1908, 577–78.

until James W. McFarlane's Oxford edition of Ibsen, published in eight volumes between 1960 and 1977.

Among the central institutional contexts for Ibsen's canonisation in the English-speaking world were, apart from the early publication of his collected works, the institutionalisation of modern drama and theatre studies within universities, and the numerous anthologies of 'great books', 'world's great masterpieces', and the like. These anthologies proliferated with the educational expansion in the decades following Ibsen's death, not least in the United States. Ibsen came to be represented in most 'world literature' anthologies and in similar drama editions he became a major editorial principle, a figure who represented a before and after. Introducing the collection *World Drama*, the editor Barrett H. Clark wrote in 1933 that its two volumes were the first in English to offer a panoramic view from the earliest epoch of documented dramatic achievement to 'the beginning of the contemporary drama – which means the first of the modern plays of Ibsen. The modern period, from Ibsen to the present day, is well covered by fifty other collections.'[40] Forty years later Myron Matlaw made similar introductory observations in *Modern World Drama: An Encyclopedia*. It was impossible to designate any one particular date for the precise beginning of the 'modern period', Matlaw stated: 'Nonetheless, Henrik Ibsen (1828–1906), though he wrote all his plays in the nineteenth century, is universally regarded as the father of modern drama.'[41]

In the theatre, the situation was very different around the turn of the century. The introduction of Ibsen in Britain was not just a matter of his being picked up by 'the independent theatre movement' – as it was, to some extent, in France; the appropriation of Ibsen was rather an integral and key element in the emergence of an 'independent', non-commercial theatre. In spite of the sensation and even artistic success of some of the early productions, Ibsen productions throughout the 1890s remained few and generally for a select audience.[42] As many as eight of the eleven Ibsen plays produced in London in the 1880s and '90s, exempting revivals, were independent matinee performances. This format in itself contributed in creating a 'new audience-constituency'.[43] It was available to and partly

---

[40] Barrett H. Clark (ed.), *World Drama* (New York: Dover, 1933), v.

[41] Myron Matlaw (ed.), *Modern World Drama* (London: Secker & Warburg, 1972), vii.

[42] Of the ten Ibsen plays given first productions on a London stage between 1889 and 1899, Archer provided translations for nine. In seven of these ten productions he supervised daily rehearsals. Including revivals, there were twenty-four Ibsen productions in these years, twenty-two of which were based on Archer's translations, see Thomas Postlewait, *Prophet of the New Drama* (London: Greenwood P., 1986), 14.

[43] Marshall, *Actresses*, 147.

dominated by women.[44] Ibsen on the whole seems to have attracted a very select middle-class theatre audience, 'leisured ladies' and 'matinee girls', as the critics would have it, and in his case strengthened by a socialist, feminist and artistic contingent.[45] A conspicuous new feature of this audience, often commented upon by conservative critics, was the serious-ness with which it treated Ibsen's drama and the fact that it was a literary audience often familiar with the play from reading: 'Many sat, book in hand, and all were serious and sober-minded'.[46]

The Independent Theatre followed up its *Ghosts* production with an acclaimed production of *The Wild Duck* in 1894, but its most dynamic period was soon over. In 1897, Elizabeth Robins founded The New Century Theatre, in association with William Archer, opening with *John Gabriel Borkman*. It ended up as a relatively short-lived experiment, however, and there was to be no production between 1899 and 1904. A somewhat more successful initiative came when The Stage Society was founded in 1899, within a six-year period producing *The League of Youth*, *Pillars of the Community*, *The Lady from the Sea*, *When We Dead Awaken* and *Lady Inger of Østråt*.[47] Very much a 'minority theatre',[48] The Stage Society proved important for the arrival of the new drama on the com-mercial stage through the Vedrenne-Barker management at the Court Theatre in 1904–1907. Both *The Wild Duck* and *Hedda Gabler* were performed during these seasons, the latter more successfully than the first. According to the historian of this theatre, Desmond MacCarthy, Ibsen was 'far from being a draw'.[49] In the next line of developments, a number of those actors and actresses involved in the experiments at the Court moved to the repertory companies that were beginning to be established in various cities. First was Annie Horniman's company in Manchester, followed by the Scottish Repertory Theatre in Glasgow (1909), the Liverpool Reper-tory Company (1910), and similar companies in Sheffield, Bristol and Birmingham. The repertory theatre replaced the customary metropolitan

[44] Susan Torrey Barstow, '"Hedda Is All of Us"', *Victorian Studies*, vol. 43, no. 3 (Spring 2001), 388; F.C. Burnand, 'Some Acting and Much Talking', *Punch*, 13 December 1905, 422.

[45] Tracy C. Davis, 'Ibsen's Victorian Audience', *Essays in Theatre*, vol. 4 (1985), 25; Barstow, '"Hedda Is All"', 391; There are a few exceptions to such descriptions of the social make-up of Ibsen's audiences, such as the *Pall Mall Gazette*'s report from the pit at the Novelty some time into the run of *A Doll's House*: 'A mixed lot of people they were, some poor and common enough', *Pall Mall Gazette*, 19 July 1889, 2.

[46] [Anon.], 'An Ibsen Service', *Daily News*, 24 February 1891, in Egan, *Ibsen*, 165.

[47] *The Incorporated Stage Society* (London: Chiswick P., 1909); Woodfield, *English*, 55–73; Anna Miller, *The Independent Theatre in Europe 1887 to the Present* (New York: Blom, 1966), 176–86.

[48] John Palmer, *The Future of the Theatre* (London: Bell, 1913), 40.

[49] Desmond MacCarthy, *The Court Theatre 1904–1907* (London: Bullen, 1907), xiii.

exports and the touring companies, and came to play 'a vital – often a dominant – role in the British twentieth-century theatre'.[50] All had Ibsen as a part of their early repertoire.

In quite a different vein, Herbert Beerbohm Tree's production of *An Enemy of the People* at the Haymarket in 1893 has been seen as something of a turning point: For the first time a leading stage-manager had chosen to take Ibsen on, and to risk a run in the commercial theatre, reaching 'the most demographically conventional of Ibsen audiences'.[51] This kind of 'popular test' had been Clement Scott and other conservative critics' challenge to the 'Ibsenites' from early on. After an initial matinee, *An Enemy of the People* replaced Oscar Wilde's *A Woman of No Importance* on the evenings of 20–22 July 1893. This production, although it soon seems to have struggled in attracting an audience, and finally to have incurred financial losses, was one of the Ibsen productions seen by the largest number of people. The claim that *An Enemy of the People* led to Ibsen being accepted 'within the official circle of London managers', is exaggerated, however.[52] No other West End manager followed Beerbohm Tree's lead. In 1894 Sir Edward Russell would still claim that 'Ibsen has against him almost the whole theatrical profession', noting that Ibsenites such as Achurch, Charrington, Robins, Lea and Waring were in a minority.[53]

The question is also which Ibsen this was. The promptbook of Tree's *An Enemy of the People* shows extensive cuts all through the play. Some of the language has been revised in order to create greater fluency, and a number of establishing clues have been cut. Culturally foreign traits, such as Aslaksen's reference to himself as a temperance man, have also been removed. Such interventions are in line with what one would expect from a production on Tree's stage. More interesting, however, is the fact that a large number of cuts have been made that seem to work towards minimising the controversial moral, and, more importantly, political, elements of the play. Dr Stockmann's extreme 'political' statements are systematically toned down.[54] The protagonist's authoritarianism and antidemocratic sentiments are hardest hit: the line in Act I about men forming judgements 'like the blindest moles', Aslaksen's description of himself as a journalist of

[50] George Rowell & Anthony Jackson, *The Repertory Movement* (Cambridge: Cambridge University Press, 1984), 1.
[51] Davis, 'Ibsen's Victorian', 33.
[52] See *Black and White*, 24 June 1893, and Chothia, *English*, 46–7.
[53] Sir Edward Russell, *Ibsen* (Liverpool: Edward Howell; London: Simpkin, Marshall & Co., 1894), 5.
[54] The cuts related to moral and social issues are relatively few compared with the political ones, see VAM, 'Ibsen – Prompt Copies', William Archer Collection GB71 THM/368/3.

'democratic tendencies' in Act II, Stockmann's reference to 'the whole democracy arrayed as one triumphant host' in Act III, the warning against the Messenger making the 'masses' think they are 'the true pith of the people' in Act IV, and, in Act V, lines such as Stockmann's claim that half the population is 'stark mad', the other 'hounds who haven't any reason to lose', and that 'the Liberals are the worst foes of free men' have all been excised. The line towards the end of Act III, on the contrary, 'Nonsense, Katrine, – you go home and look after your house, and let me take care of society,' may possibly have been cut because it was so difficult to reconcile with a progressive, feminist Ibsen.

All in all, the great number of cuts and minor revisions add up to a transformation of the play. In addition to excising controversial material, and inevitably a number of lines which had helped create the play's ironic effects, the reviews from the performances reveal that Tree inserted much comic business. One might speculate as to what extent the cuts of Stockmann's most antidemocratic and antiliberal sentiments were made in order to avoid insult, or to make the star role of the great actor-manager, who dressed up as an Ibsen look-alike, more sympathetic.

Tree's *An Enemy of the People* received its fair share of criticism from Ibsenites. Archer, for one, criticised many aspects of the acting, not least Tree's own, the unsatisfactory level of rehearsal, and, most damnably from his perspective, perhaps, that 'it was a monstrously mutilated text'.[55] Harley Granville Barker later recalled how Tree had '"clowned" the production outrageously', while other critics enjoyed his irreverent approach.[56] This was a new Ibsen, an exception to the perceived humourless creation of many a serious production, and one which Tree revived on a number of occasions over the next sixteen years.[57]

The idea that *An Enemy of the People* was a Victorian success, needs some qualification, then.[58] From textual evidence we can ascertain that it was not a faithfully translated *Enemy* that experienced some success with the average Victorian audience, it was an *Enemy* strongly adapted to accommodate to the metropolitan aesthetic, political and moral norms.

[55] Gretchen Ackerman, *Ibsen and the English Stage, 1889–1903* (New York: Garland, 1987), 304.
[56] H.G. Barker, 'The Coming of Ibsen', in *The Eighteen-Eighties*, ed. Walter de la Mare (Cambridge: Cambridge University Press, 1930), 159–95 (183 n).
[57] Tree seems very much to have enjoyed the part of Stockmann, but according to Maud Tree the play was 'always played to a loss', see Gretchen Paulus, 'Beerbohm Tree and "The New Drama"', *University of Toronto Quarterly*, vol. 27 (1957), 103–15.
[58] Moretti, *Bourgeois*, 175.

Ibsen and a British National Theatre

The strong affiliation between Ibsen and 'independent' and 'minority' theatre was a source of some trouble for British campaigners wanting to found a national theatre. One of these campaigns was the Irish one, also involving Horniman for a while and leading to the establishment of the Abbey Theatre in 1903. When W.B. Yeats in 1897, together with Lady Gregory and Edward Martyn, tried to raise money for the regular performance of Celtic and Irish plays, he alluded to the London Independent Theatre's opposition to the Lord Chamberlain's Office: this new theatrical enterprise aimed for 'that freedom to experiment that is not found in theatres of England'.[59] In 1899 this led to the production of Martyn's *The Heather Field* and Yeats's *The Countess Cathleen*, with Florence Farr over from London in the title role. The theatre's journal *Beltaine* began publication in the same year, and the Irish Ibsen pioneer George Moore joined the pioneers in Ireland.

'Independence' in Ireland, in other words, also acquired national connotations which implicated Ibsen in new and conflicting ways. In spite of the largely different artistic aims of the new Celtic drama and the Ibsen drama, there were perceived connections between the Norwegian and the Irish theatre movements, connections not made in London. These were related both to Ibsen's standing as a major writer from the periphery and to the position of the theatre in his country of origin. Two of the central contributors to the formation of Dublin's Abbey Theatre, the brothers William G. Fay and Frank J. Fay, were among those stimulated by the Norwegian example, by Ibsen and Bjørnson, by 'Ole Bull's Norwegian Theatre' in Bergen, as communicated to them by William Archer, by the status of the Norwegian language, and by the very idea of a National Theatre.[60] In his agitation for an Irish national theatre, Frank J. Fay criticised Yeats for being too much of a theorist, for not following 'the guidance of Shakespeare, Molière, and Ibsen, who were practical men first and poets after'.[61] Ibsen was seen as the product of Norway's first National Theatre, and something similar was needed in order to 'get rid of the English commercial theatre'.

But a purely 'national' Ibsen was by this time no longer available; Yeats had to relate to an Ibsen who had also become a 'realist' and 'naturalist'.

---

[59] Quoted in Lady Gregory, *Our Irish Theatre* [1913] (London: Putnam, 1914), 8–9.
[60] Robert Hogan (ed.), *Towards a National Theatre* (Dublin: Dolmen P., 1970), 10.
[61] Frank J. Fay, 'Mr. Yeats and the Stage', in ibid. 51–52; see also Fay, 'An Irish National Theatre – II', ibid. 60–65.

The Irish poet sympathised with the English reformers, but he felt that their setbacks were due to the centrality of Ibsen and the naturalists within their movement.[62] His scepticism towards Ibsen and what he perceived as his scientific, realist and non-poetic method, the 'stale odour of spilt poetry', still meant that he, with the Ibsenites Martyn and Moore, could state that 'Everywhere critics and writers, who wish for something better than the ordinary play of commerce, turn to Norway for an example and an inspiration', as they put it in their famous manifesto published in the first issue of *Beltaine* in 1899.[63] A national theatre movement had now become synonymous with the non-commercial sector, a distinction never upheld in Norway. Yeats on his part distinguished between Ibsen, the participant of a national movement producing dramas 'founded on the heroes and legends of Norway' and the later, cosmopolitan, realist figure, his remarks ranging 'from sincere expressions of admiration to equally sincere articulations of distaste', as Irina Ruppo Malone observes.[64]

Neither did Ibsen fit frictionlessly into William Archer's tireless work for an English national theatre. There was always a tension between his Ibsen agenda and his agenda for a national theatre, and it was never Archer's aim to polarise the world of the theatre. The Ibsen campaign nevertheless had such an effect, and this became a potential problem for his National Theatre programme. He had carefully to negotiate between these two activities.

Archer's aim was to achieve something like the Norwegian national theatre and to revive the native drama to a position like the one it had in Norway with Ibsen and Bjørnson. For this reason, he had always seen Ibsen more as a transitory stage than as a permanent part of the English-language canon. When in 1893 he questioned the possibility of Ibsen ever becoming popular in Britain, he noted that this was neither to be expected nor 'desired': 'for no theatre can for long live healthily on imported material. Each nation should produce its own theatre, its own criticism of its own life'.[65] Ibsen's role was to lift 'the theatre on to a higher intellectual plane', and then to disappear or be 'heard but rarely, upon the English stage'. After another decade translating and editing Ibsen,

---

[62] James W. Flannery, *W.B. Yeats and the Idea of a Theatre* (London: Yale 1976), 138; see also Tore Rem, 'Nationalism or Internationalism?', *Ibsen Studies*, vol. 7, no. 2 (2007), 188–202.

[63] See Jan Setterquist, *Ibsen and the Beginnings of Anglo-Irish Drama* (Uppsala: Lundequistska Bokhandeln, 1951), 9

[64] Irina Ruppo Malone, *Ibsen and the Irish Revival* (London: Palgrave Macmillan, 2010), 27, 39.

[65] W. Archer, 'Mausoleum', 311.

Archer may have ended up revising his own position, but in his negotiations between the foreign and the domestic, his priorities were still clear.

In 1907, Archer published the landmark *A National Theatre: Scheme & Estimates* together with the twenty-six-year-old Harley Granville Barker. *A National Theatre* had been privately printed and circulated as early as in 1904. At that time, Barker informed his readers in his new preface, they had subjected themselves to 'extreme self-denial' and had 'carefully excluded [...] Ibsen, Hauptmann, d'Annunzio, Shaw' and others from the repertory list.[66] The idea of autonomy was not to be associated solely with 'advanced theatre', but the selling point, and the novelty of the strategy, was to connect this particular autonomy with the national and a national heritage.[67] Shakespeare and his 'great epic of English history' would play a central part, while the repertoire would represent a mix of native and foreign plays, classical and modern. In an outright denial of the kind of drama which had accentuated the need for an endowed theatre, although not necessarily a national one, the two authors referred to their choice of excluding 'all plays of the class which may be called disputable'; The National Theatre should not be misconstrued as being a 'forcing-house for the esoteric drama'.[68]

The process proved a slow one, partly perhaps because the establishment of repertory companies and numerous societies had already created very different conditions from those of the 1890s. Not until 1961 was the Royal Shakespeare Company given state endowment and in 1964 the National Theatre appeared at the Old Vic. The National was not given a more permanent home until the building on the South Bank was finished in 1976.

The Effectiveness of Censorship

Why were Ibsen's plays for so long contained within the independent sector? Why did they meet such difficulties in the commercial theatre? Answering these questions, we need to reconsider how effective hostile criticism, parodies and censorship actually were.

It is orthodoxy in studies of censorship that the victim always wins, both morally and in terms of the symbolic capital accrued.[69] But British plays of

---

[66] William Archer & Harley Granville Barker, *A National Theatre* (London: Duckworth, 1907), x, xi.
[67] Ibid. 36–7.   [68] Ibid. 44–5.
[69] For example, Jonathan Dollimore, *Sex, Literature and Censorship* (Cambridge: Polity P., 2001), 95; J.M. Coetzee, *Giving Offense* (Chicago: Chicago University Press, 1996), 43.

the nineteenth century which were not granted a licence would, as we have noted, as a rule simply disappear since they did not exist as book. In Strindberg's case, the censorship of his most famous play, *Miss Julie*, meant that it took decades before he really became noticed as an acted and produced playwright in Britain. It is hard to see that this instance of censorship led to a greater attention being paid to the Swedish playwright, or to his works achieving a higher esteem.

Victorian theatre censorship helped endow the new, literary drama with a form of power, partly due to its mere existence and, more particularly, through the fact that it took it and its potential effects on the audience so seriously. But in this way censorship also had intended stifling effects. The Independent Theatre's manifesto proclaimed that it was formed expressly to produce unlicenced plays, to free the stage from the 'shackles of the censor'. But in spite of its initial provocation with *Ghosts*, it was in fact never to produce another play that did not have the Lord Chamberlain's approval.[70] Comments in the press before the performance of *Ghosts*, nervousness among theatre managers, and the lobbying of the Lord Chamberlain's Office, may explain why this loophole was never again utilised. Seeing how efficiently the censorship, with the co-operation of the theatre managers, managed to avoid a repetition, it is doubtful whether the case of *Ghosts* was quite the clear victory of progressive forces that it has seemed with the benefit of hindsight. In the aftermath of the scandal, the reception of other writers was also affected.[71] The Independent Theatre was soon criticised for doing too little for the native drama and chose to focus its energy in this direction rather than in opposing the censorship.

Why were the other Ibsen plays not refused a licence? Nearly a quarter of a century after the success of *A Doll's House* at the Novelty Theatre, John Palmer opined that 'a competent censor would never have licensed *A Doll's House*', this 'invitation to ninety-nine Englishwomen out of a hundred to abandon the beds and boards of their husbands'.[72] The Lord Chamberlain had never, Palmer continued, 'been able to forget how, in a fit of absent-mindedness, his clerk allowed *A Doll's House* to slip through and corrupt the English theatre into rebellion and contempt'.

The licence given to *A Doll's House* in 1889 most probably constituted an oversight, a wrong estimation of the impact that the play would have.

---

[70] 28 more plays were produced between 1891 and 1897, see Stephens, *Censorship*, 143.
[71] See, e.g., J.T. Grein, Letter to August Strindberg, 18 January 1893 and 6 February 1893, NLS, August Strindberg Collection, Ep. S. 53b.
[72] Palmer, *Future*, 100–2.

Once *A Doll's House* had been passed, it was difficult not to license anything but that which clearly went further in its provocations against Victorian morality and values, such as *Ghosts*. In the parliamentary hearing on the theatre censorship in 1892, Edward Pigott gave a rather surprising explanation why the other plays had passed. He claimed to have studied 'Ibsen's plays pretty carefully', and concluded that 'all the characters' in his plays

> appear to me morally deranged. All the heroines are dissatisfied spinsters who look on marriage as a monopoly, or dissatisfied married women in a chronic state of rebellion against not only the conditions which nature has imposed on their sex, but against all the duties and obligations of mothers and wives; and as for the men they are all rascals or imbeciles.[73]

But for these reasons, censorship was superfluous, Pigott concluded. Firstly, none of Ibsen's plays were profitable, and secondly, they were 'too absurd altogether' to be injurious to public morals.[74] Thus turning all the conservative reasons for censoring Ibsen on their head, Pigott was probably rationalising his decision in retrospect. If Ibsen's other plays were given a licence, they were still considered borderline cases, and exposed to deeply suspicious readings even when they were passed. After the debates around *Ghosts*, however, the Lord Chamberlain would carefully have to consider the cost of any unwanted attention provoked by the withholding of a licence. *Ghosts* was finally licensed in 1914, twenty years after Germany had given up withholding it from public performance. When the British licence was given, it was still a highly contested issue.[75]

Censorship, massive hostile criticism and parody had very clear effects across the independent/commercial divide. The most revealing evidence of these effects, and of the challenges faced when introducing Ibsen to an average English audience, can be found in the archives of The Lord Chamberlain and in extant promptbooks. A number of Ibsen plays were affected directly by the censoring of parts of the dialogue, or by voluntary cuts made in communication with the censor. A well-known example is the cut of the allusions to Hedda's pregnancy in the Lea/Robins production of *Hedda Gabler* in 1891.[76] Due to the state of the records in the Lord Chamberlain's archive before 1901, it is not known whether this was on

---

[73] *Report from the Select Committee on Theatres and Places of Entertainment* (London: Eyre and Spottiswoode, 1892), 330.
[74] Ibid.   [75] See *Ghosts*, BL, Lord Chamberlain's Correspondence, 1914/2853.
[76] See, e.g., Joanne E. Gates, 'The Theatrical Politics of Elizabeth Robins and Bernard Shaw', *Shaw*, vol. 14 (1994), 43–53.

the censor's prompting, however. In the submitted copy of *Little Eyolf*, the blue pencil has marked out Rita's reference to her 'rights' and her refusal of motherhood,[77] in addition to the entire description of the reason for Eyolf's injury, the lovers forgetting the child in the act of love-making.[78]

As we have noted, *Hedda Gabler* was a relative commercial success in British Ibsen terms, but this may be put in perspective with reference to a production which opened at Toole's Theatre on the day it closed. The young J.M. Barrie's burlesque *Ibsen's Ghosts, or Toole Up to Date*, was a mixture of a number of Ibsen plays, with parodies of the stage set, of Robins's Hedda, and it drew on the recent feud between Archer and Gosse over the translation, with the comic actor-manager J.L. Toole dressed up as Ibsen.[79] The production ran for thirty-seven performances, longer than any of the serious efforts on Ibsen's behalf.

The successful, if for some critics obscure, production of *Rosmersholm* was guided by similar principles as the production of *Hedda Gabler*, but this also involved significant alterations to Ibsen's text. The surviving promptbook of *Rosmersholm* is based on Charles Archer's translation for the Walter Scott edition of 1891, and seems to have been used for the first production of that play in the same year. This was one of the many productions in which William Archer was closely involved, and it is likely that he would have approved of the adjustments, perhaps even that he was responsible for many of them.[80] The most significant of the many changes may be catalogued under a few not always clearly distinguishable categories, such as morality, religion, heredity, dramaturgy, and, most frequently, the potentially comic.

The more directly moral concerns are expressed in minor cuts such as Rosmer's statement in Act II about how he and Rebecca 'have no concealments from each other on any subject whatever', and Kroll's possibly ambiguous statement in Act III about Rebecca's mother: 'Your mother's business must have brought her into continual contact with the parish doctor'. The parts of the dialogue that might hint towards a form of incestuous relationship between Rebecca and her foster-father have all

---

[77] *Little Eyolf*, BL, Lord Chamberlain's Correspondence, 1896/719.

[78] Whether this meant that others within the censor's office were asked to pay attention to the passages, or whether the management were explicitly told to cut them, is not known.

[79] See Chothia, *English*, 26.

[80] *Rosmersholm* (Walter Scott edition of 1891, bound with *An Enemy of the People*), VAM, William Archer Collection, GB 71 THM/368/3; It seems likely that this promptbook has been used for one of the first revivals of *Rosmersholm*, and that a number of the cuts were motivated by the audience response during the play's first staging.

been removed. Such cuts also affect comments thought to border on the blasphemous, such as those related to Rosmer's loss of faith. His confession to Kroll in Act II, 'Then I openly confess my apostacy', has been changed to 'change of view', and Kroll's reference to Rosmer 'confessing himself an apostate' in Act III has been completely excised.

Rosmersholm seems to have been particularly prone to induce laughter in the audience, and it provided fertile material for parodists, being the first play subjected to Guthrie's parodies in *Punch*. Here, much fun was had from the indirectness of the dialogue and the symbolism of the white horses, while Ibsen's mention of the absence of humour was a gift: in *Punch's* version, Rebecca gravely asseverates that 'nobody makes fun at Rosmersholm. Mr. Rosmer would not understand it', with Kroll confirming that jokes are prohibited in these parts.[81] The favourite target of the several parodies of this play, heredity, is consistently shied away from in the stage version of *Rosmersholm*, with mentions of 'hereditary' crossed out in the promptbook. This also goes for lines such as Madame Helseth's 'It runs in the family', Rebecca's references to Rosmer's 'ancestry', and Kroll's belief that 'your whole conduct is determined by your origin' in Act III.[82] In addition to these cuts, some minor revisions have to do with the bookishness of the translation, avoiding ambiguity and making some lines more fluent.

The fear of involuntary comic effect is, however, perhaps the most surprising, and the most interesting, motivation for changing the printed translation for the stage. Lines such as 'How can you sit and joke about such things?' and 'all this strikes me as ludicrous in the extreme' have been cut from Act I for obvious reasons. Other features which had to be removed for fear of the same audience reactions include references to things obscure or incomprehensible, such as Rosmer's 'It is the most incomprehensible thing in the world' in Act II, his 'I don't understand a word of this' and 'speak so that I can understand you' in Act IV. Some of the dialogue towards the very end of the play, after Rosmer and Rebecca have made the decision to end their own lives, has also been cut, perhaps because it was thought so mystical and abstract as to create comic effect. Ibsen on stage was, in this case, also protected from the easiest of attacks on another of his perceived qualities, morbidity, such as in the cutting of Act II's 'But it may become dangerous this eternal dwelling upon one

---

[81] T. A. Guthrie, *Punch's Pocket Ibsen* (London: Heinemann, 1893), 4–5.
[82] The uninitiated in the audiences of *A Doll's House* at the Novelty had found a number of comival moments, such as Rank's admission of inherited disease, see Davis, 'Ibsen's Victorian', 30.

miserable subject'. The playwright's descriptions of a humourless family were, finally, too close to antagonistic depictions of the Ibsenites to be preserved in production. The following dialogue in Act III provides a succinct example: 'Rebecca. To you, who can never laugh? R. Yes, in spite of that.'

The hostile criticism and the many parodies and burlesques clearly had an impact, then, on the activities and mediations of the Ibsenites. The strong polarisation of the theatre world encouraged a greater autonomy in the attitude towards the Ibsen drama, but some of the criticism was nevertheless taken up by Ibsen's champions.

In spite of Ibsen's gradual accommodation into the canon, such reactions lasted for a number of years, and they seem to have been brought to a head with Ibsen's puzzling move into a form of symbolism. The *Daily Telegraph* typically asked about the Independent Theatre's production of *The Wild Duck*: 'Why was it that an outburst of irreverent laughter unduly disturbed the reverential attitude of the Ibsenites?' and continued mockingly: 'No one was able to decide whether *The Wild Duck* is the very funniest play ever written, or a desperately serious problem. Has Ibsen any sense of humour at all, or is he the funniest fellow who ever put pen to paper?'[83] Archer chose to confront the *Daily Telegraph's* description head on: 'Of all the amazing delusions that ever entered mortal brain', he began, 'the most astounding, surely, is the idea that Ibsen has no humour, and that, when he writes a comic speech or scene, he does not intend it to be laughed at'.[84] He went on to argue his case in some detail, drawing attention to some of the obviously intentional comic touches in the play (Figure 8.2).

The reason why the British public at times laughed in the wrong places during Ibsen performances, Archer argued, was English provincialism, meaning a failure to 'distinguish the unaccustomed from the ludicrous', thus finding Norwegian manners comic.[85] In addition to this, there were beautiful and touching Ibsen moments that tended to trigger a vulgarity in the public, and Archer offered the scene with Mrs. Solness and her dolls in *The Master Builder* as an example. In spite of this admission, he went on

---

[83] Quoted in W. Archer, 'The Humour of "The Wild Duck"', in *The Theatrical 'World' of 1897* (London: Scott, 1898), 148. One press cutting in Archer's private collection notes of the premiere of *The Wild Duck* that the audience 'roared with laughter at the scenes intended to be serious, and they yawned ominously at the master's ponderous and heavy-handed wit', 'Ibsen's "Wild Duck" at the Royalty', 7, in VAM, William Archer Collection, GB 71 THM/368/3, Box 2: Press cuttings. See also Frank Swinnerton, *Swinnerton* (London: Hutchinson, 1937), 71.

[84] Archer, 'Humour', 146.   [85] Ibid. 150–51.

" Put that nasty pigstol down ! "

Figure 8.2   Illustration to 'The Wild Duck', *Mr. Punch's Pocket Ibsen*.
Ibsen's mixture of the comic and the tragic bewildered critics and spectators.

the offensive: 'inopportune laughter is far less to be dreaded at Ibsen performances than the absurd notion so carefully fostered by the Anti-Ibsenite faction that they are solemnities at which it is profanation to smile'. The move was brave, but it concealed the efforts at avoiding such unintended comedy in the theatre, and the destructive impact it might potentially have on the performances.[86]

As late as 1897, in a review of *John Gabriel Borkman*, Shaw discussed this question, in observing that 'the most humorous of Ibsen's work – three-fourths of "The Wild Duck", for instance – still seem to the public as puzzling, humiliating, and disconcerting as a joke always does to people who cannot see it'.[87] He blamed this on the lack of a 'thoroughly

---

[86] One critic noted about the performance of *The Lady from the Sea* that 'the ripple of laughter which was almost continuous during the fourth and fifth acts being evidently very disconcerting to the unfortunate performers', *The Standard*, 12 May 1891, in VAM, William Archer Collection, GB 71 THM/368/3, Box 2: Press cuttings.

[87] Shaw, 'The New Ibsen Play', *Dramatic Opinions and Essays* (London: Constable, 1907), vol. 2, 160.

established intellectual understanding' between Ibsen and the playgoing public. In 1899, Clement Scott nevertheless admitted that he had been part of a campaign to laugh Ibsen 'out of court', but that 'the time came when the laugh was on the other side'.[88]

Since English theatre censorship continued to exist up until 1968, every new production of a new translation of an Ibsen play would have to be approved, thus producing an archive of Ibsen's gradual adoption into the theatre canon. In 1922, in a report on *Peer Gynt*, the advisor noted that the play contained a few crude words in places, but concluded that it would be absurd to interfere with this 'European classic'.[89] 'I would suggest treating this somewhat as one would treat Shakespeare', he added in a postscript, '– parts of which if written today would appear coarse, i.e. treat it as a classic'. Besides, there was the advantage, in terms of the dangers of the play affecting the impressionable, that 'there is not the faintest possibility of its appealing to "popular" audiences'. While canonised, Ibsen, or at the very least *Peer Gynt*, was still considered a minority or elite interest within the theatre censorship.

It took yet some decades before Ibsen's modern prose plays moved into the best generic company. In 1959, Sir St Vincent Troubridge referred to Aristotle's description of the effects of tragedy as purging the soul through pity and terror when considering *Rosmersholm*. Would the Lord Chamberlain be persuaded to visit the performance of this play, he wrote, he would guarantee that 'he would totter away [. . .] a shaken but a greater man'.[90] The following year, in 1960, in a report on *John Gabriel Borkman*, Ibsen was labelled a 'noble tragic poet'.[91] When the reader of a 1965 report called *Ghosts* a 'tragedy with a strong social and ethical theme', the play can safely be said to have come a long way since 1891.[92]

Ibsen's rise to status as classic had a further consequence in the internal dealings of the Lord Chamberlain's Office: By the 1950s and '60s, he had become a standard against which the contemporary drama could be measured. Reporting on a new translation of *Little Eyolf* in 1958, C.D. Heriot concluded:

---

[88] C. Scott, *The Drama of Yesterday & To-day* (London: Macmillan, 1899), vol. 1, x.
[89] *Peer Gynt*, BL, Lord Chamberlain's Correspondence, 1922/4067.
[90] *Rosmersholm*, BL, Lord Chamberlain's Correspondence, 1959/272.
[91] *John Gabriel Borkman*, BL, Lord Chamberlain's Correspondence, 1960/971.
[92] *Ghosts*, BL, Lord Chamberlain's Correspondence, 1965/4897.

This play is the best possible answer to the question of how to discuss insatiable sex, blood-guiltiness, suspected incest, and the psychology of escape without an offensive word and with an optimistic (and a convincingly optimistic) ending. It makes the angry young playwrights of our day seem very ignorant and brittle.[93]

In a 1967 report on *Ghosts*, the same advisor commented that although it created 'a flood of protest' in 1891, quite like Edward Bond's *Saved* in 1968, it 'remains unaffected by time as a classic piece of theatre', quite unlike the latter play.[94] The judgement was pronounced one and a half years after the controversial first performance of Bond's play.

Arthur Miller's adaptation of *An Enemy of the People*, in Miller's version a transparent allegory of America in his own McCarthyite era, posed a particular challenge when it came under consideration in the late 1950s. The censor's reader was clearly in a dilemma about whether to condemn what was seen as a questionably politicised version of the play or simply to hail a classic. Miller has 'more-than-leftist leanings', the report noted, and *An Enemy of the People* was 'a natural choice' for his purposes.[95] But the reader ingeniously found a way out: even Miller could not 'altogether distort the message' of this great work of art. The reading concluded by finding as the very essence of the play a liberal message suitable for a classic: 'The passionate plea for free-speech is valid for both Left and Right.' In 1959, the British Ibsen, in his early reception so often presented as partisan, as a socialist and feminist, as the most topical of contemporary playwrights, had long been above politics.

The Revival of the Literary Drama

Even though Ibsen in the short run did not make it in mainstream British theatre, and even though a national theatre lay far ahead, he did affect the status of the native, literary drama. The translation of Ibsen into English not only coincided with a new growth in British playwriting, it must be seen as a major inspiration for it. In this respect, Britain resembles Germany. In German drama, Gerhard Hauptmann, very much inspired by Ibsen, became the leading representative of a new generation of dramatists. In France, on the contrary, while one of the goals of Antoine had been to reinvigorate the native drama, no national wave followed and

---

[93] *Little Eyolf*, BL, Lord Chamberlain's Correspondence, 1958/698.
[94] *Ghosts*, BL, Lord Chamberlain's Correspondence, 1967/1576.
[95] *An Enemy of the People*, BL, Lord Chamberlain's Correspondence, 1959/1712.

his most important contributions continued to be performances of translated authors.[96] In the 1830s, Alexis de Tocqueville had argued in his
Democracy in America (1835) that democracy would inevitably drive
literature and theatre, reading and performance, apart: 'In democracies
dramatic pieces are listened to, but not read. Most of those who frequent
the amusements of the stage do not go there to seek the pleasures of mind,
but keen emotions of the heart.'[97] Careful construction of plots and an
accuracy of style were not only superfluous, but incompatible with the
overarching goals of stirring the emotions and seeking 'perpetual novelty,
surprise, and rapidity of invention'. Tocqueville was proven right with
respect to the effects of commercialisation. What he did not foresee, was
that cultural nationalism in one of the most democratic corners of Europe
would make it a patriotic duty to contribute to the literary renewal and
elevation of the theatre. This was hard to achieve from within the theatre
institution itself, but it was possible from within a literary culture where
the writing and reading of drama had not gone out of fashion.

After a low point in English dramatic literary production had been
reached in the 1880s, there followed, from the 1890s until the second
decade of the twentieth century, a steady increase in the proportion of
'Poetry and Drama' of the total output of imaginative literature, from
12 per cent in the 1890s to 20 per cent in the 1910s. The growth from the
1890s onwards was also true of 'Poetry and Drama's' overall percentage of
the total output of books, rising from 3 per cent in the 1870s to 6 per cent
in the 1910s. Poetry became a *fin-de-siècle* genre, but the resurrected genre
of the printed play clearly also contributed to this gradual increase.

The change is evident in criticism as well, not only in that the printed
text 'gave rise to a new school of critics', but also in terms of categorisations.[98] By the middle and towards the end of the 1890s, the journals had
begun to print reviews with titles such as 'Plays for Stage and Study' and
'Plays in Print', and the publishers were beginning to advertise printed
plays under headings like 'Modern Plays', 'The Drama', 'Dramatic literature', and 'Important Plays'.[99] Whereas the contemporary printed play had
been a near unfamiliar entity when Walter Scott first published Ibsen in
1888, a decade later it was a publishing category of some significance, with

---

[96] Hemmings, *Theatre Industry*, 246.
[97] *Democracy in America*, trans. Henry Reeve, rev. Francis Bowen and Phillips Bradley (New York: Alfred A. Knopf, 1972), 82.
[98] See Anthony Jenkins, *The Making of Victorian Drama* (Cambridge: Cambridge University Press, 1991), 27.
[99] 'Plays for Stage and Study', *National Observer*, vol. 13, 6 April 1895, 559.

English and foreign plays published in about equal measure. Writing in January 1897, a rather puzzled critic concluded a review by noting that 'publishers for the masses', such as Scott and Newnes, had acquired the habit of publishing plays: 'Does that indicate that the printed play is popular?'[100]

The example of Ibsen showed that the reading of plays could compete with the reading of novels, and, as importantly, not least from the publisher's point of view, he demonstrated that the printing of plays could bring profits. Archibald Henderson, who, like so many who have written on the topic since, generally relies on Shaw's self-presentation as the author who revived dramatic literature in English, nevertheless remarks that Ibsen's example had 'a revolutionary effect upon the economic conditions of the publishing trade'.[101]

On a number of occasions Shaw volunteered his own version of how the British regained the habit of reading plays. When he had first contacted Heinemann with a suggestion that he publish 'my unacted and then-considered-unactable plays', Shaw claimed, the publisher had apparently shown him the ledger account of Pinero's plays, and given him a distinct impression that 'nobody bought plays except people who gave amateur performances of them'.[102] Shaw felt that he could not press the matter:

> I could not undertake to give the public a new habit of play-reading, though I thought that this might be done, and actually did it later on when Grant Richards (then one of Stead's young men) started as publisher, and ventured my *Plays, Pleasant and Unpleasant*, with their novel stage directions, in which the stage was never mentioned or even hinted at, and their prefaces. Their success broke the tradition.[103]

By this time, as Shaw's friend Archer had documented, Ibsen had long since become an unprecedented sales success as book, and Shaw's self-advertisement must be understood as part of his strategic positioning, both for markets and posterity; and it worked. In the *Cambridge Companion to George Bernard Shaw*, Christopher Innes claims that 'Shaw was the first modern dramatist to establish his plays as literature', noting that Shaw

[100] [Anon.], 'Plays in Print', *The Sketch*, vol. 16, 13 January 1897, 492.
[101] Henderson, *Changing*, 222.
[102] Frederic Whyte, *William Heinemann* (London: Cape, 1928), 166. Heinemann in fact showed Shaw the eighteen-pence paper edition published exactly for this purpose, and his disappointment may have been based on this first attempt at publishing an English dramatist.
[103] Ibid. 166–67. According to Archibald Henderson, Shaw would go far in establishing himself as Ibsen's equal: 'What! *I* a follower of Ibsen? My good sir, as far as England is concerned, Ibsen is a follower of mine', *George Bernard Shaw* (London: Hurst & Blackett, 1911), 61–2.

'created the conditions that attracted later authors to write for the theatre'.[104]

Shaw's own correspondence with the publisher of *Plays, Pleasant and Unpleasant* reveals that his idea of his own clear break with 'tradition' is at best overstated, and that it ignores the role played by the translated drama, and more particularly Ibsen's. When the young publisher Grant Richards approached Shaw with the aim of publishing his plays, the latter had initially been sceptical about the viability of the proposal, referring to his information from publishers like Heinemann, Lane and Scott and their experiences with publishing plays by Pinero, Wilde and George Moore. Richards insisted, however, and Shaw was soon volunteering his opinions on the physical appearance of such an edition. In a letter from 21 May 1897, Shaw explained:

> If you have a copy of Walter Scott's volumes of Ibsen's plays you will see how the style of the thing I want works at three plays to the volume. In Scott's edition the block of letterpress is not properly set on the page; but otherwise it is not so bad.[105]

Not only was the format of the book to be taken from the Scott precedent, but the shrewd Irishman even wanted to imitate the book's typography. On this note might be added a comment by Archer in his preface to the first volume of Heinemann's *Collected Works*, in which he explained that he had followed the Norwegian and German practice of using spacing for emphasis. This, he thought, was preferable to the use of italics, which created an ugly effect since they were also used for stage directions. The system, Archer explained, was first introduced in England with the translation of *John Gabriel Borkman*, but it should no longer be unfamiliar to readers, 'since it has been adopted by Mr. Bernard Shaw in his printed plays, and [. . .] by other dramatists'.[106] Shaw consciously modelled himself on Ibsen, then, even down to the finer points of the material appearance of the plays. When Richards and Shaw disagreed about pricing, Shaw insisted on the same price as that which Scott charged for his volumes in

[104] 'Preface', *The Cambridge Companion to George Bernard Shaw*, ed. Christopher Innes (Cambridge: Cambridge University Press, 1998), xvi. This is surprising since the collection contains a more guarded assessment of Shaw's pioneering efforts in this field, see Katherine E. Kelly, 'Imprinting the Stage: Shaw and the Publishing Trade, 1883–1903', ibid. 25–54.

[105] Shaw, Letter to Grant Richards, 21 May 1897, *Collected Letters, 1874–1897*, 767.

[106] W. Archer, 'General Preface', *Collected Works of Henrik Ibsen*, vol.1, xii. This practice obviously confused even experienced readers of the drama. On 3 February 1908, Arthur Wing Pinero wrote to Archer expressing his gratitude for his Ibsen introductions, but 'I've only just now discovered the reason for the "spacing"! I have been all along cursing the printer', BL, William Archer Correspondence, Add. MS. 45,294.

Ibsen's Prose Dramas, 'three & sixpence'.[107] Down to the smallest details of format and pricing, Shaw looked to Scott's *Prose Dramas*, which had begun publication eight years earlier.

In his preface to *Plays Unpleasant*, Shaw admittedly began by noting Ibsen's importance as a point of departure for the new theatre, before referring to the many 'who read with delight all the classic dramatists, from Eschylus to Ibsen' and yet rarely go to the theatre.[108] Ibsen was acknowledged as a popular dramatic writer, while at the same time being placed in the company of the classics. But Shaw's rhetorical strategy opened the field to the new and contemporary drama, represented by himself, and he proceeded by criticising Ibsen for not having put more effort into creating more reader-friendly dramatic texts, an accusation that would have puzzled Scandinavian readers. Shaw's only clear break with Ibsen was, however, in the rejection of the more detached stance of the Norwegian. One of the ways in which this manifested itself was in his long, didactic prefaces. In noting the demands put on the reader by Ibsen's drama, Holbrook Jackson was later to claim that 'intellectuals of all kinds yearned for the prefaces Ibsen might have written but didn't'.[109]

Shaw's response to the challenge of reader-friendliness lay in the extension and elaboration of stage directions, a major feature in the evolution of the so-called Shavian play-novel. The ideal was to do away with any reminders of the theatre and with the 'hideous jargon' that had blemished the old acting editions. In developing his own play-novel, Shaw had expressed surprise at what he saw as Ibsen giving his readers 'very little more than the technical memorandum required by the carpenter, the gasman, and the prompter',[110] but there is much evidence also in the early English-language reception that Ibsen's stage directions, on the contrary, appeared as conspicuously elaborate and literary. When Henderson in 1914 summed up the key developments in modern drama, he noted 'the real innovation achieved by Ibsen, Hauptmann, and the German naturalists' in employing 'the technical methods of fiction in the creation of the new drama', and stressed the fact that 'for the first time in the history of the drama, the stage direction becomes an intrinsic part of the play'.[111] The elaborate stage directions of Shaw and Hauptmann contain a 'wealth of epic detail', Henderson observed, but already from *The League of Youth* onwards Ibsen had never

[107] Shaw, Letter to Grant Richards, 25 September 1897, quoted in Richards, *Author*, 131.
[108] Shaw, *Plays: Pleasant and Unpleasant*, 2 vols. (London: Grant Richards, 1898), vol. 1, xvi.
[109] Holbrook Jackson, 'The Higher Drama', *The Eighteen Nineties* [1913], new edn (Brighton: Harvester P., 1976), 211.
[110] Shaw, *Plays: Pleasant* 1, xxii.   [111] Henderson, *Changing*, 77–8.

used stage jargon and had gradually perfected his stage directions 'from the extremely laconic to the adequately descriptive'.[112]

British critics of the late 1880s and'90s in fact often commented on 'Ibsen's curiously minute stage directions', and their salient novelty is perhaps best captured with reference to the potentially most conservative, and at times most ingenious, of literary critics, the parodists. The *Scots Observer* was among the first to ridicule this feature of Ibsen's books. The parody 'The Ghost of *Ghosts*', printed on 18 October 1890, opened as follows:

> *A spacious garden-room, with one door to the left and two doors to the right. In the centre of the room is another door, with a window rather more in the foreground. A small sofa stands in front of it. In the background are two more doors, the right-hand door leading to the conservatory, from which a door opens into the garden, from which another door opens into the street. Through a window between the first two doors one catches a glimpse of a gloomy tool-shed, from which a door leads into the conservatory. A staircase runs from the third window to the fourteenth door. There are books and periodicals on the staircase, and a piano on the hire system. So now you know exactly what the scene is like.*[113]

The main point of this parody is bluntly made at the end, and it is in line with this particular journal's consistent attitude towards Ibsen: he was a playwright who, in his realistic ambitions, left no room for the imagination. In the subsequent stage direction, however, Mrs. Alving is said to be wearing a shawl on her head, 'a little ambiguous, but you can see what is meant'.[114] The parodist is having it both ways: Ibsen is didactic and extremely detailed, while also vague and enigmatic.

The same striking feature of Ibsen's modern prose dramas was made even better use of in F. Anstey's (Thomas Anstey Guthrie) *Punch* parodies. Guthrie singled out Ibsen's habit of using stage directions to convey subtle psychological insights about his characters. Mrs. Elvsted's hair in *Hedda Gabler* is referred to as 'significant' and Mortensgård in *Rosmersholm* is said to have 'thin reddish hair', while Guthrie's new, composite character, Pill-Doctor Herdal, appears with 'slightly weak hair and expression'.[115] One reviewer praising Mr. Guthrie's comic achievement emphasised the parodist's mastering of 'the Norseman's intolerable habit of stage direction and

[112] Ibid. 228–30.   [113] 'The Ghost of *Ghosts*', *Scots Observer*, vol. 4, 18 October 1890, 561.
[114] Ibid.
[115] *Punch's Pocket*, 158. For a further discussion of these parodies, see Tracy C. Davis, 'Spoofing "The Master"', *Nineteenth Century Theatre Research*, vol. 13, no. 2 (1985), 87-102, and Tore Rem, '"Cheerfully Dark"', in Ewbank, Lausund & Tysdahl, *Anglo-Scandinavian*, 215–30.

dogged determination to leave not a garden seat undescribed'.[116] Shaw would, precisely because of such qualities, later be lauded for his innovations in making the play readable.

It is too much to claim that Ibsen gave the British back a habit of reading plays, but no contemporary figure had his success as a playwright in the book market. National narratives tend to downplay the impact of the foreign and the role of translated literature. Daniel Barrett, for example, uncritically accepts Pinero's self-advertising claim that the publication of his play *The Times* in 1891 made it 'a revolutionary document', and that he stood for the first revival of this practice since Browning's *A Blot on the 'Scutcheon* in 1843. He proceeds to present Shaw's *Plays, Pleasant and Unpleasant* as the pinnacle of this new tradition. In a more extensive investigation of the relationship between print and drama, W.B. Worthen states that 'the booking of modern drama in English begins, arguably, as does much else in modern drama in English, with Bernard Shaw'.[117]

In terms of commercial success, too, Shaw differed from Ibsen, both Ibsen at home and Ibsen in Britain. Within the first six months, Richards had sold only 756 copies. In 1934, Richards concluded that the 'rate of sales was entirely incommensurate with the amount of notice it attracted and with the reputation it helped to make for its author'.[118] Shaw's most significant part in the history of the reintroduction of the printed play lay in popularising the idea that plays could be read as literature.[119]

None of this is to ignore the importance to British dramatists of the new American Copyright Law of 1891 or the significant professional advancement which came from the introduction of new royalty laws, removing further disincentives to publish prior to performance. But the translated Ibsen, or, more precisely, his mediators, had been able to anticipate such changes by several years. The American law had a long gestation period, and when it eventually arrived it was not without built-in disadvantages for British writers, publishers and printers. It meant, however, that they could now secure copyright in America, and it was no coincidence that it was Ibsen's new publisher, Heinemann, who grabbed the initiative and, already in the autumn of 1891, ventured on the first large-scale publishing project for a contemporary English playwright, namely Pinero. The

---

[116] *National Observer*, vol. 10, 17 June 1893, 124.   [117] Worthen, *Print*, 39.
[118] Richards, *Author*, 134.
[119] It is only fair to note that others, such as Wilde, Phillips, Martyn, Galsworthy, Barker and Barrie, also followed Ibsen's example, see Miriam Alice Franc, *Ibsen in England* (Boston: Four Seas Company, 1919), 136–49.

entrepreneurial Heinemann recognised the opportunities in this field, and other publishers, like the Bodley Head, and, later, Duckworth and Methuen, soon followed suit in publishing the new drama. The result was a booking of the play, a closing of the gap between page and stage.

Franco Moretti once observed that the spatial boundaries of 'modern tragedy' and of the novel were reverse:

> Henrik Ibsen, who is usually considered (rightly so, in my opinion) the key figure of modern tragedy, belonged to a Scandinavian culture which had been left virtually untouched by the novel. The same culture also produced Kierkegaard, whose philosophy was to offer a variety of themes and accents to tragic world-views, and Strindberg, whom contemporaries perceived as Ibsen's alter ego. Conversely, the areas of Europe where Ibsen met with the fiercest resistance – 'poison', 'loathsome sore unbandaged', 'open drain', 'lazar house', as contemporary newspapers put it – were France and England; strongholds of the novel, but the most barren contributors to the new drama. Still, the most revealing example of cultural geography in the modern period is Germany. Modern tragedy, and modern tragic theory, are simply unthinkable without it, to the extent that even Kierkegaard, Ibsen and Strindberg achieved world-historical significance only through German mediation.[120]

We have certainly confirmed the very strong position held by Ibsen both in his Scandinavian context of origin and in German-speaking Europe, as well as the resistance he met in Britain and France. But to this reverse geography we have added a nuance, and an important one, we think, by highlighting the dichotomous existence of Ibsen in English. Moretti's mapping is fairly accurate if limited to Ibsen on the English stage, although the artistic importance of the Achurch and Robins productions in particular should not be underestimated. Most important, however, is the remarkable success of Ibsen as translated English literature, in terms of readership, early canonisation and effects on the native literary drama. In the long run this early English-language canonisation became at least as vital to Ibsen's standing in world literature as his German mediation. With its spread as the second language of choice around the world, English has since become the first truly global language, and ever more central to the maintenance of a world canon.[121] In this respect, Ibsen's early literary success in English earned him a lasting competitive advantage over both Kierkegaard and Strindberg.

---

[120] Franco Moretti, 'The Moment of Truth', *New Left Review* 159, 1986, 39–40.
[121] David Crystal, *English as a Global Language* (Cambridge: Cambridge University Press, 1997).

CONCLUSION

The Provincial World Poet

David Damrosch has argued that one of the aims of 'world literature', as a way of doing literary studies, is to 'get [. . .] it right in a fundamental way with reference to the source culture'.[1] Our bid on that methodological proposition is that it should encompass the need to historicise: an effort at explaining the origins of the works as well as the ways they originally managed to travel beyond their originating cultures.

Our account of how Ibsen was possible has highlighted late 'novelisa-tion' and the persistence of the drama, the national stakes in theatre and literature in Norway in particular, expanding markets allowing for the professionalisation of authorship, the favourable intersection of political and literary conflicts, the developing legal frameworks of literary property, the particular cleavages and struggles that made Ibsen an asset in appropri-ating cultures, and the great variety of 'Ibsens' across Europe by the beginning of the twentieth century. By that time, he was already assimi-lated into German culture and had become 'great' as English literature. Those were his main roads into 'the world'.

Ibsen did not move smoothly into 'the world', however. In *The Com-munist Manifesto* of 1848, Marx and Engels, recycling Goethe's concept of world literature, predicted that 'National one-sidedness and narrow-mindedness become more and more impossible, and from the numerous national and local literatures, there arises a world literature'.[2] The Ibsen case qualifies such an assessment, and maybe particularly so since he arrived from the periphery of European literary space. In the process of Ibsen's drama becoming a world drama, the distance and perceived ten-sions between originating and appropriating cultures continued to be significant. Ibsen was generally not taken as an immediately available

---

[1] *What Is?*, 288.
[2] Karl Marx & Friedrich Engels, 'The Communist Manifesto (1848)', in D'haen, Domínguez & Thomsen, *World Literature*, 17.

'cosmopolitan' author who had managed to break loose from his nationality; on the contrary, the national was made into a major code of appropriation. To his opponents, his Norwegianness would be a sufficient ground
for dismissing him as 'provincial', 'suburban' and superfluous, while his
proponents and mediators met this challenge with a range of different
strategies.

Bernard Shaw would come closest to applying the Marx-Engels formula
on Ibsen, claiming that the levelling effects of capitalism would make
national differences more and more irrelevant: 'If you ask me where you
can find the Helmer household, the Allmers household, the Solness household, the Rosmer household, and all the other Ibsen households, I reply,
"Jump out of a train anywhere between Wimbledon and Haslemere; and
there you are."'[3] To other mediators, however, the national took on a
foundational and distinguishing role. In the already cited introduction to
the first Ibsen volume in Scott's Camelot series, Havelock Ellis located Ibsen
firmly in his Scandinavian and Norwegian contexts, and went on to claim:
'To understand Norwegian art – whether in its popular music, with its
extremes of melancholy or hilarity, or in its highly-developed literature – we
must understand the peculiar character of the land which has produced this
people.'[4]

Another take on this problematic is that of Henry James, to whom
Ibsen's 'provincialism' was a recurring source of puzzlement as well as the
key to his stylistic mastery. In his 'On the Occasion of "Hedda Gabler"'
(1891),[5] James hazarded that Ibsen's ambition had been 'to tell us about
his own people', but the result was 'that he has brought about an exhib-
ition of ours'. How was such an effect possible coming from an art with
such local limitations, in being, in a memorable phrase, 'too far from
Piccadilly and our glorious standards'? Unlike William Archer, James
could not take refuge in an experience of Ibsen's poetic qualities in the
original. Ibsen, as James saw it, was first of all characterised by an absence
of style, by writing the very prose of prose. The only way to account for his
attraction was to acknowledge that this 'ugliness of surface' was proof of
Ibsen's realism, of his 'fidelity to the real in a spare, strenuous, democratic
community'. The result of the absence of aristocratic style was 'a touching
vision' of the very struggle with 'a poverty, a bare provinciality, of life'.
Eight years later, in a review of *John Gabriel Borkman*, James bemoaned
the fact that this 'provincial of provincials' had reached such 'extreme

[3] Shaw, '*Little Eyolf*', *Saturday Review*, vol. 82, 28 November 1896, 563.   [4] Ellis, 'Preface', vii.
[5] H. James, 'On the Occasion of "Hedda Gabler"', in Egan, *Ibsen*, 234–44.

"I am a Norwegian literary man, and peculiar.'

Figure C.1   Illustration to 'Hedda Gabler', *Mr. Punch's Pocket Ibsen.*

maturity', already deploring the prospect of his demise.[6] Ibsen's greatness, James again argued, lay in a peculiar tension: 'The contrast between this form – so difficult to have reached, so civilized, so "evolved," – and the bareness and bleakness of his little northern democracy is the source of half the hard-frugal charm that he puts forth'.

Reasoning in such terms was a general phenomenon. Blaise Wilfert-Portal has argued that the intensified activity of translating and reporting on foreign literature in *fin de siècle* France – its publication contexts, editing practices, the kind of expertise mobilised, the relative lack of alternative sources of information, the infant state of the social and political sciences – all contributed to making translated literature into expressions of national identities.[7] In an 1899 article on world literature, Georg Brandes lamented what he took to be a new phenomenon of writing for 'a general and unspecified

[6] James, [review of *John Gabriel Borkman*], *Harper's Weekly*, 6 February 1897, in Egan, *Ibsen*, 364.
[7] Blaise Wilfert-Portal, 'Au temps du «cosmopolitisme»?', in *L'Europe des Revues*, ed. Evanghelia Stead and Hélène Védrine (Paris: Presses Universitaires de Paris Sorbonne, 2017), vol. 2, in press.

public', and instead predicted and welcomed a world literature of the future that would be 'ever more national': Literature would become 'all the more captivating the more the mark of the national appears in it and the more heterogeneous it becomes, as long as it retains a universally human aspect as art and science. That which is written directly for the world will hardly do as a work of art.'[8] The intensified 'transnationalisation' of literature by itself produced this effect. It did not signal the end of 'national' literature, on the contrary, it rather contributed to the restructuring of literature as a nationally divided field.[9] And precisely for that reason, we should add, Ibsen could be such a rich source of prestige to Norway, quite irrespective of the perceived fraught relations between the playwright and his home country.

In the educational and publishing contexts of comparative or world literature, this has continued to be the case. This kind of literary nationalisation has, however, not inspired detailed studies of the particularities of 'national origins'. Neither has it led to close examinations of the many diverse mechanisms of mediation, translation and appropriation. Instead, it has put an extraordinary burden of representation on literature, and particularly on 'peripheral' ones. Reflecting on the problems of selection in the teaching of world literature, Werner P. Friedrich in 1960 argued that often the contributions of an entire nation would have to be built around 'the life and works of one single man': 'for Scandinavia, for instance, I am thinking of a very detailed study of Ibsen – which, in a way, would become an analysis not only of Norway, but of the whole technique of the modern drama in general.'[10]

When Ibsen's achievement has largely escaped the positing of explanatory relations and conditions, in favour of conceiving it as a basically individual effort made possible in spite of rather than because of Ibsen's Norwegian and Scandinavian origins, it attests to the extraordinary success of the agents at the time in shaping the understanding of posterity. Their symbolic constructions of the world of literature – Ibsen's poetics of distance, the Modern Breakthrough's rhetoric of rupture and confrontation – have largely succeeded in obscuring the 'local' origins of what amounts to a 'Scandinavian moment in world literature' in the late nineteenth century. When these narratives have been cultivated even in Scandinavia, part of the reason is the very cosmopolitanism of provincial intellectuals. Scandinavian intellectuals claiming a 'leading' position at

---

[8] Georg Brandes, 'World literature (1899)', in D'haen, Domínguez & Thomsen, *World Literature*, 27.

[9] Wilfert-Portal, '«Cosmopolitisme»'.

[10] Werner P. Friedrich, 'On the Integrity of our Planning (1960)', in D'haen, Domínguez & Thomsen, *World Literature*, 77.

home, will identify themselves as 'European' and cosmopolitan, implying that they are on a more advanced stage than their provincial, locally embedded contemporaries. In this respect, figures like Brandes and Ibsen and the received narratives of the Modern Breakthrough have been inexhaustible sources of reference for self-identification and self-fashioning.[11]

Resistance to historicisation has continued to prevail for many reasons, among them disciplinary divisions, methodological nationalism and the de-historicising effects of canonisation. The ingrained assumptions that historical explanation means in some way to question the autonomy of literature and that 'great literature' will make it in the world anyway, by virtue of its inherent qualities alone, have also contributed. When a literary critic like Harold Bloom holds *Peer Gynt* to be at the centre of Ibsen's contribution to the western canon and claims that '[h]is canonicity, as well as his playwright's stance, have [. . .] almost nothing to do with the social energies of his age',[12] it is worth remembering that *Peer Gynt* played almost no role in establishing Ibsen's international reputation; Ibsen himself even held *Peer Gynt* to be so peculiarly Norwegian as to be untranslatable.[13] If Ibsen had stopped writing before *A Doll's House*, he would most likely have belonged to the Norwegian canon only – or the Scandinavian at best. He would have been mentioned alongside Henrik Wergeland and Ludvig Holberg, not with Shakespeare and Molière.[14] History, canonicity and the contingencies of translation and appropriation seem to be inseparably intertwined after all.

By revaluing Ibsen's Norwegian and Scandinavian contexts of origin we have not intended to reintroduce a self-contained, unique national space as the overarching explanatory principle. On the contrary, we have rather wanted to emphasise that Ibsen's local context was always already an articulation of a space between the received vernacular, the new national and the transnational. Norway was part of the 'world republic of letters' of the eighteenth century and the 'world literature' of the nineteenth century, and from the very start of his career Ibsen was shaped by a national theatre project with a twofold transnational context. The other of the national side was Danish hegemony over

---

[11] Typically, among the much mythologised Norwegian writer Jens Bjørneboe's many planned but never completed works in the 1960s, was a book on Munch, Hamsun and Ibsen as persecuted artists and misunderstood geniuses, as well as an Ibsen biography with 'great emphasis on the painful years in Bergen and Kristiania', quoted in Tore Rem, *Født til frihet* (Oslo: Cappelen Damm, 2010), 393.

[12] Harold Bloom, *The Western Canon* (New York: Harcourt Brace, 1994), 351–52.

[13] Ibsen, Letter to L. Passarge, 18 May 1880, *Letters and Speeches*, 185.

[14] Dag Solstad makes the same point in 'Kierkegaard og Ibsen', in Niels Jørgen Cappelørn et al. (eds.), *Kierkegaard, Ibsen og det moderne* (Oslo: Universitetsforlaget, 2010), 31–2.

Norwegian theatre, the other of the artistic side was French hegemony over European theatre in general. In this study, we have wanted to make Ibsen more Scandinavian and more European at the same time.

Neither is historicisation a questioning of literary autonomy. Rather, we have tried to reconstruct the struggle for autonomy, including the symbolic constructions accompanying that struggle. We have confronted these constructions with documentary evidence of income, circulation and recognition, certainly in order to question the assumption that Scandinavia was an inhospitable environment, but not to question that Ibsen in the 1880s and 1890s was his own aesthetic legislator. Instead of questioning autonomy, we have tried to identify its preconditions and found them where their existence has not been properly acknowledged.

Finally, historical explanation should in no way be taken to deny genius or extraordinary individual talent. It will always remain a mystery, irreducible to family background, social class, 'habitus', or fortunate timing, that it was Henrik who became Ibsen, while none of his siblings would have risen above obscurity without him. But this at the same time only makes the role of the 'environment' more important. As we have suggested with reference to the world of French theatre, nothing indicates that the more 'developed' literary or theatre cultures of 'Europe' would have provided more hospitable environments for a dramatic talent without either educational or economic capital. Ibsen could cultivate 'illness', isolation and distance because he could rely on markets expanding and recognition accumulating almost continuously throughout his entire career.

'World literature' may be 'writing that gains in translation',[15] adding ever-thicker layers of meaning. But traveling also implies loss, and particularly so for world literature originating in peripheries characterised by their lack of literary and cultural resources and generally considered of little interest to 'world history'. Such assumptions will lead to an oscillation between perceiving 'peripheral' literatures as some kind of 'spontaneous' products of their 'nations', or as extraordinary individual achievements, while ruling out that literature can have relative autonomy and constitute 'worlds' of its own even in such locations. Ignoring such originating contexts, however, necessarily involves a loss of potential meanings. Trying to restore them ought therefore also to be a contribution to interpretation and a resource for any effort at historically informed actualisations of Ibsen's drama into constantly new contexts, be it by way of translation, reading, performance or scholarship.

---

[15] Damrosch, *What Is?*, 288.

Income

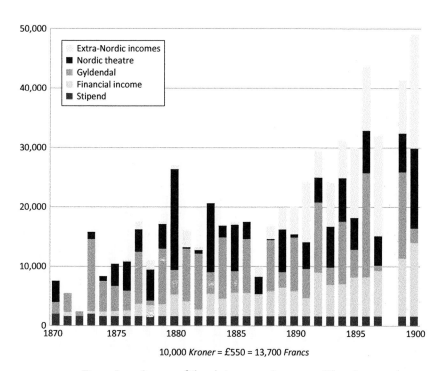

10,000 *Kroner* = £550 = 13,700 *Francs*

Figure A.1 Sources of Ibsen's income, 1870–1900. (*Kroner*)

Print Runs

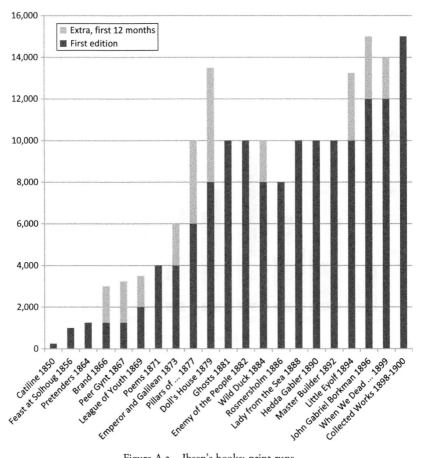

Figure A.2   Ibsen's books: print runs.

Theatre

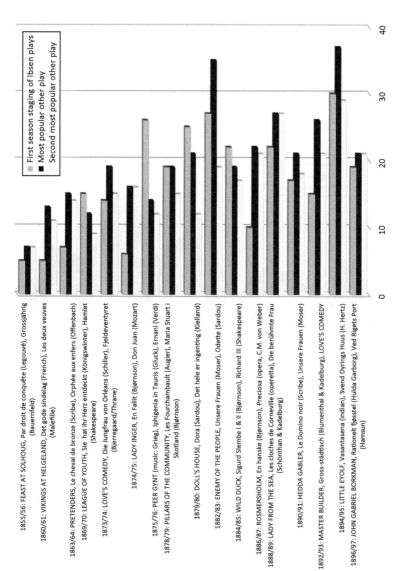

Figure A.3 Ibsen's first seasons at Christiania Theater, 1855–1897.
(Season: 1 September–31 August.)

Extra-Nordic Income

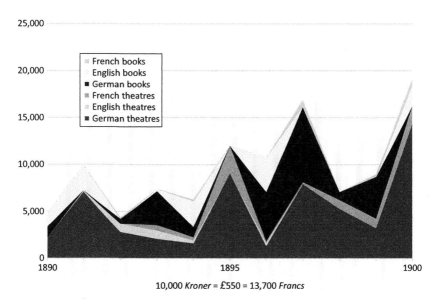

10,000 *Kroner* = £550 = 13,700 *Francs*

Figure A.4 Sources of Ibsen's extra-Nordic income, 1890–1900. (*Kroner*)

246

Archival Sources

British Library, London (BL)
- Lord Chamberlain's Correspondence
- William Archer Correspondence

National Library of Norway [Nasjonalbiblioteket], Oslo (NLN)
- H.L. Brækstad Collection, letter collection 17
- Letter collection 200 [letters to and from the Ibsen family]
- Ms 4° 2590 [letters to Henrik Ibsen]
- Ms fol 3222, Henrik Ibsen: Regnskapsbøker [Account books] 1870–1901, 2 vols.

National Library of Sweden [Kungliga biblioteket], Stockholm (NLS)
- The Carl Snoilsky Collection, Ep. S 39:14–15
- The August Strindberg Collection, Ep. S 53b

Public Record Office, London (PRO)
- Lord Chamberlain's Papers I/564 and LC I/56

The Royal Danish Library [Det Kongelige Bibliotek], Copenhagen (RDL)
- Gyldendals arkiv 1991/70. Gyldendalske Boghandel. Nordisk Forlag A/S. A: Regnskaber, 7: Forlagskladde 1850–1903, vol. H–J
- Gyldendals arkiv 1991/70. Gyldendalske Boghandel. Nordisk Forlag A/S. B: Korrespondance. NKS 3742 – 4° II Fr. Hegels Concepter 5, Henrik Ibsen 1868–87

VAM = Victoria and Albert Museum, London (VAM)
- Theatre and Performance Collection, William Archer Collection

Bibliography

Aarseth, Asbjørn, *Innledning til Kejser og Galilæer: Utgivelse*, www.ibsen.uio.no/ DRINNL_KG%7Cintro_publication.xhtml, book ed.: HIS 6k, 244–48.
Innledning til Lille Eyolf: Utgivelse: Mottagelse av utgaven, www.ibsen.uio.no/ DRINNL_LE%7Cintro_publication.xhtml, book ed: HIS 9k, 388–98.
Abret, Helga & Aldo Keel, *Im Zeichen des Simplicissimus* (München: Knaur, 1992).
Ackerman, Gretchen, *Ibsen and the English Stage, 1889–1903* (New York: Garland, 1987).
Adorno, Theodor, 'The Position of the Narrator in the Contemporary Novel', *Notes to Literature*, ed. Rolf Tiedemann, trans. Shierry Weber Nicholsen, 2 vols. (New York: Columbia University Press, 1991–92), vol. 1, 30–36.
Agerholm, Edvard, 'Henrik Ibsen og det kgl. Teater: Blade af Censurens Historie', *Gads danske Magasin* (1910–11), 276–80.
Ahlström, Gunnar, *Det moderna genombrottet i Nordens litteratur* [1947] (Stockholm: Rabén & Sjögren, 1973).
Ahlström, Stellan, *Strindbergs erövring av Paris: Strindberg och Frankrike 1884–1895* (Stockholm: Almqvist & Wiksell, 1956).
Alison, William, 'Ghosts and the Reptile Press', *Playgoers' Review*, vol. 1, 15 April 1891, 125–32.
Amdam, Per, *Bjørnstjerne Bjørnson: Kunstneren og samfunnsmennesket 1832–1880* (Oslo: Gyldendal, 1993).
Andersen, Anette Storli, 'In the Right Place, at the Right Time: Why Ibsen Worked in the Theatre for 13 Years – and Then Left It for Good', *Ibsen Studies*, vol. 11, no. 2 (2011), 84–116.
Andersen, Per Thomas, *Norsk litteraturhistorie*, rev. edn (Oslo: Universitetsforlaget, 2012).
Anker, Øyvind, *Christiania Theater's repertoire 1827–99* (Oslo: Gyldendal, 1956).
Kristiania Norske Theaters repertoire 1852–1863 (Oslo: Gyldendal, 1956).
Anon., 'Advertisement', *The Bookseller*, 4 August 1888, 864.
'An Ibsen Service', *Daily News*, 24 February 1891, in Egan, *Ibsen*, 165–66.
Announcement, *Publisher's Circular*, New Series, vol. 2, 1 August 1891, 104.
'A Play with a Purpose', *Justice*, 22 June 1889, 1.
'Drama for the Study', *National Observer*, vol. 6, 12 September 1891, 434.
'"Fruen fra Havet" paa det kgl. Theater i Berlin', *Aftenposten*, no. 148, 9 March 1889.

'Great in Little', *The Academy*, 23 March 1907, 288–89.

'Ibsen', *The Academy*, 21 March 1908, 577–78.

'Ibsen', *The Weekly Dispatch*, 9 June 1889.

'Ibsen in England', *The Academy*, vol. 60, 23 March 1901, 244.

'Nogle Tal', in Gran, *Festskrift*, 241–45.

'[Note on "Fruen fra Havet"]', *Verdens Gang*, no. 282, 30 November 1888.

'Notes', *The Playgoers' Review*, vol. 1, 1 January 1891, 25.

'Notice', *Black and White*, 24 June 1893.

'Notice', *Bookseller*, vol. 1, 9 January 1890 (Jan–Aug), 7.

'Notice', *National Observer*, vol. 10, 17 June 1893, 124.

'Notice', *Saturday Review*, 14 February 1891, in Egan, *Ibsen*, 157.

'Notice', *Sunday Times*, 9 June 1889.

'Notice', *Pall Mall Gazette*, 19 July 1889, 2.

'Notice', *Publishers' Circular*, 6 December 1889 (Christmas number), 1740.

'Notice', *The Christmas Bookseller* (Sep–Dec 1889), 269.

'Notice', *The Christmas Bookseller* (December 1890), 200.

'Notice', *The Standard*, 12 May 1891, in VAM, William Archer Collection, GB 71 THM/368/3, Box 2: Press cuttings.

['Paa Theatret opførtes Mandag...'], *Tromsø Stiftstidende*, no. 41, 20 May 1880.

'Paulo-post Ibscene', *National Observer*, vol. 6, 11 July 1891, 200.

'Plays for Stage and Study', *National Observer*, vol. 13, 6 April 1895, 559.

'Plays in Print', *The Sketch*, vol. 16, 13 January 1897, 492.

'Terry's Theatre', *Echo*, [May 1891?], in VAM, William Archer Collection, GB 71 THM/368/3, Box 2: Press cuttings.

'Theatrical Gossip', *Era*, 28 February 1891, in Egan, *Ibsen*, 170–71.

'Theatrical Notes', *Pall Mall Gazette*, 27 September 1892.

'The Ghost of *Ghosts*', *Scots Observer*, vol. 4, 18 October 1890, 561.

'The Master Builder', *Saturday Review*, vol. 75, 4 March 1893, 241.

'The Revised Translation of Ibsen', *The Speaker*, 20 April 1901, 59–60.

'Trade news', *The Bookseller*, vol. 1, 9 January 1890, 5.

Archer, Charles, *William Archer: Life, Work and Friendships* (London: Allen & Unwin, 1931).

Archer, William, 'A Translator-Traitor', *Pall Mall Gazette*, 23 January 1891.

Breaking a Butterfly (A Doll's House)', *Theatre*, vol. 3, 1 April 1884, 209–14, in Egan, *Ibsen*, 65–72.

English Dramatists of To-day (London: Sampson Low, Marston, Searle, & Rivington, 1882).

'General Preface', in *The Collected Works of Henrik Ibsen* (London: W. Heinemann, 1908), vol. 1, vii–xv.

'Ghosts and Gibberings', *Pall Mall Gazette*, 8 April 1891, in Egan, *Ibsen*, 209–14.

'Ibsen and English Criticism', *Fortnightly Review*, 1 July 1889, 30–37, in Egan, *Ibsen*, 115–23.

'Ibsen as I Knew Him', *The Monthly Review*, vol. 23 (June 1906), 1–19.

'Introduction: On the Need for an Endowed Theatre', *The Theatrical 'World' of 1896* (London: Scott, 1897), xi–lviii.

'Letter', *Pall Mall Gazette*, 3 February 1891, VAM, William Archer Collection, GB 71 THM/368/3, Box 2: Press cuttings.

'Mr. Archer Protests', *The National Observer*, vol. 8, 17 September 1892, 456.

Notice, *Playgoers' Review*, 15 April 1891, 131–32.

'The Censorship', *The Theatrical 'World' of 1895* (London: Scott, 1896), 66–73.

'The Humour of "The Wild Duck"', in *The Theatrical 'World' of 1897* (London: Scott, 1898), 146–51.

'The Mausoleum of Ibsen', *Fortnightly Review*, July 1893, 77–91, in Egan, *Ibsen*, 304–12.

Archer, William, & Harley Granville Barker, *A National Theatre: Scheme & Estimates* (London: Duckworth, 1907).

Aumont, Arthur, 'Henrik Ibsen paa danske Teatre', in Gran, *Festskrift*, 271–83.

Aveling, Edward, '"Nora" and "Breaking a Butterfly"', *To-Day*, vol. 1, (Jan–Jun 1884), 473–80.

Bang, Herman, 'De norske skuespil i Paris', *Nyt Tidsskrift*. Ny Række (1893–94), 322–33.

Banham, Martin (ed.), *The Cambridge Guide to Theatre* (Cambridge: Cambridge University Press, 1995).

Barker, H.G., 'The Coming of Ibsen', in *The Eighteen-Eighties*, ed. Walter de la Mare (Cambridge: Cambridge University Press, 1930), 159–95.

Barrett, Daniel 'Play Publication, Readers, and the "Decline" of Victorian Drama', *Book History*, vol. 2 (1999), 173–87.

Barstow, Susan Torrey, '"Hedda Is All of Us": Late-Victorian Women at the Matinee', *Victorian Studies*, vol. 43, no. 3 (Spring 2001), 387–411.

Beecroft, Alexander, 'World Literature without a Hyphen: Towards a Typology of Literary Systems', *New Left Review* no. 54 (2008), 87–100.

Bentley, Eric, *The Playwright as Thinker*, [1946] (Minneapolis: University of Minnesota Press, 2010).

Berg, Thoralf, *Debatten om et norsk scenespråk i Christiania 1848–1853 med hovedvekt på Knud Knudsen og hans arbeid for et norsk scenespråk ved Den norske dramatiske Skoles Theater i sesongene 1852/53*. Unpublished dissertation (Trondheim: Universitetet i Trondheim, NLHT, 1977).

'Teater og underholdning i Tromsø, Hammerfest og Vadsø', in Claes Rosenqvist (ed.): *Artister i norr: bottnisk och nordnorsk teater och underhållning på 1800-talet* (Umeå: Kungl. Skytteanska Samfundet, 2008), 303–443.

Bergsøe, Vilhelm, *Rom under Pius den niende: Skizzer og skildringer* (Copenhagen: Gyldendal, 1877).

Bjørnson, Bjørnstjerne, *Artikler og taler*, ed. Chr. Collin & H. Eitrem, 2 vols. (Kristiania: Gyldendal, 1912–13), vol. 2.

Brevveksling med danske 1854–1874, ed. Øyvind Anker, Francis Bull & Torben Nielsen, 3 vols. (Copenhagen: Gyldendal, 1970–74), vol. 2.

Brevveksling med svenske 1858–1909, ed. Øyvind Anker, Francis Bull & Örjan Lindberger, 3 vols. (Oslo: Gyldendal, 1960–61), vol. 2.

Gro-tid: Brev fra årene 1857–1870, ed. Halvdan Koht, 2 vols. (Kristiania: Gyldendal, 1912–13).

Blanc, Tharald, *Henrik Ibsen og Christiania Theater 1850–1899* (Christiania: J. Dybwad, 1906).

Bloom, Harold, *The Western Canon* (New York: Harcourt Brace, 1994).

Bourdieu, Pierre, 'The Field of Cultural Production', in Finkelstein & McCleery, *Book History Reader*, 99–120.

The Rules of Art: Genesis and Structure of the Literary Field, trans. Susan Emanuel (Stanford: Stanford University Press, 1996).

Brahm, Otto, *Kritische Schriften*, ed. Paul Schlenther, 2 vols. (Berlin: S. Fischer, 1915), vol. 1.

Brandes, Edvard, 'Henrik Ibsen: "En Folkefjende": Skuespil i fem Akter', *Morgenbladet* (Copenhagen), no. 285, 7 December 1882.

Brandes, Edvard and Georg Brandes, *Georg and Edv. Brandes brevveksling med nordiske forfattere og videnskabsmænd*, ed. Morten Borup, 8 vols. (Copenhagen: Gyldendal, 1939–42), vols. 1–3 and 6.

Brandes, Georg, *Breve til Forældrene 1872–1904*, ed. Morten Borup & Torben Nielsen, 3 vols. (Copenhagen: Reitzel, 1978–94). *Correspondance de Georg Brandes: Lettres choisies et annotee*, ed. Paul Krüger, 3 vols. (Copenhagen: Rosenkilde & Bagger, 1952–66), vol. 2: *L'Angleterre et la Russie* and vol. 3: *L'Allemagne*.

'"Et Dukkehjem" i Berlin', *Udvalgte skrifter*, ed. Sven Møller Kristensen, 9 vols. (Copenhagen: Tiderne Skifter, 1984–87), vol. 8, 24–30.

'Henrik Ibsen', *Verdens Gang*, no. 184, 6 August 1889.

Hovedstrømninger i det 19de Aarhundredes Litteratur (Copenhagen: Gyldendal, 1872).

'Indtryk fra London', *Tilskueren*, vol. 3 (June 1896), 430.

Levned, 3 vols. (Copenhagen: Gyldendal, 1905–08), vol. 2: *Et Tiaar*.

'Literatur: Bjørnstjerne Bjørnson: "En Fallit" og "Redaktøren"', *Det nittende Aarhundrede* (1875), 241.

'World literature (1899)', in D'haen, Domínguez & Thomsen, *World Literature*, 23–27.

Brandon, Ruth, *The New Women and the Old Men: Love, Sex and the Woman Question* (London: Secker & Warburg, 1990).

Bratton, Jacky, et al. (ed.), *Melodrama: Stage, Picture, Screen* (London: BFI Publishing, 1994).

Brauneck, Manfred, *Die Welt als Bühne: Geschichte des europäischen Theaters*, 6 vols. (Stuttgart: Metzler, 1993–2007), vol. 3.

Bredsdorff, Elias (ed.), *Sir Edmund Gosse's Correspondence with Scandinavian Writers* (Copenhagen: Gyldendal, 1960).

Breve fra og til Holger Drachmann, ed. Morten Borup, 4 vols. (Copenhagen: Gyldendal 1968–1970), vol. 1.

Britain, Ian, 'A Transplanted *Doll's House*: Ibsenism, Feminism and Socialism in Late-Victorian and Edwardian England', in Ian Donaldson (ed.), *Transformations in Modern European Drama* (London: Macmillan, 1983), 14–54.

Brooks, Peter, *The Melodramatic Imagination* (London: Yale University Press, 1976).

Buchanan, Robert, 'The Dismal Throng', in *The Complete Poetical Works*, 2 vols. (London: Chatto &Windus, 1901), vol. 2, 399–401.

Bull, Francis, *Tradisjoner og minner* (Oslo: Gyldendal, 1945).

Burckhard, Max, 'Begegnungen mit Ibsen', *Neue Freie Presse*, no. 15007, 3 June 1906, 12–13.

Burnand, F.C., 'Some Acting and Much Talking', *Punch*, 13 December 1905, 422.

Bushnell, Rebecca, *Tragedy: A Short Introduction* (Malden, MA.: Blackwell, 2008).

Byrnes, Robert F., 'The French Publishing Industry and Its Crisis in the 1890s', *The Journal of Modern History*, vol. 23, no. 3 (1951), 232–42.

Cancik, Hubert & Hildegard Cancik-Lindemayer, '"Was ich brauche, sind Fakta" (Ibsen): Die antiken Quellen zu Leben und Werk des Imperator Julian Augustus', in Richard Faber & Helge Høibraaten (eds.), *Ibsens "Kaiser und Galiläer": Quellen – Interpretationen – Rezeptionen* (Würzburg: Königshausen & Meumann, 2011), 39–64.

Casanova, Pascale, *The World Republic of Letters*, trans. M.B. DeBevoise (Cambridge, MA: Harvard University Press, 2004).

Charle, Christophe, 'Le champ de la production littéraire', in Henri-Jean Martin & Roger Chartier (eds.), *Histoire de l'édition française* (Paris: Fayard/Cercle de la Librairie, 1985), vol. 3, 137–75.

Chothia, Jean, *English Drama of the Early Modern Period, 1890–1940* (London: Longman, 1996).

Cima, Gay Gibson, *Performing Women: Female Characters, Male Playwrights, and the Modern Stage* (London: Cornell University Press, 1993).

Clark, Barrett H. (ed.), *World Drama: Ancient Greece, Rome, India, China, Japan, Medieval Europe, and England* (New York: Dover, 1933).

Coetzee, J.M., *Giving Offense: Essays on Censorship* (Chicago: Chicago University Press, 1996).

Colin, René Pierre, 'Un éditeur naturaliste. Albert Savine (1859–1927)', *Les Cahiers naturalistes*, vol. 46, no. 74 (2000), 263–70.

Crane, Walter, *An Artist's Reminiscences* (London: Macmillan, 1907).

Crystal, David, *English as a Global Language* (Cambridge: Cambridge University Press, 1997).

Daae, Ludvig, *Politiske dagbøker og minner*, 5 vols. (Oslo: Grøndahl, 1934–59), vol. 1: *1859–1871*.

Daae, Ludvig [Ludvigsen], *Professor, Dr. Ludvig Daaes erindringer og opptegnelser om sin samtid*, ed. Nic Knudtzon (Oslo: Novus, 2003).

Dahl, Per, 'Georg Brandes' fire indtryk', in Jørgen Dines Johansen, Atle Kittang & Astrid Sæther (eds.), *Ibsen og Brandes: Studier i et forhold* (Oslo: Gyldendal, 2006), 39–62.

Dahl, Per Kristian Heggelund, *Streiflys: Fem Ibsen-studier* (Oslo: Ibsen-museet, 2001).

Damrosch, David, *What Is World Literature?* (Princeton: Princeton University Press, 2003).

Davis, Tracy C., *Actresses as Working Women* (London: Routledge, 1991).
'Ibsen's Victorian Audience', *Essays in Theatre*, vol. 4 (1985), 21–38.
'Spoofing "The Master"', *Nineteenth Century Theatre Research*, vol. 13, no. 2 (1985), 87–102.
de Figueiredo, Ivo, *Henrik Ibsen: Masken* (Oslo: Aschehoug, 2007).
D'haen, Theo, Cesar Domínguez & Mads Rosendahl Thomsen (eds.), *World Literature: A Reader* (London: Routledge, 2013).
d'Amico, Giuliano, *Domesticating Ibsen for Italy: Enrico and Icilio Polese's Ibsen Campaign*, Biblioteca dello spettacolo nordico, Studi 6 (Bari: Edizioni di Pagina, 2013).
Dietrichson, Lorentz, *Svundne Tider*, 4 vols. (Kristiania: Cappelen, 1896), vol. 1.
Dingstad, Ståle, *Den smilende Ibsen: Henrik Ibsens forfatterskap – stykkevis og delt*, Acta Ibseniana IX (Oslo: Centre for Ibsen Studies/Akademika, 2013).
'Ibsen and the Modern Breakthrough – The Earliest Productions of *The Pillars of Society, A Doll's House*, and *Ghosts*', *Ibsen Studies*, vol. 16, no. 2 (2016), 103–40.
'Mytene etableres: De første Ibsen-biografiene', in Astrid Sæther et al. (eds.), *Den biografiske Ibsen*, Acta Ibseniana VI (Oslo: Centre for Ibsen Studies/ Unipub, 2010), 79–101.
Dollimore, Jonathan, *Sex, Literature and Censorship* (Cambridge: Polity Press, 2001).
Dostoevsky, Fyodor, *Notes from the Underground*, trans. David Magarshack, in *Great Short Works of Fyodor Dostoevsky* (New York: Harper & Row, 1968).
Selected Letters of Fyodor Dostoyevsky, trans. Andrew R. MacAndrew, ed. Joseph Frank & David I. Goldstein (London: Rutgers University Press, 1987).
Due, Chr., *Erindringer fra Henrik Ibsens Ungdomsaar* (Copenhagen: Græbes bogtrykkeri, 1909).
Eagleton, Terry, 'An Octopus at the Window', *London Review of Books*, vol. 33, no. 10 (2011), 23–4.
Edel, Leon, 'Foreword', *The Complete Plays of Henry James* (Philadelphia: Lippincott, 1949), 9–11.
Egan, Michael (ed.), *Ibsen: The Critical Heritage* (London: Routledge & Kegan Paul, 1972).
Eide, Elisabeth S., *Bøker i Norge: Boksamlinger, leseselskap og bibliotek på 1800-tallet* (Oslo: Pax, 2013).
Eliot, Simon, *Some Patterns and Trends in British Publishing 1800–1919*, Occasional Papers, no. 8 (London: The Bibliographical Society, 1994).
Ellis, Edith Lees, *Stories and Essays* (Berkeley Heights: Free Spirit Press, 1924).
Ellis, Havelock, 'Preface', in Ibsen, *The Pillars of Society, and Other Plays*, ed. Havelock Ellis (London: Scott, 1888), vii–xxx.
'Women and Socialism', *To-Day*, vol. 2 (July–Dec 1884), 351–63.
Eltis, Sos, *Acts of Desire* (Oxford: Oxford University Press, 2013).
Elton, Oliver ['O.E'], 'The Master Builder', in *The Manchester Stage, 1880–1900* (London: Constable, 1900), 197.

Eriksen, Anne, *Minner fra Den evige stad: Skandinavers reiser til Roma 1850–1900* (Oslo: Pax, 1997).

Ewbank, Inga-Stina, 'The Last Plays', in McFarlane, *Companion*, 126–54.

Ewbank, Inga-Stina, Olav Lausund & Bjørn Tysdahl (eds.), *Anglo-Scandinavian Cross-Currents* (Norwich: Norvik Press, 1999).

Farfan, Penny, 'From "Hedda Gabler" to "Votes for Women": Elizabeth Robins's Early Feminist Critique of Ibsen', *Theatre Journal*, vol. 48 (March 1996), 59–78.

Fay, Frank J., *Towards a National Theatre: The Dramatic Criticism of Frank J. Fay*, ed. Robert Hogan (Dublin: Dolmen P., 1970).

Felski, Rita, 'Introduction', in Rita Felski (ed.), *Rethinking Tragedy* (Baltimore: Johns Hopkins University Press, 2008), 1–25.

Finkelstein, David & Alistair McCleery (eds.), *The Book History Reader* [2002] rev. edn (London: Routledge, 2006).

Fischer, S., 'Der Verleger und der Büchermarkt', in *S.F.V. Das XXVte Jahr* (Berlin: S. Fischer, 1911), 24–33.

Fischer-Lichte, Erika, *History of European Drama and Theatre*, trans. Jo Riley (London and New York: Routledge, 2002).

Flannery, James W., *W.B. Yeats and the Idea of a Theatre* (London: Yale 1976).

Flaubert, Gustave, *Correspondance 1871–1877*, in *Œuvres complètes de Gustave Flaubert* (Paris: Club de l'Honnête Homme, 1975), vol. 15.

Fleischhacker, Sabine, 'Ibsen im Lichte der Münchener Presse (1876–1891)', *Ibsenårbok 1983/84*, 113–31.

Fontane, Theodor, *Sämtliche Werke*, 23 vols. (München: Nymphenburger Verlagshandlung, 1959–70), vol. 22.

Foucault, Michel, 'What Is an Author?', in Finkelstein & McCleery, *Book History Reader*, 281–91.

Franc, Miriam Alice, *Ibsen in England* (Boston: Four Seas Company, 1919).

Friedell, Egon, *Vår tids kulturhistorie* [Cultural History of the Modern Age; orig. German edn 1927–31], 3 vols. (Oslo: Aschehoug, 1933–34), vol. 3.

Friedrich, Werner P., 'On the Integrity of Our Planning (1960)', in D'haen, Domínguez & Thomsen, *World Literature*, 74–82.

Frye, Northrop, *Anatomy of Criticism* [1957] (Princeton: Princeton University Press, 1971).

Fulsås, Narve (ed.), *Biografisk leksikon til Ibsens brev – med tidstavle*, Acta Ibseniana X (Oslo: Centre for Ibsen Studies, 2013).

Historie og nasjon: Ernst Sars og striden om norsk kultur (Oslo: Universitetsforlaget, 1999).

'Ibsen Misrepresented: Canonization, Oblivion, and the Need for History', *Ibsen Studies*, vol. 9, no. 1 (2011), 3–20.

Innledning til brevene, www.ibsen.uio.no/brevinnledninger.xhtml, book ed.: HIS 12k–15k.

'The De-Dramatization of History and the Prose of Bourgeois Life', *Nordlit*, no. 34 (2015), 83–93.

Fulsås, Narve & Ståle Dingstad, *Innledning til brevene. Bosteder. Dresden 1868–1875*, www.ibsen.uio.no/BRINNL_brevInnledning_3.xhtml, book ed.: HIS 13k, 70–76.

Innledning til brevene. Eksil, forfatterrett og oversettelser – 1870-årene. Deutsche Genossenschaft Dramatischer Autoren und Componisten, www.ibsen.uio.no/ BRINNL_brevInnledning_7.xhtml, book ed.: HIS 13k, 107–10.

Garff, Joakim, *Søren Kierkegaard: A Biography*, trans. Bruce H. Kirmmse (Princeton: Princeton University Press, 2013 [2007]).

Gates, Joanne E., 'Elizabeth Robins and the 1891 Production of Hedda Gabler', *Modern Drama*, vol. 28, no. 4 (December 1985), 611–19.

'The Theatrical Politics of Elizabeth Robins and Bernard Shaw', *Shaw*, vol. 14 (1994), 43–53.

Gatland, Jan Olav, *Repertoaret ved Det Norske Theater 1850–1863* (Bergen: Universitetsbiblioteket i Bergen, 2000).

Gedin, David, *Fältets herrar: Framväxten av en modern författarroll: Artonhundratalet* (Stockholm: Brutus Östling, 2004).

Gjervan, Ellen Karoline, 'Ibsen Staging Ibsen: Henrik Ibsen's Culturally Embedded Staging Practice in Bergen', *Ibsen Studies*, vol. 11, no. 2 (2011), 117–44.

Goethe, Johann Wolfgang (von), 'On World Literature (1827)', in D'haen, Domínguez & Thomsen, *World Literature*, 9–15.

Goldman, Harvey, *Politics, Death, and the Devil: Self and Power in Max Weber and Thomas Mann* (Berkeley: University of California Press, 1992).

Gosse, Edmund, 'Bibliographical Note' in *The Master Builder*, New [second] edition (London: Heinemann, 1892), xi.

'Ibsen, the Norwegian Satirist', *Fortnightly Review*, vol. 19 (January 1–June 1 1873), 74–88.

'Ibsen's Social Dramas', *Fortnightly Review*, vol. 45, 1 January 1889, 107–21, in Egan, *Ibsen*, 77–93.

Gran, Gerhard (ed.), *Henrik Ibsen: Festskrift* (Bergen: John Grieg, 1898).

Gregory, Lady, *Our Irish Theatre* [1913] (London: Putnam, 1914).

Grein, J.T., 'The Independent Theatre', *Black and White*, 14 March 1891.

Gross, John, *The Rise and Fall of the Man of Letters* (London: Weidenfeld and Nicolson, 1969).

Grube, Max, *Geschichte der Meininger* (Berlin: Deutsche Verlags-Anstalt Stuttgart, 1926).

Grundy, Sydney, *The Play of the Future by a Playwright of the Past* (London: French, 1914).

Guthrie, T.A. ['F. Anstey'], *Punch's Pocket Ibsen* (London: Heinemann, 1893).

Guttormsson, Loftur, 'The Development of Popular Religious Literacy in the Seventeenth and Eighteenth Centuries', *Scandinavian Journal of History*, vol. 15 (1990), 7–35.

Guy, Josephine M. & Ian Small, *Oscar Wilde's Profession: Writing and the Culture Industry in the Late Nineteenth Century* (Oxford: Oxford University Press, 2000).

Hadley, Elaine, *Melodramatic Tactics* (Stanford: Stanford University Press, 1998).

Haffner, Vilhelm, *Albert Cammermeyer: Hans liv og virke* (Oslo: Cammermeyer, 1948).

Hagen, Erik Bjerck, 'Brand-resepsjonen 1866–1955', in Erik Bjerck Hagen (ed.), *Ibsens Brand: Resepsjon – tolkning – kontekst* (Oslo: Vidarforlaget, 2010), 11–32.

Halvorsen, J.B., 'Ibsen, Henrik Johan', *Norsk Forfatter-Lexikon 1814–1880* (Kristiania: Den norske Forlagsforening, 1892), vol. 3, 1–89.

Hamsun, Knut, 'Mot overvurdering av diktere og diktning', *Samlede verker*, ed. Lars Frode Larsen (Oslo: Gyldendal 2009), vol. 25, 144–56.

Paa turné: Tre foredrag om litteratur, ed. Tore Hamsun (Oslo: Gyldendal, 1971).

Hansen, Johan Irgens, 'Det literære Reportervæsen', *Dagbladet*, no. 405, 18 November 1884.

'Ibsen i Tyskland IV', *Dagbladet*, no. 95, 28 March 1888.

Hardy, Thomas, *The Collected Letters of Thomas Hardy*, ed. Richard Little Purdy and Michael Millgate, 7 vols. (Oxford: Clarendon, 1978–88), vol. 1.

Haugan, Jørgen, *Dommedag og djevlepakt: Henrik Ibsens forfatterskap – fullt og helt* (Oslo: Gyldendal, 2014).

Heinemann, William, Letter, *Pall Mall Gazette*, 24 January 1891, VAM, William Archer Collection, GB 71 THM/368/3, Box 2: Press cuttings.

Helland, Frode, *Melankoliens spill: En studie i Henrik Ibsens siste dramaer* (Oslo: Universitetsforlaget, 2000).

Hemmer, Bjørn, *Ibsen: Kunstnerens vei* (Bergen: Vigmostad & Bjørke, 2003).

'Ibsen and the Realistic Problem Drama', in McFarlane, *Companion*, 68–88.

Hemmings, F.W.J., *The Theatre Industry in Nineteenth-Century France* (Cambridge: Cambridge University Press, 1993).

Henderson, Archibald, *George Bernard Shaw: His Life and Works: A Critical Biography* (London: Hurst & Blackett, 1911).

The Changing Drama: Contributions and Tendencies (New York: Henry Holt and Co., 1914).

HIS = *Henrik Ibsens skrifter*, ed. Vigdis Ystad [et al.], 16 vols. (Oslo: Aschehoug, 2005–10).

Historisk statistikk 1968 (Oslo: Statistisk sentralbyrå, 1969).

Hoare, Eileen, 'A Doll House in Australia', *The Ibsen Society of America*, www.ibsensociety.liu.edu/conferencepapers/adollhouse.pdf.

Hobsbawm, E.J., *The Age of Empire 1875–1914* (London: Cardinal, 1989).

Holledge, Julie, Jonathan Bollen, Frode Helland & Joanne Tompkins, *A Global Doll's House: Ibsen and Distant Visions* (London: Palgrave, 2016).

Ibsen, Henrik, '*A Doll's House* and *An Enemy of the People*', in *A Doll's House and Other Plays*, trans. Deborah Dawkin & Erik Skuggevik, ed. Tore Rem (London: Penguin, 2016).

From Ibsen's Workshop: Notes, Scenarios and Drafts of the Modern Plays, trans. A.G. Chater and ed. William Archer, in *The Collected Works*, 12 vols. (London: Heinemann, 1912), vol. 12.

Ibsen's Poems, in versions by John Northam (Oslo: Norwegian University Press, 1986).

Klein Eyolf (Berlin: S. Fischer Verlag, 1895).

Letters and Speeches, ed. Evert Sprinchorn (London: MacGibbon & Kee, 1965).
Letters of Henrik Ibsen, trans. John Nilsen Laurvik & Mary Morison (New York: Duffield & Comp., 1908).
'*Rosmersholm*', in *An Enemy of the People, The Wild Duck, Rosmersholm*, trans. James W. McFarlane (Oxford: Oxford University Press, 1999).
Samlede verker, Hundreårsutgave, eds. Francis Bull, Halvdan Koht & Didrik Arup Seip, 21 vols. (Oslo: Gyldendal, 1928–57), vol. 15: *Artikler og taler* and vol. 16: *Brev 1844–1871*.
Samlede værker, 10 vols. (Copenhagen: Gyldendal, 1898–1902).
The Master Builder, in *The Master Builder and Other Plays*, trans. Barbara J. Haveland & Anne-Marie Stanton-Ife, ed. Tore Rem (London: Penguin, 2014).
The Oxford Ibsen, ed. James W. McFarlane, 8 vols. (London: Oxford University Press, 1960–77), vols. 1–5.
www.ibsen.uio.no/brev.xhtml, book ed.: HIS 12–15.
www.ibsen.uio.no/dikt.xhtml, book ed.: HIS 11.
www.ibsen.uio.no/sakprosa.xhtml, book ed.: HIS 16.
www.ibsen.uio.no/skuespill.xhtml, book ed.: HIS 1–10.
Innes, Christopher, 'Preface', in Innes, *Cambridge Companion to Shaw*, xvii–xviii.
(ed.), *The Cambridge Companion to George Bernard Shaw* (Cambridge: Cambridge University Press, 1998).
Jackson, Holbrook, 'The Higher Drama', *The Eighteen Nineties: A Review of Art and Ideas at the Close of the Nineteenth Century* [1913] (Brighton: Harvester P., 1976).
Jakobsen, Kjetil, *Kritikk av den reine autonomi: Ibsen, verden og de norske intellektuelle*. Dr.art. dissertation (Oslo: University of Oslo, 2004).
James, Henry, 'After the Play', *New Review*, vol. 1, June 1889, 30–45.
Henry James: Letters, ed. Leon Edel, 4 vols. (London: Macmillan, 1980), vol. 3.
'On the Occasion of "Hedda Gabler"', in Egan, *Ibsen*, 234–44.
[Review of *John Gabriel Borkman*], *Harper's Weekly*, 6 February 1897, in Egan, *Ibsen*, 363–65.
Jan, Sara, 'Naturalism in the Theatre: Ibsen's *Ghosts* in 1890s England', in Ewbank, Lausund & Tysdahl, *Anglo-Scandinavian*, 159–73.
Jelavich, Peter, *Munich and Theatrical Modernism: Politics, Playwriting, and Performance 1890–1914* (Cambridge, MA.: Harvard University Press, 1985).
Jenkins, Anthony, *The Making of Victorian Drama* (Cambridge: Cambridge University Press, 1991).
Jerome, Jerome K. ['A Dramatist'], *Playwriting: A Handbook for Would-Be Dramatic Authors* (London: The Stage Office, 1888).
Johnston, Brian, 'Introduction' to *Ibsen's Selected Plays* (London: Norton, 2004), xi–xxi.
Text and Supertext in Ibsen's Drama (London: Pennsylvania State University Press, 1989).
'The Ibsen Phenomenon', *Ibsen Studies*, vol. 6, no. 1 (2006), 6–21.
Jongh, Nicholas de, *Politics, Prudery & Perversions: The Censoring of the English Stage 1901–1968* (London: Methuen, 2000).

Joyce, James, 'Ibsen's New Drama', *Fortnightly Review*, 1 April 1900, in Egan, *Ibsen*, 385–91.
Letters of James Joyce, ed. Stuart Gilbert & Richard Ellmann, 3 vols. (London: Faber and Faber, 1957–66), vol. 1.
Selected Letters of James Joyce, ed. Richard Ellmann (London: Faber & Faber, 1975).
Jæger, Henrik, *Henrik Ibsen* (Copenhagen: Gyldendal, 1888).
'Henrik Jægers opptegnelser fra samtaler med Ibsen', in Hans Midtbøe, *Streiflys over Ibsen og andre studier* (Oslo: Gyldendal, 1960), 141–64.
Kafka, Franz, *Diaries, 1910–1923*, ed. Max Brod, trans. Joseph Kresh, Martin Greenberg & Hannah Arendt (New York: Schocken Books, 1976).
Kaplan, Joel H. & Sheila Stowell, *Theatre and Fashion* (Cambridge: Cambridge University Press, 1994).
Kapp, Yvonne, *Eleanor Marx*, 2 vols. (London: Lawrence & Wishart, 1972–76), vol. 2.
Karpantschof, René & Flemming Mikkelsen, 'Folkelige protestbølger og demokrati i Danmark seet i et internationalt perspektiv 1700–2000', in Nils Rune Langeland (ed.), *Politisk kompetanse: Grunnlovas borgar 1814–2014* (Oslo: Pax, 2014), 105–39.
Keating, Peter, *The Haunted Study: A Social History of the English Novel 1875–1914* (London: Secker & Warburg, 1989).
Keel, Aldo, 'Reclam und der Norden. Autoren, Titel, Auflagen 1869–1943', in *Reclam. 125 Jahre Universalbibliothek 1867–1992*, ed. Dietrich Bode (Stuttgart: Philipp Reclam jun., 1992), 132–47.
Kelly, Katherine E., 'Imprinting the Stage: Shaw and the Publishing Trade, 1883–1903', in Innes, *Cambridge Companion to Shaw*, 25–54.
Kielland, Alexander L., *Brev 1869–1906*, ed. Johs. Lunde, 4 vols. (Oslo: Gyldendal, 1978), vol. 2.
Kittang, Atle, *Ibsens heroisme: Frå* Brand *til* Når vi døde vågner (Oslo: Gyldendal, 2002).
Koht, Halvdan, *Life of Ibsen*, trans. and ed. Einar Haugen & A.E. Santaniello (New York: Blom, 1971).
Knudsen, Jørgen, *Georg Brandes: I modsigelsernes tegn: Berlin 1877–83* (Copenhagen: Gyldendal, 1988).
Georg Brandes: Symbolet og manden: 1883–1895 (Copenhagen: Gyldendal, 1994).
Kristensen, Sven Møller, *Digteren og samfundet i Danmark i det 19. århundrede*, 2 vols. [1942–45] (Copenhagen: Munksgaard, 1970), vol. 2: *Naturalismen*.
Lange, Sven, 'Henrik Ibsen og det unge Europa: Spredte Indtryk', in Gran, *Festskrift*, 225–33.
Larsen, Lars Frode, *Tilværelsens Udlænding: Hamsun ved gjennombruddet (1891–1893)* (Oslo: Schibsted, 2002).
Larsen, Peter, *Ibsen og fotografene: 1800-tallets visuelle kultur* (Oslo: Universitetsforlaget, 2013).
Lausund, Olav, 'Edmund Gosse: Ibsen's First Prophet to English Readers', in Ewbank, Lausund & Tysdahl, *Anglo-Scandinavian*, 139–58.

Leary, Patrick & Andrew Nash, 'Authorship', in *The Cambridge History of the Book in Britain* (Cambridge: Cambridge University Press, 1999–), vol. 6, 172–213.

Ledger, Sally, 'Eleanor Marx and Henrik Ibsen', in John Stokes (ed.), *Eleanor Marx (1855–1898)* (Aldershot: Ashgate, 2000), 53–68.

Henrik Ibsen [1999] (Tavistock: Northcote, 2008).

Lie, Jonas, *Brev 1851–1908*, ed. Anne Grete Holm-Olsen, 3 vols. (Oslo: Novus, 2009), vol. 1.

Lindberg, Per, *August Lindberg: Skådespelaren och Människan* (Stockholm: Natur och kultur, 1943).

Lindberger, Örjan, 'Ibsen och två svenska teaterchefer', *Nordisk tidskrift för vetenskap, konst och industri*, vol. 40, no.6 (1964), 376–86.

Lindau, Paul, *Nur Erinnerungen*, 2 vols. (Stuttgart & Berlin: Cotta, 1916–1917), vol. 2.

Listov, A., *Ordsamling fra den norske æsthetiske Literatur siden Aaret 1842, alfabetisk ordnet og forklaret* (København: Gyldendal, 1866).

Lord, H.F., 'Life of Henrik Ibsen', in *Nora: A Play* (London: Griffith and Farran, 1882), vii–xxiv.

Loué, Thomas, 'Un modèle matriciel: les revues de culture générale', in Pluet-Despatin, Leymarie & Mollier, *Belle Époque*, 57–68.

Lyons, Charles S., *Henrik Ibsen: The Divided Consciousness* (Carbondale & Edwardsville: Southern Illinois University Press, 1972).

Lyons, Martyn, *A History of Reading and Writing in the Western World* (Basingstoke: Palgrave Macmillan 2010).

Le Triomphe du livre : Une histoire sociologique de la lecture dans la France du XIXe siècle (Paris: Promodis, 1987).

Lønnum, Erlend, 'Knudsen og Ibsen', *Språknytt*, vol. 40, no. 2 (2012), 29–31.

MacCarthy, Desmond, *The Court Theatre 1904–1907: A Commentary and Criticism* (London: Bullen, 1907).

McCarthy, Justin Huntly, 'The Lady from the Sea', *The Hawk*, 19 May 1891.

McDonald, Jan, 'The Actors' Contributions', *Scandinavica*, vol. 15 (1976), 1–17.

McFarlane, James W., 'Berlin and the Rise of Modernism', in Malcolm Bradbury & James W. McFarlane (eds.), *Modernism: 1890–1930* (London: Penguin, 1991), 105–19.

Ibsen and Meaning (Norwich: Norvik Press, 1989).

(ed.), *The Cambridge Companion to Ibsen* (Cambridge: Cambridge University Press, 1994)

Malone, Irina Ruppo, *Ibsen and the Irish Revival* (London: Palgrave Macmillan, 2010).

Matlaw, Myron (ed.), *Modern World Drama: An Encyclopedia* (London: Secker & Warburg, 1972).

Marker, Frederick J. & Lise-Lone Marker, *The Scandinavian Theatre: A Short History* (Oxford: Basil Blackwell, 1975).

Marshall, Gail, *Actresses on the Victorian Stage* (Cambridge: Cambridge University Press, 1998).

Marx, Karl & Friedrich Engels, 'The Communist Manifesto (1848)', in D'haen, Domínguez & Thomsen, *World Literature*, 16–17.

Matos, T. Carlo, *Ibsen's Foreign Contagion* (Bethesda: Academia Press, 2012).

Mendelssohn, Peter de, *S. Fischer und sein Verlag* (Frankfurt am Main: S. Fischer, 1970).

Meyer, Michael, *Ibsen: A Biography* (London: Penguin, 1974).

Miller, Anna, *The Independent Theatre in Europe 1887 to the Present* (New York: Blom, 1966).

Mix, Katherine Lyon, *A Study in Yellow: The Yellow Book and Its Contributors* (London: Constable, 1960).

Moi, Toril, *Ibsen and the Birth of Modernism: Art, Theatre, Philosophy* (Oxford: Oxford University Press, 2006).

Moisy, Sigrid von, *Paul Heyse: Münchener Dichterfürst im bürgerlichen Zeitalter* (München: C.H. Beck, 1981).

Mollier, Jean-Yves, 'La revue dans le système éditorial', in Pluet-Despatin, Leymarie & Mollier, *Belle Époque*, 43–56.

Montague, C.E., *Dramatic Values* (London: Methuen, 1911).

Moore, George, 'Our Dramatists and Their Literature', *Fortnightly Review*, vol. 52 (November 1889), 620–32.

Moretti, Franco, *Atlas of the European Novel 1800–1900* (London: Verso, 1998).
   The Bourgeois: Between History and Literature (London: Verso, 2013)
   'The Moment of Truth', *New Left Review*, no. 159 (1986), 39–48.

Nansen, Peter, *Mine 20 Aar i Gyldendal* ([Copenhagen]: L. Levison Jun, [1918]).

Neue deutsche Biographie (Berlin: Duncker & Humblot, 1953–).

Nissen, Martinus, 'Statistisk Udsigt over den Norske Litteratur fra 1814 til 1847', *Norsk Tidsskrift for Videnskab og Literatur* (1849), 177–207.

Nordhagen, Per Jonas, *Henrik Ibsen i Roma* (Oslo: Cappelen, 1981).

Northam, John, *Ibsen: A Critical Study* (Cambridge: Cambridge University Press, 1973).

Nygaard, Jon, '. . . af stort est du kommen': Henrik Ibsen og Skien*, Acta Ibseniana VIII (Oslo: Centre for Ibsen Studies/Akademika, 2013).

Nygaard, Knut, *Holbergs teaterarv* (Bergen: Eide, 1984).

Nygård, Stefan & Johan Strang, 'Facing Asymmetry: Nordic Intellectuals and Center-Periphery Dynamics in European Cultural Space', *Journal of the History of Ideas*, vol. 77, no. 1 (2016), 75–97.

Nyholm, Kela, 'Henrik Ibsen paa den franske scene', *Ibsenårbok 1957–59*, 7–78.

Næss, Trine, *Christiania Theater forteller sin historie 1877–1899* (Oslo: Novus, 2005).

Orme, Michael, *J.T. Grein: The Story of a Pioneer 1862–1935* (London: Murray, 1936).

Paasche, Fredrik, *Norges Litteratur: Fra 1814–1850-aarene* (Oslo: Aschehoug, 1932).

Palmer, John, *The Future of the Theatre* (London: Bell, 1913).

Papazian, Eric, 'Språkreformatoren Knud Knudsen', *Språknytt*, vol. 40, no. 2 (2012), 19–22.

Parker, Louis N., *Several of My Lives* (London: Chapman & Hall, 1928).

Pasche, Wolfgang, *Skandinavische Dramatik in Deutschland: Björnstjerne Björnson, Henrik Ibsen, August Strindberg auf der deutschen Bühne 1867–1932*. Beiträge zur nordischen Philologie, herausgegeben von der Schweizerischen Gesellschaft für skandinavische Studien, 9 (Basel: Helbing & Lichtenhahn, 1979).

Paulsen, John, *Mine erindringer* (Copenhagen: Gyldendal, 1900).

Paulus, Gretchen, 'Beerbohm Tree and "The New Drama,"' *University of Toronto Quarterly*, vol. 27 (1957), 103–15.

Pettersen, Hjalmar, *Skrifter af Henrik Ibsen*, Bibliographia Ibseniana (Kristiania: [Det Mallingske Bogtrykkeri] 1922), vol. 2.

Pfäfflin, Friedrich & Ingrid Kussmaul, *S. Fischer, Verlag, von der Gründung bis zur Rückkehr aus dem Exil: Eine Ausstellung des Deutschen Literaturarchivs im Schiller-Nationalmuseum Marbach am Neckar, 1985*, Marbacher Kataloge, no. 40 (Marbach: Deutsche Schillergesellschaft, 1985).

Pluet-Despatin, Jacqueline, Michel Leymarie & Jean Yves Mollier (eds.), *La Belle Époque des revues 1880 1914* (Paris: Éditions de L'Imec, 2002).

Postlewait, Thomas, *Prophet of the New Drama* (London: Greenwood P., 1986).

Powell, Kerry, *Oscar Wilde and the Theatre of the 1890s* (Cambridge: Cambridge University Press, 1990).

Puchner, Martin, 'Goethe, Marx, Ibsen and the Creation of World Literature', *Ibsen Studies*, vol. 13, no. 1 (2013), 28–46.

Stage Fright: Modernism, Anti-Theatricality, and Drama (London: Johns Hopkins University Press, 2002).

Qvistgaard, Magnus, *Pioneering Ibsen's Drama: Agents, Markets and Reception 1852–1893*. Unpublished dissertation (Florence: European University Institute, 2015).

Raven, James et al. (eds.), *The Practice and Representation of Reading in England* (Cambridge: Cambridge University Press, 1996).

Ray, Catherine, 'Henrik Ibsen', in *The Emperor and Galilean: A Drama in Two Parts*, trans. Catherine Ray (London: Samuel Tinsley, 1876), iii–xiv.

Rem, Tore, 'Bjørnson, bønder og lesning: Om gotiske meningsdannelser', *Edda*, vol. 92, no. 3 (2005), 243–58.

'"Cheerfully Dark": Punchian Parodies of Ibsen in the Early 1890s', in Ewbank, Lausund & Tysdahl, *Anglo-Scandinavian*, 215–30.

Forfatterens strategier: Alexander Kielland og hans krets (Oslo: Universitetsforlaget, 2002).

Født til frihet: En biografi om Jens Bjørneboe (Oslo: Cappelen Damm, 2010).

'Hot Property: Reading Ibsen in the British Fin de Siécle', http://ibsen.nb.no/id/98024.

'Nationalism or Internationalism? The Early Irish Reception of Ibsen', *Ibsen Studies*, vol. 7, no. 2 (2007), 188–202.

Repertoardatabase, http://ibsen.nb.no/id/1998.0 (accessed in 2014; transferred to https://ibsenstage.hf.uio.no in 2017)

Report from the Select Committee on Theatres and Places of Entertainment (London: Eyre & Spottiswoode, 1892).

Rhys, Ernest (ed.), *Malory's History of King Arthur and the Quest for the Holy Grail* [Morte D'Arthur] (London: Walter Scott, 1886).

Richards, Grant, *Author Hunting* (London: Hamish Hamilton, 1934).

Riley, Denise, '*Am I That Name?*': *Feminism and the Category of 'Women' in History* (Houndmills & London: Macmillan, 1988).

Ringdal, Nils Johan, *By, bok og borger: Deichmanske bibliotek gjennom 200 år* (Oslo: Aschehoug, 1985).

Roberts, Chalmer, *William Heinemann: May 18th, 1863–October 5th, 1920: An Appreciation* (London: Privately printed, 1920).

Robins, Elizabeth, *Ibsen and the Actress* (Edinburgh: Neill, 1928).

Rode, Ove, 'Ibsen-Ugen i Berlin', *Politiken*, nos. 76 and 77, 17 and 18 March 1889.

Rowell, George and Anthony Jackson, *The Repertory Movement* (Cambridge: Cambridge University Press, 1984).

Russell, Edward, *Ibsen: A Lecture Delivered at University College, Liverpool* (London: Simpkin, Marshall & Co., 1894).

Ræder, Trygve, *Ernst Sars* (Oslo: Gyldendal, 1935).

Rønning, Helge, *Den umulige friheten: Henrik Ibsen og moderniteten* (Oslo: Gyldendal, 2006).

St Clair, William, *The Reading Nation in the Romantic Period* (Cambridge: Cambridge University Press, 2004).

St John, John, *William Heinemann: A Century of Publishing 1890–1990* (London: Heinemann, 1990).

Salmonsens Konversationsleksikon, 2nd ed., 25 vols. (Copenhagen: J.H. Schultz, 1915–28), vol. 2.

Sangerfestkomiteen, *Beretning om den femte store Sangerfest afholdt i Bergen 14–18 Juni 1863*, Udg. ved Sangerfestkomiteen (Kristiania: Joh. D. Behrens, 1963).

Sapiro, Gisèle, 'Autonomy Revisited: The Question of Mediations and Its Methodological Implications', *Paragraph*, vol. 35, no. 1 (2012), 30–48.

'Translation and the Field of Publishing: A Commentary on Pierre Bourdieu's "A Conservative Revolution in Publishing"', *Translation Studies*, vol. 1, no. 2 (2008), 154–66.

Sars, Ernst, *Norges Politiske Historie 1815–1885* (Kristiania: Oscar Andersens Bogtrykkeri, 1904).

Schoonderwoerd, N.H.G., *J.T. Grein: Ambassador of the Theatre 1862–1935: A Study in Anglo-Continental Relations* (Assen: Van Gorcum, 1963).

Schreiner, Olive, *Olive Schreiner: Letters 1871–9*, ed. Richard Rive (Oxford: Oxford University Press, 1987).

Schwartz, Fritz, 'Die Ausdehnung des internationalen Urheberrechtsschutzes', *Vorbericht. IV. Internationaler Verleger-Kongress zu Leipzig vom 10.–13. Juni 1901* (Leipzig: Brockhaus, 1901), 63–66.

Scott, Clement, '*A Doll's House*', *The Theatre*, 1 July 1889, N.S., 21.

Editorial Comment on *Ghosts*, *Daily Telegraph*, 14 March 1891, in Egan, *Ibsen*, 189–93.

The Drama of Yesterday & To-day, 2 vols. (London: Macmillan, 1899), vol. 1.

Scott, Joan Wallach, *Only Paradoxes to Offer: French Feminists and the Rights of Man* (Cambridge, Mass.: Harvard University Press, 1996).

Setterquist, Jan, *Ibsen and the Beginnings of Anglo-Irish Drama* (Uppsala: Lundequistska Bokhandeln, 1951).

Shaw, George Bernard, 'An Aside', in Lillah McCarthy, *Myself and My Friends – A Life on the Stage* (London: T. Butterworth, 1933), 3.

Bernard Shaw: Collected Letters, ed. Dan H. Laurence, 4 vols. (New York: Dodd Mead, 1965–88), vol. 1.

'*Little Eyolf*', *Saturday Review*, vol. 82, 28 November 1896, 563.

Plays: Pleasant and Unpleasant, 2 vols. (London: Grant Richards, 1898), vol. 1.

'The New Ibsen Play', *Dramatic Opinions and Essays*, 2 vols. (London: Constable, 1907), vol. 2, 154–62.

Shepherd-Barr, Kirsten, *Ibsen and Early Modernist Theatre, 1890–1900* (Westport, Conn.: Greenwood Press 1997).

'Ibsen in France from Breakthrough to Renewal', *Ibsen Studies*, vol. 12, no. 1 (2012), 56–80.

'The Development of Norway's National Theatres', in S.E. Wilmer (ed.), *National Theatres in a Changing Europe* (Houndmills: Palgrave Macmillan, 2008), 85–98.

Smidt, Kristian, *Silent Creditors: Henrik Ibsen's Debt to English Literature* (Oslo: Aschehoug, 2004).

Solstad, Dag, 'Kierkegaard og Ibsen', in Niels Jørgen Cappelørn et al. (eds.), *Kierkegaard, Ibsen og det moderne* (Oslo: Universitetsforlaget, 2010), 25–35.

Steen, Ellisiv, *Den lange strid: Camilla Collett og hennes senere forfatterskap* (Oslo: Gyldendal, 1954).

Steiner, George, *The Death of Tragedy* (London: Faber & Faber, 1961).

Stephens, John Russel, *The Censorship of English Drama, 1824–1901* (Cambridge: Cambridge University Press, 1980).

Stokes, John, *Resistible Theatres* (London: Paul Elck, 1972).

Stråth, Bo, *Union og demokrati: Dei sameinte rika Noreg-Sverige 1814–1905* (Oslo: Pax, 2005).

Symons, Arthur, 'Henrik Ibsen', *Universal Review*, April 1889, 567–74.

'Ibsen on the Stage', *The Scottish Art Review*, vol. 2 (1889), 40.

Swinnerton, Frank, *Swinnerton: An Autobiography* (London: Hutchinson, 1937).

Tanum, Johan Grundt & Sverre Schetelig, *Den norske bokhandlerforening: 1851 – 10. januar – 1926* (Oslo: Foreningen, 1926).

Templeton, Joan, 'Antoine versus Lugné-Poë: The Battle for Ibsen on the French Stage', in Maria Deppermann et al. (eds.), *Ibsen im europäischen Spannungsfeld zwischen Naturalismus und Symbolismus*, Kongressakten der 8. Internationalen Ibsen-Konferenz, Gossensass, 23.–28.6.1997 (Frankfurt aM: Peter Lang 1998), 71–82.

Ibsen's Women (Cambridge: Cambridge University Press, 1997).

The Incorporated Stage Society: Ten Years 1899 to 1909 (London: Chiswick Press, 1909).

Thwaite, Ann, *Edmund Gosse: A Literary Landscape, 1849–1928* (London: Secker & Warburg, 1984).

Tocqueville, Alexis de, *Democracy in America*, trans. Henry Reeve, rev. Francis Bowen and Phillips Bradley (New York: Alfred A. Knopf, 1972).

Todd III, William Mills, 'The Ruse of the Russian Novel', in Franco Moretti (ed.), *The Novel* (Princeton, NJ: Princeton University Press, 2006), vol. 1, 401–23.

Tolstoy, Leo, *War and Peace*, trans. Rosemary Edmonds (Harmondsworth: Penguin, 1982).

Torp, Arne, 'Skandinavisten Knud Knudsen', *Språknytt*, vol. 40, no. 2 (2012), 23–25.

Torsslow, Stig, *Ibsens brevväxling med Dramatiska teatern* (Stockholm: [Kungliga dramatiska teatern], 1973).

Trüper, Henning, *Topography of a Method: Francois Louis Ganshof and the Writing of History* (Tübingen: Mohr Siebeck, 2014).

Turner, John R., *A History of the Walter Scott Publishing House*. Unpublished dissertation (Aberystwyth: University of Wales, 1995).

'The Camelot Series, Everyman's Library, and Ernest Rhys', *Publishing History*, vol. 31 (1992), 27–46.

The Walter Scott Publishing Company: A Bibliography (Pittsburgh, Pa: University of Pittsburgh Press, 1997).

Tveterås, Harald L., *Bokens kulturhistorie: Formet av forfattere, forleggere, bokhandlere og lesere, 1850–1900. Den norske bokhandels historie* (Oslo: Cappelen, 1986), vol. 3.

Norske forfattere på danske forlag, 1850–1890. Den norske bokhandels historie (Oslo: Cappelen, 1964), vol. 2.

Vestheim, Geir, *'(...) der er Gift paa Pennen hans': Kampen i Stortinget om diktargasjane 1863–1962* (Oslo: Unipub, 2005).

Vibe, Johan, 'Henrik Ibsen som Forfatter af Nutidsdramaer', *Vidar: Tidsskrift for Videnskab, Literatur og Politik* (1887), 481–502.

von Vegesack, Thomas, 'Sweden', in Derek Jones (ed.), *Censorship: A World Encyclopedia*, 4 vols. (London: Fitzroy Dearborn, 2001), vol. 4, 2353–56.

Wagner, Hans, *200 Jahre Münchener Theaterchronik 1750–1950* (München: Wissenschaftlicher Verlag Robert Lerche, 1958).

Walkley, Arthur Bingham, *'A Doll's House*: Henrik Ibsen in English – Miss Janet Achurch as Nora', *The Star*, 8 June 1889.

['Spectator'], *'The Lady from the Sea'*, *The Star*, [May 1891?], VAM, William Archer Collection, GB 71 THM/368/3, Box 2: Press cuttings.

Ward, T.H., 'Review of Studies in the Literature of Northern Europe', *The Academy*, vol. 15, 10 May 1879, 294.

Weber, Max, 'Politics as a Vocation', *Max Weber's Complete Writings on Academic and Political Vocations*, trans. Gordon C. Wells, ed. John Dreijmanis (New York: Algora Publishing, 2007), 155–207.

White, Hayden, 'Against Historical Realism: A Reading of "War and Peace"', *New Left Review*, no. 46 (July–August 2007), 89–110.

Whitebrook, Peter, *William Archer: A Biography* (London: Methuen, 1993).

Whyte, Frederic, *William Heinemann: A Memoir* (London: Cape, 1928).

Wilfert-Portal, Blaise, 'Au temps du «cosmopolitisme»?: Les revues parisienne et la litterature etrangere, 1890–1900', in Evanghelia Stead and Hélène Védrine (eds.), *L'Europe des Revues: Réseaux et circulations des modèles* (Paris: Presse Universitaires de Paris Sorbonne, 2017), vol. 2, 257–75, in press.

'Une nouvelle géopolitique intellectuelle. Entre nationalisme et cosmopolitisme', in *La Vie intellectuelle en France*, ed. Christophe Charle and Laurent Jeanpierre (Paris: Le Seuil, 2016), vol. 1, 560–91.

Williams, Simon, 'Ibsen and the Theatre 1877–1900', in McFarlane, *Companion*, 165–82.

Wilson, William, 'Preface', in *Brand: A Drama*, trans. William Wilson [1891] (London: Methuen, 1894), v–xv.

Wirsén, Carl David af, 'Henrik Ibsen: En Folkefiende: Skuespil i fem akter', *Post- och Inrikes Tidningar*, nos. 289 and 290, 12 and 13 December 1882.

'Literatur: Henrik Ibsen: *Gengangere*', *Post-och Inrikes Tidningar*, no. 1, 2 January 1882.

Wittmann, Reinhard, *Buchmarkt und Lektüre im 18. und 19. Jahrhundert: Beiträge zum literarischen Leben 1750–1880* (Tübingen: Max Niemeyer, 1982).

Geschichte des deutschen Buchhandels (München: C.H. Beck, 1999).

Woodfield, James, *English Theatre in Transition 1881–1914* (London: Croom Helm, 1984).

Worthen, W.B., *Print and Poetics and Modern Drama* (Cambridge: Cambridge University Press, 2005).

Young, Robin, 'Ibsen and Comedy', in McFarlane, *Companion*, 58–67.

Ystad, Vigdis, *Innledning til Catilina: Bakgrunn*, www.ibsen.uio.no/DRINNL_C1%7Cintro_background.xhtml, book ed.: HIS 1k, 13–42.

Innledning til De unges Forbund: Utgivelse: Mottagelse av utgaven, www.ibsen.uio.no/DRINNL_UF%7Cintro_publication.xhtml, book ed.: HIS 6k, 31–39.

Innledning til Et Dukkehjem: Bakgrunn, www.ibsen.uio.no/DRINNL_Du%7Cintro_background.xhtml, book ed.: HIS 7k, 191–210.

Innledning til [Olaf Liljekrans] [1877/78]: Tilblivelse, www.ibsen.uio.no/DRINNL_O3%7Cintro_creation.xhtml, book ed. HIS 2k, 670–72.

Zola, Émile, 'From *Naturalism in the Theatre*' [1878], in Eric Bentley (ed.), *The Theory of the Modern Stage: An Introduction to Modern Theatre and Drama* [1968] (Harmondsworth: Penguin, 1976), 351–72.

Østvedt, Einar, *Fra 1814 til ca. 1870: Skiens historie* (Skien: Skien kommune, 1958), vol. 2.

Index

266